Robert Pepper's **2ND EDITION**

4WD
HANDBOOK

BOILING BILLY
PUBLICATIONS

www.boilingbilly.net.au

WOODSLANE

www.travelandoutdoor.bookcentre.com.au

Boiling Billy, a licensed imprint of
Woodslane Press Pty Ltd
10 Apollo Street
Warriewood NSW 2102 Australia
Email: info@woodslane.com.au
Tel: 02 8445 2300 Fax: 02 9970 5002
www.woodslane.com.au

1st edition published 2010 by Woodslane Press
Revised edition published 2012 by Woodslane Press
2nd edition published 2014 by Woodslane Press
Text copyright © Robert Pepper 2010, 2014
Photographs and figure © Robert Pepper 2010, 2012, 2014 unless otherwise credited
Design & layout: Ryan Morrison

If you have any suggestions, corrections or ideas for future editions of this book please write
or email us at:

Boiling Billy Publications
Nimmitabel NSW 2631
Ph/Fax: 02 6454 6162
e-mail: info@boilingbilly.com.au
web: www.boilingbilly.net.au
or contact the author via www.4wdhandbook.com and facebook.com/4WDHandbook

National Library of Australia Cataloguing-in-Publication entry

Author: Pepper, Robert
Title: Robert Pepper's 4WD Handbook : the complete guide to
             understanding, setting up and driving your
             4WD vehicle / by Robert Pepper ;
             Photographs by Robert Pepper
Edition: 2nd edition
ISBN: 9781922131584 (pbk.)
Notes: Includes index.
Subjects: Four-wheel drive vehicles--Australia--Handbooks, manuals, etc, Four-wheel drive
             vehicles--Handbooks, manuals, etc, Four-wheel driving--Australia.

Dewey Number: 629.22042

Printed in China by Everbest

Cover photo: This book is about 4WDs in general, so here's a selection that just all happen
to be orange.

contents

introduction

There is a dream, an intention. A desire. The primeval urge to explore, to leave behind, to set out and explore, away from the teeming hordes, off the beaten path.

For many people, a 4WD vehicle is the key to fulfilling that dream, but it's all too easy to let month after month tick by, and never really try it.

After all, isn't it dangerous? Isn't the vehicle too nice to be risked offroad? Is my 4WD good enough? Is it environmentally "correct"? Do we have time? Doesn't next month have an "r" in it?

You can do it.

It doesn't matter what sort of vehicle you have. Don't worry if you have a small "softroader" that isn't really designed for the rough stuff. You can still enjoy the bush, as long as you accept, and drive within, the vehicle's limitations, although the real limitation is usually the driver's ability.

There's no need to go and buy the best 4WD on the market (whatever "best" means), and you don't need to spend vast amounts of cash on accessories. A 4WD is about using what you have, not a spending competition.

This book shows you how, step by step, and assumes no prior knowledge whatsoever. You'll learn how your 4WD works, and how to drive it offroad responsibly and safely.

Enjoy your offroad adventure!

This is one image that sums up why we own a 4WD – social adventure. Our 4WD can take our family and friends to places hardly anyone goes, like our own private toboggan run, up in the Victorian High Country. This funride was was over 100 metres long, and our little convoy didn't see another soul after we turned off the bitumen. I can't think of another recreation that combines independent adventure and travel for the whole family at such a reasonable cost.

who this book is for

This book is written for anyone who drives a vehicle offroad, especially – but not exclusively – offroad tourers in Australia. It is designed to provide a solid base of knowledge before, during and after practical training and experience.

how to use this book

You can read the book from cover to cover, or you can just skip to the sections that interest you. The early chapters cover terms and concepts that the later sections draw upon. It's all cross-referenced and there is an index at the back, and a glossary provided online at www.4wdhandbook.com

about this book

Everything in this book has come from my personal experience. Every photograph, with just a couple of exceptions, was either taken by me or is of me driving. Some photographs are deliberately set up to illustrate a point, but many are just images I've collected over the years on trips, road tests, product tests, training courses and various events.

There is nothing recommended in this book that I have not personally tried and found to be effective, but that doesn't mean to say there isn't another way. In my work as an offroad instructor the one thing I've learned is that you never stop learning. I'm also in the fortunate position of being a motoring journalist, specialising in offroad vehicles, so I have had extensive first-hand experience driving many brand new press cars in difficult terrain and on trips, in addition to my own vehicles. Being a journo also means I've had access

It doesn't matter what 4WD you own, you can still explore the world. Here is a stock-standard Evoque together with a Wrangler Rubicon which is capable enough out of the box, but this example is highly modified for even more ability.

to technical insights from car manufacturers, and have had the privilege to work with many fine people in the aftermarket industry. I hope that through this book I can pass on some of that learning, and that readers will join the offroading community to experience the joys of exploring Australia and the world by 4WD.

support website

This book's support website is www.4wdhandbook.com and there you can find:

- Errata – I hope I've not made any mistakes, but if I have this is where you'll find corrections. Nothing's eror three.

- Extras and updates – sometimes there's another way, another point of view, and those can be worth looking into.

- Contact details – if you have enjoyed this book and found it useful, please tell me, and why, so I can keep on doing whatever it was that worked. Conversely, if you feel something's wrong or could be better explained or you have a different point of view, let me know that, too (unfortunately, I can't provide general advice to readers). You can also follow along at facebook.com/4WDHandbook for regular updates on 4WDs, touring, new vehicles, techniques and a bit of fun!

 Find us on **Facebook**

summary of contents

This book is split into four Sections with 42 chapters:

Section 1 – How 4WDs work:

This is really all about ensuring the terms and concepts used in the Driving Techniques section make sense. You can't be an effective offroader unless you have some knowledge of how things work, and that's what this section is all about. This technical knowledge will also help you with buying accessories and modifying your 4WD.

Section 2 – Driving techniques:

This is the heart of the book, and discusses how to drive on all sorts of terrain, why certain techniques work and why some don't.

Section 3 – Recovery:

Because no matter how good a driver you are, some day you'll need to know how to get yourself (or others) out of difficulty.

Section 4 – Going touring:

Choosing a 4WD, setting it up with accessories and how to start offroad touring.

what's not in the book

Where to go touring – there are plenty of good books and magazines that list a variety of treks (see page 521 for some from this publisher and author) but they don't explain 4WD theory or techniques. That's the purpose of this book.

4WD Glovebox Guide

A companion volume to this book is the *4WD Glovebox Guide*. This is designed as a quick reference to be used in the field, and is aligned with the National Competencies for training. It does not have the detailed explanations of the *4WD Handbook*. The Guide contains some information not in the Handbook that is more useful in a field guide, for example communications, navigation, tyre repair and jumpstarting techniques.

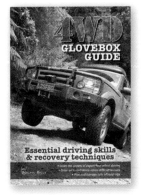

SECTION 1

WHAT A 4WD IS AND HOW IT WORKS

CHAPTER 1

WHAT IS A 4WD?

What's a 4WD? How does it differ from a road car and why is that important? What is all this jargon?

4x4s, 4WDs, softroaders and AWDs

There is no industry standard definition for any of the terms above. What follows is an explanation of what they are generally taken to mean:

- **4X4:** The term 4X4 means "four wheels, four driven" and is a used as synonym for 4WD. 4X2 means four wheels, two driven, and 6X4 is six wheels, four driven. 8X8 means a lot of fun. 4X0 is no fun at all. 4X2s are either RWD (rear wheel drive) or FWD, front wheel drive. It's a pity "front" and "four" start with the same letter, as it does tend to confuse things.

- **4WD:** The term 4WD now tends to mean a four-wheeled vehicle, designed for offroad use,

Subaru make true all wheel drives which drive all four wheels, all the time. In slippery conditions such as this skidpan, AWD cars grip much more effectively.

that can have all four wheels driven and has low-range – a set of crawler gears. Sometimes 4WDs are 2WD on bitumen and 4WD off, and those are known as "part-time" or "selectable" 4WDs. This will be explained later.

- **AWD:** The term "AWD" stands for "all wheel drive" and is used for vehicles that drive all four wheels, but are not designed for offroad use. Confusingly, 4WDs which can drive all four wheels when on the bitumen are often said to have an AWD mode, and AWD is also known as "constant 4WD", as all four wheels are driven all the time. Road cars like Subaru Imprezas and some Audis are, technically, 4WDs, but they fall firmly into the AWD bracket.

- **Softroader:** these are offroad vehicles without low-range. Typically they look like a 4WD, have some offroad capability, but aren't really designed for the heavy-duty rough stuff

Despite being much the same size, the Suzuki Grand Vitara is a 4WD with low-range, while the Land Rover Freelander 2 doesn't have low-range, and so is known as a softroader.

because they are optimised more for on-road performance. Manufacturers don't like the term "softroader", so they have coined terms like crossover instead. This is still a softroader, but the name implies that the best of both worlds can be had from a road car and a 4WD. That's never the case.

- **SUV:** From North America we have the term SUV, which means "Sports Utility Vehicle"; and these are anything that looks like a 4WD. Some are even 2WD, and now in Australia we have 2WD versions of AWDs (e.g. the Ford Territory and Hyundai Tucson). The term "SUV" is never used in Australian 4WD clubs or the industry.

Marketing people have invented plenty more terms but fortunately most of those monikers don't go much further than their fevered imaginations and glossy brochures.

A common misconception is that 4WDs are always big. Some models, like the Nissan Patrol and Toyota Land Cruiser, are indeed larger than the average car, or at least taller if not longer or wider. However, small vehicles like the Suzuki Grand Vitara and Jimny, and the first-generation Kia Sportage, are just as much a "real 4WD" – immensely capable offroad and an awful lot smaller. Conversely, some larger vehicles that look the part aren't very good offroad.

Whatever type of vehicle you have, you can still enjoy the bush.

why drive all four wheels?

Compared to 2WD, AWD cars have better traction and roadholding. They accelerate quicker initially, especially in slippery conditions, as they can get their power to the ground more effectively where a 2WD would simply spin wheels. As vehicles become ever more powerful this is more and more of an advantage. Around corners AWDs grip better than 2WD, especially if the driver needs to change throttle mid-bend. It is often said that an AWD is of no use under braking, but this is incorrect. If the engine is used for braking in slippery conditions by selecting a lower gear then all four wheels are being asked to turn slower than the current pace, whereas with a 2WD the engine braking is restricted to one set of wheels. This effect is also true even if the brake pedal is also depressed; if you perform an emergency stop in third gear from 100km/h you'll stop more quickly than if you put the vehicle in neutral.

The reason why all cars aren't AWD is because AWD uses extra parts, namely the drive to the other set of wheels. AWD is therefore more expensive to manufacture and maintain. AWD vehicles weigh more because of the extra components – perhaps another 50-100kg or so – and there is more mechanical friction. All else being equal, the AWD's fuel consumption is also increased, and it will be slower, except in low-traction conditions, which is why AWD cars are so successful in rallying.

offroading, 4WDing and 4WDriving

The English language is cumbersome in places, such as when we need to describe taking a 4WD off the beaten track.

In this book, and in general use, the term **"offroad"** is used to mean travelling over tracks, and rougher terrain than bitumen and well-formed gravel roads; basically 4WD-only territory. These "offroad" tracks are still defined roads.

In reality, there are very few circumstances in which you should ever drive off a track – sand dunes are one, and only when specifically permitted. In all other circumstances, keep to the track/trail/road. It's safer and more environmentally responsible.

Other terms you might hear are wheeling (from "four-wheeling", especially in the USA), 4WDriving or similar spellings. They all mean the same thing as offroading, as defined above. They do not mean randomly driving wherever you please. That's known as bush-bashing or, more correctly, environmental vandalism – this gives all offroaders a bad name and leads to track closures.

This is a legally defined road. It just happens to be one that really needs 4WD and low-range. "Offroad" means "roads that normal cars cannot handle", not actually driving off defined roads.

what makes a 4WD a 4WD?

If a "4WD" is a "a vehicle intended for offroad use" then it's going to have some different design features compared to a normal car, given that a road car isn't designed for offroading.

Understanding the design differences is important, because they translate directly into the different driving style required for 4WDs compared to road cars, and all offroading requires more knowledge of how vehicles work than just plain road driving. The problem with all the differences is that they are almost exactly the opposite of what is good for a road car. Softroaders in particular make offroad compromises, for example, by definition none have low-range gears, and few have decent under-body protection. That doesn't mean softroaders can't go offroad, it just means they are less capable than 4WDs.

A Nissan Patrol demonstrating axle-flex – keeping all four wheels on the ground to stabilise the vehicle and ensuring all four wheels are helping drive it.

differences between a 4WD and a road car

Design Feature	Why you need it
Bigger wheels (taller, not necessarily wider)	The larger a wheel is, the easier it is to climb over obstacles, for example rocks. Also, the vehicle's ground clearance is improved.
Ground clearance	Ground clearance is the distance between the lowest point of the vehicle and the ground. The more there is, the more able the vehicle is to pass over obstacles.
Low gearing	Usually achieved by a set of low-range gears, which allow the vehicle to travel very slowly, yet have the engine operating at high enough revs to be effective. Going very slowly is very important when offroad. It's not called "adrenaline at five km/h" for nothing.
Under-body protection	Ground clearance is all well and good. If you have 220mm, which is a lot, that's perfect until you find something 225mm high. At which point you need under-body protection. It'll happen, and you'll hear it.
Suspension travel	Travel? Where's it going? Up and down, is the answer. Take a look at the Patrol on page 9. Obviously, if all four wheels can be kept on the ground, all four wheels can contribute to moving the vehicle. So 4WDs have long suspension travel, to maintain an even keel over rough terrain.
4WD transmission	Sounds obvious, but there needs to be a mechanism to send drive to all four wheels.
Tyre tread pattern	Not just larger, but a different grip pattern designed for offroad use as well as on-road. However, almost all 4WDs come from the factory with road-oriented tyres. Most owners change them for more offroad-oriented tyres.
Taller profile	All that clearance adds up to a taller vehicle, which means you sit higher up and have better visibility.
"Torquey" engine	We'll get into torque and power later, but this means the engine is designed for lots of turning force at low rpm, not for high revs. If you attend dragster meetings you'll note the lack of offroad vehicles competing.

driving differences between a 4WD and roadcar

These differences translate into a different driving technique for 4WDs:

Difference	Why?	What the driver has to do
Body roll around corners	The tall vehicle, long travel suspension and big tyres add up to more body roll around corners.	Reduce speed before the corner, smoothly enter and exit the corner.
Better visibility	You can see over the tops of cars, over fences and all sorts of obstructions that leave a normal car blind.	Use the visibility!
Less need to rev engine	Unlike small cars, 4WD engines, especially diesels, simply don't need to be revved hard to 4,000rpm or more.	Change gear earlier than you would in a road car. For example, some (older) diesels aren't worth taking much beyond 2,000rpm. You get the noise, but nothing else.
Longer stopping distances	Factors like a greater weight and tyres with an offroad bias contribute to longer stopping distances.	Use that extra visibility
More affected by wind	Those warnings for high-sided vehicles will begin to mean something now!	Be aware on high bridges, or when large trucks pass in the opposite direction.
Less grip	Body roll, offroad tyres, other factors.	Slow down, be smooth. Modern 4WDs are nearly carlike, but old ones are really little trucks and should be driven as such.

Some 4WDs drive very similar to a road car, others more like a truck. In general, the older the 4WD or the more offroad-capable it is, the more different it will be to a road car. In any case, a 4WD handles differently to a normal road car, and needs to be driven slower and more carefully. It's the same as trying to drive a road car in the same manner as a high-performance sports car; the sports car will go faster, stop quicker and generally be a different driving experience.

angles and measurements

There are some important measurements and angles to consider with 4WDs. These are:

Wheelbase: The wheelbase is the distance between the front axle and the rear axle.

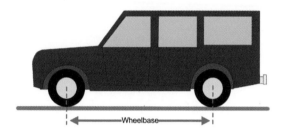

Track: Distance between the centre of the tyres on an axle, not the width of the vehicle. The track may vary slightly from front to rear. Track is important to know when towing a trailer. The width of a vehicle is the width of the bodywork, as the tyres should be inside the body. Width may be quoted with and without mirrors folded.

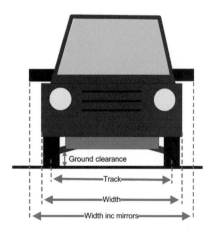

Ground clearance: This is usually measured in millimetres, with the standard tyres at the manufacturer's recommended pressures, and is the distance from the ground to the lowest point of the vehicle except for the tyres, wheels, hubs or mudflaps, fully laden. This definition is not fixed, so again it is worthwhile knowing which definition has been used for comparison purposes, and looking under your own vehicle so you know what the lowest point is, before you find out the hard way on a track.

Clearance is how big an obstacle the vehicle can drive over, and is often important when following wheel ruts, as this Pathfinder demonstrates.

Angle of approach (or attack, depending on your nature): This is the angle at which the vehicle can, in theory, climb over an obstacle without touching the front. This might be as much as 60 or 70 degrees. No stock 4WD is going to climb a hill that steep, at least without a run-up. (Diagram on pg 12).However, a good angle of approach is definitely a worthwhile asset.

Breakover or ramp angle:
This is a measure of how acute an angle the vehicle can cross without being hung up. It can be measured in one of three ways as shown in the diagram.

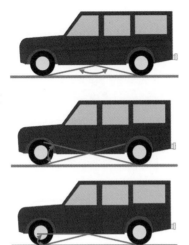

Departure angle: The angle the vehicle can descend without touching the rear. It is typically several degrees less than the approach angle and even less when towbars and tongues are fitted which is why the latter are removed before offroading.

Santa Fe in the High Country almost scraping its backside – running out of departure angle.

Range Rover Sport demonstrating ramp angle.

Nissan Patrol close to the limit of its approach angle. The angle is improved over stock (showroom condition) by the larger tyres and suspension lift, as well as the bull bar; and if he did hit the mud wall there won't be any panel damage!

why a 4WD?

Why buy a 4WD over a road car? There are many reasons, but one of the important reasons is the vehicle's ability to access offroad destinations. If you intend to go on the beach, into the forests or around the outback there are many places that

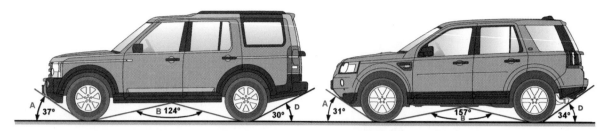

The diagram shows a Discovery 3 (with air suspension at offroad height) and Freelander 2, to scale, with approach angle A, breakover angle B and departure angle D. Typically, the softroader has a short rear overhang, giving a good departure angle, but the breakover angle is always a softroader problem.

are accessible by 2WD, and many that are 4WD-only. Even those that are accessible by 2WD may be best done in a 4WD vehicle, as 4WDs typically carry more weight and bulk more easily than road cars. If you had to carry four people, all their personal effects, two spare tyres, food, water and emergency kit down 500km of outback dirt road with washouts, what sort of vehicle would you prefer, regardless of whether the terrain was rough enough to actually warrant using low-range?

On the touring front, 4WDs can be easily customised for touring, with long-range tanks, dual batteries, uprated suspension and more. Most of these modifications (or "mods" as they're known – Chapter 40 has more detail) are technically possible with road cars, but they aren't as suited to the changes and there will be less aftermarket support for fitting (for example) a set of cargo shelves and a fridge to the back of a Commodore than to your average 4WD wagon.

As bitumen has spread over Australia, the modern car has become less and less suited for dirt road travel as it becomes lower, is shod in fragile high-speed tyres, has a thirst for premium fuel and is

simply not designed for rough work. Car magazines used to include dirt-road testing; no longer.

There are other reasons to opt for a 4WD. Some of the largest and heaviest trailers are best towed with a 4WD, although powerful road cars can tow a lot, too, but often only with special tow setups. Simply having a V8 engine and the power available does not necessarily make the car capable of towing heavy loads.

Safety is a consideration, too. 4WDs may or may not be safer in a crash than a road car. It all depends – on the type of crash, the model of 4WD and so on. Larger vehicles are not necessarily safer, although having been rear-ended by a B-double I'm not sure I'd be alive had I not been in a 4WD.

While 2WDs can get to many remote places, think about it this way; you could do a 5km bush hike wearing patent leather shoes and still make it. But wouldn't it make more sense to wear footwear appropriate for the task?

Even when not travelling in rough terrain, the 4WD's ability to easily carry a camping load makes it a great touring choice.

body styles

long wheel base (LWB) and wagons

A LWB 4WD is one that has a long wheelbase, or enough length for five doors, in which case it is a wagon. LWBs can be any body style, for example utes or wagons.

short wheel base (SWB)

SWBs are shorter than LWBs, as the name suggests. They have only two passenger doors, and although most can seat passengers in the rear, the cargo compartment is strictly limited by comparison to a LWB. Many owners remove the rear seats and use SWBs as two-seaters. SWBs are often known as "shorties". (However, LWBs are not referred to as a "longies".)

Short wheelbase Land Rover 90 and Jeep Wrangler.

mid wheel base

A longer version of a SWB, not quite a LWB. Known as "middies", not to be confused with the drinking term.

ute

Every Aussie knows what a ute is! A utility truck (pickup in US parlance), or a "bakkie" if you're in South Africa.

dual, twin or double cab and extra-cab utes

A double cab (or dualcab) ute has passenger seats but a shorter tray. An extra-cab ute has a small storage area behind the front seats.

Single-cab ute in black, double cab in grey and a two-door wagon long wheelbase in green.

trayback

A trayback ute has a separate, removable flat bed like a tray, hence the name.

A Discovery 2 converted to a single-cab trayback ute

summary

- 4WDs are designed for offroad work.
- "4X4" and "4WD" mean the same thing in common parlance.
- AWD means all wheel drive, the ability to drive all four wheels all the time, same as "constant 4WD".
- 4WDs which drive in 2WD on bitumen are known as part-time or selectable 4WDs.
- Approach, ramp and departure angles are a measure of a vehicle's ability to negotiate uneven terrain.
- Clearance is the gap under the vehicle; what it can drive over.
- A softroader is an offroad vehicle without low-range.
- The wheelbase is the distance between the front and rear axles.
- "Offroad" really means off the beaten track on rough terrain, not bush-bashing.
- 4WDs make excellent touring vehicles, even on the bitumen, as well as great tow cars.

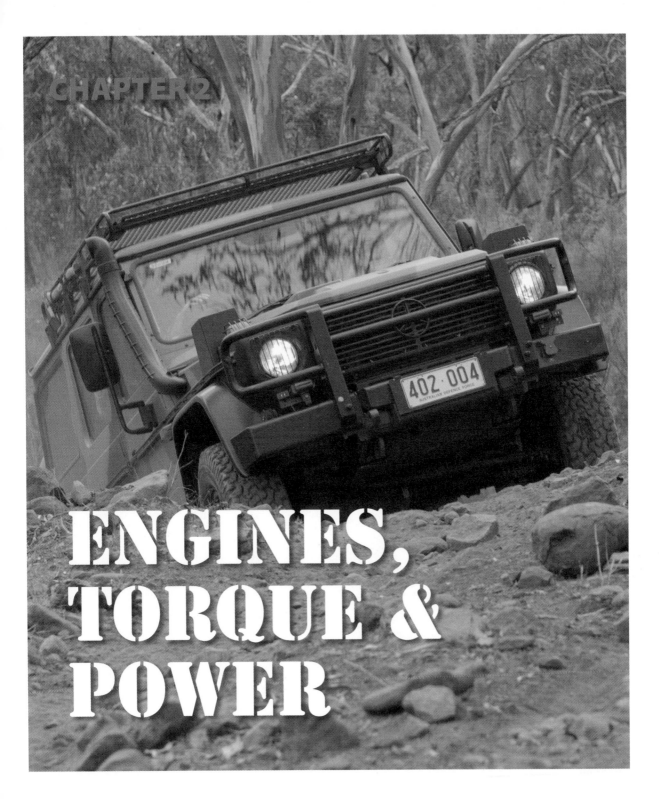

CHAPTER 2

ENGINES, TORQUE & POWER

You don't need to be around 4WDs or cars for very long before you hear about power and torque. It is important to understand these terms as they are frequently used in vehicle specifications and as part of descriptions of offroad devices and driving techniques.

force, torque and power

force

The pressure of one object against another. Imagine a shut door, and someone pulling it open. That pull is force. It's force whether or not anything moves. Force is measured in newtons (from Sir Isaac). The more newtons (N), the greater the force. A person standing on the ground generates force courtesy of gravity; the ground generates an equal upwards force. If it doesn't, you fall downwards. Every kilogram of mass generates just under 10N of force downwards, and a 75kg person is generating around 735N on the earth's surface.

torque

A turning force. If you are using a spanner to tighten a bolt you are applying torque. A vehicle engine produces torque; it has a driveshaft that turns the wheels via some cogs. Torque is measured in Nm (newton metres). That's just the force (in newtons) multiplied by the distance from the centre of rotation. Why distance? Well, try opening a door by pushing it near the hinge. Easier to open it further away from the hinge, isn't it?

The mighty Volkswagen Touareg R50 has a V10 turbo-diesel engine that can develop a massive 850Nm of torque.

The same goes for tightening a bolt. If you use a long handled spanner you can apply the same force, and the extra distance gives you more leverage and more torque.

As an example of torque, imagine a person weighing 75kg standing on the end of a wheel brace (tool used on the nuts that secure a wheel to the car) that is 33cm long. A 75kg person translates to about 735 newtons of force. The distance from the centre of rotation is 33cm or a third of a metre, so we multiply 735 by 0.33 and get 243Nm.

That means you can generate a 243Nm force quite easily. If that same person stood on the end of a two-metre long lever, the torque would be almost 1,500Nm. And you thought a 500Nm engine was something special! It is, for reasons that become clear a little later.

work:

The definition is:

Work = force x distance.

So if you exert a force and something moves, then that's work. If you pull on a door and it doesn't move, that's force. If the door moves, then that's work.

If you are loosening a nut and trying to turn the spanner, no work is done until the nut actually turns.

power:

How quickly you can do work! In the torque example, we generated 243Nm of force pretty easily, which is more torque than a small car's engine. Feeling pretty good, aren't you? But the difference between you generating that force and a car engine is that the car engine can do it at 4,000 revs per minute. Can you do anything 4,000 times a minute, let alone rotate something 360 degrees with that amount of force? Now you can see why the 500Nm engine is impressive.

Imagine your vehicle on a flat piece of road. Could you push it 20 metres? Yes you could. You could also drive it that distance.

Whether you drive it or push it the same amount of work is done. The difference is that the engine can do the work quicker than you can, thus it is more powerful.

Another example is when winching. You can hand-winch your vehicle up a hill. It takes hours – I've done it with friends after a car was broken – but you can do it. Or you could drive it. In both cases the same amount of work is done; the difference is the speed it's done, and that's power.

Power is measured in kilowatts, and is basically torque multiplied by revs. The exact formula is:

Power in kW = (torque in Nm x rpm)/9,558

For example, an engine that generates 300Nm at 1,950rpm creates 61kW.

torque/power curve

The graph below is an example of a 4WD engine's torque and power curve; that is, the torque and power plotted against revs. The vehicle is the Freelander 2 and the graphs show the curves for petrol automatic, diesel manual and diesel automatic. It is normal for modern engines to be tuned slightly differently when mated to manual or

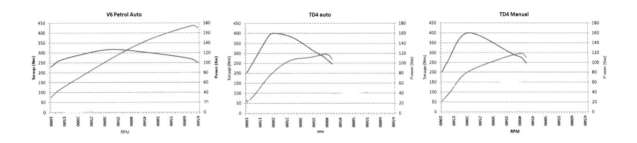

automatic engines and in this case the diesel in auto tune holds a higher torque curve for longer than the manual. The petrol actually has more off-idle torque than the diesel, but the diesel quickly improves.

An automatic diesel Freelander.

In all cases torque rises to a peak, which is 3,200rpm for the petrol and 2,000 for the diesels. However, power continues to rise after the torque peaks as the extra revs compensate for the reduction in torque – power is just torque multiplied by revs. Eventually the torque drops off so much that the extra revs don't produce any more power, thus there's no point revving the engine beyond this limit. The reason for torque decrease is because the engine begins to spend more energy in overcoming internal friction. If that doesn't make sense, think about someone cycling. You can pedal faster and faster, but eventually you end up just using the energy to push your legs round, not move the bicycle any faster.

torque and power in practice

Torque is the turning force an engine can produce. 4WDs often need a lot of turning force at the wheels, for example when in soft sand, towing, climbing a steep hill or even all three at the same time. How quickly that turning force is applied is not particularly important, so 4WD engines are generally tuned to produce lots of torque at relatively low revs, which means you don't need to be driving them at high revs at low speeds, and you can drive slower (a very good idea in rough terrain). In contrast, the torque required to move a race car or road car is quite low as the car is light and the track or road hard, fairly flat and smooth. However, that torque must be delivered very rapidly, so the race or road car's engine may not generate much turning force, but it must do so at high revs. For racing there's no point having an engine that can generate 1,500Nm of torque at only 300rpm, unless the race was to see who could drive the slowest up a really steep hill without stopping, which is exactly the sort of operating conditions you find with 4WDs.

Torque is also used to describe how much force should be used to tighten bolts, for example wheel nuts. This is expressed in Nm (force) because it doesn't matter how quickly you do up the nuts (power), it's how much force is used to tighten them correctly.

Slogging through soft sand, up slopes and dragging a trailer requires a powerful turning force at the wheels. That's why 4WD engines are tuned for torque, and why they have low-range.

This Impreza WRX doesn't need a lot of torque to move its light weight on a hard surface, but it does need to develop that torque at a high rpm so it can move quickly! It can develop 195kW and 343Nm of torque, but at 6,000 and 4,000rpm, ideal for driving fast, but not for driving slowly.

summary

- Force is the pressure of one object against another.

- Torque is a turning force.

- Work is movement of one object to place to place.

- Power is how quickly work is done – in the case of car engines, it's basically rpm x torque.

- 4WD engines are typically designed to produce more torque at low revs, as opposed to race car or road car engines, which don't need as much torque but need it at higher revs.

CHAPTER 3

HOW 4WD
WORKS

This chapter is not a mechanical thesis. It tells you what you need to know about how a 4WD works so you can drive it better and more safely. Rather than give you a set of rules, this book helps you understand the basic principles so you can apply them to any situation. This, in turn, helps you to drive over rough terrain with minimal impact to the environment, your vehicle and your passengers.

It is possible to bimble along in your road car and not care about how it works. 4WD is far more demanding of the driver's skills, and the vehicle, and so it is important that the driver has an understanding of what is happening and why. You'll remember this when you're sliding sideways down a hill, and it'll be too late to read this chapter, unless it's a very long hill.

what's what?

Everything has jargon. There's no alternative but to learn it, at least to some degree. Here is a quick guide to 4WD terms. Give it a glance, but don't worry about trying to memorise it now. You can always return here when an unfamiliar term is used.

Almost all touring 4WDs are modified to a greater or lesser extent. This tough Nissan Patrol (as shown on page 24) is definitely at the "greater" end of the scale, making it a good vehicle to point out some common modifications.

how a 4WD works: in brief!

All this is explained in more detail in the following chapters.

- The 4WD's engine transmits torque (turning force) to all four wheels via the transmission.

- Some 4WDs cannot be used in 4WD on bitumen. This is because the front axle travels further than the rear axle when going around corners, yet the transmission tries to drive both axles at the same speed. This causes stress on the transmission, called "transmission windup", or "axle bind". These 4WDs run in 2WD on the bitumen, and only in 4WD offroad, where the front and rear axles can slip enough to equalise the difference in speed around corners.

- All 4WDs have differentials, a system of cogs which allow drive to go to both wheels on a given axle even though the inside wheel will go much slower than the outside around a bend. Unfortunately, the differential system sends most drive to the wheel that's easiest to turn, so if a 4WD is offroad and loses traction on one wheel that wheel spins, its partner on the axle with traction gets very little to no drive and the car loses momentum or stops. There are various means to overcome this.

#	Item	Description
1	Bull bar	Primarily to protect the vehicle against animal (usually roo) strike, but also makes a handy platform on which to mount other accessories
2	Driving lights	Essential for offroading or dirt roads where there are no streetlights
3	UHF radio	Several radios fitted here, but UHF is the common radio for travellers
4	Roof-mounted lights	Fitted to some vehicles for offroad work
5	Snorkel	Essential for any tourer in case of deeper than expected water – cheap engine insurance
6	Roof rack	Full-length version shown, some are without the sides, just flat
7	Recovery gear	Sometimes carried internally, or on the rack
8	Sidesteps (rock sliders)	Rock sliders are tough enough to support the vehicle's weight as it moves over rocks – standard sidesteps are not
9	Steering damper	The bigger wheels mean the steering can kick back so this damper keeps it under control
10	Offroad tyres	Offroad tourers choose stronger tyres and a more offroad-oriented tread – in this case the tyres are substantially larger than normal
11	Winch	Winch fairlead (bottom) and control box (top) (actual winch hidden from view)
12	Rear work light	For reversing and camping
13	Dual wheel carrier	Two spares is the way to go for tourers
14	Towbar	A recovery point as well as for towing
15	Aftermarket suspension	The standard suspension is not designed for this work so four new coils and dampers are required
16	Long-range fuel tank	For longer trips and sheer convenience
17	Aftermarket rear bar	Replaces the flimsy plastic version and allows mounting of the dual wheel carrier

- All 4WDs have a gearbox, like normal cars, either automatic or manual. 4WDs also have a transfer case, which lowers all the gears, like changing the front cog on a geared bicycle. Normally, road car style is high-range, while offroad is low-range, the same four, five or six gears but much lower, a crawler set. Softroaders by definition do not have low-range.

- Low-range usually has second gear set slightly lower than first gear when in high-range. The purpose of a transfer case is to allow the engine to develop maximum torque (turning force) while the vehicle moves very slowly, which is what you want for many offroad situations.

how 4WD works: in detail

the two problems

Each manufacturer has their own particular 4WD mechanism and a flashy name to go with it. Mitsubishi has Super Select, Jeep has Quadra-Trac, Honda has Real-Time and so on.

The good news is that all these impressive-sounding systems are solving the same two basic problems in slightly different ways. If you understand those two problems, not only will you immediately be a long way towards understanding all 4WD systems on the market and the limitations of the various solutions, you will also learn concepts which will help you drive offroad more safely and effectively. This chapter explains the two problems and their solutions.

Six 4WDs, six different 4WD systems, but all solve the same basic set of problems.

problem 1: wheels on an axle

Forget 4WD for a moment. Imagine an axle with two wheels, one at either end. This is what it looks like in 3D:

But we'll just look down on it from the top. The grey colour of the axle indicates it is not moving.

We do need to drive the axle, so we add a very simple driveshaft and two cogs. The colour of the axle has changed to green to signify it is being driven.

The axle moves forwards in a straight line. Both wheels travel the same amount of distance. Easy.

Now imagine the axle turns through a circle.

This is now a problem. **The inside wheel travels less distance than the outside wheel**, and its circle is considerably smaller than the outside wheel's. Yet both wheels must take the same amount of time to turn the corner.

Have you ever seen a group of marching soldiers take a corner? The soldiers on the inside need to slow right down, almost marking time, and the guys on the outside need to speed up. Same principle here.

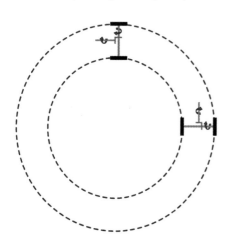

So why is it a problem? With the situation as it stands, both wheels connected to a single axle, the inside wheel cannot slow down, because it's directly connected to the outside wheel, so both wheels must turn at the same speed. So what happens is that the inside wheel spins and scuffs, as it is forced to rotate at the same speed as the outside wheel, yet only travel a fraction of the distance.

Clearly this is not an acceptable state of affairs. If cars had that sort of arrangement they would be going through tyres very quickly, and enormous stress would be placed on the axle. Not to mention loss of traction on the side wheel as it is slipping, resulting in poor handling.

One solution would be to drive only one wheel. Which would work, but would tend to cause the vehicle to veer in one direction, and cars really need at least two wheels driven for traction anyway.

solution to problem 1: wheels on an axle

The real solution is a differential, henceforth known as a "diff", represented as a magenta circle on the diagram. The line coming into the diff is known as a driveshaft, and the lines coming from the wheels to the diff are known as axles. The definition of an axle is a shaft on which a wheel rotates.

A diff replaces the simple cogs we had as our drive mechanism. The diff's cog arrangement is complex, but it is not important to understand how the diff works. It is important, however, to understand the effect it has, so we'll concentrate on that.

The diff transmits drive to both wheels, just like our simple cog system. However, the diff also allows one wheel to slow down and another to speed up while going around a corner; and it maintains drive to both wheels, all the time.

In other words:

- One input shaft (from the engine) goes into the diff's cog arrangement.
- Each wheel has its own entirely separate axle ending inside the diff.
- Both axles are driven, and can be driven at different speeds.

The diagram below shows a differential in action. The size of the curly blue arrow indicates the speed the two axles are being driven at.

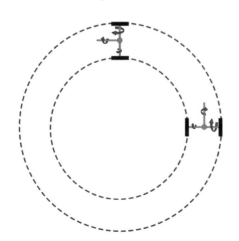

The differential housing "pumpkin" is clearly visible on the front axle of this Patrol, offset towards the driver's side. All 4WDs have differentials on the front and rear axles, but the pumpkin may not be quite as visible as this example.

summary

- Two wheels on a fixed axle must rotate at the same speed.
- When an axle goes around a corner, the inside wheel travels slower than the outside wheel.
- Differentials (diffs) allow two axles to be driven at the same speed, or one axle to speed up and the other to slow down. They are the solution to the problem, but cause other issues which are important and will be explained shortly.

differentials: the trouble with the solution

There had to be, it was too good to be true. Actually, this section should be titled "The Trouble Offroaders Have with Differentials" because it's not much of a problem for normal road users.

The problem is that if two wheels on an axle have different amounts of traction, the diff sends more drive to the wheel with the least traction.

You can think of the drive to the wheels as water flowing through a pipe. Water always takes the path of least resistance, and it's exactly the same with drive going through a differential.

This time a wheel is in mud (the brown blob). This makes it much easier to turn than its partner on firm ground, so all the drive goes to the wheel that's easiest to turn. This is shown on the diagram by a green axle, with grey showing no drive to that axle.

If one wheel on an axle is on mud, and another on rock, then the wheel on mud is easier to turn because it's on a more slippery surface. So the diff, being lazy, tends to rotate the wheel in the mud. Which is a pity, because as a result the wheel with the traction on rock doesn't get very much drive and the vehicle goes nowhere. The bigger the difference between the traction on the wheels, the more drive goes to the wheel with less traction.

To be precise, both wheels get exactly the same amount of torque, and that amount is exactly the amount needed to turn the wheel that is easiest to turn.

That means with a wheel on slippery mud a very small amount of drive is going to the wheel with traction, and the net result is that the two wheels on that axle are not helping move the car at all. With any luck the other axle will have two wheels with reasonable traction so the vehicle can still move.

This means your 4WD could easily become a 2WD, with two rotating wheels on the front and rear axles, helplessly spinning while the other two wheels with traction are comfortably resting, not moving at all. A common example is when the vehicle is balanced on two diagonal wheels, say front left and rear right, with both spinning uselessly, but you could also see a situation on a sideslope where both the uphill wheels are spinning. If all four wheels are spinning then that's a basic loss of traction and nothing to do with the differential problem.

The diff problem in action. The passenger side wheel is stationary, but its opposite wheel is rotating fast. The diff is sending the power to the wheel with least traction, the one easiest to turn, instead of the one with traction. The reason the driver's wheel is easier to turn is because it has less of the car's weight on it than the passenger side, and the more weight on a tyre, the greater the traction.

That is the problem with differentials, and understanding it is absolutely essential for all 4WD drivers because many driving techniques work around the limitations of the differential, and there are many solutions for overcoming the problem.

solutions to the differential problem

Now we understand the problem, it's easy to understand the various methods of solving it. The basic differential as we know it so far is called an "open diff". There are plenty of other types, starting with:

cross-axle differential lockers

The diff on an axle can be fitted with a locking mechanism, technically known as a "cross-axle differential lock" but more often just referred to as a "locker". When activated, the diff in effect ceases to exist. Both wheels on the axle turn at the same speed, whether the vehicle is turning or not. Obviously this makes it hard to turn on a high-traction surface as the wheels on the axle can no longer turn at different speeds, but that doesn't matter; lockers are typically only used in a straight line, on loose surfaces and for short periods of time, so a bit of tyre scuff isn't a problem. When the locking diff is deactivated it behaves like a normal diff, known as an "open" diff.

There are two basic types of cross-axle locker (hereafter referred to as just a "locker"):

- Manual lockers
- Autolockers

manual lockers

Manual lockers require some form of driver control to lock and unlock and are what we've discussed up until this point. The best known example is ARB's Air Locker, so named because the lock/unlock mechanism works on compressed air, but some

4WD manufacturers provide manual lockers as an option. These are often electric. When not locked, manual locking diffs behave exactly the same way as open diffs.

autolockers

Autolockers are locked all the time, and unlock when required (i.e. when going around a corner). The internal gears are arranged so they work like this:

- A wheel on an axle is allowed to rotate faster than its partner by freewheeling (no drive to it), but never slower. A normal diff doesn't ever permit freewheeling like this.

- When the vehicle goes around a corner, the outside wheel speeds up. The diff unlocks to allow this. The inside wheel is driven and the outside wheel freewheels.

- If you're offroad and one wheel hits slippery ground and the other has traction, then both wheels are turned at the same speed. The diff is locked, automatically, hence its name.

Autolockers are simpler, and therefore cheaper than manual lockers. So why doesn't everyone use them?

problems with autolockers

Many people like the ability to control the locking of the differential. Lockers aren't always wanted, even if they manually unlock. Chapter 9 has details on driving with lockers.

Also, autolockers do change the handling of the vehicle because only the inner wheel is driven around corners, not both wheels as in a normal, open diff.

  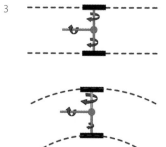

1   Normally when a vehicle raises a wheel this high in the air the differential would send all the drive to it and the front axle no longer contributes towards moving the vehicle. In this case the Patrol is fitted with twin ARB Air Lockers so that doesn't happen and the wheel on the ground continues to be driven, thus the vehicle can continue to move.

2   Switches for the popular aftermarket manually-operated locker, the ARB Air Locker. These are driven by compressed air, hence the switch for a compressor.

3   When going around a corner the auto-locker's outside wheel freewheels.

Autolockers are also not suitable for fitting to the front of constant-4WD vehicles, or the rear of short wheel base vehicles. When a vehicle corners there is a weight shift to the outside, and the inside wheels become lighter. The less weight there is on a wheel, the less traction it has. Remember that autolockers only drive the inside wheel which, when cornering, is the one with less traction. So, it's quite likely that the inside wheel will get more power than it can handle. The outside wheel, moving faster, is freewheeling. But if the inside wheel spins, as it is more likely to do so now it's partner is just freewheeling, then as it spins it will very rapidly catch up to the outside wheel. As it does so, the diff will lock. Suddenly, the outside wheel goes from freewheeling to driving. And both wheels are turning at the same speed, because in effect the differential has ceased to exist. If this sounds like a recipe for a handling disaster you would be dead right. Exactly what would depend on a few factors but it would certainly take unwary drivers by surprise. Therefore, autolocked vehicles should be driven with care; never apply power around a bend, especially in the wet.

Autolockers can make life difficult in slippery conditions, too. Imagine a vehicle on flat, but very slippery mud. When it turns, an open diff would send torque to both wheels on the axle; and both would turn, because both have about as much traction as each other. There'd be a bit of wheel-spin, but it would move.

The autolocker would drive only the inner wheel. Now that's a problem, because the outer wheel would be doing nothing, just trying to freewheel; which is easy on bitumen, but in the mud it's likely to just act as a brake. It can't be driven any faster than the inside wheel, and the friction of the mud slows it from freewheeling. So it rotates at the same speed as the inside wheel. Which isn't what you want for a vehicle to turn; you need the outside wheel to go quicker. So turning on an autolocker on a slippery surface is harder than with open diffs.

limited-slip diffs

An open differential easily allows one wheel to travel quicker than the other. A Limited-Slip Differential, or LSD, works the same way but restricts that movement a little. There are several types but the most common one is the clutch type.

Imagine the diff working as we know it, letting the two wheels turn at different speeds around a corner. Now imagine that there is a strong man grasping the two axles in either hand, and he's going to try and stop them from turning at different speeds if he can. This is the clutch pack inside the diff, and now the wheels can still turn at different speeds, but they're being restricted from doing so a little because while that guy is strong, he's not strong enough to totally stop the axles from slipping a bit through his hands. The effect is to restrict the differential action a little, which is why you don't generally find LSDs on the rear of short wheel base vehicles, as the slight handling effect of not wanting to turn a corner is more pronounced with a shorter vehicle. It is not noticeable with a long wheelbase vehicle. This restriction on differential operation is known as "preload", and it is always there. Preloaded LSDs work even with one wheel off the ground.

When offroad, the LSD comes into its own. The principle of a differential is this; it will always send equal amounts of driving force (torque) to both wheels. So, with an open diff, one wheel on the mud and one on dry rock, then the wheel on dry rock will only get as much drive as the wheel

on mud can support. Put another way, however difficult the wheel on mud is to turn, that's how much drive the wheel on the rock gets. An LSD doesn't change this principle, but what it does is preload the diff so the two axles connected to it are already hard to turn at different speeds.

With an open diff the wheel in mud may have a resistance of X, so the wheel on the rock gets X drive. With an LSD the resistance to turning may be 1.5X, so the wheel on the rock gets 1.5X. In other words, the wheel that is hardest to turn now has drive equivalent to the amount required to overcome the clutch in the LSD. That is a lot better than nothing. And it gets better, because as the diff spins the clutch packs move together and provide more resistance, restricting the differential action even more, and thus sending even more drive to the wheel that is hardest to turn, the one with traction.

There are other types of LSD such as geared or viscous, but the basic principle is they all restrict, but not stop, differential action.

LSDs are very often fitted to the rear axle of Japanese LWB 4WD vehicles as standard and can be bought aftermarket, although most people would spend the money on a locking differential instead.

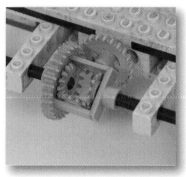

Model of a differential. The axles are turned by the input shaft, but are additionally free to rotate relative to each other.

LSDs can often mean the difference between making a tricky section or not.

electronic traction control (ETC)

Electronic Traction Control is a development of ABS (anti-lock brakes). ABS-equipped vehicles have sensors which tell a computer how fast each wheel is rotating. That information is used also for ETC. When the computer detects that a wheel is spinning quicker than it should be then it will apply the brakes to that spinning wheel, around 30 times a second if need be, and only to that wheel. This has the effect of making the spinning wheel harder for the diff to turn.

The diff, being lazy, decides to send more drive to the wheel which isn't spinning, which happens to be the one with more traction. Therefore, progress is continued. It is not dissimilar to a computer-controlled LSD, but more powerful. In other words, as soon as a wheel spins, the computer brakes that wheel, which in effect sends drive to the other, opposite, wheel on the axle. The diff equalises torque between the two wheels, so the harder the spinning one is to turn as the brakes are applied

to it by the computer, the more torque the other wheel gets. There is more on ETC in Chapter 9.

This Touraeg's passenger front wheel is spinning as the diff finds it easier to turn than the driver's side. However, the traction control computer is applying the brakes to the spinning wheel, sending torque to the opposite wheel. Same at the back, except it's the driver's side rear that's spinning. Thus, the vehicle is able to keep moving. Without traction control the driver would need to use momentum to conquer this little set of rocks, or choose a better line up the rocks.

The diagram shows the diff and axles again, in mud with a wheel spinning. The gold bars represent the brakes. After a fraction of a second the ETC computer realises the wheel in mud is spinning quicker than the other one and applies the brakes to that first wheel, making it harder to turn. The differential turns both wheels with the same torque so the braking in effect means the wheel not in mud gets extra torque and the vehicle can continue.

problem 2: front and rear axles

Now we have diff theory is explained, it's time to look at the second basic problem.

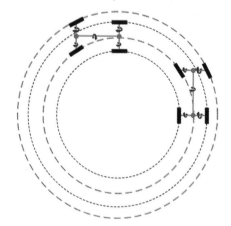

When the vehicle turns a corner the front axle travels a greater distance than the rear.

On each axle the outside wheel is travelling further than the inside wheel (as shown by the relative size of the blue arrows), but we've fixed that with differentials. But when the vehicle turns a corner the front axle travels a greater distance than the rear. Have you ever clipped a kerb with the rear wheels of a vehicle but not the front? Or followed a big truck around a tight bend and seen the rear wheels cut the corner? That's the rear wheels taking a shorter arc.

This means the **front wheels must turn quicker than the rear wheels when the vehicle corners.**

This is no problem for 2WD drivers, but it is for 4WDs because **if the front axle is driven, and so is the rear axle, both are going to rotate at the same speed. Yet, cornering demands different speeds.** This is true whether the vehicle turns left, or right, travels forwards or backwards.

If the 4WD was turning on low-traction surfaces like ice or dirt then the tyres could scuff, letting the front and rear axles turn at the same speed. However, on bitumen, which is high traction, the axles still want to turn at different speeds, but they can't really because the tyres are gripping the road so well. So you have a sort of "immovable object meets unstoppable force" situation, and what happens is that the transmission is stressed; the metal parts are literally wound up like a spring, which is why this state of affairs is called "windup". Imagine a long length of pipe metal with two extremely strong men on each end, one twisting it clockwise, the other stopping his end from twisting. The pipe would be in some tension, and this is what is happening to the transmission when a 4WD is driven on bitumen or other high-traction surfaces.

Here are some numbers, using a Discovery 3 which has a turning circle of 11.45 metres kerb to kerb, a wheelbase of 2.885 metres and a track of 1.6 metres.

Wheel	Dist wheel travels 360 degrees	%
Inner rear	23.8	0%
Outer rear	33.9	42%
Inner front	25.9	9%
Outer front	36.0	51%

Overall, the front axle travels 7% further than the rear after a 360° turn at full lock. And that's the second problem. Understand that, and you've got the key to understanding much 4WD theory, which helps with your driving. Of course, some 4WD vehicles can be driven on bitumen, so clearly there is a solution. In fact, there are several.

1   *Almost any dirt road is loose enough for windup not to be a concern.*

2   *Bitumen, even when soaking wet, is sufficiently high-traction for windup to occur.*

3   *Offroad, but relatively smooth rock is flat, high traction and thus a risk of windup, even after turning 90 degrees sharply.*

solutions to the front and rear axle problem

There are two basic solutions to this particular issue; part-time 4WD and constant 4WD.

part-time 4WD

Drive in 2WD (usually rear wheel drive) on the road, 4WD off it. Drive is simply disconnected to the front axle, shown in the diagram by a break in the front driveshaft. There is no chance of windup now because the front axle is disconnected entirely from the rear and can rotate at whatever speed it chooses.

This solution is simple, cheap, effective and somewhat out of date, also known as "selectable 4WD". Found in many older 4WDs, Nissan Patrols up to the GU models, the Holden Colorado 7, Toyota FJ Cruiser and most 4WD utes.

The reasons that this system has fallen out of favour are to do with safety and handling. Simply put, an all-wheel-drive vehicle is far more able to grip the road than a 2WD. At some point you have probably seen a ute or powerful 2WD car lose the

back end around a wet roundabout, even if it's not being driven particularly hard. If that vehicle had been AWD then the loss of traction would have been very unlikely to occur, and much more

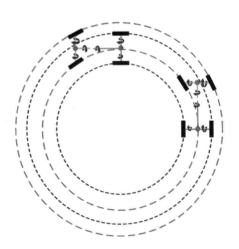

Part-time or selectable 4WD systems are simply 2WD on the road. The front axle is in grey because it is not driven and just freewheels, which avoids windup. The size of the blue arrows indicates the relative speed of each wheel. The outside wheels travel faster than the inside wheels, and the front wheels travel faster than the rear. The front driveshaft, in grey, is freewheeling faster than the rear driveshaft in green.

easily controllable even if it did. Older 4WDs had such poor handling and little power that being 2WD on the road didn't matter; nowadays even the basic utes have 130kW, five or six speeds and a lot of torque, which is more than enough to break traction. Add taller suspension designed for carrying weight with offroad tyres and the solution is very definitely AWD.

constant 4WD

In Chapter 1 we talked about an "all wheel drive" vehicle, one that has all four wheels driven, yet is designed for road use. So it must be possible to drive all four wheels on bitumen. The solution has already been mentioned, and that is a differential.

Constant 4WD systems use a third differential (or something that does much the same job) between the front and rear axles.

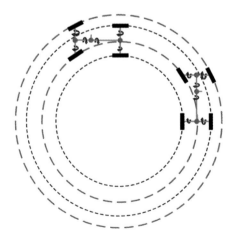

The addition of a third, centre, differential solves the problem. Now both front and rear axles can be driven at different speeds. The little green shaft on the right of the centre diff represents the drive coming from the engine. Note the relative sizes of the blue arrows showing relative rotation speed.

The centre diff works in exactly the same way as the ones on the axles, which means it is a special arrangement of gears which permit drive to be transmitted to both the front and rear axles, allowing them to turn at different speeds. So all four wheels are driven without windup. This is the basis of how AWD cars work on the road: there's something between the front and rear axles that drives their driveshafts at different relative speeds depending on whether the vehicle is turning or not.

free-wheeling hubs

This isn't a solution to the differential problem, but it's a variant on part-time 4WD that's extremely important to understand.

When in 2WD, the part-time 4WD system is inefficient. The front part of the transmission (axles and driveshaft) is rotated by the front wheels, wasting energy. Free-wheeling hubs solve this problem by disconnecting the front wheels from the axles when in free mode. The hubs can be manual (which means you need to get out of the vehicle and turn the switch on the wheel to and from free and lock) or automatic (which means that's done for you). Automatic hubs lock when the vehicle is put into 4WD and driven forwards or backwards a metre or so to engage the hubs. They disengage when the vehicle is put into 2WD and again moved. Manual hubs are either in or out depending on whether they are set to lock or free, and do not lock or unlock dependent on whether the vehicle is in 4WD or moving.

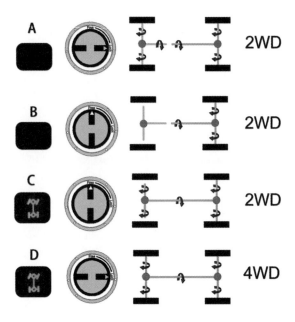

A | 2WD
B | 2WD
C | 2WD
D | 4WD

Free-wheeling hubs are manually locked or unlocked (set to "free") by turning the dial.

Land Cruiser 76 Series with manual-locking hubs and a part-time 4WD system.

Diag A: *The front wheels of a part-time 4WD rotate, which in turn rotates the front axle, differential and driveshaft for no good effect, just wasting fuel. The hubs are set to "Locked", and the dash light display does not show 4WD.*

Diag B: *Free-wheeling hubs disconnect the wheels from axle so the wheels freewheel, and the axle can remain stationary. Hubs are set to "Free". This is shown by the front axle not quite reaching the wheel, but in reality it's just a mechanical disengagement. The principle, however, is the same.*

Diag C: *If you engage 4WD and forget to lock in the hubs then you'll be turning the front driveshaft, the front diff and the axles…but not the wheels! Hubs are set to "Free". Dash light display says you're in 4WD but what it really means is you're turning the front driveshaft.*

Diag D: *4WD engaged and hubs locked – what you want for offroad.*

Typical symbol that appears on the dash when 4WD is engaged on part-time 4WDs, or sometimes it just says "4WD". With manual hubs, that doesn't mean to say all four wheels are driven! Note there is no 'X' between the axles which would mean a centre diff is locked.

summary

- 4WD means driving the front axle and the rear axle at the same time.
- When a vehicle goes around a corner, the front axle travels further than the rear axle.
- If both axles are driven at the same speed, this causes transmission windup. This is a problem.
- The basic two ways to deal with the "4WD problem" are:
  - Drive in 2WD on bitumen
  - Use a centre differential or equivalent
- Free-wheeling hubs are used on part-time 4WD vehicles to disconnect the wheels from the drivetrain in order to save fuel.

centre diffs: the trouble with the solution

The solution of putting a differential between the front and rear axles works reasonably well on-road, but it doesn't work offroad. As we know, a differential will send drive to the shaft or axle that's easiest to turn, which is invariably where it's least needed. Vehicles that have a centre diff have the same problem.

Consider a constant 4WD vehicle with a front wheel in the air.

Drive goes from the engine to the centre diff. The centre diff will send drive to wherever it is easiest. Think of the rear of the vehicle. Both wheels are on the ground. At the front, one wheel is in the air. What happens is that all the drive goes to the wheel in the air, and none to any of the three wheels on the ground. This situation will be

referred to later on as 3WOTGA1S, or "3 Wheels On The Ground And 1 Spinning".

A centre diff is fine as long as all four wheels have roughly equal amounts of traction, such as on the road. As soon as one or more wheels have significant differences in traction – which happens all the time offroad – then the three diffs in the transmission (one centre, two on the axles) combine to send drive to where it's least needed, to the wheel(s) with the least traction.

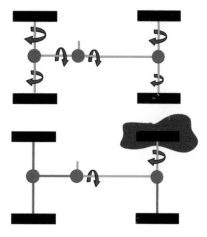

The diagram above shows a constant 4WD, or all wheel drive system with a normal centre diff, unlocked. This works fine so long as all four wheels have the same or close to the same amount of traction, such as on flat bitumen. However, when offroad each wheel may have vastly differing traction, and the lower diagram shows the vehicle with one wheel in mud. That's now by far the easiest wheel to turn so all the drive goes to that wheel, none to the other wheels, and no progress is made.

solutions to the centre diff problem

There are several solutions to this problem which fall into a fewer number of groups, described below. While we have described the device which distributes torque front and rear as a centre differential, and in many cases it is, there are other devices which do exactly the same job but aren't differentials. The correct term is "coupling", or "torque splitter".

lockable centre diffs

This is the simplest solution. The centre diff is simply locked and unlocked, usually by a lever in the cabin. When it is unlocked it acts as an open differential, turning both front and rear driveshafts while permitting them to turn at different speeds around a corner. However, it is vulnerable to the 3WOTGA1S situation – so when offroad it is locked in exactly the same way as a cross-axle locker. When locked the centre diff, in effect, ceases to exist, and both the front and rear shafts turn at the same speed. The car is working exactly the same as a part-time 4WD with the hubs locked and 4WD engaged. This means that if driven on a high-traction surface the vehicle will certainly get transmission windup – but it also means that the 3WOTGA1S cannot occur, as drive is sent equally to front and rear axles. It is still possible to come to a halt if you have one wheel on each axle losing traction (say front left and rear right), but that's much better than coming to a halt as soon as one wheel loses traction.

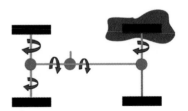

Now the centre diff is locked, so it no longer acts as a diff. The shafts now have to turn at the same speed. While this doesn't fix the problem on the rear axle – the rear diff is still sending all rear drive to the wheel easiest to turn – the front wheels still have good traction and can pull the car through. You can think of the drive to a wheel as being like pressurised water with each of the wheels being a tap; if the tap is open (wheel easy to turn) the water will escape.

A slippery, wet surface which shortly moves into bitumen. The Defender has constant 4WD so it has all-paw traction on all surfaces. In really slippery conditions the centre diff would be locked, but with pretty much equal traction on all four wheels on a flat surface the car does a good job of dividing power equally between all four wheels, great for traction which means good handling and safety.

viscous couplings

A viscous coupling is like a centre diff, even though it's not a differential. It allows the front and rear driveshafts to be driven at different speeds.

However, as the speed difference between the shafts increases, the viscous coupling starts to lock up, beginning to act like a locked centre diff.

Viscous couplings are quite simple. The front and rear driveshafts each have a plate at the end and the plates rotate in some fluid. If the two plates rotate as the same speed, the fluid also goes around at that speed, but if one plate starts to rotate significantly slower than the other, then that heats up the fluid which changes its viscosity (thickness, like from water to honey) which in turn starts to "glue" the plates together, and so the coupling becomes like a locked centre differential.

This is great, because if a viscous coupling is used instead of a centre diff, the coupling allows the front and rear driveshafts to turn enough to avoid transmission windup, as when the car is turned through a corner the speed difference is quite small. It also helps in the 3WOTGA1S situation. After the front wheel in the air has spun a little, the front driveshaft is going much quicker than the rear, and instantly the viscous coupling locks up, sends drive to the other shaft, and on we go.

So if a viscous coupling is so good, why do we need anything else? Why bother with a centre diff lock, which is manually operated? Good questions, and the answer lies in the operation of the viscous coupling.

The coupling permits some difference in shaft speed before it begins to lock up.

This means, for example, in the 3WOTGA1S situation, the front wheel in the air has to spin a little before any drive goes to the back. Not very much, and according to manufacturers it's

instantaneous, imperceptible and so on – words that should ring immediate alarm bells.

But the problem is that no matter how quickly the system reacts, it is reacting to a situation that has already developed. A locked centre diff, on the other hand, is already distributing drive 50/50 front and rear, so there isn't that momentary spin.

Softroaders often use viscous couplings because it saves on the weight and expense of a lockable centre diff. It's also easier for the driver to understand, just drive and let the 4WD system do its thing. Viscous couplings can be very effective, but aren't usually found on heavy-duty 4WDs, or, if they are, there are other mechanisms too.

torsen diffs

"Torsen" is a registered trademark of the Toyoda-Koki company. The word means "Torque Sensing".

The torque sensing bit comes into play when one wheel on an axle loses traction, and therefore accepts less torque. Then torque bias happens; let's say it's a 5:1 ratio. That then means that the wheel with traction gets five times the torque of the wheel with less traction.

This is exactly what we want to happen; more torque going to the wheel with traction. It's instantaneous, too, no waiting for traction control or an LSD to work – it's entirely mechanical.

So why isn't everyone running Torsen diffs?

Because $5 \times 0 = 0$. If a wheel is in the air, then it requires so little torque to turn it that the partner wheel gets almost nothing, and you're going nowhere. Torsen diffs are also expensive and complex. They are also being replaced by something that a computer can more easily control. Torsen diffs are often used as centre diffs (notably in the Toyota Prado 120 and Volkswagen Touareg) because the chances of completely losing all traction on one axle compared to the other are a lot smaller than losing traction on one wheel compared to another. In that case, the Torsen works very well.

A Prado 120 with a Torsen centre diff. This does a much better job of distributing torque front and rear than a conventional diff, but like all mechanical systems is largely reactive; it can't predict or work out what's happening from other parts of the vehicle.

electronic centre couplings

All the systems described thus far have been mechanical. Computers are very much a part of modern vehicles and can now control the torque difference between front and rear driveshafts using something like an electrically operated clutch, which can be entirely open or entirely locked, or anywhere in between. The computer's input comes from many sensors; relative speeds of all the wheels, steering wheel input, engine torque and more, then it works out what the best front/

rear torque distribution is and operates the centre clutch to that effect. When correctly designed these are the most effective systems on the market as it is not always ideal to have an exact 50/50 front/rear torque split – this assumes the front wheels have exactly the same traction as the rear, which is very rarely the case, for example when ascending a hill. The computer can also pre-empt what will happen, for example, when accelerating hard from standstill – it may bias the torque towards the rear even as the accelerator pedal is depressed. A mechanical system would need to wait until there was front wheel slippage before reacting.

The current state of the art is the Range Rover. This doesn't have a centre differential as such; instead it has an electronically operated clutch that can instantly vary the torque front and rear, controlled by a computer.

on-demand 4WD

An on-demand 4WD system is one that drives one axle, usually the front, and lets the other axle freewheel. When necessary, the other axle is driven. This arrangement is most commonly found on softroaders, which allow the rear axle to trail for fuel economy reasons, although Nissan employs a RWD variant of on-demand in some operation modes with its All-Mode 4WD. The decision to drive the other axle is usually controlled by a computer on modern vehicles which can determine when the driving axle is slipping. The centre coupling is not usually a differential, but an electrically operated clutch and computer-controlled clutch, which works on a similar conceptual principle to a differential, but can better vary the torque front and rear. While there are marginal fuel economy advantages with on-demand (and again manufacturers claim their systems are instant-response), the problem is again they have to react to a problem once it has developed. True AWDs may never break traction in the first place so are much preferred, and AWD handling is even safer than FWD. The better on-demand 4WDs have a manually operated system that locks the centre clutch, although these tend to disengage at around 40km/h and often cannot withstand sustained use without overheating. For these reasons on-demand is not ideal for offroading, especially sustained use such as long beach runs.

The Volvo XC90 drives the front wheels for fuel efficiency and safe, conservative handling. This is all fine up until you get into a slippery situation which calls for all wheels to be

driven. By the time the rear wheels kick in it can be a little late. True AWD cars already drive all four wheels all the time.

summary

- Differentials send drive to the axle that is easiest to turn. If one wheel is on a slippery surface, that wheel gets a lot of drive and the other wheel gets a lot less.

- That causes a problem because it could turn an AWD into a one-wheel drive.

- Some centre diffs can be locked, so they do not act as diffs at all; then exactly 50% of the drive is sent to the front and rear axles. This mode must not be used on bitumen because of transmission windup.

- Viscous couplings are devices that permit a bit of slip between two axles, enough for cornering, but then quickly lock up and act like a locked centre diff.

- Electronically operated, computer-controlled central clutches distribute torque front and rear according to the computer's direction, based on many sensors around the vehicle. These are the way of the future.

- On-demand systems drive one set of wheels, usually the front, and only drive the other when required. Sometimes they can be manually set to drive both at low speeds.

petrol and diesel engines

There are differences between petrol and diesel engines that translate into differences in driving techniques and accessory selection. This section explains those differences in detail.

Petrol and diesel engines work in the same basic manner; a small explosion is created inside a cylinder which forces the cylinder down, which turns a crankshaft, which turns a driveshaft, which turns differentials, axles and wheels. The major difference is that with petrol, a mixture of fuel and air is ignited by a spark, but with diesel the mere injection of fuel into the compressed air is what creates ignition.

differences in theory

There are significant differences between the two engines, although modern technology is blurring the line.

Energy content: A litre of diesel contains about 18% more energy than a litre of petrol. Diesel is also an oily fuel, which is why diesel engines are sometimes referred to as "oilers" or "oil burners".

Compression ratio: The fuel/air mixture in both engines is compressed by the piston before ignition. The amount of compression is expressed as a ratio, for example 12:1, meaning it is compressed 12 times more than atmosphere pressure. The higher the compression:

- the more energy required to start the vehicle
- the better the engine braking
- the worse the effect of ingesting water into the engine

The compression ratio of diesels is higher, thus diesels need more energy to start (bigger batteries), brake better downhill and while any water ingress will damage any engine, it'll be worse for diesels.

Stroke: The stroke is the distance the cylinder moves up and down. Long-stroke engines can develop lots of torque at low speed, but become inefficient at higher engine speeds. Diesel engines tend to have longer strokes than petrol engines.

Flash point: Diesel has a much higher flash point than petrol, which means it takes more heat and effort to ignite diesel than petrol. That's good for safety.

differences in practice

Modern diesels have greatly improved the disadvantages of diesels like noise and vibration. Intercoolers and turbos have improved power and torque. Petrol engines have also eroded the advantages of diesels but to a lesser degree; electronic engine management has improved low-down torque and fuel efficiency. However, the differences remain:

Fuel efficiency and range: Diesel vehicles are anywhere between 10-40% more efficient than their petrol equivalent. The difference in differences for specific vehicles are mainly due to the relative age of the engines; a vehicle offered with a very new petrol engine and an ageing diesel will have specifications much closer than another vehicle with two engines of the same vintage, and the quality and design of the gearbox (especially autos) plays a part too. It is important to note that the harder an engine is worked, the greater the fuel consumption, but diesels do not increase their fuel consumption under load as much as petrol engines, an important point when considering towing, sand driving or carrying a heavy load.

Many Australian trips involve long distances while heavily loaded. Under these conditions diesels are far more fuel efficient than petrol engines, which is why offroaders pay higher premiums for diesels. It's not just the fuel cost, it's the fact you need to carry a lot less fuel. Our Defender made it over the Simpson using 65L of diesel, and we took 140L. A petrol vehicle would have needed to find room for quite a bit of fuel which would also weigh more.

Torque: Diesels produce their torque lower down the rev range than petrol engines. They are generally better for towing, and for crawling at low speeds offroad.

Power: Petrol engines are generally more powerful, so better suited for general road use. This is because they are better able to rev higher.

Engine braking: Diesels are better at engine braking because of the higher compression ratios.

Weight: Diesel engines weigh more than petrol engines, not least because they often also have intercoolers and turbos. Diesel fuel also weighs more per litre than petrol.

Responsiveness: A petrol engine, with a shorter stroke, less compression and no reliance on a turbo, will respond more quickly to accelerator inputs than a diesel.

Noise and vibration: Diesels are noisier and tend to vibrate more than petrol engines.

Starting: Because of the high compression, diesels need more power to start; that's why keeping your battery in good condition is very important for diesel owners.

Safety: Petrol is a lot more flammable than diesel. This particular difference is of interest to 4WDers in case you need to carry jerry cans of fuel. Of course, the extra range of a diesel means fewer jerries are necessary in the first place.

Anything that involves speed usually means petrol engines are a better bet, and powering along through sand is where a powerful petrol engine is ideal, especially with its quick response to throttle input. This heavy LX570 makes easy work of the sand, albeit with an expert driver at the helm.

common-rail diesels

There are many interesting diesel and petrol technologies, but the term "common-rail diesel" is, well, common, and so needs a short explanation. The rail is a long thin tube and filled with diesel at extremely high pressure. That diesel is let out into the cylinders, controlled by a computer. The advantage of the design is that fuel can be very precisely controlled, even down to small additional injections of fuel before and after the main injection. All this translates to reduced noise and improved economy and power. This is often represented by manufacturers using designations such as CRDi.

diesel and petrol: a comparison

The table below is a comparison of three Toyota Land Cruiser 100 Series vehicles, all in mid-spec GXL trim. The only difference is the engines, which are:

4.2 standard: a plain 4.2 litre diesel engine

4.2 tdi: the same engine, but with an intercooler and turbocharger (see below)

4.7 petrol: a petrol engine of 4.7L capacity

Points to note:

- The turbo and intercooler improves power by better than 50% and torque by about 50%.

Makes a big difference! However, that model is heavier, which reduces the payload and takes the edge of the more powerful engine.

- Both diesels' torque peaks much lower down the rev band than the petrol. The petrol produces easily the most power, but at a higher rpm.
- The fuel consumption is about 50% better on diesel than petrol. The extra efficiency of the tdi offsets the greater weight. This 50% disparity would be increased when offroad.

So what's best? For towing and offroad, the turbodiesel. It has the most torque and it's all available at a low 1,800rpm. The petrol has to rev almost twice as hard to produce a little less torque. That will drive fuel consumption even higher.

Where would the petrol be best? For quicker acceleration. It has an extra 20kW, and is 200kg lighter than the turbodiesel.

There is never, ever, one generic answer to whether petrol or diesel is best. It very much depends on the vehicles being compared and the uses the vehicles will be put to.

LPG

Liquid Petroleum Gas is a mixture of butane and propane and is an option for some petrol engine

Model	Kerb weight (kg)	Fuel/100km	Fuel tank capacity	Range (km)	Power (kW @ rpm)	Torque (Nm @ rpm)
4.2	2,356	14	145	1,036	96 @ 3,800	285 @ 2,200
4.2 tdi	2,618	12	141	1,175	151 @ 3,400	430 @ 1,800
4.7 petrol	2,406	19	145	763	170 @ 4,800	410 @ 3,400

vehicles. The advantage is that because it is very environmentally friendly, it's very cheap. The disadvantages are that it's not particularly efficient, so fuel consumption is 15-25% greater, it's not available in the more remote locations and the engine runs a fair bit hotter. When offroad many owners switch to petrol for the additional power. Not all vehicles can be converted to LPG.

engine features

turbochargers and superchargers

A turbocharger has a fan that sits in the way of the exhaust gas and spins as the exhaust flows past. The fan drives a compressor that compresses the air before it gets into the engine. The greater the volume of air in the piston, the greater the amount of fuel needed to maintain the correct fuel/air ratio: the more the fuel, the bigger the bang and the more the power. Turbos can increase an engine's power by about 30-40%, but don't do very much for off-idle torque as there isn't a sufficient quantity of exhaust gas to get the compressor going. You'll hear people talk about "turbo lag" – this is the sudden increase in power as the turbo kicks in, which can be disconcerting, or could mean boost threshold, which is an apparently slow response to the throttle until the turbo starts to help. Modern engines are much better in this respect than older ones, and modern diesels are almost always fitted with turbochargers, usually sophisticated versions like twins or variable-vanes which are designed to mask boot and threshold problems.

A supercharger is exactly the same as a turbocharger but doesn't have a fan. Instead, the compressor is driven directly by the engine.

A Range Rover Sport with a supercharged V8 petrol engine, capable of sprinting from 0-100 in around 7.5 seconds.

turbo timers

A turbo timer is a device fitted to a turbocharged engine which idles the engine for a certain time after the car is stopped, the driver exits and locks the vehicle. The reason for this is to allow the turbo to spool down. However, they are not needed. Turbos do need to spool down but they do so very quickly and certainly don't need two or three minutes – even just coming into a driveway will do it. Manufacturers just recommend not revving the engine high and then immediately shutting it off, but that's bad practice with any engine. Turbo timers also mean the vehicle relies only on its park brake to immobilise the vehicle instead of also using the gearbox by leaving the vehicle in gear.

A Range Rover Sport with a turbocharged V6 diesel engine, capable of ambling from 0-100 in around 13 seconds. It also has an intercooler.

intercoolers

An intercooler is a device for cooling air before it gets to the cylinders of the engine. The cooler the air, the more that can be sucked into the engine, the better the compression and the bigger the bang; more torque at any given rpm, and more power! These are almost always fitted to modern diesel engines.

engine braking

If you are driving a vehicle at any speed and then release the accelerator, the vehicle will slow down. There are many reasons why this is the case, such as aerodynamic drag, but one of the major reasons is engine braking. If you are driving at 100km/h in fifth gear and come off the throttle you'll slow; if you were in third gear at the same speed you

would slow down a lot quicker. This is engine braking, or slowing down using the internal friction of the engine and the lower gears. The lower the gear, the higher the engine is forced to rev, the greater the friction and the quicker you slow down.

This is the main reason why the car at 100km/h in third gear slows down a lot quicker than the one in fifth, even though other factors like the aerodynamic drag are the same. In other words, the wheels suddenly want to make the engine run faster than it was before and that creates resistance, which slows the vehicle.

Engine braking is not taught very often to road drivers as modern brakes are more than enough to slow a vehicle (another difference between offroad driving and road driving), but it still has its place on the road when towing or descending long, steep hills, or both. Engine braking is an important part of offroad driving because it means the vehicle can be slowed with less risk of a wheel locking.

Descending a steep hill in a very low gear means you may not need to apply the brakes at all in order to maintain a slow speed, and that means more control – the engine is turning the wheels as opposed to you applying the brakes, which may induce a skid. The steepness of a hill that can be descended in this manner depends on how low the gearing is, and how much the engine resists being forced to turn at a higher speed that it would for a given throttle opening. The latter is largely governed by the compression ratio (see above), which is why diesels, which tend to compress the air inside the cylinder more than petrol engines, typically provide better engine braking.

CHAPTER 4

GEARING & TRANSMISSIONS

4WDs have low-range gearing. What is this, and why is it important?

about gears

A 4WD's engine spins very fast; at idle, even a diesel is doing about 700 rpm, or revs per minute. If the engine drove the wheels directly, then that would translate to a speed of about 38km/h. At idle.

Clearly, it would be a good idea to have a minimum speed a bit slower than 38km/h. And it would be good to operate the engine at, say, 2,000rpm, where it can develop much more torque; that's around the peak torque rev band for the average diesel.

What we need is gearing; the ability for the engine to rev at a speed where it can develop some useful torque, yet deliver that torque so the wheels are driven at a slower rate.

There is a major benefit to gearing for 4WDs, and that's the torque increase. That's easy to understand by thinking of riding a bicycle. If you need to cycle up a steep hill, you need a larger turning force applied to the wheel, or more torque. So what you do is to keep pedalling with the same force, but change down a gear. You now move slower, but generate more torque which is what you need to get up the hill. If you have a high-power, low-ish torque engine you can gear down, producing more torque. So why the obsession with 4WD engines, lots of torque and low down in the rpm range? Because the more torque produced the less gearing needed, the easier the engine is to drive, the less fuel it uses and the quieter it is. What would you prefer; driving up a hill at 1,500rpm, or

moving at the same speed but with the engine doing 5,000rpm? Even if you were to gear down that far, you'd lose a lot of mechanical efficiency in the gears.

The disadvantage of using very low gears is the small speed range. To go from 1,000rpm to 4,000rpm in first low is only a few km/h. In 5th high, 1,000rpm to 4,000rpm may go from about 50-130km/h. That's why the best engines for 4WDs produce a lot of torque at very low rpm, so you can move slowly while having the entire rev range available so you can speed up if necessary. However, all that torque in low-range means the transmission has to be strong enough to cope with the stress, which is why abrupt and large throttle openings in low-range are definitely not recommended.

4WD gears

From the engine to the wheels there are usually three main sets of gears involved:

- Gearbox
- Transfer case
- Differential

All three of these gears increase torque and slow the shafts down.

- The gearbox is what you're familiar with; it has five, but sometimes four or as many as nine ratios plus reverse, and for the purposes of this section it doesn't matter whether it is automatic or manual.
- The transfer case is something special for 4WDs. It houses the high/low-range gears.

- The differential also does its part in slowing the drive down to a reasonable speed at the wheels.

The table below shows the gearing for automatic and manual petrol and diesel Prado 150 GXLs. The numbers represent the ratios, eg "4.171" means the output gear turns once for every 4.171 turns of the input gear.

Prado 150

Prado 150 GXL								
	3.0 TDI				**4.0 V6 Petrol**			
	6spd Manual		**5sp Auto**		**6spd Manual**		**5sp Auto**	
	High	**Low**	**High**	**Low**	**High**	**Low**	**High**	**Low**
1st	4.171		3.52		3.83		2.804	
Transfer	1	2.566	1	2.566	1	2.566	1	2.566
Diff	3.909		3.727		3.909		3.727	
Crawl Ratio	16.30	41.84	13.12	33.66	14.97	38.42	10.45	26.82
Weight (approx)	2290-2330 kg				2210-2250 kg			
Power (Kw) @ RPM	127 @ 3400				202 @ 5600			
Torque (Nm) @ RPM	410 @ 1600-2800				381 @ 4400			
Compression ratio	17.9:1				10.4:1			
Fuel economy (L/100km)	8.8		8.5		13.0		11.5	

The "crawl ratio" is the lowest gear the vehicle has. It is found by multiplying three items; the first gear, the low-range and the diff ratio. The lower the better; the slower you go for any given engine speed, and the better the engine braking. These two Prado automatics are five-speeders, so they have a much higher first gear than the six-speed manuals. The difference is that you can't slip the clutch for long in a manual without wearing it out, but an automatic is designed to operate without the engine being directly connected to the driveshaft (see later in this Chapter), so you can achieve the same low speed – as with a manual gearbox – of the engine operating in a good rev band yet the vehicle moving slowly. This does not negate the need for low-range in automatics, but it does lessen it.

The transfer ratio is 1:1 in high-range, so it makes no difference, but first low is 2.566 times lower than first high; and that's a useful reduction.

Don't assume that petrol engines run the same diff ratios as diesels, either. The auto petrol has a different ratio to the rest of the range. Because diesel engines and petrol engines deliver their torque and power differently across the rev range, and automatic transmissions works differently to manual, it's by no means uncommon to have different diff ratios across a range of otherwise identical cars.

The weight, power and torque are included for interest. As usual, the diesels are heavier than petrol engines, the autos heavier than the manual, and although in this case the petrol engine produces a little more torque, it's further up the rev range than diesel. In this case the autos return better fuel economy than the manuals which is unusual, but rapidly becoming less so. The compression ratio is quite different too, so where manual diesel has a 1:41 crawl ratio vs the petrols 1:38 the diesel's greater compression ratio will improve still further its ability to engine brake.

The crawl ratio is an indication of how good the vehicle is at low-speed work, for example coming down steep hills or climbing over rocks. It's not the only factor by any means. Other things to consider are:

- **The engine:** Diesels have higher compression ratios than petrol engines, so they will descend slower under engine braking.
- **Weight of the vehicle:** The heavier the vehicle, the more torque it needs to move and

the more difficult it will be to restrain coming downhill.

- **Tyres:** Larger tyres effectively lower the crawl ratio, which is why a set of aftermarket crawler gears are usually fitted to vehicles with 35" and 37" diameter tyres.

how low-range works

Low-range is there to allow the vehicle to move slowly with its engine operating in or around the maximum torque band, and with the clutch fully up. It is also fantastic for engine braking and securing a vehicle on a hill.

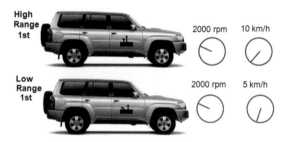

Same revs, lower speed…how much lower depends on the transfer case reduction ratio. In the Patrol that's 1:2.02 as standard.

Low-range is selected by a number of means. Sometimes it's a button, sometimes it's a lever. In all cases stopping, selecting neutral on the main gearbox, and not rushing it will help ensure a successful range change. Sometimes selecting low-range will automatically lock a centre diff (if fitted, and that's most vehicles), sometimes it won't – examples of the latter are Land Rover Defenders and Discovery Series 1 and 2/2a. Some vehicles vary, for example there are many variants of LC100, with everything from part-time 4WD to constant 4WD with a centre diff that is locked in low-range. Sometimes you simply select low-range and there's a separate button to lock the centre diff. The Prado variants will either automatically lock their centre diff or not, depending on year and trim spec.

The best advice is to read the owner's manual carefully and follow its instructions. You will know when you're in low-range as the car's gearing will feel different, requiring more frequent gear changes. However, with a modern automatic vehicle even experienced drivers can accidentally drive in high range when they think they're in low, so a positive check is important – look for a dash light or other indicator.

Jeep Wrangler about to attempt a rocky downhill. Clearly, high speed is not a great idea and low-range allows the driver to move the vehicle slowly and in control.

low-range vs high-range

How low is first low – or second low – relative to first high?

It depends, of course, on the various ratios. Two example vehicles, a Land Rover Defender TD5 and a Nissan Patrol GU, are compared below. Both have five-speed manual gearboxes.

An LC100's range selector level showing high-, neutral- and low-range.

The Holden Colorado and Isuzu D-Max utes have push-button selectors for 4WD (they are part-time 4WD) and for low-range.

When a constant 4WD vehicle has its centre diff locked, or a part-time 4WD vehicle is in 4WD, you typically see an information light such as this one on the dash. The orange icon has an X between the axles which indicates this vehicle has a constant 4WD system with a centre diff lock. Contrast the green icon with no X on

part-time 4WD on page 36. There is not usually any light to denote a vehicle being either in high- or low-range.

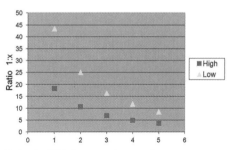

Defender TD5, five-speed manual

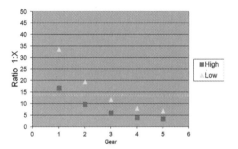

Patrol GU TD6, five-speed manual

The graphs show that the Defender has first and second low well and truly lower than first high. This is because of the massive 3.32 reduction in the transfer case, or the input shaft turning 3.32 times for every rotation of the output shaft. The Patrol's second low is lower than its first high, but not by as much; 2.02 isn't a particularly good reduction. Both of them have gears third to fifth low under third high. It's worth noting the Patrol has a big 4.2L engine as opposed to the Defender's smaller 2.5L, so the Defender would lose some of its gearing advantage as it has to rev higher. However, to balance that again, the Defender is about 500kg lighter!

As a rough rule of thumb the high/low-range relationship is something like this:

- Second low is a little lower than first high
- Third low is a little lower than second high
- Fourth and fifth low are between second high and third high
- Fifth low is a lower gear than third high
- First gear is generally a little lower than reverse.

It pays to know what's relative to what as sometimes you need to move to high-range to utilise the different set of gear ratios.

Caution: As you can see, fifth low is about equal to third high, but that's equal in gear ratio only. Fifth gear is designed for cruising, and that means relatively little load from the engine. When was the last time you accelerated hard in fifth and took the engine to high revs? In the words of one gearbox mechanic, "fifth gear is not the strongest set of cogs in your box".

So be wary of using fifth low for the sort of acceleration and load you'd normally use third high

for. It's not designed for it. Gentle cruising is fine, but not high-revving sand work. Switch to high-range if you find you need fourth and fifth low.

A crawl ratio of better than 1:45 is pretty good for a 4WD, but not good enough for the rock crawlers. There are aftermarket kits to get the crawl ratio down to 1:100 or better. Sometimes two transfer cases are joined together for this purpose.

The death of low-range? This VW Amarok has an 8-speed automatic and no low-range. Yet it is a superb offroader, certainly can't be classified as a softroader and is more capable in tough, steep conditions than many low-range vehicles. The same is true of the new Range Rover Sport which is available without low-range in some variants. Low-range will eventually be deleted, probably when each wheel on a vehicle is individually driven by an electric motor, something we're seeing as hybrid diesel and petrol/electric vehicles come onto the market.

manual and automatic transmissions

manual transmissions

Manuals have two basic components; the gearbox and clutch. The gearbox has a set of gears; four on old vehicles, but these days usually five or six.

clutch

To change gears a clutch is used. A clutch is basically two shafts with large plates on each end. When the plates are apart, no drive is transmitted. That's when the clutch is fully down. When the clutch is fully up, the plates are very firmly pressed together so effectively the two shafts become one.

When the clutch is partially up, the two plates are together, but the driving plate is spinning faster than the driven plate. That's "slipping the clutch" and means you can drive slower than you would if the clutch was fully up.

However, you've probably smelt the disadvantage of this for long periods; fried clutch. The clutch is designed to be either up or down, with only short periods in between. Slipping the clutch continually is not a good idea as it quickly wears down what is an expensive bit of kit. Also, if an obstruction is encountered, for example a rock, the vehicle is likely to stop dead or stall. If you approached the same obstacle in low-range with the clutch up, the vehicle is far more likely to crawl over it.

automatic transmissions

There are two basic types of automatic transmissions; conventional and DSG, or Direct Shift Gearing.

There are also two basic types of driver control; conventional and manual-select, or "manumatic".

A Santa Fe, without low-range, edging over some rocks. Clearance isn't a problem so long as speed is kept very low, and the auto allows the driver to do just that. The manual would require the clutch to be slipped. Still, low-range would be better.

conventional automatics

A major difference between the automatic and manual transmissions is the clutch mechanism. With a manual, it's two plates held together with varying amounts of pressure, depending on whether the clutch is up or down or somewhere in between.

The automatic has a fluid clutch, which is also basically two plates, but the plates have vanes, are a fixed distance apart and are in a fluid-filled chamber. The one driven by the engine is called the pump and the other one, connected to the wheels, is called the turbine. The pump is connected to the engine's flywheel, so as the engine turns, the pump turns – this rotates the fluid and, because the turbine is also in the fluid, it turns too, but there is no direct mechanical linkage (most of the time), only fluid.

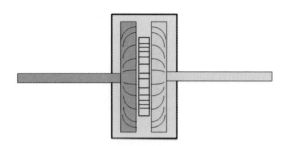

Simplified automatic transmission. The bright green shaft is driven by the engine, which turns the pump inside a chamber filled with fluid, shown in light grey. That fluid rotates, and thus turns the turbine, shown in lighter green, which is connected to the gearbox and thus the wheels. In between is the stator, also with vanes.

That's why automatic transmissions are sometimes called "slushboxes". It also explains why autos aren't often as fuel efficient as manuals. The fluid clutch is also known as a "torque converter" as there's an extra, static set of vanes in between the pump and the turbine called a stator which redirects fluid flow between pump and turbine during periods of high slip, such as when you're starting off in first gear, and increases the torque output.

The turbine doesn't quite spin at the same speed as the pump, so energy is wasted, unlike a manual. However, modern autos have a lock mode which locks out the fluid clutch when the speed of the turbine is close to that of the pump, and then the turbine and pump spin at the same speed. This is great for cruising and is generally known as "torque convertor lockup" and is where you want to run your automatic for best efficiency. You'll see when the convertor locks up as you'll be in the same gear as before but suddenly the revs will drop a bit.

As there isn't a direct connection between engine and propshaft, you don't need to worry about "slipping the clutch", right? Right – for shortish periods. However, the transmission fluid can heat up and then the fluid clutch starts to lose its effectiveness. Automatic 4WDs need low-range, but it's true that the fluid converter does compensate for lower gearing to some extent, which is why the best softroaders have automatic gearboxes. And it's easy to see why engine braking isn't as good with autos compared with manuals, as there's no direct link from the wheels to the engine.

The automatic gearbox system decides when a gear change is necessary by monitoring how hard the engine is working, the speed of the vehicle and where the accelerator pedal is. The monitoring can be mechanical via hydraulics, valves and vacuums, or (in the case of modern vehicles) electronically with a computer making the calls.

shift patterns

Conventional, older autos have a shift pattern of (assuming 4 speeds):

P – park
R – reverse
N – neutral
D – drive (car selects all four gears)
3 – drive (car selects from bottom three gears)
2 – drive (car selects from bottom two gears)
1 – drive (car is locked into first gear)

For most on-road driving conditions, most drivers would never use the 3, 2 or 1 positions. That will change for offroad, where it can be useful to restrict the gears the vehicle can use.

Some four-speed autos have P, R, N, D, 2, 1. An example is the 3-litre Nissan Patrol. Despite the absence of a "3", you can in fact select third gear by selecting "D" and then clicking the overdrive button on the gearshift – in effect a fourth gear. An overdrive is a high-speed cruising gear, so named because the ratio is less than 1:1. However, it is usually used as just another gear option.

2nd start

Conventional automatic gearboxes fitted to 4WDs may also have a "2nd start" button. This forces the transmission to pull away in second gear, either in high- or low-range. This is extremely useful in slippery conditions.

power and snow

Some conventional autos have a "power" mode. This generally does not actually make the engine any more powerful, but rather delays the gear changes so the engine revs longer in each gear. Sometimes this is known as a "sport" mode. A "snow" or "slippery conditions" mode is the reverse; the transmission will "short change", which means changing up gears earlier than normal, so as to avoid wheelspin.

1   *Ford Territory six-speed manumatic with P, R, N and D. For manual control move the level to the left and then pull it back to change up, forwards to change down.*

2   *The Hyundai Santa Fe is the same as the Ford except you push forwards to change up.*

3   *Jeep is different again; to get into manual mode you pull the selector back past neutral and then move left to change down, right to change up.*

4   *A conventional automatic on a Nissan Patrol. The shifter has 1, 2 and D. In position 1 the car is locked into first gear and cannot select a higher gear. In 2 it cannot select a gear higher than second. The D position uses all four gears, unless the overdrive is deselected by clicking the small button on the right of the selector lever, below the larger one which is the override for moving into R or P, making it a three-speed. Clicking the button again re-engages the overdrive, making it a four-speeder again. The Power A/T Hold button simply makes the engine hang on to the gears a little longer than normal.*

5   *The way of the future, a 2012 Range Rover with a dial to select Park, Reverse, Neutral, Drive and Sport. If you want to manually select a gear you use paddle shifters (pg 58).*

6   *Mercedes-Benz ML350 with a stalk-mounted gearshift. Press in a button at the end for the park brake, and the dash displays the gear selected.*

A "power second" button on an LC200. Choose between starting in second gear (useful offroad) or power. "Power" doesn't give you any more power, it just delays upshifts.

manumatics

A "manumatic" is a manually-selectable automatic gearbox. The typical pattern is:

Automatic mode

P – park

R – reverse

N – neutral

D – drive (car selects from all gears)

Manual mode

+: driver selects this momentarily to shift up a gear

–: driver selects this momentarily to shift down a gear

The current gear is usually displayed on the instrument panel in manual mode and sometimes automatic. Because the driver can select a gear there is no need for the 3, 2, 1 pattern found on conventional automatics.

The manumatic is sometimes incorrectly referred to as Tiptronic, which is Porsche's trademarked name for this system. Other manufacturers have different names, for example Land Rover use Command Shift

and BMW call theirs Steptronic. It is a pity that the manufacturers could not decide on a single name, but a real shame that they have not standardised how the gears should be shifted. Some, like BMW and Ford, use a lever back–shift up–lever forwards–shift down system, but Land Rover and Hyundai have the exact opposite. Jeep has a side to side mechanism for shifting up and down.

Manumatics work in one of two ways. Land Rover, Ford, Hyundai and others permit the driver to select a gear, say third, and the vehicle will then remain in third gear as long as it can. This is a "gear select" manumatic. Toyota is an example of a different approach. If third gear is selected that means the transmission will choose from gears one, two and three, but not four, five or six – this is a "maximum select" system. That is why manumatic Toyotas still have a 2nd start button – selecting "2" on the transmission means the vehicle will still pull away in first. With the other approach, Land Rovers for example, selecting third gear means you'll pull away in third. The system won't let you pull away in fourth – that's just getting silly.

Both systems have computer overrides. Should the speed drop too low, or the engine hit the rev limiter, the computer will change up or down as appropriate, but it will not re-select the original gear when it can. How cautious the computer is varies greatly; Land Rovers will in some situations let you stall the automatic, which is ideal, given you've selected the gear, whereas others change up and down as the computer sees fit with little regard for the driver's gear selection. In no case is the gear selection quite as "manual" as that for a true manual gearbox, and this is most notable when driving for

Modern adaptive automatics change shift points automatically depending on the conditions and driving styles. Going downhill or uphill they may delay upshifts, providing engine braking. They can also select a gear before you accelerate out of a corner, so you don't get that pause when the car needs to shift down as you exit the bend. With non-adaptive automatics it is often best to use sport mode going uphill, and lock out some of the higher gears coming downhill.

economy, when you would want to trickle along at 1,200–1,400rpm. Manumatics don't let you do that, although a modern automatic should get close to or even exceed the fuel economy of a manual vehicle, especially when cruising.

adaptive and sport modes

Manumatics are also typically adaptive, which means the computer monitors how the car is being driven and modifies the gear changes to suit. For example, it may decide you are driving quickly and hold on to gears longer, or detect a hill and select a lower gear to provide engine braking. A sport mode is giving the adaptive system a hint that you'll be driving quicker than usual, but it has uses elsewhere (as explained in the chapters on driving techniques). The adaptive learning is continuous,

so if you enter town after a spirited country drive the auto will quickly learn you're now driving gently. There is no need to be concerned that your other half will "teach" the car bad habits.

stop/start systems

The very latest automatics now shut the engine off when the vehicle is halted in order to save fuel. These modes are typically disabled when offroad systems are selected as it is useful to have the engine running at all times. There is however no need to be concerned at the duty cycles on the starter motor or battery as both are designed for multiple stop/start cycles.

paddle shifters

Some manumatics have paddles attached to the steering for shifting up and down gears. These do exactly the same thing as moving the gearlever forwards and backwards (or left and right in a Jeep). Some manufacturers fix the paddles so they turn with the wheel, others do not. For offroading the latter is better so they are easy to find when turning the wheel. I prefer fixed for sportscars, as fitted to the Ferrari 458!

Volkswagen Touareg paddles (top), separate from wheel and Range Rover (bottom), fixed to wheel.

DSG – direct shift gearboxes

The DSG automatic is the same as a manumatic from a driver's perspective, with P, N, D and +/- to allow the driver to select a gear. However, it is quite different mechanically as it is two manual gearboxes each with half the gears; one has one, three and five and the other two, four and six. When the vehicle is in one gear, say second, the other gearbox is not in use but has pre-selected third gear. When the time comes to

change up there is no need to change gears – rather the drive is changed from one gearbox to another by means of a clutch, like a manual transmission, not a fluid clutch like a conventional automatic. The overall effect is impressive because gearshifts are extremely fast, not even requiring a drop in engine revs, and there is no loss of efficiency as with the fluid clutch. If the transmission needs to change down, this is done in a similar manner to a normal automatic transmission, but is not as time-critical as an upshift.

DSGs are the first automatics to better the manual equivalents in fuel consumption and acceleration. But for offroad driving there is little difference between a normal manumatic and a DSG.

parking automatics

When a manual vehicle is parked on a hill and left in gear the engine acts as a park brake, the effectiveness of which varies and shouldn't be relied upon. Gravity attempts to move the vehicle downhill, which means the wheels try to turn. For the wheels to turn the entire transmission has to rotate, including moving the pistons up and down in the cylinders. This is a lot of friction, difficult to conquer and thus the vehicle is fairly well immobilised.

Automatic transmissions only have a fluid clutch which, at rest, can spin freely and does not directly connect the wheels to the engine. Thus, there is no engine braking from an automatic, which is why the P position disconnects the engine and instead inserts a small pin into the automatic transmission, preventing the wheels from turning at all. The problem with this approach is that once in park on a steep hill the vehicle will rock back onto the pin, and it may be impossible to move the shifter from Park.

Avoiding this situation in the first place is covered in Chapter 22, but should it occur then the "Shift Lock" button found on some automatics may release the pin and allow you to move the vehicle from Park.

manuals or automatics?

For the pros and cons of automatics vs manuals refer to Chapter 31.

Manuals:

- have better engine braking, although modern six- and seven-speed autos are far better than the four-speeders of old;
- can be push-started, although that's rarely needed these days;
- are slightly lighter;
- are usually cheaper (at new);
- usually have slightly better fuel economy due to no fluid clutch and slightly lighter weight;
- offer control over the gears (although most manumatics permit a lot of control, too).

Automatics:

- are easier to drive in all conditions, especially difficult terrain;
- can be inched extremely slowly over obstacles, slower than any vehicle in first low;
- can't be towed for long, because the turbine is not designed to effectively "drive" the pump unless there is a special tow mode;
- are definitely preferred for softroaders, which do not have the benefit of low-range.

Gone are the days when autos were markedly inferior to manuals on or offroad. Most experienced offroaders prefer automatics, or at least admit they are easier to drive.

This Jeep Wrangler is a manual, but there's nowhere it can go that the automatic version couldn't follow. In some driving situations the manual is better, in others the auto is superior, although even the crusty old wizards who have tried autos now say they wouldn't switch back. However, manuals are lighter on the fuel, simpler, cheaper and in some cases, just more fun.

In rocky terrain like this automatics are great, low range is fantastic and the combination of the two is best of all. This Jeep is a manual, and has oversize tyres which raise the gearing, so first low isn't as low as it once was. To compensate the final drive (diff ratio) has been increased to 1:4.56.

CHAPTER 5

SUSPENSION

Engines get all the glory, with their kilowatts and torque figures, but what really makes a 4WD capable often has more to do with the suspension than vast amounts of tyre-shredding power.

what suspension does

The suspension does two jobs:

- absorbs and dampens shocks from uneven terrain for a comfortable journey (ride)
- keeps all four wheels solidly on the ground to provide traction, turning control and braking, while reducing body roll and inspiring driver confidence (handling)

There are lots of suspension systems with lots of components, but the most important parts are the spring and the shock absorber.

springs

The spring absorbs the bump in the road by compressing, allowing the wheel to move up relative to the rest of the vehicle. That's great, but then the spring rebounds, compresses, rebounds… and the vehicle behaves like a kangaroo. To damp this rebound/compression cycle there are shock absorbers, known as shocks or, more accurately, dampers. In a way shocks are misnamed – although they do help absorb the bumps, it's the spring that does most of that work and the shocks dampen the resulting bounce. The springs also carry the weight of the vehicle, so if you removed the shocks you wouldn't notice much difference until you went over a bump! Actually, you'd notice even on a billiard

table-smooth surface because of the weight shift when a vehicle accelerates, brakes or corners – it'd feel something like a cross between a seesaw and a swing.

There are several different types of spring, but all do the same basic job. The most common types are:

- **Coil spring:** most commonly used, found in the front of virtually all 4WDs. Provides good handling and flex but requires a relatively complex locating system as the coil spring by itself cannot keep the axle in one place relative to the chassis. Used with independent or live axles (see later in this chapter).

- **Leaf spring:** simplest design, good for load carrying and can locate the axle correctly relative to the chassis, although not very precisely, which is one reason it doesn't handle very well. Another reason is that as the spring compresses the leaves rub together, generating friction, which damps the effect of the compression. This is not good because exactly the same effect happens at any speed, whereas with, for example, a coil spring that damping effect is precisely controlled by sophisticated valves in a shock tuned to respond differently for different conditions and situations.

- **Torsion bar:** a long bar fixed at one end and connected to an independent suspension arm at the other. The twisting moment provides the spring. Used in the front of independently-sprung vehicles.

- **Air spring:** an airbag, inflated to varying pressures for varying situations. Still requires a shock absorber. More and more offroad vehicles use air suspension because of its ability to vary ride height.

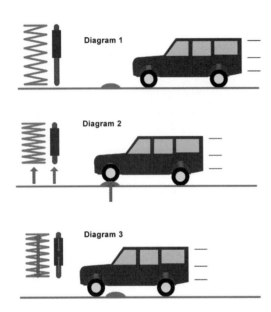

Diagram 1: *Coil spring at normal extension, shock at normal extension.*

Diagram 2: *Vehicle moves over bump. Wheel forced upwards, compressing the spring and the shock.*

Diagram 3: *Over the bump the spring expands. The shock resists the spring's tendency to cycle through expand-contract oscillations.*

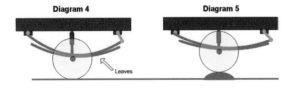

Diagrams 4 & 5: *Leaf setup with two leaves (most have more). When the spring compresses the additional leaves*

are brought into play. Although the inter-leaf friction has a damping effect a shock absorber is still required.

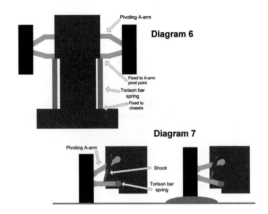

Diagrams 6 & 7: *A torsion bar is a long bar that provides a spring effect through a twisting motion.*

Suspension absorbs shocks, and the tyres can be thought of as part of the suspension system too.

Suspension should ideally keep the weight on all four wheels all the time. Here the inside wheels have less weight and are spinning up, reducing the vehicle's ability to accelerate.

Leaf springs (four leaves) attached to the top of an axle. The yellow shock is clearly visible and to the left is the pyramid-shaped bumpstop. The friction of the leaves under compression goes a little way to dampening the bumps, but that's not a good thing as there is no variability in this damping effect, unlike a sophisticated shock absorber with many sets of valves for specific situations.

LC100 with new black coils, with the bumpstop inside the coil. The swaybar (see later in this Chapter) is partially disconnected and hanging down.

Torsion bar on the right connected to a Terracan's A-arm. Bumpstop visible to the left.

shock absorbers

Shocks come in monotube, twintube, single, double and all sorts of other flavours, but they all dampen out the effects of a spring compressed by the vehicle moving over uneven terrain. Nitrogen gas is used as it is inert (does not expand) when hot, and is even in many shocks that don't feature a variant of the word 'nitrogen' in their name. "Gas shocks" generally refer to nitrogen shocks, even though the cheaper alternative, air, is also a gas.

An airbag inside a coil to assist with carrying a heavy load, but not to give a lift. Bumpstop to the left and swaybar in the foreground.

Coils within coils for a variable spring rate on a Defender. Used for very heavy loads where there is a great difference between loaded and unloaded weights.

The splines on the torsion bar can be clearly seen. The bar is fixed into the chassis at one end and attached to a pivoting A-arm at the other. The bar twists, giving the spring effect.

monotube and twintube shocks

Both monotube and twintube (bi-tube) shocks compress and rebound, and as they do so they force fluid through small gaps. This is similar to operating a coffee plunger or a bicycle pump. If you've used the latter you'll recall pumps become hot during use, and that's exactly what happens with a shock; the energy absorbed has to go somewhere, and it becomes heat. Dissipating that heat is a major task of shock designers, as is tuning the shock for optimum operation in a variety of conditions and loads. The shock tuning is done by determining the number, size and type of valves for the oil to flow through. Larger valves let more oil through, as does using a greater number of valves. There are mechanisms to prevent return flow and open or close extra valves depending on piston rod speed. The shock also needs to work in both directions, for compression and rebound. In short, it's a skilled job and something of a black art to work out the best combination of valves for any given vehicle setup.

Speed-sensitive shocks mean the speed of the rod up and down, how quickly the shock compresses or extends, not the vehicle speed. Low rod speeds are less than 0.1 metres/second, equivalent to twists and turns at 80km/h. A medium rod speed is 0.1-0.3m/s, say a speedhump at 50km/h. High rod speeds of 0.3-2m/s would be corrugations.

Shocks have to deal with two other problems; aeration – which is mixing of gas with fluid and, foaming and cavitation – which is when the piston moves so quickly the fluid cannot keep up, creating a low-pressure cavity. Both reduce shock performance and can damage the shock.

the great shock debate

Each design has its advantages. The monotube has more of the oil touching the outer tube which means it is better at heat dissipation, something that kills shock performance and, by extension, vehicle performance. As the oil and gas are entirely separate aeration is impossible, so performance is maintained. If gas and oil mix by aeration the result is in effect a thinner oil, which means there is less damping. This is known as shock fade, and is apparent to the occupants by a far bouncier (and more dangerous) ride, with much less handling control.

When a monotube overheats it hardens up rather than softens because the oil expands but cannot aerate. The relatively high gas pressure in the shock also helps prevent overheating in the first place.

As a monotube has something like twice or three times the gas pressure (gas reaction force) of a twintube, it is constantly trying to extend, and that's what you want offroad, when it forcibly pushes the wheel down. For this reason monos are also quicker to react than twins. Finally, a monotube can be mounted in any direction. Twins can only be mounted at around a 45 degree angle from vertical.

The main twintube advantage is shock travel. For a given overall length, there will be more piston travel with a twin as the gas doesn't take up vertical space. Twintubes are also cheaper to manufacture, so for both those reasons original-equipment shocks are almost always twins.

One of the offroading world's ongoing wars is about whether monotubes or twins are best, but of more importance is the quality of the valve tuning and construction. Buy based on those criteria.

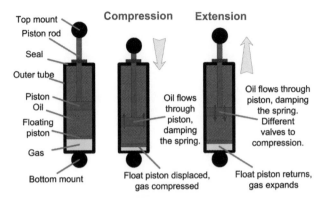

Compression   **Extension**

Top mount
Piston rod
Seal
Outer tube
Piston
Oil
Floating piston
Gas
Bottom mount

Oil flows through piston, damping the spring.

Oil flows through piston, damping the spring. Different valves to compression.

Float piston displaced, gas compressed

Float piston returns, gas expands

Monotube shocks, so named because there's just the one tube filled with oil, with a piston inside. Similar to a coffee plunger, the piston moves up and down in the tube. As it does so the piston rod moves further into the tube, which displaces the oil, causing the bottom piston to compress the nitrogen gas. The speed at which the piston moves through the oil is controlled by a complex series of valves.

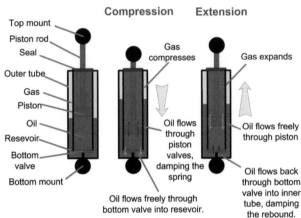

Compression   **Extension**

Top mount
Piston rod
Seal
Outer tube
Gas
Piston
Oil
Reservoir
Bottom valve
Bottom mount

Gas compresses

Gas expands

Oil flows through piston valves, damping the spring

Oil flows freely through piston

Oil flows freely through bottom valve into reservoir.

Oil flows back through bottom valve into inner tube, damping the rebound.

The twin tube shock operates on a similar principle to the monotube, but has a second tube inside the main tube, inside which is smaller piston. As the piston rod moves down into the inner tube it pushes oil through the bottom valve, compressing the nitrogen gas. Like the mono, the main piston has a complex series of valves, and so does the bottom valve.

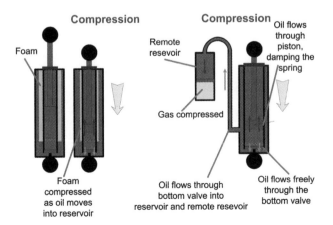

Compression   **Compression**

Foam

Remote resevoir

Oil flows through piston, damping the spring

Gas compressed

Foam compressed as oil moves into reservoir

Oil flows through bottom valve into reservoir and remote resevoir

Oil flows freely through the bottom valve

Foam cell shocks are the same as twin tubes but instead of using gas to compress and expand as the rod moves into the tube, foam is used. Remote-reservoir shocks are the same as twintubes (or monotubes) with the exception that additional oil is stored in a remote canister, where it can be more easily cooled due to a greater volume of oil and larger surface area

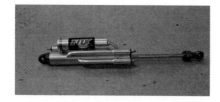

This diagram shows the complex arrangement of valves and shims which control how quickly oil moves through the piston head, and thus the damping effect of the shock.
Image courtesy ARB Corporation.

A twin tube shock cutaway. The top of the shock is simply a shroud for the rod to shield it from dirt and debris. The inner and outer tubes can clearly be seen, as can the piston's valve assembly.

Remote-reservoir shock, as used on high-performance offroad racing 4WDs. Overkill for the average tourer.

It is said that monotubes aren't as strong as robust as twin tubes, and if a stone hits a monotube it will damage it whereas a twintube has an outer tube protecting the piston. Using the all-purpose scientific tool known as a hammer we put this to the test and, after a good belting, this quality monotube survived intact. Conclusion; monotubes are more than robust enough for offroad use.

bumpstops

Springs are great, but there's a limit to how far the spring can compress, and that limit is set by a little bit of inverted-pyramid shaped rubber called a bumpstop. When the moving part of the suspension hits the bumpstop you've bottomed out, and you'll feel and hear that if it hits hard – one of those "where did that washout come from" moments. The reason the bumpstop is pyramid shaped is because it has a small amount of last-resort shock-absorbing capability itself, so cutting it down might get a few more mm worth of articulation, but will place extra stress on the vehicle if (when) the suspension bottoms out.

variable-rate suspension

So far so good; we've damped out the effects of the rough terrain. However, a suspension engineer's life isn't that simple because suspension is a compromise. Take, for example, weight. With a heavily loaded vehicle you need stiff springs, otherwise you'll bottom out all the time. But if you then took the load out you'd have a vehicle that just doesn't absorb shocks, and would skip over rough terrain, making the handling potentially dangerous. That's where variable-rate suspension comes into its own. Examples are air springs, twin-coils (coils within coils) and progressive coils (easy to compress initially, then becoming progressively stiffer).

variable-height suspension

Many modern 4WDs have variable-height suspension. The advantages are many; the lower centre of gravity with a low ride height improves stability and handling at high speeds, the suspension can self-level when loaded and it can be raised for offroad use and even dropped low for access to car parks (and under trees!). Most systems use air springs with a varying amount of air in them controlled by a compressor. Air springs still require shocks, which may be mounted inside the air spring, for example the Discovery 3 or 4. Some systems are only mounted on the rear wheels, for example Prado 120 Grandes, but most are on all four wheels. These systems automatically lower from their offroad heights at speed which in Australian conditions is not always a good idea. As the springs are stiffer when inflated further to raise the ride height, the offroad ride tends to be firmer than the equivalent car with raised coil suspension, but of course the variable car can simply lose its extra ride height when the offroading is complete.

The LX570 has variable height suspension but, unusually, uses the shocks (dampers) to adjust height with conventional coil springs.

The front air suspension on a Discovery 3. Inside the metal cylinders are air springs, and inside those are shock absorbers.

Jeep Grand Cherokee showing three of its suspension modes; Park, Normal and the higher of two Offroad settings. The vehicle will auto-lower from the offroad heights at speed.

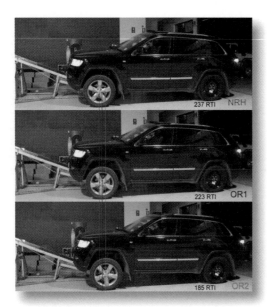

Variable-height suspension is usually self-levelling so vehicles remain level when loaded or towing.

Air suspension fitted to the rear of a highly modified competition 4WD. The rubber bag and air hose are clearly visible, as are the shocks, diff pumpkin and rear driveshaft.

The Grand Cherokee on a ramp which flexes the suspension to the maximum at its three settings of Normal Ride Height, Offroad 1 and Offroad 2. As the suspension is raised the suspension travel reduces, and while the photo doesn't show it, the ride becomes harsher. The Grand has very limited suspension travel, but makes up for it with excellent traction control.

articulation

4WDs also need suspension articulation, which is how far each wheel can travel relative to the body. It is known by a variety of names; travel, articulation or flex. It is very important for keeping all four wheels firmly on the ground, which means traction isn't lost as weight shift is minimised. The ideal for most situations is fairly soft, long-travel suspension, although short-travel suspension has its place in some situations as it often keeps the chassis further away from the ground. Unfortunately, that long-travel, soft setup is exactly what you don't want on-road, because it leads to undesirable traits like excess body roll, nose-dive under braking and generally woolly handling.

Some Volkswagen Touraegs have air suspension. Here one such model is compared with a conventional coil-sprung version. The improvement in approach, ramp and departure angles is clear, but not so obvious is an improvement in clearance. This Touraeg also has the very good idea of a door-mounted spare wheel. The Touraeg does not auto-lower until it reaches a sensible 70km/h.

Flex has been important as long as 4WDs have existed. Here an early '60s Nissan Patrol G60 flexes its ancient leaf springs ahead of a 2008 Nissan Patrol GU with coils. Both have live axles front and rear.

swaybar

The partial solution to body roll around corners is an anti-roll bar, or swaybar, a simple metal rod that connects one wheel with the body on the opposite side. The idea is that as the car rolls away from the turn, the swaybar restricts the ability of the outside spring to compress as it rises with the inboard side of the vehicle's body. However, at low-range speeds all a swaybar does is restrict articulation, which is why many people remove it or fit a disconnect system for offroad use. Some vehicles such as certain Range Rover Sport models have a automatic disconnect/reconnect system.

Unsprung mass is another factor in a vehicle's handling. This means any weight of the vehicle that isn't supported by the springs. Sprung mass is everything else. For example, a live-axle vehicle has wheels, axle, diff and some of the propshaft weight as unsprung mass. As a general rule, the more unsprung mass a vehicle has the harder the suspension has to work, and the poorer the handling, hence the move to independent suspension.

Swaybar fitted to a Defender 130 – the metal bar running from under each coil around the fuel tank. Swaybars are usually just a simple piece of metal that connects one end of an axle to another. As the axle articulates the swaybar resists movement; ideal on-road, not so good offroad.

The controls in the Wrangler for the swaybar – just an on/off switch. The swaybar reconnects at speed and disconnects again after you slow down. Also seen here are the controls for the front and rear lockers (press the top or bottom of the switch) and the stability control off button. All have corresponding dash lights.

Jeep Wrangler showing front axle flex with and without the swaybar disconnected. The JK Wrangler has a factory disconnect option, although this particular vehicle has an aftermarket solution.

This Wrangler has a swaybar disconnect but with the swaybar unlocked for maximum articulation it didn't make it up this rutted hill because the flex meant the belly was lowered sufficiently to touch the ground and stop the car. Reconnecting the swaybar reduced the flex, and kept the belly from touching. The wheel was further in the air, but the traction control pulled the car through regardless. Maximum articulation is not always good.

live axles and independent suspension

A live axle is a solid beam from one wheel to another. They are also known as beam axles, or solid axles. An independent suspension setup has a smaller axle for each wheel which can then move independently of its partner, hence the name.

There are three main suspension configurations:

- Live axle front and rear
- Independent front suspension (IFS), live axle rear, known generally as IFS (although this term does not specify a live rear).
- Fully-independent suspension; IFS plus IRS, independent rear suspension.

While it is technically possible to run independent at the rear and a live at the front, this makes no engineering sense.

In an attempt to get the best of both worlds, older 4WDs used live axles front and rear, which gave way to IFS, allowing the handling advantages of independent on the front with the axle flex and strength on the rear. Now IFS is giving way to fully-independent suspension. While independent suspension doesn't offer the flex of live axles, sophisticated traction control systems mean having a wheel in the air is no longer the disadvantage it once was. Independent suspension is far better for handling than live axles because if a wheel is disturbed by a bump, that effect is not transmitted to the rest of the vehicle. Independent suspension also offers less unsprung weight, and on a live axle the wheels, axle and differential are all unsprung weight. With independent suspension only the wheel and a short stub axle are unsprung. Unsprung weight is not good for on-road handling.

A disadvantage for hardcore offroaders is the ability to modify the suspension. If you want to lift an independent suspension vehicle you have limitations, whereas the limitations are much less with a live axle vehicle which can be lifted higher.

Y62 Patrol with fully independent front and rear suspension.

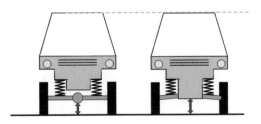

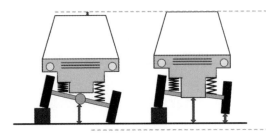

doesn't happen with the independent vehicle – there's nothing to force the other wheel down except gravity and the natural extension of the spring. Independent systems typically don't flex as well, but in some cases this is an advantage – as the diagram shows, there can be more clearance under the body, and the vehicle is raised a little higher, although it's less stable as the weight is not so well distributed across the wheels. It's all about driving to the vehicle's strengths.

Live (solid) and independent suspension suspensions compared. Independent vehicles typically have a better ground clearance, and while there is a diff pumpkin it's hidden away so the underside of the vehicle is quite flat. On a live axle vehicle, when the suspension flexes one wheel comes up, which naturally pushes the other down. This

Land Rover Defender showing live axles front and rear.

Live-axled, coil spring Defender; independent air-spring Discovery 3; and coil-spring Discovery 3 compared. The live axle has the best flex by far, keeping the tyre square to the ground. However, clearance is not improved. The air-sprung Discovery's clearance is by contrast improved on the passenger side even if the flex isn't so good. The coil-sprung Discovery comes nowhere near, as it doesn't benefit from the air D3's ability to cross-link the suspension in low-range – that means when the air D3's wheel starts to move up on one side, the air suspension pushes the other wheel down to match and thus provide better stability. The air D3's greater flex is almost all on the passenger side due to this effect.

RIGHT: A Discovery 2 (live axles), Pajero (fully independent), Patrol (live axles), LC100 (live axles) and LC200 (IFS), all up on the same ramp. The LC200 put in an impressive performance to out-ramp all the others, proving that an independent front end doesn't necessarily mean no flex. The LC200 is aided to its win by Toyota's KDSS system which interlinks diagonal wheels to push one down when the other is pushed up. It should be noted that the LC200 is the only vehicle without an aftermarket suspension lift.

suspension lifts

A suspension lift is simply lifting the entire vehicle above the wheels by extending the springs. Why would you do this? Well, there are many reasons:

- More clearance; better angles all round
- Clearance to run larger tyres
- To reset the vehicle back to where it rides unladen when it is laden (add say a 50mm lift to the rear, put lots of gear it and it'll be back to normal)
- Improved ground clearance (independent suspension only).

Technically, this would give a reduction in handling performance due to a higher centre of gravity. However, the actual height increase is less than 3% for a typical 4WD, and not all of that height increase translates into a centre of gravity increase. Thus, the higher centre of gravity doesn't make much of a difference – in fact the benefits of the vehicle being able to carry load more effectively mean a net improvement in handling, as borne out by countless owner experiences.

It's important to note that suspension-lifting a live-axle vehicle won't improve minimum clearance, as the differentials will still be the lowest point. Also, not all aftermarket suspension kits lift a vehicle.

Of course, there are disadvantages, which are largely proportional to the size of the lift. A small lift, say 30-50mm for a medium 4WD will give the benefits above with minimal disadvantages below:

- The driveshafts will be operating at new angles which they weren't designed for.
- With independent suspension the downward wheel travel may be restricted, or require additional modification.

The greater the lift, the greater the advantages and disadvantages. It's also an insurance issue. Often there is no mechanical, handling or insurance problem with lifts of up to 50mm, but as always, you need to check your individual circumstances. Many people lift the rear a little more than the front to compensate for the load they carry in the back.

Make sure that both springs and shocks are replaced during a suspension lift. If the damper is too long, the coil can fall out, and shocks should always be matched to springs.

My Defender before and after a 2" suspension lift. Often by the time a lift is done the original suspension has sagged so the actual lift is more than 2". The handling was improved in all conditions, particularly when loaded or towing.

summary

- Suspension is there to absorb shocks from irregularities in the road surface.
- A spring absorbs the shock.
- A shock absorber dampens the spring action.
- Monotubes and twintubes are the main types of shock absorber.
- 4WDs need long-travel suspension. The distance a wheel can travel relative to its normal position is called articulation, flex or travel.
- Long-travel suspension gives poor handling on-road. Swaybars help to prevent body roll, but prevent articulation and so are sometimes disconnected.
- Live axles are also known as beam or solid axles, and directly connect the two wheels on an axle. Independent suspension gives each wheel its own axle.
- IFS is Independent Front Suspension.

The original and aftermarket coils for the Defender. The replacements are taller and have thicker coils, so can bear more weight. The coils are evenly spaced so these are linear springs.

CHAPTER 6

WEIGHTS

If you're going 4WD touring you need to understand weights to keep your vehicle legal and safe.

what weight?

Your vehicle has a basic weight (kerb, or tare weight), and a maximum permitted weight (GVM, or Gross Vehicle Mass). The difference between the two is the payload. Out of that payload comes everything added to the vehicle beyond showroom standard (stock), and whatever you're carrying. That means kit like bull bars, snorkels, larger tyres, rock sliders, winches all eat into your payload. And then there's the occupants of the vehicle, and after that your recovery gear, camping gear, tools, fridge, water… It all adds up and you need to ensure it stays below the GVM, or have the vehicle modified so it has a higher GVM.

The GVM is usually, but not always, less than the sum of the front and rear axle loads to permit some element of uneven loading.

Unfortunately, there is no worldwide standard definition of kerb and tare. Some texts define tare as an empty weight, and kerb as empty plus a full tank of fuel, fluids and a driver of a defined weight, but generally the terms are used interchangeably. Other definitions say the vehicle has 10L of fuel in it. Even if there was a clear definition, accessories such as sunroofs, towbars, electric seats or tyre options would change the tare, which is why some manufacturers specify a range for a tare instead of a specific weight. It is important to know which definition is being used for comparative purposes, and do not assume your vehicle weighs at empty the same as the manufacturer's tare. Find a weighbridge and work it out for yourself. Some European vehicles are quoted with the EC kerb weight, which incorporates a 68kg driver and 7kg of luggage, for example my Discovery 3, the loading of which is shown in the table overleaf. All weights are in kg.

Weight	Definition
Tare/kerb weight	Weight ready to roll; full of fuel, oil etc. but no driver or payload.
GVM	Gross Vehicle Mass. The heaviest the vehicle is permitted to weigh by law. This will be on a placard on the vehicle, usually around the driver's door.
Payload	How much you can carry; the difference between GVM and kerb weight.
Front axle load	The maximum load that can be placed on the front axle.
Rear axle load	The maximum load that can be placed on the rear axle.

example touring load (Discovery 3)

Accessories		Camping gear		Totals	
Bullbar	41	Food	15	D3 tare	2,455
Winch	32	Cooking gear	7	GVM	3,230
Cargo barrier	14	Personal bags	20		
Roofrack	45	Filled water tank	30	Payload	775
Ladder	5	Sleeping bag/mat	15	Total weight	555
Dual battery	20	Misc stuff	10	Difference	220
UHF radio	3	Tent	30		
Electric brake controller	1	Chairs	10		
Cargo system	20	Fridge (empty)	16		
Snorkel	5	Filled fuel tank	78		
Tyres (extra)	20	Table	6		
Rear carrier	30	Recovery gear, tools	25		
Second fuel tank	38				
Towbar	6				
Compressor	3				
Shovel holder	10				
TOTAL	**293kg**	**TOTAL**	**262kg**		

Notes:

- The basic modifications to the vehicle total 293kg; camping and 4WD gear adds another 262kg and then we need to get in. Fortunately our combined weight is less than the remainder.

- The extra fuel tank is 104L capacity but diesel isn't as dense as water so it doesn't add 104kg.

- The bull bar weighs 55kg, but 14kg of trim and a bracing bar is removed to fit it so there's a net weight gain of only 41kg.

- Land Rover quotes tare weights including the 75kg driver so that figure has been deducted and this car has a few non-standard options for the trim level so 5kg has been added to compensate.

- All weights have been rounded up to be conservative, and include wiring, brackets etc.

The D3 in touring mode.

Defender on a public weighbridge. Some servos have them, and sometimes just taking a load of rubbish to your local council tip can involve driving over a weighbridge. If you can, get front and rear axle loads as well. It is probably best to weight the vehicle empty of its usual load, then weigh items such as camping gear and people on scales so you can see where the weight goes.

MAX. ALLOWABLE VEHICLE LOADINGS (INCLUDING OPTIONS & ACCESSORIES)		FRONT AXLE	REAR AXLE	MAX. OPERATING MASS
STANDARD SUSPENSION		1200kg	1850kg	3050kg
LEVELLED SUSPENSION		1200kg	1750kg	2950kg
RECOMMENDED TYRES	RIM SIZE	NOTE:- THE SUM OF THE LOAD CARRYING CAPACITIES OF THE TYRES FITTED TO ANY AXLE OR AXLE GROUP OF THIS VEHICLE SHALL NOT BE LESS THAN THE RELEVANT LOAD SHOWN ABOVE. THE TYRES FITTED TO THIS VEHICLE SHALL HAVE A SPEED CATEGORY NOT LESS THAN 'N' (140km/h). THE FRONT AND REAR TYRES SHALL BE OF THE SAME TYPE AND CONSTRUCTION.		
7.50 R 16	5.50 F x 16			
7.50 R 16	6.50 J x 16			
235/85 R 16	6.50 J x 16			
235/85 R 16	7 J x 16			
RECOMMENDED TYRE PRESSURES ON ROAD AND OFF ROAD		FRONT 193kPa (28PSI)		REAR 331kPa (48PSI)

Land Rover Defender 110 placard showing a front axle max load of 1,200kg, rear of 1,850kg and max operating mass (GVM) of 3,050kg for standard suspension. Although the vehicle is fitted with aftermarket suspension that doesn't change the ratings in a legal sense, which is important – the limit is what's on the placard. In any case there is far more to a vehicle's load carrying ability than stiffer suspension; brakes, chassis strength and more are all factors which need to be assessed before the vehicle can properly be said to be able to carry more than its rated load.

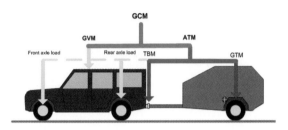

Vehicle weights (refer to table on page 75 for vehicle wieghts and table on page 79 for towing weights))

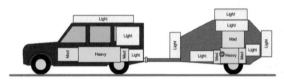

An idealised load pattern for a vehicle – heavy weights are low and centred. It will not always be possible to follow this, but if it isn't then at least the driver should be aware of the effects of handling and drive accordingly.

models and weights

You'll often find that all models in a vehicle range have the same GVM. However, as the trim spec increases from basic to luxury, so does the kerb weight. That drops the payload, as all those electric motors in the driver's adjustable seat weigh a fair bit.

Manuals are slightly lighter than autos and petrol engines are lighter than diesels. So a luxury-spec automatic turbodiesel isn't likely to have anywhere near as much payload capacity as basic petrol manual. Here are some examples from Toyota's Prado 120 range:

Prado 120				
Engine	3.0L tdi		2.7L petrol	4.0L petrol
Trans	auto	auto	man	auto
Trim	GX	Grande	GX	Grande
Kerb (kg)	2,151	2,289	1,936	2,197
GVM (kg)	2,900	2,900	2,800	2,850
Payload (kg)	**749**	**611**	**864**	**653**

The GVM is pretty much the same, as you'd expect from the same basic vehicle. But the extras on the Grande compared to the GX weigh 138kg (comparing the two diesels), or almost two thin adults! The weightlift king is the base model manual petrol, which has a payload of 253kg more than the luxury turbo-diesel auto.

All that extra weight translates to slower acceleration, worse fuel consumption, and worse offroad performance, too. The auto petrol Grande owner certainly has more power and torque than the GX's 2.7L engine, but the edge is taken off it by the 261kg (13%) difference in weight. That's more than three 80kg adults, mainly in electric luxo-doohickeys.

The best trim level for 4WD is perhaps not the luxury. There's no need to go all-out with the poverty-pack models though; most want air conditioning and some luxuries. However, some people do buy top-range vehicles and enjoy the bush in considerable style, so that's definitely an option too. As ever, you pay your money, you take your choice!

Utes are designed for load carrying and typically have a larger payload than wagons. This Colorado has a payload of 1,028kg – even after allowing for the touring accessories shown there will be plenty of capacity left for a family and touring gear.

All the gadgets and trim – electric everything, soundproofing, gizmos, better seats, sunroofs and more – found on a luxury 4WD carry a weight penalty, so usually these vehicles have a small payload. This Range Rover TDV8 can carry only 480kg.

towing weights

When you tow there are some more weights to be concerned with:

Weight	Expansion	Definition
ATM	Aggregate Trailer Mass	The total weight of the trailer, how much it'd weigh if you put it on a weighbridge.
GTM	Gross Trailer Mass	Weight of the trailer taken by the trailer wheels (ATM minus TBM).
TBM	Towball Mass	Weight of the trailer on the tow car's hitch.
GCM	Gross Combination Mass	Total permitted weight of the trailer and tow car. Set by the tow car manufacturer.
Unbraked tow capacity	N/A	How heavy a trailer the car can tow without brakes on the trailer wheels. For most medium to large 4WDs this is 750kg, but may be less for smaller vehicles.
Braked tow capacity	N/A	How heavy a trailer the car can tow with brakes on the trailer wheels. This varies from around 1,500kg to a maximum of 3,500kg.
Hitch and car TBM ratings	N/A	The car manufacturer will specify maximum TBMs. However, the hitch/towbar itself also has to be rated to the same amount. Whichever is the smaller is the value to work with, for example a vehicle may according to the manufacturer be able to handle a TBM of 350kg but if the hitch fitted is only 150kg, then the figure to work with is 150kg.

The trailer manufacturer should supply the ATM and that should be on a placard on the trailer. They should also recommend a TBM. The vehicle manufacturer will state the GVM and the tow capacity, braked and unbraked. The rear axle load limit is one to watch as it can easily be exceeded with a heavy TBM.

Hitch on a Hyundai Santa Fe which states the vehicle (and hitch) can be used to tow a trailer of GTM 2,500kg with a 200kg TBM but only with five occupants in the car. This is more properly expressed as "not fully loaded". With six or seven occupants the TBM drops to 150kg and a GTM of 2,450kg. Without brakes it's only 700kg – unusual since most 4WDs of that size are 750kg.

The LC200 has a small payload for its size, so several aftermarket manufacturers offer GVM upgrade kits. This is the Ironman test car demonstrating an emergency stop.

Despite the weight shift forwards and the weight of the bull bar the vehicle is not yet out of suspension travel on the front wheels, so if a bump is hit control can be retained.

The revised placard for the LC200 showing an increase in GVM of 280kg (from 3300kg to 3580kg). However, the maximum axle loads remain unchanged so that extra carrying capacity can only be used with a careful weight distribution.

Remote touring in Australia with four or so on board means carrying a lot of fuel, water and gear. Keeping within payload limits is difficult, which is one reason trailers are popular. However, you can't take trailers everywhere as towing makes the vehicle less agile.

The Nissan Patrol is a good example of different braked tow weights. The 4.2L diesel manual can tow 3,500kg, as can the 4.8L petrol auto. The 3.0L diesel manual can do 3,200kg, but the 3.0L diesel auto only 2,500kg. Front and rear axle limits for the 2010 models are 1,500kg and 1,800kg respectively. Tare weight is between 2,366kg and 2,512kg, and GVM 3,000kg to 3,060kg depending on model. Maximum TBM is 350kg, but Nissan say you must reduce load below GVM by 290kg. Otherwise, use a 300kg TBM, reduce below GVM by 220, 250kg TBM by 150kg and at GVM the vehicle can handle a 200kg TBM.

Summary

- Ensure you know your vehicle's GVM (check the placard) and stay within it.

- The onus is on the driver to ensure that all the figures are within limits;
  - Front axle load not exceeded
  - Rear axle load not exceeded
  - GVM not exceeded.

- If towing add;
  - ATM of trailer within limits for tow car, braked or unbraked tow rating
  - TBM of trailer within limits for the lower of the tow car's rating or hitch rating
  - Total weight of tow car plus trailer within limits of the GCM.

CHAPTER 7

WHEELS: TYRES & RIMS

If the tyres don't grip, nothing else matters.

tyre and rim jargon

Tyres and rims have their own special jargon and that needs be dealt with first:

Term	Definition
Rim	The metal wheel on which the tyre is fitted
Bead	The part of the tyre that seals against the rim
Sidewall	The vertical side of the tyre, from bead to shoulder
Tread	Part of the tyre that touches the road
Tread block	A single block of rubber, many of which together form the tread
Shoulder	Part of the tyre between the tread and the sidewall
Tyre information	Raised letters on the side of the tyre
Studs	Threaded rods onto which you place the rim and then screw on the wheel nuts
Stud pattern	The diameter and number of the studs and the size of the circle they form – the size of the circle is defined by its PCD, or Pitch Circle Diameter
Wheel nuts	Nuts that screw onto the studs, holding the rim in place (4WDs usually use five or six)

which tyre when?

The first thing to understand is that the tyres your vehicle comes with out of the showroom are rarely suitable for any offroading. This is because they are designed for good on-road performance, a quiet, smooth ride and fuel economy – not all-terrain grip, robustness, strength and load carrying. Also, tyres are not something that people base buying decisions on, so manufacturers tend not to spend a lot of money on high-specification tyres.

There are several decisions to make when choosing offroad tyres:

- construction
- tread class
- size
- rim size.

Your vehicle will have a placard which shows the manufacturer's recommended tyres in terms of size and rating. Road authorities typically do not permit much deviation from the size, but the construction, aspect ratio and tread pattern can be varied so there is much more choice available than the placard may indicate.

Discovery 3 placard saying the vehicle must be fitted with one of four tyres, for example 235/70/17 on a 17x7 rim. It also states the load rating must be at least 1,030kg (109) and the speed rating not less than H. Fortunately, Australian authorities permit a lower speed rating (N) for 4WDs. Australian D3s are permitted a tyre load rating of 109; European models must be 110, which proves that you should always check the limits for the vehicle in your country as specifications do differ from market to market.

tread pattern

The first choice to be made when selecting tyres is the tread pattern. In general, the more open and deeper the tread pattern, the better the performance offroad and on dirt roads. The downside is quicker wear, onroad ride and handling penalties, increased fuel consumption and noise. There are four classes of tyre spanning the tread range:

road/all-season

Road pattern tyres simply aren't designed for offroad work as their shallow and close tread won't provide much grip off bitumen. All-season tyres are no better.

all-terrains (ATs)

These are the first recognisable offroad tyres, with more widely spaced tread blocks and a deeper tread pattern than road. Pretty much every even halfway serious offroader runs at least all-terrain tyres, and even if you don't plan on serious offroading traction, the extra tread depth and traction is always good to have even on dirt roads. While ATs compared to road tyres are more costly, noisier, and grip less on the bitumen, the modern all-terrain is a very versatile tyre and those differences in road handling are not particularly noticeable and certainly very easy to live with. The all-terrain is the base offroading tyre.

mud terrains

The next step is mud terrains. The advantage of "muddies" over ATs is only greater offroad grip. You pay for that with a greater purchase price, reduced life, greater on-road noise and less on-road grip. But they are quite liveable on the road, especially if you have good soundproofing, and many people run them on their vehicles all the time, as I have done for some years. Muddies are used for more difficult offroad work, not just for mud.

extreme

This sort of rubber is what you'd put in a trailer, tow to the forest and then swap the wheels over; it'd be too expensive, painful and dangerous to run them on bitumen for very long. However, when offroad, there is nothing to compare to their ability to grip.

Road, all-terrain, mud and extreme tyre tread examples.

A mud tyre at home. The open tread means it can bite into a soft surface and easily self-clean where a more closed tread would simply clog up. However, there's a penalty to pay on-road with wear, noise and handling, although modern muddies are now quite "streetable".

There is no fixed industry classification of what tyre is classified as what. Some tyres could fall into either camp and nobody has yet invented a tyre that does not compromise some aspect of performance, so beware "do it all" claims. Beware also claims by some manufacturers that their tyres are "all-terrain" pattern when in fact they are very similar to road pattern. The photographs show what is generally accepted as the different tread types.

As a general rule, we'd take mud tyres for shorter trips involving steep hills, mud, state forests and the like, but opt for all-terrains for longer trips. If in doubt, err on the side of the more open-tread tyre as there may well be difficult times offroad when you'll really regret not having maximum traction, whereas the times on-road that you'll regret not having road tyres are much fewer. Also, the combination of modern mud tyres and a modern vehicle is by no means unliveable on a daily basis. An exception to the mud-is-best rule is sand, which needs a close-pattern tread. Here road tyres are actually the best, but with the correct technique and pressure muddies work nicely on sand too. The other exception is slick rocks, not common in Australia.

construction

Tyres come in two types of construction; P for Passenger, and LT for the stronger Light Truck.

The Passenger construction tyres are better on-road. They have thinner sidewalls, so dissipate heat better than the thicker, stronger, LT. The P is also lighter, and that makes a difference to performance and economy as it's all rotating weight. The P tyre is likely to have a higher speed rating, but the LT tyre's rating will be more than adequate for legal Australian road speeds.

However, offroading demands a strong tyre; rocks, dirt roads, heavy loads, wheelspin and uneven weight distribution all need a strong tyre. The LT class is recommended for offroaders; only buy P or XL (Extra Load) if there are not LT tyres available. Remember, the tread pattern is not linked to construction. While Passenger construction tyres are better for on-road use, the dynamics of modern vehicles and technology of modern LT tyres is such that handling isn't really a problem with LT tyres.

LT tyres will be marked as such, but P tyres are often not marked.

A light-truck (LT) construction 245/70/17 radial (R) tyre rated at 119 (1360kg, single tyre on wheel) and 116 (1250kg, double wheels), speed rating Q (160km/h).

radials and cross-ply

Pretty much all tyres these days are radials, as opposed to cross-ply. Cross-ply tyres have layers

of cord (ply) crossed, which is strong, but as the cords rub each other they generate heat. The radial's cords don't cross but have extra belts for strength. On the tyre markings should be a letter designating the design.

Class	Description
R	Radial
B	Belted
D	Diagonal

tyre sizes

With a tyre size we're concerned with diameter, width and profile. As the standard tyres on a 4WD are likely to be unsuitable for any serious 4WD work, you'll need to change tyres and knowing the size is important. For tyre selection purposes the diameter is calculated from the specifications and the width is the width of the tread, not including the sidewall bulge. The profile is the height of the sidewall relative to the width.

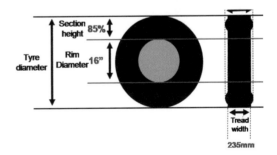

There are two types of tyre size definitions; metric and imperial. We'll deal with metric first, using this example:

235 / 85 / R16 120 N

This means:

Code	Description	Unit
235	Width of the tyre.	mm
85	Aspect ratio. 85 means that the height of the tyre is 85% of the width (see diagram on pg 85).	%
R	Radial. You won't see much else, and it might be omitted.	N/A
16	Diameter of the rim, in inches. Yes, we're mixing metric and imperial. No, I don't know why.	Inches

The 120N is the speed and load rating, which will be explained shortly.

To get the diameter of the tyre in mm, the formula is:

Rim size in inches x 25.4	406mm	16 inches, 25.4mm per inch
	+	
(235 x 0.85) x 2	400mm	85% of 235mm, x 2 for the total diameter (see diagram)
	=	
Total diameter	806mm	Calculated, actual may vary due to tread wear or design

This figure gives you the theoretical diameter of the tyre. The actual diameter of the tyre will vary a little from that figure as for every 1mm of tread wear the diameter reduces by 2mm, and if a tyre had 16mm of tread depth (mud terrain, for example) its diameter would vary quite a bit from new to worn. Therefore, the more aggressive the tyre, the typically larger actual diameter it has compared to what the tyre markings would indicate. This is of most interest to people who have spare tyres

stored under or inside the vehicle as often that room is quite restricted. For example, they may find a 265/65/17 road tyre fits, but a 265/65/17 mud won't, unless it is deflated. The rolling diameter is different again and that is a function of inflation pressure. Usually it is two to four percent smaller than the unloaded diameter.

There is another, older, simpler method for tyre size definition, and that's the imperial method:

32 x 11.5 x 15 which means:

Code	Description	Unit
32	Diameter of the tyre	Inches
11.5	Width of the tyre	Inches
15	Rim diameter	Inches

and yet another is:

Code	Description	Unit
9.50	Tyre width	Inches
R	Tyre construction (R is for Radial)	N/A
16	Rim diameter	Inches

Total tyre diameter is 16 + 9.5 + 9.5 inches, as this assumes a 100% profile (aspect ratio).

speed ratings

A speed rating for a tyre is the maximum speed it can be driven at for its maximum load, for 10 minutes. The tyre is new, correctly balanced and inflated so it is an idealised condition.

Speed ratings are important because you must fit tyres to your vehicle that have a speed rating as specified by the manufacturer. However, most Australian road authorities may permit you to use a lower-rated tyre on an offroad vehicle, regardless of the manufacturer's recommendations, for example an N-rated tyre.

The table below shows some of the common speed ratings. Even mud tyres have no problem meeting an N rating.

Speed rating	Max speed (km/h)
F	80
G	90
J	100
K	110
L	120
M	130
N	140
P	150
Q	160
R	170
S	180
T	190
U	200
H	210
V	240
Z	240
W	270
Y	300

High-performance vehicles are designed for high speeds and come with high-performance tyres, even though there's no public road in Australia on which you could even begin to approach the limits.

This Range Rover Sport V8 is a very quick vehicle and has 275/40/20 tyres rated to 106Y – or only capable of carrying 960kg, but able to reach 300km/h. It's not actually that quick but the idea is to over-rate the tyre's speed capability. In Australia, that's way over-rated, unless you spend your weekends trying to break the lap record for offroad vehicles at Philip Island.

The LC200, a vehicle of similar weight to the Sport V8, comes with 285/65/17 tyres rated to 116H – a load capacity of 1,250kg with a speed rating of 210km/h.

load ratings

A load rating is how much your tyre can carry, assuming it is in good condition and appropriately inflated. You must ensure the tyres you fit match or exceed the manufacturer's recommended load rating, which shouldn't be a problem with any form of offroad tyre – these typically carry more load than the equivalent road tyre. Essentially, tyre designers trade high-speed capability for strength and load-carrying capacity. Unlike the speed rating, there's no exemption for offroad vehicles, nor does there need to be. A list of the most common ratings for 4WDs is shown in the table.

Index	Rating (kg)	Index	Rating (kg)
90	600	112	1,120
91	615	113	1,150
92	630	114	1,180
93	650	115	1,215
94	670	116	1,250
95	690	117	1,285
96	710	118	1,320
97	730	119	1,360
98	750	120	1,400
99	775	121	1,450
100	800	122	1,500
101	825	123	1,550
102	850	124	1,600
103	875	125	1,650
104	900	126	1,700
105	925	127	1,750
106	950	128	1,800
107	975	129	1,850
108	1,000	130	1,850
109	1,030	131	1,950
110	1,060	132	2,000
111	1,090		

load ranges

Light-truck tyres may also have a load range, which describes the number of plies in a tyre. Load Range A is 2 plies, B is 4, C is 6 and so on to N which has 24. The amount of plies is not directly relevant to either strength or load carrying capability, so load range is best ignored. Focus instead on the load carrying index and the general construction of the tyre. It may be better to have fewer, stronger plies than many weaker ones.

tyre age

Tyres rely on flexibility for grip and over time this flexibility is lost. That means tyres older than around 5 to 7 years should never be used, regardless of tread depth. You can identify the tyre's age from the DOT (US Department of Transport) code. In the photo the code is PJAH D21V 3012. The last four digits refer to the week and year, so the 30th week of 2012, so July 2012.

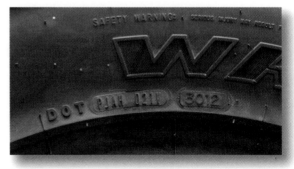

A code of 4008 would be the 40th week of 2008. The PJAH D21V refers to the manufacturer, location of manufacture and type of tyre – don't try to look it up, the date is the useful part. The full code is often found only on one side of the tyre – you may just see a partial code on the other side. There was an older system for tyres before 2000, but none of those should be in use now!

low- and high-profile tyres

Nobody used to be all that bothered about high-performance handling in the 4WDs of the '80s, but today, with hundreds of kilowatts and sophisticated suspension, it's a different story. Modern 4WDs are capable of sustaining double-ton speeds, have loaded weights of beyond three tonnes, yet can also handle fluidly through the bends and traverse the roughest terrains. The problem is that the tyre qualities needed for each of these situations are diametrically opposed, and a major factor is the profile, or the height of the sidewall relative to the width. However, for offroading we're more concerned with the actual height of the sidewall, not its percentage. For example, the Toyota LC200 may run a 285/60/18 tyre, and the Discovery 3 a 255/60/18 – both 60-profile, but it's 60% of 285mm and 255mm respectively so the sidewall heights are 171mm and 153mm, or 12% different. That's significant.

To compare high- and low-profile we can use a Discovery 4 3.0L's 255/55/19 as an example; taking 55% of 255mm gives us 140mm when the tyre has no weight on it. From this we can calculate an overall diameter of 763mm, given there are 25.4mm to an inch. A common misconception is that fitting a larger rim increases the overall diameter – it doesn't need to, so in this case if we used a 20" rim the tyre size would be 255/50/20, or going the other way, 255/60/18. We can go one further and use 255/65/17 with an unloaded sidewall height of 172mm, which fits the Discovery 3 and Discovery 4 2.7L, and that size is what we'll use as our second example to compare to the 255/55/19.

We'll assume the 255/55/19 and 255/65/17 are of precisely the same construction and design. This

is never going to be the case in practice, as low- and high-profiles even of the same model and manufacturer necessarily require different designs, but it is important to get a couple of points out of the way. The first is that for a given inflation pressure the contact patch will be precisely the same length and width regardless of the profile. This is because the contact patch is a function of the weight on the tyre and its pressure, although the volume of air inside the tyres is different. As we're assuming all else is equal, including weight, both these theoretical tyres should be run at exactly the same pressure to achieve that contact patch. There is no difference between a low- and high-profile tyre until the vehicle begins to move, and the differences become more apparent the faster you go (and the latest 4WDs can move very quickly!).

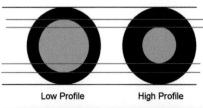

Low Profile   High Profile

A 255/55/19 next to a 265/65/17. Same overall diameter (the 19 is slightly worn) but different rim sizes. Note the distance the bottom of the rim is from the ground. The 19" looks all right at the moment, but wait until it's on the car and you have most of the car's weight balanced on it offroad.

advantages of a low-profile tyre

A low-profile tyre has a large-diameter rim relative to the tyre diameter, and thus a short sidewall. Exactly when a tyre is classified as low-profile is open to debate, but in general any aspect ratio of 60 or less would be classed as low-profile. In general, a low-profile tyre will handle better than a high-profile tyre (like the sort seen on serious off-roaders), at least on smooth terrain and at high speed. One reason is steering response. When you turn the steering wheel, it turns not the tyre but the rim.

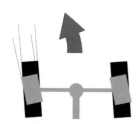

The tyre only turns because it's attached to the rim, and as low-profile tyres have little distance between the rim and the contact patch on the road, steering response and feedback is improved. Then there is tyre slip angle; when a vehicle corners it naturally resists the change in direction (inertia) and the force required to change direction (centripetal force) is provided by the tyres through the contact patch. This means the rim moves relative to the contact patch, and that's not good for handling.

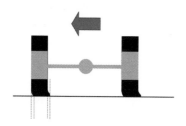

Low-profile tyres move less relative to their rims, so provide better handling on high-speed bitumen.

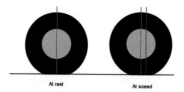

Pneumatic trail. Higher-profile tyres distort more at speed and under braking or cornering loads, which upsets the balance and handling of the vehicle.

Tyres also change shape at speed, and that, too, affects handling. A tyre's contact patch covers a lengthways area on the ground, and when the tyre isn't moving the centre of the patch lines up to the centre of the wheel. When the tyre is moving at high speed it takes a little time for the tyre to deform to flat as it hits the ground, and after it leaves the ground it takes a little time for it to reform to round. Thus, the contact patch moves backwards relative to the centre point of the wheel –again, that's not good for high-speed handling as it changes the steering geometry. This is known as the pneumatic trail, and it is minimised by use of wide, low-profile tyres as opposed to narrower, higher-profile tyres. A similar effect happens under heavy acceleration or braking.

Low-profiles are typically wider than the equivalent high-profile, so their contact patch is wide and short as opposed to long and thin. This is another factor, meaning less rim/tyre movement (slip). The extra width also means the tyre's deformation at the ground is less, because it has a short contact patch albeit a wide one, and the longer the contact patch the greater deformation and thus heat build up. This means there's again less build up of heat. However, in the wet, a wide tyre is at a disadvantage because it has a wider area of water to move out of the way before it can grip the surface, and then not much contact patch length left after that is done. Low-profiles are also made with relatively shallow treads, not the 12-16mm of offroad tyres. This again is to improve handling; the entire car rests on the tread blocks, so the deeper the tread the more "squirmy" the tyre and the greater the heat build up.

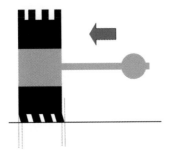

However, wide low-profiles are not all advantage for handling. They have a grip advantage in the dry, but once that limit is reached the loss of grip is quite sudden, unlike a narrower higher-profile tyre in which that loss is more gradual. The low-profile also does not absorb minor undulations and irregularities well on the road, so on dirt roads, uneven surfaces and the like they are at a disadvantage.

Finally, low-profile tyres also look better (apparently), and that's probably a major factor for their popularity. It's a pity to spend all that money on a fire-breathing sports 4WD and then ruin the handling with offroad tyres. Then again, it's a pity not to maximise the offroad capability of your vehicle by tip-toeing around in the rough on racetrack tyres.

advantages of a high-profile tyre

When you're offroad very often you want a greater contact patch for flotation in sand or mud. You do that by lowering tyre pressures, which also means benefits in ability to mould the tyre to the terrain, better impact resistance, improved ride comfort through less bouncing, which means more traction and even slightly improved articulation – the tyre with weight on it compresses more than it otherwise would, whereas the tyre without weight remains free to expand to its unweighted diameter as usual. This trick is often used in suspension flex competitions, which is why all four tyres are checked for even pressures by the judges.

Time and time again cars have failed an obstacle, let the tyres down and then cruised up. Lower pressures also mean improved puncture resistance – try puncturing a balloon blown up hard or soft. Incidentally, slower speeds also reduce the risk of punctures. The analogy there is placing an axe blade on a piece of wood, or slamming it down; the principle is the same with a sharp rock on a tyre.

The problem with low-profiles and tyre pressures is that the rim gets very close to the ground and can be damaged, so low-profile pressures need to be kept up to prevent that happening. Provided the width and diameter are the same, the contact patch of a low-profile is in theory the same as a high-profile but in practice there are differences due to tyre construction.

The major problem is the sidewall height. Our 255/65/17 has an unladen sidewall height of

172mm vs the 255/55/19's 140mm. Only 26mm difference, but that's 20%, quite a percentage difference. At 40psi on a D3 that would change to 131mm and 112mm; and the 19 would look all right on the flat, still some distance between rim and ground, so you'd wonder what all the fuss was about. To find out just cross-axle the vehicle so it is resting on two diagonal wheels. Then each wheel would support around 1,500kg instead of 750kg, and you'd see that rim come very close to the ground. If the rim touches the ground it may well be bent out of shape. Keeping the rim away from the ground is extremely important and this is the primary reason why low-profiles do not work well offroad. In order to make sure the rim doesn't touch you need to ensure there is plenty of air in the tyre, which means not airing down very much. If you don't air down then the contact patch cannot increase which means traction problems in soft terrain and, just as important, increased rolling resistance. It also means the tyre is more likely to bounce around, leading again to traction problems, and the higher the pressure, the greater the chance of a puncture. The short sidewall also means the tyre is prone to "pinching" or "rim crush", where the rim cuts down into the sidewall and damages the tyres, or even causes a puncture. This is even more the case with wide tyres which may not be flat to the surface.

The cross-axled example above gets worse if you're on a slope. If a 3,000kg 4WD is on a 30 degree flat slope then instead of having, say, 1,500kg on each axle on the flat it may have around 1,750kg on the downhill wheels, or 875kg per wheel instead of 750kg. That's assuming the load is equally spread, and it generally isn't, so the load on one wheel

could shoot up well above 1,500kg even before we consider acceleration factors. In other words, just because a 255/55/19 looks pretty good on the flat and level that doesn't mean to say it still protects the rim when you're into hills or rocks, and the only solution is keeping the pressure up which has the disadvantages already described. For example, I've tested a vehicle with 275/40/20 tyres and concluded it is simply infeasible to air them down in any terrain except one due to rim damage concerns. The one exception is sand, where a vehicle's weight is generally more evenly distributed than in rocks or forest hills. Sand is softly forgiving so the chances of rim damage are far less. Since the low-profile has pretty much the same contact patch as a high-profile, the reduction in rolling resistance is the same for both types, thus the low-profile works in sand. Sand driving is more about reduction of rolling resistance than increasing traction, as evidenced by the fact that mud tyres don't perform as well as a more closed tread. However, even in sand low-profiles are still vulnerable to the odd rock or stick, when the tyre cannot protect the rim.

High-profiles are typically designed to carry more weight than low-profiles, and this is critical for touring offroaders where strength and load carrying is more important than ability to sustain high speeds.

The fact that low-profiles are typically wider is also a usually a disadvantage. While the contact patch area is the same, it is shorter and wider. This means the tyre is less likely to be flat to the ground on uneven terrain – not a problem on a flat racetrack, but all that width cannot often be used.

Secondly, consider a tyre with a patch length of 260mm (a 235/85/16 at 20psi) vs one with 209mm (a 255/55/19 at 20psi). Both are rolling over a loose stone of 60mm diameter. The first tyre will still have around 200mm of tread length left to try and make contact with the ground so it won't balance on top of the stone anywhere near as much as the 255/55. This assumes we've aired the 255/55 to 20psi – we probably can't, so if it were left at 35psi we'd have a patch length of 170mm. While it's not particularly important for offroading, a tall, narrow tyre is more efficient than a short wide one; just have a look a bicycles, hybrids and solar-powered vehicles. A wider tyre is also slightly more puncture-prone because it presents a wider face to the terrain.

low-profile tyres: what to do

It is now clear why we see so many punctures with road-spec low-profile tyres. It is because they are designed for high speed and thus are thin and easily punctured, and there is little protection for the rim, which means they cannot be aired down very far or at all, increasing the probability of a puncture as does their width, and because of sidewall pinch. An offroad-spec low-profile tyre would fix the thin-construction problem and go some way to being able to air down, but it would have very strong sidewalls to protect the rim and thus not have the pliable flexibility of its low-profile cousin, which would mould itself to the terrain and thus grip better and bounce less. However, that's the only solution available if your vehicle cannot run high-profiles. The good news is that if you have a modern vehicle with low-profile tyres and fit offroad rubber to it then you'll find the vehicle so capable it can still run with the older vehicles,

but it's in spite of, not because, of their tyre profile. Conversely, on my Discovery 3 I've fitted 17" rim and all-terrain tyres – this has taken the edge off the road handling but it is still very good and more than enough for my purposes.

wide or narrow?

For offroad use, narrow tyres are, in general, better than wide ones.

The wide tyre cannot get all its tread in contact with the ground.

To explain – all else being equal, a wide tyre has exactly the same contact patch as a narrow tyre. The difference is the shape of the patch. A

245/70/17 tyre may have a width of 245mm and a contact patch length of 180mm, and a 265/65/17 may have 265mm and 166mm.

As contact patch area is the same then the flotation is also the same. However, wide tyres have several disadvantages for offroad use. The first is rolling resistance – obviously a wide tyre creates a wider track than a narrow one, so there's greater rolling resistance. Then comes deformation. A long contact patch will act like a mini caterpillar track, enveloping small undulations (refer photos on page 103/104). A wide but short track won't do that. Then there's situations where the tyre isn't flat to the road, which is most of the time in the rough. As the photo shows, tyres hang on by their crown and sidewalls. In those situations narrow tyres have longer contact patches so more rubber in contact with the road compared to wide ones. A narrow tyre and rim weighs less than the equivalent diameter-wide tyre and rim too, which is one reason why economy-oriented vehicles run narrows.

All this is why specialist offroad vehicles have narrow tyres – think Defender, 79 Series, most military vehicles, even tractors. Wide tyres have numerous advantages for high-performance and onroad use, which is why they are fitted to sportscars.

While the physics does say the contact patch area between narrow and wide is the same, what varies it in practice is the construction of the tyre. Nevertheless, the advantages of narrow tyres hold true. It is possible to have a narrow low-profile tyre, but as both low-profiles and wide tyres are good for onroad handling that's what you find on sportscars, whereas narrow high-profile tyres are found on offroad vehicles.

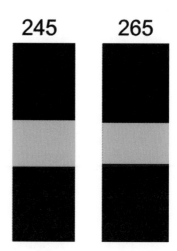

A scale diagram of the contact patch on a 245/70/17 tyre compared to 265/65/17.

TUSTs and run flats

tusts

These are Temporary Use Spare Tyres, otherwise known as space-saver spares, and more correctly referred to as a dangerous waste of space. A TUST is a tyre and rim that is narrower, shorter and lighter than the normally fitted tyre. Manufactures use them because they are cheap and light, and because modern tyres are much more resistant to punctures. Many road motorists go years between punctures. However, not many offroaders go years between punctures, and when they have a puncture they may be many hours or even days drive from the nearest settlement; in any case, small country towns are not known for having a ready supply of every type of tyre. The TUST is designed only to be used for a short period of time, at a low speed, with a low load. Clearly this is not acceptable if you are changing a flat anywhere

1   A 275/40/20 tyre on a Range Rover Sport on a rock, at 40psi, starting to pinch the rim. We took the decision not to air these down as there was simply no way we could do so and still protect the rim.

2   Buying four rather than five tyres is a false economy for 4WDs. This Pathfinder has the standard spare and four larger mud tyres. Should the spare be needed the vehicle is instantly unroadworthy and unsafe. Braking will be affected, as will handling. Moreover, as the rolling diameter is different the transmission will be worn and the electronic stability control could be thrown out. Instead, buy five tyres and rotate them.

3   An alloy rim bent on the inside. This crack would worsen and leak air. Typically such damage is not repairable.

classed as offroad. While a TUST can work around town, fitting one offroad is the equivalent of trying to go bushwalking while wearing one hiking boot and one thong. The vehicle's capability will be dramatically limited, and it gets worse – the chances of having a second puncture in a TUST are much greater than a normal tyre. But the woe doesn't end there. After changing the tyre you then need to take your normal wheel with you. But where? It probably won't fit into where the TUST was stored because that is likely to be a small compartment just big enough for the TUST. The manufacturers say you could put it in the back, which is something of a sick joke when you consider what space is likely to be available in a fully loaded offroader.

It should be clear that TUSTs have absolutely no place whatsoever on a touring 4WD. If you own a vehicle with a TUST then you should take a proper spare tyre with you on even the shortest offroad trips, maybe on the roof.

run-flats

Run-flat tyres are designed to continue operating after a puncture. This may work around town, but isn't going to work offroad. A typical town puncture may be a small nail. An offroad puncture could be a small nail, or it could be a tyre gashed open across its width. Moreover, the run-flats have a harsher ride and cannot be aired down as far. Simply, they are not suitable for offroad use and are in no way substitutes for a proper spare tyre.

larger diameter tyres

You may consider running larger-diameter tyres on your vehicle than standard, which instantly improve offroad capability in most situations. However, there are pros and cons:

Pro/con	Notes
+ Greater clearance under the diff	Bigger tyres are the only realistic way to achieve under-diff clearance.
+ Better angles (departure, ramp, attack)	Can also be achieved in ways other than tyres such as suspensions lifts.
+ Greater "clamber over" ability	Bigger tyres make obstacles look smaller!
+ Greater body clearance	Everything is higher up.
+ Better flotation	Pressures can be dropped even further for better flotation in sand, this also works well on other surfaces as the tyre moulds itself to the terrain. However, pressures may need to be dropped a long way anyway to get a decent sized contact patch, which means keeping the tyre on the rim would be a problem. In this case beadlocks, devices which fix the tyre to the rim instead of relying on air pressure, may be required. Only internal beadlocks are legal in Australia.
- Speedo error	Changing the tyre diameter will make the speedometer read differently. However, most under-read by default so it might get closer to reality. Check it at a few different speeds, using, for example, a GPS receiver on a flat, straight road.
- Higher gearing	The bigger the tyre, the lower the gearing. Reduced engine braking. Low-range won't quite be as low.
- Performance	Bigger tyres are heavier. This has an effect on performance and economy, especially as it's rotating weight, and leads to more drivetrain stress, possibly causing a failure later on.
- Handling	A higher centre of gravity won't help with the handling.
- Rubbing	Tyres too large might rub against the guards; this needs to be tested on full lock at maximum articulation.
- Electronic systems	ABS, stability control, trailer sway control and the like all rely on individual wheel speed sensors. These sensors measure the rotation speed of the wheel – but they cannot measure how far the vehicle travels per wheel rotation, which will be longer with larger-diameter tyres. There is no question that this reduces the system's effectiveness, as the vehicle is travelling faster than what the sensors indicate, so their reaction could be anything from sub-optimal to inappropriate. The larger-diameter tyres also affect general handling which would not have been accounted for. That said, there is also no question that the systems are not precisely sensitive to an exact diameter and can still work effectively with slightly different size. The reports of owners who have had no problems with large-diameter tyres may well be true, but they are unlikely to have fully tested the emergency features. The best advice is not to fit oversize tyres to ESC-equipped vehicles, or if you do, to be aware of the implications as described above.

1   *A Temporary Use Spare Tyre.*

2   *An XC-90 showing a TUST. Many softroaders have TUSTs; be sure to check for yourself the speed and load rating of the spare tyre matches that of the others.*

3   *No more than 80km/h and for temporary use only.*

4   *Where do you put the damaged original tyre?*

Larger-diameter tyres are one of the most effective upgrades for improving offroad capability, which is why competition trucks run 35"-37" tyres as opposed to standard vehicles, which run 29"-32". However, the modifications required by the rest of the vehicle to reliably and safely function are extensive and become more so as the diameter increases – it's by no means just bolting the bigger rubber on and calling it good. Most tourers will stick with a tyre size close to standard.

This module from American Expedition Vehicles modifies the speedometer of Jeep Wrangler JK models so it reads correctly and also passes the correct values to the stability control system. However, larger tyres still affect the vehicles handling.

Two Jeep Wranglers. The older model is a much-modified TJ including 37" tyres. It has no electronics. The newer model is a JK and has the full range of modern electronics, including stability control, so modifications need to take this into account.

Another consideration is legality. Most states only permit vehicles to fit tyres that are 15mm greater diameter than the maximum diameter the manufacturer specified for that series of vehicles, so options may be limited anyway. However, note the word "series"; if you bought a base-model vehicle that comes with small tyres, the higher-spec models might run marginally larger-diameter tyres, and you can check this out by looking at the vehicle's tyre placard (this should be somewhere around the driver's side door jamb). In other words, you can legally upgrade to that tyre size. If you investigate this, note that the lower-spec vehicle often has different diff ratios (see Chapter 4) to compensate for the smaller tyres, so if you go up tyre sizes you'll actually be higher-geared than the equivalent model which had that tyre size to begin with.

directional and asymmetric tyres

Most tyres are bi-directional, which means they work as well forwards as they do in reverse, and the spare can be put on any wheel. There are some uni-directional tyres that can only be run in one direction. These outperform bi-directionals when going the "right" way, but are much worse when going the other way, either reversing or if you get a flat and have to fit your spare on the "wrong" side. Offroad tourers are probably better off with conventional bi-directionals just for that reason. Competition trucks use uni-directionals for maximum performance. Then there are asymmetric tyres that split the tread into two, a wet half and a dry half, each optimised for the specific condition. While each optimised half of the tyre would grip better than half of a conventional tyre in its special condition, the other half wouldn't, so overall, it's just another compromise, not the final answer to tyre design.

1   The Cooper XST, an asymmetric design (image courtesy Cooper Tires).

2   The Baja Claw, a uni-directional design (image courtesy Cooper Tires).

3   The LX570's tyres need to be smooth, quiet and perform everywhere. The Wrangler can afford to focus more on offroad prowess, but the Cherokee drivers will value fuel efficiency, cost and on-road handling. There's no perfect tyre.

winter tyres

Winter tyres are designed for low temperatures as well as snow and ice, and they dramatically outperform normal tyres. One reason is a different tread pattern, but the main reason is that winter tyres are designed to retain their flexibility in low temperatures (as in below around 7 degrees Celsius) by using more rubber for a softer compound. Flexibility means grip, so winter tyres can be thought of more as low-temperature tyres, offering up to 20% more grip in certain conditions. Winter tyres can be used in higher temperature conditions but will wear more quickly than normal tyres. Winters come in various grades designed for different temperature ranges, up to tyres that can be fitted with screw-in studs for amazing ice traction – don't confuse winter tyres with specialist snow/ice tyres. Most 4WD offroad tyres are rated "M+S" for Mud and Snow and should work well in cold conditions.

tyre pressures

why are they important?

Tyre pressures are incredibly important to all vehicles and especially 4WDs. Not just for bitumen running, but especially for offroad driving. The correct pressures can mean the difference between an easy drive up a hard track, and spending time winching. They can mean the difference between a long tyre life and early (expensive) replacement of tyres, maybe even a major blowout at the side of the road. Tyre pressures have an effect on how comfortable the ride is, fuel efficiency, handling in all conditions, load carrying ability and most definitely safety.

The problem with tyre pressures is determining the "correct" pressure. There are no fixed rules (20psi here, 40psi there) as the correct pressure depends on many factors, some of which are listed below along with guides about whether the pressures should be increased or decreased, all else being equal:

- Size of the tyre (internal volume: the diameter, width and profile) – the smaller the tyre, the greater the pressure. The larger the tyre fitted, the lower the pressure required.

- Weight on the tyre – more weight, more pressure required to maintain the tyre's shape and support the load.

- Speed to be driven – the higher the speed, the higher the pressure. High pressure means minimal deformation as the tyre rolls: deformation causes heat, heat causes tyre failure. High pressures also mean a stiff sidewall and precise handling.

- Construction of the tyre – the tougher and heavier the tyre, the less able it is to dissipate heat from deformation and the higher the pressure required for a given speed.

- Terrain – many terrains demand a specific pressure for flotation, notably sand. The softer the terrain, the lower the pressure should be in order to reduce the vehicle sinking into the soft surface, which increases rolling resistance. This is usually a more important factor than increasing traction. When pressures need reducing, so must speed be reduced to avoid handling problems and tyre damage through heat generation.

As a general rule, the manufacturer's recommended pressures are too low for a touring 4WD. This is because the tourer will typically add 200kg-400kg of equipment and accessories and be running tougher, heavier tyres less able to dissipate heat. Depending on the situation, adding about 10% to the recommended pressures will be approximately correct, but check with 4WD tyre specialists for your specific vehicle and situation. The average tyre shop is typically a place where tyres are fitted and may not have any specialist knowledge; often tyres are simply inflated to either the placard recommendation or to their maximum safe pressure. The correct pressure will certainly be somewhere in between.

One occasion when pressures should certainly be raised is when the vehicle is heavily loaded or towing, and will be spending a lot of time at highway speeds on the bitumen (this is especially true for hot days). This is the classic time for tyre failures. The damage done may not be apparent until later, so increase pressures in these situations to retain the same contact patch area as when unloaded.

The best way to check the tyre pressures are correct is to draw a chalk or similar line width-wise across the tyre and then drive in a straight line. The mark should be evenly worn; if it's worn more in the centre the tyres are overinflated – on the outsides, underinflated. Another way to check is the "4psi rule"; a tyre's cold pressure – when the vehicle hasn't been driven for an hour or more – should be about four psi less than its hot pressure, measured after it has been driven for half an hour. If the pressure is less the tyre is not heating up very much which means it is not deforming very much, and that means it is not moulding to the road and gripping it particularly well. If the difference is much more than four psi, the tyre pressure is too low, which will damage the tyre, worsen handling and reduce fuel economy. In any case, regularly check your tyres for even wear; if they are wearing mainly at the centre then chances are the pressures are too high, on the edges and maybe it's too low. Any type of uneven wear should be discussed with a real tyre expert as it may also be incorrect alignment.

Around 10% to 20% of the energy required to maintain a 4WD at 100km/h is soaked up by the tyres. Of that energy around 90% to 95% goes in rotational deformation, which is why hybrids and other cars focused on fuel efficiency also have tyres specially designed for low rolling resistance – usually at the expense of grip.

It is not possible to give recommended pressures as vehicles vary so widely. For example, road pressure on a tiny Suzuki Jimny is around 22psi. On a Defender 130 it's around 50psi, and then you have vehicle loading and tyre type as well. That's why this section explains principles, after which you can work out the best pressure for yourself.

why lower the pressure?

Most of the time offroaders will be lowering tyre pressures. Lower pressures have the following effects:

- Larger (longer, not wider) contact patch
- A softer, more flexible tyre
- Reduced ground clearance
- The tyre is less firmly fixed to the rim.

the advantages of lower pressure are:

- **Better flotation:** A larger contact patch means the weight is spread over a wider area, so the tyre sinks in less. This is useful in sand and mud. The main advantage of flotation is reduced rolling resistance in soft terrain. It is this, rather than an increase in traction, which allows vehicles at low pressure to drive where high pressure tyres cannot go. The loss of ground clearance by lowering pressures is offset in soft conditions by reduced sinking.

- **Potentially better traction:** On loose, fragile surfaces the terrain cannot support a high shear force; each square centimetre of ground can handle only so much "tearing" which is what a tyre does as it is driven. Therefore, a larger contact patch spreads the shear load.

- **Improved resistance to punctures:** Imagine blowing a balloon up until it's stretched and full of air. Wouldn't take much to burst it. With lower pressure in the balloon, it's hard to burst it.

- **Ability to mould to the terrain:** A low-pressure tyre will mould itself around and over small stones and sticks. A high-pressure tyre could easily be balanced entirely on a small, loose rock.

- **Shock absorption:** Drop a highly-inflated ball on concrete and it will bounce high and keep on bouncing. A partially inflated ball won't bounce as high and will stop bouncing sooner. Precisely the same effect is seen with tyres, and this is particularly noticeable on rocks. The bouncing means a loss of traction and additional drivetrain stress.

the disadvantage of lower pressures are:

- **Restriction on speed:** Lower pressures means the tyre deforms more, which means heat can easily build up and damage the tyre. In addition, there is more slip between rim and tyre around corners. So if you have to run low pressures on the road, keep the speed down.

- **Handling:** The car will feel horribly woolly and vague if driven at any speed above about 20km/h and the steering will feel heavier. It feels wrong and it is.

- **Possibility of the tyre coming off the rim:** This may be because the tyre is pinched in a rut, because of abrupt manoeuvring or because the vehicle is slipping sideways. Some tyres are more prone to it than others. Careful, gentle driving is the key. Putting a tyre back on a rim is easy to do but it's generally something to be avoided.

1   Corrugations are the bane of an offroader's life. You find them in all sorts of places, including sand. Nothing you can do will
    eliminate them, but softer tyre pressures help alleviate the discomfort for you and stress on your vehicle.

2   Tyres do part company with the rim on occasion. It's not a big problem and doesn't generally cause a crisis.

3   A Santa Fe coming downhill on a 235/65/17 tyre at 20psi. As most of the vehicle's weight is on the front wheels the tyre has
    flattened out and the rim is close to the ground. The passenger front wheel has even more weight on it. Therefore, even if the
    rim-to-ground distance looks ok when the vehicle is on the flat, that doesn't mean the tyre will continue to provide adequate
    clearance to protect the rim on uneven terrain.

- **Slight decrease in ground clearance:**
  However, the tradeoff is worth it.

- **Sidewall bulge:** This is often cited as a reason
  not to lower pressures on dirt roads, but in fact
  the additional bulge from road pressure to dirt
  pressure is in the order of 7mm, not enough to
  worry about. At very low pressures the bulge
  becomes significant, but remember that the
  tyre is softer so it is inherently more resistant to
  punctures. Overall, lower pressures and lower
  speeds, offroad, result in fewer punctures. It's
  that simple. This is the logic side of things; the
  experience side of things comes from that of
  tour operators who used to run a high pressure,
  experienced many punctures on their tours,
  then dropped pressures and reduced the
  numbers of punctures. Consistent experience
  and consistent results.

The chapters in the following section deal with tyre
pressures for specific terrains and situations.

measuring tyre pressure

Tyre pressures are measured in psi (pounds per
square inch) or bar. The most common measurement
is psi, even in this age of metric, so we'll use that. For
reference, the conversion factor is:

1 psi = 0.068947 bars

1 bar = 14.5038 psi

You can see why psi is the more popular
measurement, given 4WD tyre pressures typically
range between 15 and 45 psi or 1.03 and 3.10 bar!

pressures vs contact patch

The contact patch of a tyre is an elongated oval,
and the pressure exerted by the tyre is not equal all
the way around the oval but greatest at the centre,
reducing towards the edges.

265/65/17 contact patch, Discovery 3

A typical tyre contact patch showing an oval shape.

Taking five psi out of a tyre doesn't increase the contact patch by a given amount. If that change is from 40 to 35, it won't make much difference. But from 25 to 20 is a big percentage difference, and from 20 to 15 even bigger. It's that last five psi or so that makes all the difference.

yielded on average another three per cent or 12mm of contact patch length. The low-profile 19" tyre clearly lets the rim closer to the ground than the other two tyres, and thus should not be lowered as far in order to avoid rim damage. The higher-profile 235/85/16 is of the strong, light-truck construction, is the narrowest tyre and is also on a slightly lighter vehicle so results are not directly comparable. However its contact patch figures are not too far away from the others. The total contact area is closer than the graph shows as the 235/85/16 is narrower, and naturally has a longer contact patch. The sidewall bulge shows little variation from high to low pressure; from 40psi to 25psi (a lowish pressure for dirt-road driving), the average bulge increases by only 7mm. Add another 2mm to get to 20psi.

The actual sidewall height of the unladen 235, 265, and 255 tyres is, respectively, 172mm, 200mm and 140mm. At 40psi that reduced to 134mm, 154mm and 114mm. The average height loss from 40psi to 25psi is 11mm or, put another way, the rim is 11mm closer to the ground and the vehicle loses 11mm of ground clearance. See page 104 for images of the tyres.

This chart shows the contact patch length (top), distance from the ground to the bottom of the rim (middle) and "bulge" – distance from the outermost tread block on the ground to the actual width of the tyre. Three tyres on two vehicles are shown; a 235/85/16 LT mud tyre on a Defender weighing 2,400kg, a 265/65/17 all-terrain and a 255/55/19 mud tyre, both Passenger construction on a 2,700kg Discovery 3. The graph shows that the increase in contact patch area is non-linear; taking averages, going from 45psi to 40psi increases the contact patch by four percent, whereas from 35psi to 30psi it's six percent, from 25psi to 20psi it's 13%, 20psi to 15psi is 21% and from 15psi to 10psi another 24%. The point is that once you get below 25psi another two psi makes a difference, and even more so when you get below 15psi. Dropping the pressures from 10psi to 8psi

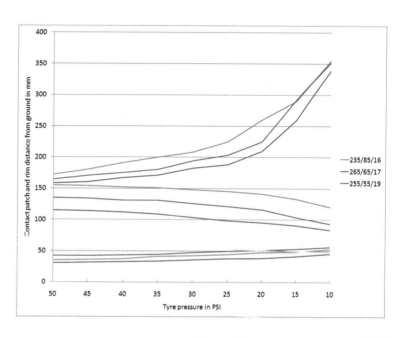

	40psi	30psi	25psi	20psi	15psi	10psi
255/55/19						
265/65/17						
235/85/16						

The sets of tyres showing non-linear increase in contact patch as the pressures are lowered. The chart shows the results.

To demonstrate how well a tyre at low pressure moulds to the terrain I jacked up my Discovery 3 and put a small rock under the front wheel, I began with the tyre at 45psi, then aired down to 20psi. The difference is dramatic. At 45psi the tyre balances on the rock – the equivalent of a human standing on a cricket ball; the wheel will rotate and spit the rock backwards. At 20psi the tyre is still balancing, but only just, and has wrapped around the rock. In a real-life situation at 20psi more of the tyre would be touching the ground instead of just balancing on the rock. Another advantage of low pressures is the lack of bouncing when a wheel lifts and comes back to the ground, and from the photos it is also apparent the vehicle's body is not lifted as far up at 20psi to get over the little rock, which contributes to stability, albeit at the cost of a little ground clearance. Therefore, lower pressures have more advantages than just pure flotation in soft conditions – they also work well on rocks.

Front-on view of two tyres at eight psi. Only the tread is touching the ground. Contact patches only get longer, never wider. That said, if the ground is soft the sidewall will touch the ground, which is why 4WD tyres have tread on the sidewall. Also, if the ground is soft then the higher the tyre pressure, the greater the amount the tyre sinks in. Look also at the images on page 104 of the tyre on a rock at 20 and 40psi - very little sidewall bulge.

tyre grip

Tyres grip in one of two ways: adhesion and deformation, or mechanical. Adhesion is the stickiness of a tyre to a surface, and mechanical is the tyre moulding itself to the terrain, much like two cogs intermeshing, but at a fine level with the tread pattern intersecting with the ground. Offroad tyres mostly rely on mechanical grip as they run cold, unlike for example sportscar tyres. Adhesive tyres can actually be detrimental to traction in loose surfaces as they pick up mud and stones in the tread, but would be an advantage in slick rock driving.

rims

The rim is the metal wheel that the tyre is fitted to. Rims have load ratings and any aftermarket rim must have at least the same load rating as the original rim. This is typically measured in kg and stamped on the rim.

Rim sizes are expressed in diameter x width, e.g. 15x8 is a 15 inch diameter rim, 8 inches wide. Ensure the tyres fitted to a rim are designed not only for the rim diameter, but also the width – the tyre manufacturer's website will list permitted rim sizes.

Rims also have a PCD, or Pitch Circle Diameter. This is the diameter of a circle that passes through the centre of each wheel nut, as shown below:

PCDs are expressed as number of nuts x diameter, e.g. 5 x 100 is 5 nuts, 100mm diameter. It is also important that the nuts on any aftermarket rims engage the threads for at least as many turns as the original nuts.

Rims also have an offset, which is explained in the diagram below:

rim offset

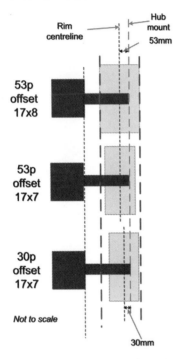

The offset is the distance the rim mount face is away from the rim centreline. Away from the car is positive, towards the car is negative. The standard offset for a Discovery 3 is 53p (positive). Fitting a 30p 17x7 rim doesn't increase the width of the car very much as the rim is narrower, although further out than the 53p. However, track is the distance from wheel centre to wheel centre (Chapter 1), so track is increased by 43mm. A rim of 45p leads to an increase of 16mm, within the 25mm limit. The width of the rim has no effect on track, just overall width of the vehicle. A different offset does change the track. Aside from the legal consideration the offset must be correct so as not to affect handling and minimise driveline stress.

The standard 17x7s are 53P, which means that the rim mount face is 53mm towards the outside of the rim.

split rims & tubeless tyres

Older 4WDs used split rims and tubed tyres. A split rim is one that comes apart in two pieces, in order to fit the tyre. A solid rim is exactly that; one solid, usually forged, piece of metal alloy. Tubed and tubeless tyres are exactly what you'd imagine; one has an inner tube, much like a bicycle tyre, while the other does not.

Split rims and tubed tyres have fallen out of favour even with old, experienced hands. This is because if you put a split rim back together incorrectly, which is easy to do, then during tyre inflation it can explode and injure anyone in its path. Tubed tyres are also more complicated to work on, and the tube itself can rub and puncture. Modern solid rims and tubeless tyres are reliable and easy to work with, and small punctures can quickly be repaired using plugs.

Do not use tubes in tubeless tyres except in emergencies. This is because tubeless tyres have a rough interior which can damage tubes, and because the tubes will increase the tyre operating temperature.

1   A steel rim can be knocked back into shape with a hammer. However, it's often weaker than an alloy so is more likely to need a repair, and even when repaired may not seal properly. This steel rim has been bent out of shape by a wedge of wood. We knocked the bead off, removed the stick and hammered it back into shape.

2-3   A red Wrangler TJ with black steel rims and a silver Wrangler JK with silver alloys. The alloys fill out the tyre more than the steels.

solid rims: alloy or steel

Technically, an alloy is any combination of metals. In rim terms it means wheels made up of aluminium, magnesium or most often a combination (alloy) of the two. Steel wheels are just plain steel, usually with an inner section welded to an outer. Alloys may be cast in one piece or two, or forged. Once upon a time steels were the only sensible option, but many years of offroading later and quality alloys have well and truly proven themselves, so there is no need to replace them with steels. While steel rims, if bent, can be hammered back into shape, the average steel wheel is weaker than a quality alloy so it is more likely to need that repair. On the other hand, alloy rims are significantly lighter, stronger and look better. In short, alloys work in the bush. Note; do not use wheel nuts designed for alloy rims on steel rims and vice-versa. The nut must be designed for the rim, otherwise it will not hold and could damage the stud or rim. Another tip; aftermarket rims are often around a third of the price of manufacturer equivalents. Alloy rims also permit better heat dissipation than steels as they are more open and for that reason it may not be wise to fit steels to high-performance 4WDs. Alloy rims are also known as "mag" wheels as magnesium is often used as one of the metals alloyed.

A 265/65/16 tyre on a steel rim with a 235/70/17 on an alloy rim. The steel rim is less open than the alloy and so cannot dissipate brake-generated heat as well.

tyre wear

As you inspect your tyres, look for even wear across the tread width. If the centre section is over-worn in relation to the outer parts, this indicates over-inflation. Over-worn outer sections indicate under-inflation. If one side is worn it indicates an alignment or balancing problem. Also check for cuts, bulges, tread blocks torn off and anything else unusual as it's nice to spot these things before they cause a problem.

A ripped treadblock. The tyre is not unserviceable yet but you need to keep an eye on it.

A tyre that has been on a vehicle with poor alignment, shown by the significant shoulder wear on the right side of the tyre. Regular inspection should pick up the early signs before it gets this bad.

preventing a puncture

While you should know how to repair a puncture, here's how to reduce your chances of needing those skills in the first place:

Strong tyres: Use light-truck construction tyres. Passenger construction tyres are lighter and weaker, built for speed, not strength. Stronger tyres are also easier to fix; I once spent a solid hour repairing around 30 punctures in a set of Simex extreme tyres after an Outback Challenge run. However, I found it impossible to repair a small hole in a high-speed passenger tyre because the tyre was so thin it simply tore around the plugged hole as it was inflated.

Run the right pressures: On high-speed dirt roads consider using 75% of manufacturer's recommended pressures, in low-range half that and sand even lower. Conversely, at high speed on bitumen, especially when heavily loaded, consider going above manufacturer's recommended, but never above the max-inflation of the tyre. The lower the tyre pressure, the greater the resistance to punctures.

Slow down: The slower you go, the less force on the tyre when it hits something like a rock, and the less chance of a puncture.

Tread depth and wear: The shallower the tread depth, the greater the chance of a puncture. The legal limit is usually 1.6mm; replace your tyres well before that at around four millimetres or earlier.

Inspect your tyres: If you don't, you won't know what condition they're in or if there are any alignment problems developing!

Watch your line: Your 4WD isn't a tank. Avoid upturned rocks, tree roots at nasty angles and anything else that looks likely to damage tyres. Your lower speed helps here too.

Keep to the track: Foraging off-track is a good way to pick up a puncture, damage the environment and get yourself into trouble.

A common worry is that the sidewall bulge created by airing down presents a puncture risk. It is true the sidewall bulges more; by seven millimetres for the 235/85/16 LT mud (bottom pics) from 50psi to 20psi, and nine millimetres for the 265/65/17 P AT (top pics) from 45psi to 20psi. This is not really a significant amount and is offset by the softer tyre being naturally more puncture-resistant. Also, for dirt roads you would run at 25psi to35psi, so the difference would be more like five and seven millimetres. Bottom line; lower tyre pressures on dirt roads with the corresponding lower speeds mean fewer punctures, greater grip and a smoother ride.

1   *Eventually, it'll happen. Be prepared.*

2   *Correct and frequent wheel alignment – modified as required to account for non-standard tyres and suspension work – goes a long way towards a long tyre life, good handling and even fuel efficiency. Offroaders are more likely to need more frequent alignments than road cars.*

3   *Remote pressure monitors can warn of slow leaks.*

4   *Inspect tyres for signs of damage, which need not be cuts. This tyre has an unusual bulge, probably due to carcass damage. It was immediately replaced – you simply cannot afford to risk your life and those of others.*

spare wheel carriers

Modern vehicles usually mount the spare wheel under the rear body. That's because it means a lower centre of gravity, better visibility to the rear, easier opening doors, a shorter car and they can hide those hopeless TUSTs.

There are several problems with this approach for the offroad tourer. Firstly, merely accessing the spare can be difficult as the car may not have had a flat on nice, level, hard ground. Secondly, aftermarket tyres, if slightly wider or larger, may not fit. Thirdly, the access mechanism may well be hidden under a carload of drawers and gear. So it makes sense to move the spare wheel up onto the back, solving all these problems and opening up the space for a tank to carry extra fuel or water. Most vehicles have several spare-wheel carrier options and some units can also take jerry cans, or two wheels. Only accept those carriers that are Australian Design Rules (ADR) compliant, as there are strict regulations about the rear lights and how visible they must be. You should also look for units that are strong enough to take a work light and perhaps a spade carrier, as well as the wheel.

There are two basic types of carrier; those that replace the entire rear bumper and those that add to the existing bodywork. The former are strong, and often have a towbar built in. Unfortunately they are also heavy, and that amount of steel at the back does nothing for the car's handling, especially when mounted with twin spare wheels. That's where the lighter units come in, but those don't strengthen or protect the rear of the car.

An LC100 with a spare carrier integrated into the rear bar. In this case the second mount is being used for a jerry can holder, although it could hold a second spare instead.

choosing a tyre and rim combination

In brief:

1. Check your tyre placard to find the permissible sizes, load ratings and speed ratings.

2. Consult your local road regulations to determine how far you can go outside the placard, eg in Australia offroad vehicles can use N-rated tyres, and there may be leeway to legally fit larger tyres.

3. Make a list of the:
   - tyre sizes, construction and tread patterns eg 245/70/17 LT all-terrain and 255/55/19 P road, with manufacturer and price.
   - rims available eg 17x7, 19x8.

4. Decide which tyre/rim combo you want. Note that not all rims fit all tyres, eg you may require a 17x8 (17" tall by 8" wide) rim for wide tyres or a 17x7 for narrower ones. The tyre manufacturer's website will list allowable rim sizes.

5. If you are choosing an aftermarket rim then check the following is within legal limits: offset, load rating, pitch circle diameter and number of turns for each nut.

6. Make your final choice from the shortlist of possible options. Always buy five tyres for offroad use.

summary

- Tyres come in road, all-terrain, mud and extreme tread patterns. There is no fixed standard for which is which.

- Construction is Passenger (P) or Light Truck (LT), which is stronger.

- There are several ways of marking tyres for size.

- Tyres are speed- and load-rated.

- Low-profile tyres work well on-road and for high speed performance, but poorly offroad.

- Temporary Use Spare Tyres (TUSTs) should never be used with 4WDs.

- Larger-diameter tyres improve offroad capability in many ways, but may require many other modifications to be reliable and safe in proportion to the additional size.

- Tyre pressures are critically important for offroading.

- Rims can either be split or solid. If solid, they can be either alloy or steel.

- There are many state regulations to comply with for tyres.

This photo was snapped by chance as the Discovery went over a normal rock on a normal Flinders Range trail. The tyre is at 25psi, but it is clear how the tyre is absorbing the shock and moulding over the rock. A low-profile tyre would have had rim damage, or had to run much higher pressures, leading to bouncing, traction loss, and an increased risk of punctures.

Tyres will be punctured, so carry a set of plugs which can often be used for repairs. The companion book 4WD Glovebox Guide has repair instructions.

CHAPTER 8

BRAKES

What speeds up must slow down, and brakes are better than trees.

types of brake

There are two common types of brake, disc and drum. Both do the same job of slowing a vehicle down by converting kinetic energy to heat. Quite a lot of energy is converted, which is why brakes get so hot and hybrid drive vehicles go to the trouble of storing that energy for later use. As 4WDs become faster and heavier the problem of overheating becomes more and more apparent, and the manufacturers' typical solution thus far has been to fit ever-larger brakes, which means ever-larger rims and lower profile tyres.

disc brakes

Disc brakes are quite simple. There is a disc attached to the wheel called the rotor. The rotor rotates with the wheel. Positioned next to the rotor are two clamps, called the pads. When the pads are squeezed together they slow the rotor, and thus the wheel.

drum brakes

Drum brakes also have pads, but these are inside the drum and press outwards onto the inside of the drum which slows the vehicle.

discs and drums compared

Disc brakes are superior because they are far less prone to gunk up with mud, clear debris and water quicker, provide better stopping power and can better dissipate heat. Some cheaper vehicles have discs on the front and drums on the rear (still common on utes), but almost all modern 4WDs have four discs all round. Fewer and fewer vehicles have drum brakes at all, and no modern ones use them on the front wheels.

VW's Amarok has an Offroad Mode which recalibrates the ABS, improving stopping distances in this case by 20% on dirt roads. Modern ABS systems are effective on many terrains, unlike the earliest systems.

park brakes

Park brakes are there to prevent the vehicle moving when it's stopped. Where possible, don't park on steep hills and if you need to, leave your manual in gear and chock your vehicle anyway. See Chapter 22 for a discussion of autos on steep hills.

Park brakes generally work on one of two items in the transmission:

- Wheel
- Transmission output shaft.

A transmission park brake activates a brake on the transmission. If you're in 4WD, then all four wheels are locked.

Wheel park brakes simply apply pressure to the brakes on the rear wheels only.

pros and cons

Transmission brakes lock all four wheels as they immobilise the transmission and the brake is up out of the way of dirt and mud ingress. However, if you have a constant 4WD vehicle and jack one wheel up then the vehicle is no longer immobilised as the differentials will permit the other three wheels to rotate. That is why centre diffs should always be locked before jacking, and preferably any other locking diffs engaged as well.

Wheel park brakes only operate directly on the rear wheels (though some cars have them on the front wheels) but they do brake all four wheels if 4WD is engaged; if the rear two wheels are immobilised when the centre diff is locked or part-time 4WDs are in 4WD it will not be possible to turn the front two either. Still, wheel park brakes are generally regarded as inferior to transmission park brakes for holding a vehicle on a hill. Regardless of the park brake type it pays to leave autos in park, manuals in first low and the wheels with weight on them securely chocked – park brakes are not to be trusted.

Some modern vehicles disconnect the centre coupling when stopped and that means only two wheels are secured by the park brake instead of four, which could well mean the vehicle cannot be secured on a hill by the park brake, especially if the braked wheels are uphill of the unbraked wheels.

Transmission park brakes are relatively rare, but are found on vehicles including Nissan Patrols, Land Rover Defenders and Land Rover Discoverys.

operating park brakes

There is a reason why the term "park brake" is used and not "handbrake" – it's because the park brake is not necessarily operated by the hand. Many softroaders have foot-operated park brakes, where you depress a pedal with your left foot to engage, pressing it again a little further and letting it come back on a spring to disengage. Examples include the Santa Fe 2, XC90, Touareg and Kluger. This is done to free up room around the gearshift, but it doesn't make the vehicle any easier to drive offroad.

An XC90 showing its foot-operated park brake.

Land Rover Discovery 1 with conventional, hand-operated, non-electronic park brake, and old-style "T-bar" automatic shifter.

A Hummer H3 with a manually operated park brake. To the bottom left of the steering wheel is a beige handle; pull that to operate the park brake, then turn the handle 90 degrees to lock it in. This is a common system on utes.

Some new vehicles, notably the Land Rover, have electronic park brakes, or EPBs. These are one-touch toggle switches which electronically operate a park brake. In the case of Land Rover the electronics have some tricks; if you pull away with the EPB engaged it will automatically disengage, and applying it at speed will not engage the park brake; instead, the computer will slow the car down using the normal brakes. Handy if the driver suffers a heart attack. Whatever type of park brake you have, do not assume it can hold you on a hill.

An electronic park brake.

brake bias

A typical car or 4WD does not operate the front and rear brakes with equal force. There are two reasons for this; firstly, when a vehicle brakes there is a weight shift to the front which increases the traction of the front wheels and decreases the weight on the rear, so the front wheels can handle much more of the braking effort than the rears. This is why the front wheels of vehicles typically have larger-diameter brake callipers than the rear.

The second reason is that should a wheel lock up it is better for the driver if the front wheels lock up and the vehicle ploughs straight on, rather than the rears locking, which could see the vehicle spin. If you're going to crash, it's always better to crash head-on than sideways, or to roll. This brake bias does mean that there is unused braking capacity on the rear axle, a problem solved by EBD (see next chapter).

From an offroading perspective it is important to know that the front brakes are considerably more powerful than the rear as in some situations rears will have more traction, for example when reversing down a hill (see Chapter 22 for more details).

There is also a dirt-road driving consideration. When a 4WD is driven with a locked centre diff or if part-time, in 4WD, then the front wheels cannot both lock unless the rears also lock, as the front axle must rotate at the same speed as the rear. Therefore, you get that "lost" braking power from the rear axle, but run the risk of instability under hard braking – when you lock up it won't just be the rears, it'll be all four wheels. Vehicles with ABS should alleviate this problem.

Top image shows an 80 Series braking hard with the centre diff unlocked – notice the rear wheels are still rotating, and the fronts are locked. Directional control is maintained by the rear wheels. In the lower pic the centre diff is locked, so all four wheels easily locked. Better braking but potential loss of directional control.

summary

- Wheel brakes are either disc or drum. Discs are better because they stop more efficiently and are less prone to fill up with debris.

- Park brakes are called park brakes because some are foot operated (preventing them from being called "handbrakes").

- Park brakes may be transmission or wheel operated.

- Always put vehicles into 4WD and preferably low-range before jacking a wheel, and engage any other locking differentials.

- Never rely on park brakes.

- Electronic park brakes may do more than just act as a park brake.

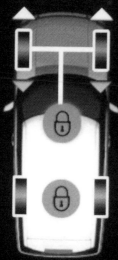

CHAPTER 9

7:16 PM   12°C

A: Average Fuel   15.3 l/100km

ELECTRONIC DRIVING AIDS

Whether you like it or not, electronics are taking over 4WDs. The newer models are bristling with acronyms; ETC, ESC, DSC, ABS, HDC and more. All of these are EDAs, or electronic driving aids.

There are actually only a few types of EDA, but each manufacturer likes to invent their own marketing names for the same thing. We'll use the generic names in this article (some of which are manufacturer names that have become generic terms) and cover the manufacturer-specific names later on.

So why are electronics taking over from drivers? The short answer is that EDAs improve a vehicle's capability both on the road and off it, making it safer and easier to use. Why complicate the controls with locking diffs if traction control can do the job, is cheaper to produce and easier to use?

It should also be remembered that, like locking differentials, no EDA can increase traction. All they can do is try to maximise the available grip, so good tyres, correctly inflated and the right driving techniques are still very important.

The effectiveness of EDAs varies widely too, and it's definitely not a case of "seen one, seen them all", any more than it is for tyres. The newer ETCs on the Pajero and Discovery 4 are generations ahead of the earlier efforts, which have in some cases earned the technology a poor reputation it no longer deserves. It's like driving a mid-'80s Hilux and concluding that all diesel vehicles are slow.

A few years ago EDAs were the domain of top-spec models but now virtually every vehicle on the market has some form of EDA. Very few EDAs, if any, are available aftermarket.

While the major reason for introducing EDAs is to make 4WDs easier to drive, an understanding of how and why they work is important to get the most out of them, or avoid their limitations.

electronic traction control (ETC)

the problem it solves

Standard (open) differentials send drive to the wheel that's easiest to turn, i.e. the one with least traction! This means your "four" wheel drive may only be sending drive to two wheels, and those two are the two with least grip (one may be in the air!). Refer to Chapter 3 for more detail.

The D3's ETC has braked the airborne wheel, making it harder to turn. This means it requires more force (torque) to turn so the wheel on the opposite axle gets the same amount of torque and thus the vehicle can proceed. Without ETC the front axle would be useless, with the airborne wheel madly spinning.

how it works

A computer detects a significant difference in speed between two wheels on an axle and brakes the quicker wheel only (the one uselessly spinning), using the same sensors as ABS (see later in this chapter). This makes that wheel harder to turn and thus it requires more turning force (torque) to overcome the brakes. As differentials distribute torque evenly the wheel not spinning (the one with traction) gets this increased amount of turning force and the vehicle can continue.

If all four wheels are spinning evenly, then traction control won't engage because it can't see a need to; it's not a magic carpet and all it does is try and equalise the traction between wheels. Lockers wouldn't help in that situation either. You're out of traction and that's solved by something like airing down further or changing to tyres with more grip.

The brakes are operated by a small reservoir of energy. When that reservoir is depleted, no more traction control. So if you're been giving it heaps up a long, rocky hill, you might find your ETC deserting you before you reach the top.

Traction control is great because it works on all four wheels and doesn't require any driver input. However, it is a reactive system. It needs to wait for a wheel to spin, and that little delay can mean the difference between momentum being maintained or not. One of the major differences between newer and older systems is that the newer systems react much quicker, one reason why they're more effective.

In addition, traction control sometimes isn't as effective as a locker. If you're in an extreme situation, you may be able to drive out with lockers where traction control, at least the older types, won't save you. That said, modern traction control is now so good that situations which are beyond it are becoming increasingly rare. Put it this way; if I had to drive a very difficult section I would choose a good traction control system (all four wheels) over a rear cross-axle differential lock (only two wheels). Certainly a vehicle with ETC will go a lot further than the same vehicle without. Many crossover and softroaders rely on it to overcome their lack of wheel travel. Without it, they'd be spinning wheels in the air much of the time.

Late-model Pajeros, Tritons, the new Ranger and the Prado 150 are examples of vehicles that combine an optional rear differential lock with traction control. Actually, they don't combine it; if the rear locker is engaged the traction control is disabled. In many cases the traction control does a better job of keeping the vehicle moving than the rear locker, with one exception being long, steep shale climbs.

Some modern Land Rovers like the Discovery 4 have an optional rear locking differential (actually just a strong clutch pack, but the effect is the same). However, the "e-diff", as Land Rover calls it, works with, not instead of, the traction control as an integrated whole. This D4 with e-diff was able to ascend this difficult hill, whereas a D3 without was not. The stronger, 3.0 diesel engine of the D4 helped as it was able to use second gear rather than first low, but the e-diff was the primary advantage.

What's just been described is often known as something like Brake-ETC, designed for rough-terrain use when one wheel on an axle has traction and the other does not. There's also Engine-ETC - when the computer detects that all driven wheels are spinning it'll reduce power accordingly. This is part of ESC (described later on in this chapter). Brake-ETC always works well offroad and only ever brakes one wheel at a time (the spinning one), Engine-ETC can cut power and thus hinder progress in conditions such as deep mud, which is why its intervention rate is reduced when vehicles are modes such as centre diff locked or low range.

A few traction control myths:

- Traction control doesn't really increase brake wear very much, as it only comes in occasionally and all it has to do is stop a wheel with no or little weight spinning, which doesn't take much effort, nowhere near the amount required to slow a heavy vehicle.

- Traction control also does not slow progress. It only brakes wheels which are uselessly spinning anyway, so in fact you're maintaining speed you'd otherwise have lost.

- Traction control is not a negative on sand, at least in my experience, which spans many years of operating many traction-control vehicles on that surface. Typically problems with traction control can be traced to driver error, usually too-high tyre pressures.

- Fitting an aftermarket locker to a traction control-equipped vehicle works fine. As the wheels on the locked axle will never turn at different speeds the traction control will never engage on that axle. However, an exception is for highly sophisticated vehicles which manage traction control across all four wheels along with a front/rear torque split and other factors. These systems will not understand a locking rear diff and they will probably still work, but not as optimally as before.

- Traction control is definitely not the same as stability control (see later in this chapter). Unfortunately, many refer to "disabling traction control" when what they are really doing is disabling stability control.

how to drive it

Like many EDAs you don't have to do much, just drive and let it work. However, if you come to a halt, or are likely to do so then revving the engine a little will help wake up the ETC and may see you through. Sometimes a lower gear than you'd otherwise choose is more effective with ETC than the classic technique of the highest gear the engine can manage.

For best effect with ETC don't come to a complete halt in the first place – as with many offroad situations continuous, controlled momentum is better than stop-start progress. That means looking out front and anticipating the obstacles that will slow or stop the car, like ledges and roots, and using judicious momentum and a good choice of line.

Unlike lockers, ETC has no effect on steering and can safely be used in tight situations and on sideslopes.

This Freelander has run out of wheel travel on the ascent which would normally mean a failed climb, or using much more momentum. However, the ETC system is braking the spinning wheels (front driver's side and rear passenger's) which transfers torque to the wheels with traction, and so the little Landie makes the climb.

ETC may give up if overworked due to overheating or running out of brake energy. Give the car a rest, switch it on and off, and it will typically return to life.

pros and cons

ETC is far more effective than an open diff, can beat a LSD and the best versions are as good as cross-axle lockers in almost every situation. ETC is easier to drive than a set of lockers, and you can turn corners. As ETC limits wheelspin the chances of a fast-spinning wheel hitting the deck and breaking something are reduced – but not eliminated! Although ETC is always active, it cannot be used continuously and may require a break to recharge on some models, although most can be driven almost indefinitely without it cutting out. This need for a break is particularly noticeable on older vehicles that rely on ETC for their offroad capability, especially those that cannot lock centre diffs so the computer has to work extra hard to balance torque across four wheels at once instead of two sets of two. All in all, ETC is definitely something worthwhile having on your vehicle's spec sheet. I haven't seen any 4WDs that have a specific "disable ETC" button, but in some cases ETC is disabled when stability control is switched off, or is disabled when the switch is held in for a few seconds. Some of the adaptive terrain systems (see later in this chapter) change the point at which ETC kicks in and how it operates.

cross-axle lockers vs ETC

There's no winner. In some cases, ETC will be better, in some cases lockers will. Typical examples for ETC are conditions that require manoeuvrability or some momentum such as sand, shallow mud, sideslopes and loose surfaces. Lockers win in really slow going with good traction, specifically rocks and deep ruts. The two are complementary – don't make the mistake of assuming lockers always beats ETC.

torque vectoring

the problem it solves

Exactly the same as ETC – standard (open) differentials send drive to the wheel that's easiest to turn, i.e. the one with least traction! This means your "four" wheel drive may only be sending drive to two wheels, and those two are the two with least grip – one may be in the air. Refer to Chapter 3 for more detail.

how it works

While the problem torque vectoring solves is the same as ETC, the solution is different. Rather than brake a spinning wheel, torque vectoring uses redesigned differentials and electrically controlled clutches to send torque wherever it's needed. This is a major advance over ETC, which has to wait for a wheel to spin before acting, and when it does detect a problem there's a limit to the amount of braking it can do to the spinning wheel, which ultimately limits its effectiveness to increase torque on the wheel with traction. Torque vectoring doesn't need to brake any wheel, it just sends torque exactly where it's needed and, since it is instantaneous and computer controlled, this can be predicted and linked to other

systems. For example, when driving around a corner a torque vectoring system will send more torque to the outside wheel than the inside – a conventional differential equalises torque. The system could also sense diagonal wheels are about to lift and proactively send torque to their opposite partners. This ability to send torque exactly where it's needed and before it's needed is an offroad designer's dream. The technology is still new and only available in a few vehicles but will become mainstream.

how to drive it

As per traction control.

pros and cons

No cons! This can beat cross-axle lockers and is more intelligent and efficient than ETC.

hill descent control (HDC)

the problem it solves

Coming down a steep hill you somehow need to slow the vehicle. Traditionally this was via engine braking in low-range for manuals, or by overdriving the brakes in autos (Chapter 22). Both techniques force the wheels to turn at a slow speed, as opposed to braking them to a slow speed.

HDC control on the Range Rover Evoque—the length of the green bar shows the speed set.

The Freelander lacks low-range so descending this steep, unrutted, off-camber, gravelly hill is dangerous. However, the driver just flicked HDC on, and was very careful to steer straight and let the electromagic do its job.

how it works

HDC is basically cruise control with the brakes only. You set a speed, and the system keeps the vehicle there, and sometimes it changes gears in automatics to suit. If one wheel slows down relative to the rest that means it is slipping and the brakes are released for an instant on that wheel, then reapplied. That way each wheel is braked to the best of its tractive ability.

Dashboard light indicating Toyota's hill descent control system in operation (green icon below the 0 on the speedo).

Button to activate Jeep's HDC, next to the hazard lights. The stability control off switch (see below) is also shown.

how to drive it

At the top of the hill, activate the HDC – usually there's a button (Land Rover, Toyota, Ford) while sometimes it's always on like in the Pajero, and sometimes it engages automatically, as with the VW Touraeg. Point yourself down the hill. Some older systems disengage if you touch the brakes, others like that on the Discovery 3 allow you to do what you like, for example applying the brakes yourself. When you finish manual braking HDC will take over again. Some newer ones allow you to vary the speed, for example Land Rover has +/- 0.5km/h increments controlled by the cruise control system. Jeep's HDC uses the gear lever for much the same effect and Nissan's Pathfinder also uses the cruise control system. If the hill is not steep, increasing the HDC speed may not have an effect as HDC only stops the vehicle going faster, it doesn't accelerate the vehicle to the target speed. Don't use HDC for dune descents as it will brake the vehicle, dipping the nose into the sand. Just use low first gear or second instead and drive down. When switched off, older HDCs would instantly release the brakes, but newer ones do so gradually. HDC may be rough and noisy in operation, especially older versions, and it is often not difficult to be smoother by taking manual control. If you do use HDC, always use it with an appropriate gear. It may still try and work with third low when you could be in first low, but it will need to do more braking and that increases the chance of a wheel locking or skidding.

The hill descent control (Descent Assist Control, in Toyota-speak) button on a Prado Grande. Also seen are the suspension settings and suspension height adjustment which is this case work only on the rear axle.

pros and cons

Older HDCs are fine for those High Country slogs where the hills aren't particularly rutted and you don't mind hurtling down at four to eight km/h. However, for those rutted, rocky ledges you'll be wanting to inch over at a snail's pace and that's where the old HDCs cannot help because they don't slow down to a real crawl. You need to resort to key on/key off, overdriving the brakes or brake normally (Chapter 22).

If you're using one of the newest HDC systems (Jeep Grand Cherokee, Toyota LC200) then these can now inch a vehicle downhill better than the best drivers, individually applying braking pressure to each wheel, something the driver cannot do and not even ABS modulation can help here, even if it works at very low speeds which is unlikely. I'd use these modern HDC systems in the toughest conditions, but have my foot over the brake just in case.

A major HDC disadvantage is the time taken to vary the speed. If the driver brakes normally it is very quick and easy to modulate the brake pressure during a descent as the terrain changes. An example is coming down a steep part into a momentary flatter washout; you would want to

apply maximum braking as it flattens to reduce speed, then ease off the brakes slightly to avoid wheel lock for the next steep part. In a crisis you may even need to come off the brakes entirely and accept a high rate of descent. It is not as easy and quick to modulate speed and brake pressure with HDC even if you can override it with normal braking and acceleration.

electronic stability control (ESC)

the problem it solves

ESC keeps the car heading where you want it to go and, along with curtain (side) airbags, is one of the most important safety advances in recent years.

When a car skids out of control it will either understeer, which is when the car ploughs straight on, or oversteer, which is when the back starts to overtake the front. ESC is there to keep the car going where you want it to!

how it works

There are various sensors on the vehicle which monitor things like yaw (rotation around a vertical axis), throttle position, brakes, steering wheel angle, lateral acceleration and so on. When the computer decides that the vehicle isn't going where the driver wants it to it brakes one or more wheels. For example, to tighten the cornering radius to correct understeer it may brake the inside front wheel and reduce braking on the two outside wheels. It can also reduce the throttle input. I've had a couple of cars in a test situation where my foot has been to the floor around a corner yet there has been no engine response due to ESC.

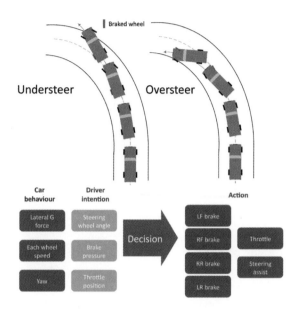

Understeer   Oversteer

Car behaviour	Driver intention		Action	
Lateral G force	Steering wheel angle		LF brake	
Each wheel speed	Brake pressure	Decision → Decision	RF brake	Throttle
Yaw	Throttle position		RR brake	Steering assist
			LR brake	

Stability control systems steer a car by braking each wheel individually for a fraction of a second. They can also reduce the throttle, even if the driver floors the accelerator pedal. The system gathers data about precisely what the car is doing from a wide variety of sources, and not just what it's doing now; it looks at what it has been doing for the last few seconds, and at the driver's input. In short, the computers know precisely what is happening to the car and know before the driver has had a chance to think. Computers have their limitations, but slow reactions are not among them and they never get tired. Once the computer has decided the car is not responding appropriately to driver control it then takes corrective action. It returns the vehicle to driver control when it senses the car is again responding to driver input and not sliding or about to slide.

Some sports vehicles have multiple modes of ESC, from normal driving to sport to track day. 4WDs tend to have a binary switch; ESC is either on or off. However, even when it's turned off the system is only desensitised, not usually entirely deactivated.

how to drive it

ESC saves lives, which is why it will be standard in vehicles from around 2012 in places where it is not already. At speed, it does a better job of keeping a car pointing where it should be than any human could hope to. The only reason to switch it off when travelling above about 30km/h would be if you specifically want to hang it out around corners or you are in sand. However, in low-range territory it should generally be disabled because as the car slides, slips and generally moves around over rough terrain the ESC can cut in and literally stop you from making progress. Most vehicles permit ESC to be disabled with a dash switch, except some such as a few Toyotas which disable it via locking the centre diff. Once disabled there will be a small instrument console warning light, and it may automatically re-enable at speed (Pajero) or when the engine is next switched off and on. With any electronic system be careful that it stays in the mode you meant to set it to.

To the left of the emergency indicator switch is the Discovery 4's ESC on/off switch. Most new cars have a similar button while older vehicles often have an acronym such as "VDC" or "ESC". Watch for the indicator light to come on in the instrument panel. Sometimes the button needs to be held down for a second or two while on other cars it toggles instantly.

A typical instrument panel light indicating ESC is disabled. When you see the indicator it means ESC is off, contrary to usual indicators when the presence of the icon means something is turned on.

A little later we found a slippery, rutted uphill. The Kluger had the clearance and traction to get up when allied with a little momentum, but again the ESC kicked in at the wrong time, braking the wheels so hard the car fell into the ditch on the left. Several attempts later we made it, but it was much harder than it needed to be.

This is where ESC is worth its weight in gold, on high-speed dirt roads.

As a driver, if you never need to take evasive action (the mark of a good driver) and don't drive particularly hard you'll never know ESC is there. If you do drive hard enough for it to cut in, the way it does so will vary. For example, early Toyotas systems were harsh; an abrupt chop of the throttle accompanied by warning lights and bells, with significant braking. The Land Rover and Volvo systems have no warning of their operation other than the fact you feel a brake being gently applied and the throttle is less responsive.

ESC is not infallible. When testing a car I tried a dirt corner deliberately quickly with ESC off. Sure enough, the back end came out, but a quick correction and all was well. Then I reached over to switch the ESC back on – and saw I'd made a mistake and it was already on! Dirt roads are so unpredictable they can catch out anything.

There are also circumstances that the computer may not be programmed to handle, such as complete tyre failure, or loss of a single sensor on a wheel – in which case, you're on your own and back to basics with old-fashioned car control (Chapter 12).

Beware some ESC systems that also disable ETC. Here you have a choice of having ESC, which may restrict progress, but keeping ETC that may pull you through, or the reverse – no ESC and no restrictions on the car's ability to slide or manoeuvre, but no traction assistance with ETC. The choice will depend on the driver and the situation, but be aware of the effects of disabling ESC. Some ESC systems disable traction control immediately ESC is disabled, others require a second or longer press to disable ETC in the unlikely event that is required.

pros and cons

There's no real disadvantage to ESC except in cases when it can't be disabled for offroad work. Other than that, keep it on at all times. Like all EDAs, ESC has to wait for a problem to develop before it corrects; it cannot look ahead to see that loose off-camber gravel patch like a good driver.

Hook into a corner too fast and ESC will intervene to try and save the situation, but it can only operate within the laws of physics. You still need to drive sensibly and run the right tyres and pressures, using ESC as a final safety measure you hope you'll never need.

anti-roll mechanisms

Anti-roll systems are just a development of ESC tuned to detect conditions likely to lead to a rollover.

anti-lock braking system (ABS)

the problem it solves

If you brake too hard you can lock the wheels. On a dry bitumen road locking the wheels will stop you quickly, but not as quickly as if the wheels are braked to a point just before they lock. However, on a dirt road locking the wheels helps as the tyres dig into the soft ground. On a wet road a locked wheel is dangerous as the tyre cannot disperse water and is likely to aquaplane (skate over the top of the

water), dramatically increasing braking distances and losing steering control and thus direction control as well. Similarly, while locking a wheel on dirt may decrease stopping distances, no vehicle can be steered with a locked wheel so the chances of avoiding a problem are nil, and there is a risk of rolling if one wheel digs in more than the other.

Older ABS systems were not good on dirt roads, but newer ones are far more effective.

how it works

A computer monitors each wheel's speed relative to each other when braking. When a wheel begins to slow down significantly relative to the rest that means it is about to lock up. The computer then releases the brakes for an instant on that wheel and reapplies, so the wheel doesn't lock, brakes at its maximum capacity and, as it is still rotating, the driver can steer the vehicle.

This Subaru WRX has had its ABS disabled for a demonstration. The front wheels have been locked by a harsh application of the brakes and the front wheels are now skidding over the top of the puddles. The driver has no steering capability whatsoever, and stopping distances are very much lengthened. The reason the front wheels locked first is because road cars are designed to lock those first rather than the rears as the resulting plough-on understeer skid is easier and safer to deal with than losing the back end, which would mean the car spinning (Chapter 12). Race cars have a brake bias setting to utilise more of the rear wheel traction, and EBD (see pg128) does much the same thing.

how to drive it

Try and ram your foot through the firewall as hard as possible and as quickly as possible. Ignore any pulsing effect through the brake pedal; that's normal and just the effect of the computer selectively applying the brakes.

ABS is effective on all bitumen surfaces, especially when wet. Older systems can be ineffective on dirt roads, where they do not lock up enough to let the tyre bite into the softer ground, skating over corrugations, increasing stopping distances. Newer

systems are far more intelligent and can work out what sort of surface they are on and permit a greater or lesser amount of tyre lock. However, as with any computer-based system, don't assume that because yours seems to work well in most situations this will always be the case. And again, there's no substitute for decent tyres at the right pressures.

Few cars permit ABS to be disabled, but some of the newer ones do vary its responsiveness according what other control selections the driver has made.

A major advantage of ABS is the ability to brake and steer. If you try to steer, the system will release the brakes sufficiently to let you do so, but that will increase overall stopping distance. Chapter 12 explains this in more detail.

If ABS is active in low-range, for example descending hills or stopping on slippery ground, the brake pedal can be squeezed hard with little fear of lockup, although all other hill descent techniques such as the correct line and gear must still be used. As ever, the electronic aids are supplementary to the basics.

Hard braking, two wheels on dirt, two on tar. The computer has to correctly distribute the braking force. Not all ABS system handle this situation!

pros and cons

ABS is fantastic. The only disadvantage is on some dirt roads, especially over corrugations. The newer systems very rarely get in the way in any offroad situation, and overall make the vehicle more capable.

electronic brake distribution (EBD)

the problem it solves

In most vehicles, more braking force is sent to the front wheels because those are the ones with the effective weight when braking. This is known as brake bias. The reason for bias to the front is that if one set of wheels has to lock it, it's better that it be the front so you hit the problem head-on as opposed to spinning into it sideways. However, the front/rear brake bias means that the front wheels can be braking to their maximum, yet the rear wheels still have some braking traction left. Conversely, in slippery conditions the reverse may be momentarily true. There is no way to pre-tune a brake system to consistently lock all four wheels exactly at the same time in all conditions, as so many factors vary the braking force each wheel can take, so having a computer control it in real time is the solution.

EBD is what you want when you need to slow down in a hurry.

how it works

Yet another computer monitors the relative braking performance of the front and rear axles and sends braking force to where it's needed as appropriate, which is usually to the rear wheels. All ABS does is stop a wheel locking, it doesn't send extra braking force anywhere.

how to drive it

As per ABS, just put your foot to the floor and keep it there!

pros and cons

No disadvantages, it's a Good Thing!

electronic brake assist (EBA)

the problem it solves

In an emergency stop situation, not all drivers brake hard enough to stop in the shortest possible distance.

how it works

The computer decides if it's panic time by seeing how quickly you slammed the brakes on, and even how quickly you came off the accelerator. If the microchip thinks disaster is impending, it'll help you out by applying the brakes for you as hard as the car can handle. Some vehicles will also pre-tension seatbelts and do various other things in the expectation of a crash.

how to drive it

Brake as normal. EBA can assist even the fastest reacting drivers.

pros and cons

No disadvantages, it's a Good Thing!

hill start assist

the problem it solves

On a steep hill when you take your foot off the brake to move it to the accelerator the vehicle will roll backwards, whether it's a manual or an automatic. The park brake may be used, but may not be powerful enough to hold the vehicle. Hill Start Assist systems momentarily apply the footbrake while you move your foot from one pedal to another.

how it works

The vehicle has a gradient sensor and can detect when the footbrake is applied. It simply applies the brake for you as required. Some work on any slope, others only on certain gradients.

Toyota's Hill Start Assist was unable to hold the vehicle on this gradient, like most similar systems.

how to drive it

Don't. These systems are not reliable, as they don't always work on steep hills, and may be deactivated by a light touch on the accelerator, an accidental gear change or other control movement – or they could just time out. There are better ways to perform hill starts in most situations (Chapter 22).

pros and cons

This is a solution to a problem better solved by other driving techniques (Chapter 22).

gradient release control (GRC)

the problem it solves

When a vehicle is descending a steep hill and the footbrake is released the vehicle will gather speed quickly. If the driver is regulating the speed using the footbrake that is no problem as the footbrake is not fully released, but if the driver is using Hill Descent Control then the vehicle will accelerate up to the HDC target speed, at which point HDC will kick in and rapidly slow the vehicle. This rapid change of speed can destabilise the vehicle and cause a traction loss.

how it works

When the footbrake is released on a steep hill (usually around 18 degrees), then the vehicle will not instantly release the brakes but will ease them off so the vehicle doesn't hurtle down the hill, irrespective of whether the driver has their foot on the brake or not. Land Rover's implementation works both forwards and in reverse and requires the HDC system to be activated.

Discovery 4 with GRC. If HDC was being used without GRC to descend this slope then when the driver releases the brake pedal the vehicle would accelerate up to HDC speed before slowing down. GRC makes the transition more even and smooth, but even a driver with basic training would be able to do a better job.

how to drive it

Simply take your foot off the brake and let the GRC system smoothly move the vehicle off up to the HDC descent speed.

pros and cons

GRC is only of use when used with HDC. If HDC is not enabled then drivers should ease off the brakes anyway, doing manually exactly what GRC does. If HDC is enabled then GRC is a convenient way to smoothly get to the HDC descent speed. GRC can get in the way by applying the brakes when you don't wish them to be applied, or applying an inappropriate amount of brake pressure. An example would be easing down into a gully where you would want to accelerate down the last little bit of slope in order to gain momentum for the climb out. However, that situation is avoided by simply not using HDC or not stopping on the downward slope so GRC is never activated. Drivers

may never want to use GRC, but like other EDAs they may find it working when not expected so need to understand it anyway.

other systems

launch control

High-performance sports cars have had launch control for some time. This is a system that operates the gears and throttle in order to provide the quickest possible acceleration from start. Some offroad vehicles offer a similar system designed to get you moving on certain surfaces. An example is Land Rover's launch control system for sandy surfaces which carefully reduces wheelspin on launch so as not to dig the wheels into the soft surface. A skilled driver could do the same as these systems, which cannot always be deactivated and always have to assume conditions are the same. However, sand texture and gradient varies widely. The driver can assess those conditions and make a call, but the electronics cannot (yet) do that.

Driving off in sand is tricky. Sand launch control makes it easier, but a driver with basic training should not need it.

crawl control

Toyota have a crawl control system on most 200 Series and some Prados. This is cruise control for offroad. The driver selects one of three speeds in older versions, or five in newer versions, ranging from about 1 to 5km/h – and the system keeps the vehicle at that speed, whether uphill or down. When descending it acts like a HDC, but unlike HDC it will drive the vehicle uphill or on the flat and it operates at very slow speeds. The system does nothing a skilled driver cannot do, but for those not experienced offroad the throttle control is a real bonus. Even old hands can benefit from using it when crossing boulder-strewn rivers, where your throttle foot would be bounced around and in turn the throttle would be varied. Crawl control keeps a nice, even throttle control no matter what. The only temptation may be to over-use it when in many situations more momentum would be required.

The LC200's Crawl control and switch with selections for 1, 3 and 5 km/h.

rock crawl pre-charge

This is a Land Rover function, activated with the rock crawl terrain response mode, which applies a small amount of brake pressure at all times when the vehicle is travelling very slowly. The engine in effect has to drive through the brakes; it's the same as applying the accelerator with your left foot on the brakes (a technique described later in this book). The advantage is much greater control as the wheels do not "fall off" but are already braked (see Chapter 17).

cornering brake control (CBC)

A development of ESC which keeps a vehicle on the desired neutral path through a corner. Unlike ESC, CBC activates very subtly before any control is lost. Land Rover also have something called Fast Off which detects how quickly a driver comes off the accelerator to the brake and holds a lower gear to assist with braking.

gradient acceleration control (GAC)

Introduced on the Range Rover Vogue MY2011 this is a safety net for steep descent. If a steep descent

Many offroad situations need precise throttle control at low speeds, and that's exactly what crawl control delivers.

is started without HDC being engaged then the car would normally be accelerated quickly down the hill by gravity. GAC detects the gradient and applies the brakes to prevent runaway behaviour.

turn assist

Toyota's Turn Assist works in low-range with the centre diff unlocked and tightens turning circles by braking the rear inside wheel. An LC200's turning circle was measured at 11.8m with the centre diff unlocked, 12.7m with it locked,

and 11.3m with it unlocked and turn assist operating – about a 5% improvement.

adaptive terrain systems

Modern vehicles are controlled by an array of computers which react to situations. Adaptive vehicle controls are ways the driver can pre-set the vehicle to adapt it for certain situations, for example driving on rocks, sand or snow. Newer systems also have settings for the road situations such as economy or sports

A Range Rover Vogue Terrain Response rocker switch. The centre button with the red vehicle and yellow mark is HDC, to the left is the suspension height selector with a lock to keep it at access height after the engine is switched off, to the right is the high/low-range switch.

These are driver-controlled systems that preset the various mechanisms on the vehicle to best deal with certain types of terrain. There are an increasing number of systems on the market. Not all vehicles from a manufacturer have the technology or a full implementation.

Jeep Grand Cherokee in ruts, using its Sand/Mud mode

Nissan's All-Mode adaptive terrain system showing the four modes of Road, Rock, Snow and Sand with the 4WD mode (high-range, high-range centre diff locked and low-range), rear cross-axle locker, ESC off switch and HDC switch around the outside.

The table shows some common adpative terrain systems:

Manufacturer	Name	Modes
Land Rover	Terrain Response	Normal, Mud/Ruts, Sand, Grass/Gravel/Snow, Rock Crawl (not Freelander/Evoque)
Toyota	Multi-Terrain Select	Off, Mud and Sand, Loose Rock Mogul Rock
Jeep	Selec-Terrain	Auto , Sand/Mud, Sport , Snow, Rock
Nissan	ALL-MODE	On-road, Sand, Snow, Rock
Ford	Terrain Management System	Normal, Mud, Sand, Snow
Peugeot	Grip Control	Standard, ESP Off, Offroad, Sand

In each case, the driver select the best mode using an in-cabin control. The effect of that is demonstrated by this table from Land Rover:

	Normal	Grass/gravel/snow	Mud and ruts	Sand	Rock crawl
Terrain characteristics	Hard surfaces with no loose coating, wet or dry	Firm underlying base, but loose, slippery material on top	Slippery, rutted, uneven terrain but not extremely slow going	Soft ground with no hard base	Dry, solid, extremely uneven terrain that may raise wheels in the air
Use/examples	Normal driving	Slime, grass, gravel, shallow snow, shale, sand on hard surfaces	Most mud conditions, wet sand	Most sand, deep gravel	Crawling over rocks, extremely rutted and slow terrain
Engine management	Normal	More gradual torque delivery	Progressive torque delivery	More aggressive response to throttle	Cautious torque delivery allowing good speed control
Automatic transmission	Normal	Starts in second high or third low, early shift up	Tuned for mud driving	Holds onto gears longer, downshifts sooner	Start in first, late shift up
Centre diff	Normal	Increased pre-load	Increased preloading, aggressive response to slip	Normal	Increased preloading, aggressive response to slip
HDC	Off	On (low-range only)	On (low-range only)	Off	On
Gear range	High	High or low	High or low	High or low	Low-range only
ETC, DSC	Active	High sensitivity to slip	Low sensitivity to slip	DSC control modified to reduce engine intervention	High sensitivity to slip
Air suspension	Normal	Offroad (low-range)	Offroad (low-range)	Offroad (low-range)	Offroad

Toyota's Multi-Terrain package is summarised below:

	MTS Off	Rock	Mogul	Loose Rock	Mud & Sand
Terrain characteristics	Normal driving	Slow, very uneven, rocky terrain where clearance is a problem	Generic offroad mode	Loose rocks	Mud, dirt, sand, deep snow

Jeep's Selec-Terrain system, air suspension, HDC select and low range select.

The Snow setting is for hardish, slippery surfaces. In deep snow Normal, Mud/Ruts and even Rock Crawl work better. The suspension has been tricked into the higher Extended mode to make life easier.

The changes made to each of the systems according to a different Terrain Response setting are, individually, small. However, the combined effect is quite noticeable as the car is worked harder – you won't notice much just idling around on the flat. It's almost as if you've driven into a garage and out again in a different car. In sand mode, for example, the shift points are higher and traction control sensitivity is reduced. In rock crawl mode the throttle sensitivity is reduced and traction control sensitivity is increased.

how to drive it

The obvious answer is to simply look out the window and decide what sort of terrain you're driving on, then twiddle the dial, but that approach only takes you so far. What about rocks covered with mud, and where's the water setting? Here are some guidelines.

- **Water:** Select the program for whatever terrain is under the water. Disable stability control to avoid unwanted braking by the computer.

- **Hills:** If unsure, for steep hills select rock programs as these are most sensitive to wheelspin and provide the torque necessary for the climb. The rock crawl modes also tend to pre-lock the centre coupling which is very important on hills.

- **Stability control:** Disable in sand and mud where the vehicle will slip naturally, even if the program desensitises it.

- **Rocks:** If it's so rocky you need to be in first or second low, minding your clearances, and the vehicle is riding up and down climbing over boulders, then you need rock mode regardless of other terrain characteristics. Does not apply to small pebbles.

- **Muddy rocks:** Use rock settings if you're crawling over rocks, muddy or otherwise.

- **If in doubt:** Select the "off" setting, as the vehicle will still react and work effectively, and by opting for a neutral setting you won't have given it a setup which is not optimal. And finally, break all these rules if it seems the right thing to do!

If you select the wrong setting you won't break the vehicle but it may struggle more than it otherwise would, for example selecting grass/gravel/snow mode in sand will see the car try and shift gears too early, straining the engine.

A Range Rover TDV8 on sand. Although sand mode does desensitise the stability control it is always best – and Land Rover recommend – that it be manually disabled in sand.

A Range Rover Sport TDV6 crossing a river. Select the mode most appropriate to the terrain under the water and disable stability control as the last thing you want is the vehicle being slowed down if it slides a little! Raising the suspension is also a very good idea.

The best way to use these systems is to understand exactly what settings they change (see the Land Rover chart on p133) and then experiment with the different modes before you get into a situation where you really need to. Think of the modes not so much as for named terrains, but types of terrain. For example, grass/gravel/snow is for flattish, slippery terrains, which could also be sand on flat rock, or a thin coating of mud on a hard flat surface. Rocks is for terrain that is extremely uneven and slow – which could also be a section of dirt with lots of ditches, dugouts and moguls. Sand is for soft terrain where the vehicle sinks in – which also describes some types of snow, and mud. The mud modes activate the traction control earlier than the sand modes because sand is very loose – but not all the time, so in some types of sandy situations where the sand is thick mud mode may be better in sand. And perhaps you are stuck in mud, cross-axled, but the traction control isn't doing enough to pull you out despite the fact a tyre or two still has traction. Maybe a switch to rock mode could help. Again, it's all about experimentation. You still need to pick lines and drive the car, and selecting gears manually can also be beneficial.

Land Rover's latest iteration of Terrain Response, version 2, now automatically detects the terrain and places the vehicle into the most appropriate mode, and advises the driver to change vehicle height or select low-range as required. Manual override is still available, at least for the moment.

EDAs: aka (also known as)

The basic concept of each EDA is the same across vehicles, but its sensitivity and general feel does vary even from model to model. Also, each manufacturer tends to have a different name for it. On page 137 is a quick guide to some of the major brands.

EBD and EBA are not listed because they are almost always called just EBD and EBA, or sometimes Brake Assist.

		Collective name for EDAs	Electronic Traction Control	Anti-lock braking	Electronic Stability Control	Hill Descent Control	Hill Start Assist	Adaptive terrain system
Manufacturer	Ford	-	E-TCS, BTCS	ABS	DSC	HDC	HSA	Terrain Management System
	Hyundai	-	TCS	ABS	ESP	-	-	-
	Jeep	Selec-Terrain	TCS/ BTCS/ELSD	ABS	ESP	HDC	HSA	Selec-Terrain
	Land Rover	Terrain Response	ETC	ABS	DSC	HDC	HSA	Terrain Response
	Mercedes	-	4ETS	ABS	ESP	DSR	-	-
	Mitsubishi	MATT	ATC	ABS	ASC	EBAC	-	-
	Nissan	-	TCS	ABLS	VDC	HDC	-	All-Mode
	Subaru	-	TCS	ABS	VDC	-	HSAC	-
	Suzuki	-	ETC	ABS	ESP	JDC	HHC	-
	Toyota	DAT	A-TRC	ASB	VSC	DAC	HAC	MTS
	Volkswagen	-	ASR	ABSPlus	ESP	HDA	HHA	-
	Volvo	-	TRACS	ABS	DSTC	HDC	-	-

Exactly what each one of those acronyms stands for isn't covered here, but think of words like Active, Assist, Braking, Control, Driver, Electronic, Dynamic, Start, System and Traction.

other terms

Some other terms you may see in manufacturer brochures:

- **Xenon headlights:** HIDs (see Chapters 26 and 40). Worth having.
- **Adaptive cruise control:** Keeps you at a set distance behind the cars in front.
- **RSC:** Roll Stability Control, variant of ESC.
- **TSA:** Trailer Sway Assist, variant of ESC designed to stop dangerous trailer sway.
- **RSCA:** Roll Sensing Curtain Airbags. Switch to disable curtain airbag deployment sensors to avoid deployment when offroading at significant sideslope angles.
- **AEB:** Autonomous Emergency Braking. Detects obstacles and automatically brakes for you (in theory). May need to be disabled for offroad use.
- **Eco modes:** Some vehicles switch off the engine automatically when stopped and restart instantly. This saves fuel in stop/start traffic but such modes should be disabled for offroad use to retain full control of the vehicle at all times.
- **Wade Sensing:** Land Rover system that uses sensors mounted under the wing mirrors to measure the distance from the water to the mirror, and thus deduce its depth. The system reports water depth to the driver and warns if it is too deep. I've not tested this as yet, but would suggest it is no substitute for a good old fashioned recce.

does the driver know best?

Many EDAs do not permit driver override. For example, manually locked centre diffs on the X-Trail and Santa Fe 2 unlock at around 30-40km/h plus. The air suspension on the new Land Rovers lowers to normal height above 50km/h. Some stability control systems cannot ever be switched off. The Freelander's centre clutch unlocks at rest, leading to problems on steep hills. The Pajero automatically re-enables its stability control at high speed without driver input.

Experienced and knowledgeable drivers may be frustrated by these restrictions on occasion, because there is no way the vehicle designers can possibly anticipate every offroad situation and to have certain options unavailable simply because of a design decision could, in extreme cases, threaten safety.

Drivers should therefore be aware that some EDAs may, in some situations, work against the best interests of the driver. They should also remember that the computer may decide to change their settings if certain conditions are met. You can't expect modern vehicles to stay the way you've set them, unlike the old ones where, once you shifted a lever, it stayed shifted and there was no electronic brain deciding it would sneak it back without your consent. Some modes require other systems to be switched on or off first, for example Land Rover's GRC requires HDC to be enabled first and then it only works on steeper hills. The VW Touareg requires its ESP to be switched on so its hill descent system can operate. There is no fixed set of rules, not necessarily any easy way to find out, and often very few people will be familiar with the vehicle in offroad situations.

A careful read of the owner's manual is highly recommended, although this does not necessarily contain all the information that expert offroad drivers require, and even if it did it would be difficult to remember all the permutations. Again, it's a matter of getting to know the vehicle. Owners' web forums can be a great place for tips, but they're not always correct. Overall, EDAs are definitely making modern 4WDs more capable, safer and easier to drive, but also quite different to the models of previous years.

During testing we discovered the centre coupling on the Freelander 2 unlocks at rest. This means on a steep hill the front wheels lock and the rears do not, which means a loss of steering control. If the centre coupling locked then the rear wheels would force the front wheels to keep turning, as the rears have much better traction because the bulk of the car's weight is on them. Unfortunately, there is no way to override the computer's unlocking of the coupling. While modern electronics are mostly wonderful and dramatically increase the safety and capability of vehicles, they do have their limitations and this is just one example.

CHAPTER 10

VEHICLE
EXAMPLES

This chapter completes the section with a look at some example vehicle designs.

land rover defender 110 TD5

This Defender TD5 has twin beam axles, coil springs, a five-speed manual gearbox, ABS and traction control. It is AWD but with a simple centre diff so it is best to lock it on many dirt roads, unlike the more sophisticated Torsen unit in cars like the LC200.

The Defender's transfer case has five modes: high- and low-range with the centre diff unlocked; high and low with the centre diff locked; and neutral. The vehicle's centre diff can be locked or unlocked on the move simply by shifting the lever left and right, and lifting off the accelerator to let it engage. Low-range with the centre diff unlocked is very useful for backing a trailer. The car can also be shifted from low to high-range on the move using a series of double-declutch manoeuvres – refer to the owner's manual.

VW amarok

One of the new breed of utes, this Amarok has no low-range, yet with its 8-speed automatic, effective HDC and well-calibrated ETC is much more capable offroad than many low-rangers. This points to the future of offroaders. The vehicle has a lockable rear differential, and an "offroad" mode which changes the calibration of things like the ABS for dirt-road use, resulting in much shorter stopping distances according to our tests. Unusually for a ute, this Amarok is all wheel drive with a Torsen centre differential, but like most utes it has old-school drum rear brakes and leaf springs with a live rear axle.

toyota land cruiser LC100

The LC100 is a good example of a vehicle that at one end of the trim range is a basic workhorse – part-time 4WD, manual gearbox, manual hubs, twin beam axles – all the way to a powerful automatic turbodiesel, with variable-height suspension (independent at front), stability control and traction control like the Sahara model pictured.

This LC100 is showing the automatic gearbox set to second start. Stability control (VSC in Toyotaspeak) is off. Some Toyotas do this automatically when the centre diff is locked, others have a switch. The variable-height suspension is raised and the centre diff is locked as denoted by the icon to the left of the VSC off display. There is nothing to say the vehicle is in low-range, but the position of the transfer case lever should give that away, as will the driving characteristics.

jeep wrangler

The JK Wrangler Rubicon is notable for its factory-fit extensive offroad features: swaybar disconnect, front and rear locking differentials, crawler gears and more. It has a part-time 4WD system, traction control, stability control and, very rarely these days, beam axles front and rear.

This Rubicon is showing both front and rear cross-axle lockers engaged. Only factory-fit lockers have dash displays. The photo also shows the swaybar is disconnected, and next to it stability control is off (the skid icon). The Wrangler is a part-time 4WD and is now in 4WD, as shown by the icon below the N in the gear indicator. On the right is a basic compass showing west and a temperature display. In-car compasses suffer from calibration problems so aren't very accurate. GPS technology doesn't suffer from the same problem it can provide far better direction indication than a compass.

nissan patrol Y62

Nissan's Y62 Patrol is another vehicle with fully independent suspension, and is constant 4WD in its Auto mode which biases drive to the rear. The 4H mode locks the centre diff, and the 4L is low-range. The rear differential is lockable although this disables traction control on the front axle too. The vehicle has an adaptive-terrain system with sand, snow, rock and road modes. A hill descent control feature is included. The only engine is a V8 petrol. The Y62 also features HMBC, or Hydraulic Motion Body Control. This is a suspension system that works in a similar way to Toyota KDSS, resisting body roll (weight on vehicle on either left or right wheels) but permitting axle flex (weight of vehicle on diagonal wheels).

mitsubishi pajero

The Pajero was a pioneer of the fully-independent suspension and monocoque chassis design back in the early '00s. The concept has stood the test of time.

The Mitsubishi Super-Select 4WD system is used on the Pajero, second-gen Challengers and some newer Tritons. This is one of the more complex systems on the market. It has the following modes:

2H – rear wheel drive, 4X2

4H – constant 4WD, or AWD, centre diff not locked

4HLC – 4WD high-range, centre diff locked

4LLC – 4WD low-range, centre diff locked

Most owners tend to drive around in 2H. However, the fuel savings are insignificant as vehicles are not fitted with manual free-wheeling hubs. The problem is that these modern vehicles produce plenty of power, too much in some conditions for 2WD. As an example, I was asked to look at why a Pajero had "just stopped" while the driver was making a 90 degree turn from a sidestreet into a quick main road. It turned out the conditions were quite wet and off-camber, and the driver had accelerated the vehicle quickly. This is exactly how one gets a vehicle to do circlework, or a donut. The stability control had quickly intervened, braking and chopping the throttle. Unfortunately, a large truck was bearing down on the driver and gave her a bit of a fright. The solution was simply to drive the vehicle in AWD mode, or 4H, on the road. There's no way the back end would have started to come out had all four wheels been driving. I also found someone else who had the same experience but on a dirt road – AWD is the answer.

The auto shifter works in a similar manner to that of the Discovery with a manumatic mode. The stability control "off" switch is in front of the shifter, next to the electric antenna up/down switch and is marked with the usual car-skid icon.

On the right is the controls for a Mitsubishi Challenger 2, with the same Super Select system as the Pajero but this time the ESC-off button is labelled "ASC OFF" (in Mitsubishi-speak, Active Stability Control). The R/D lock button is the rear

crossaxle difflock which disables traction control.

subaru outback

Subaru pretty much invented the car-based offroad vehicle and this 2013 Outback is the latest iteration. The Outback is a lifted Liberty, and boasts traction control and stability control. Unfortunately, the centre diff relies on the ETC to distribute torque front and rear as opposed to just left/right on each axle, and that's not as effective as a centre lock, viscous coupling or Torsen centre. The Outback has paddle shifters on its automatic gearbox, the park brake is electronic and operated by finger and it has a hill-hold assist activated by a button instead of automatically operating. Of particular interest is the EyeSight system which is two stereo cameras that detect hazards and can automatically brake the car (autonomous braking), and maintain a set distance behind other vehicles in cruise. This needs to be switched off for offroad use as otherwise it may generate a false alarm, for example by low-hanging branches.

land rover discovery 4

An entire book could be written on the D4 alone. It has seven suspension height settings, three of which are normally used, a highly sophisticated traction control and centre coupling, electronically locking rear diff, stability control with TSA, surround-camera view, a powerful turbodiesel, Terrain Response, cross-linked air suspension in low-range, fully-independent suspension, HID headlights and more.

The manumatic auto box has a conventional automatic mode, but in some Terrain Response settings you can move it to the left and it goes into sport mode. Over to the left it can be moved forwards to manually change up a gear and backwards to change down, computer permiting. On the right of the shift is the electronic park brake, which automatically disconnects as you drive off, and if pulled up at speed puts the car into an emergency stop. At the top is the Terrain Response dial with the five TR modes. In common with most modern vehicles there is no way to manually lock the centre coupling as Land Rover has decided the driver should let the computer worry about that, and they're right. For the most part.

toyota land cruiser LC200

Toyota's flagship retains the IFS setup of its LC100 predecessor, and builds on it with a more powerful engine and better electronic aids. Many LC200s also have the KDSS – Kinetic Dynamic Suspension System – which when diagonal wheels are lifted forces their opposing numbers down, improving axle flow. The system also works on-road as a swaybar to prevent body roll when two wheels on the same side of the vehicle want to flex upwards. Most LC200s also have crawl control (see Chapter 9, EDAs).

Toyota LC200 showing its H4 and L4 transfer case operation. The LC200 has a Torsen centre diff which does a good job of torque distribution, but can also be locked by means of the button in the second picture. Thus, the LC200 has complete flexibility; high- or low-range and centre diff locked or unlocked. Next to the centre diff lock button is the stability control disable switch. See earlier in this Chapter for the Turn Assist feature.

SECTION 2

DRIVING TECHNIQUES

CHAPTER 11

THE BASICS

This section is all about how to drive your vehicle offroad, with chapters dedicated to many terrains, starting with some generic points.

what you need to know about your 4WD

You need to be much more familiar with your 4WD if you're going to drive it offroad. Some points to check out:

- Where are the two or three lowest points under the vehicle? Are they lined up?

- Does it have low-range and if so, how is low-range engaged?

- Are there any vulnerable bits of trim, towbars or anything that could fall off?

- Does the vehicle have any traction aids like cross-axle lockers, LSDs, traction control?

- Does the vehicle have stability control?

- Are there any electronic aids that may help or hinder? For example most Toyota LC200s have crawl control, Land Rover Discovery 3 and 4 have cross-linked air suspension in low-range and many vehicles have height-variable suspension.

- Where is the air intake (for water crossings)?

- Is the park brake functional?

- Does the vehicle have auto or manual free-wheeling hubs?

- What sort of engine does it have? A large diesel drives quite differently to a small petrol engine.

- What sort of tyres does it have? How far can they be aired down? What sort of grip are they likely to provide?

Section XXX has more details on how to drive unfamiliar 4WDs.

Six 4WDs. One is part-time 4WD, two can be either part-time or constant. All have stability control. One has a disconnecting swaybar. One has a rear locker, two others have the option. Most are automatics, but with different gearbox systems. One has variable-height suspension. One has a big, torquey petrol engine and another has a revvy little diesel. Each vehicle has different strengths, weaknesses, vulnerable points, driver aids and more. Although many driving techniques are the same for all vehicles, it is important to understand the differences and drive to a vehicle's strengths and minimise the weaknesses.

A towbar hanging down that'll reduce departure angle, a trailer plug about to fall off and a vulnerable reversing light. Items to fix before any offroading is done.

In order to maintain forward movement a 4WD must have:

- **Traction:** grip at the wheels.
- **Clearance:** little to no contact with the ground, other than the tyres.

Traction is maintained by taking a good "line" (route through the obstacle), using the appropriate control inputs such as steering, gears and throttle, and setting up the vehicle for the obstacle, such as adjusting tyre pressures.

Clearance is largely maintained by choosing the correct line.

This section is all about techniques to maximise traction and clearance. But here's some general advice based on years of doing it right and wrong!

- Very few times will you get back in your vehicle and think "well, walking the track was a complete waste of time".
- The patron saint of 4WDs punishes those that do not prepare.
- Try slowly first; better three goes than one big effort and a breakage.
- What works for one vehicle and driver may not work for another.
- The greater the ego, the greater the danger.
- Any niggling doubt at the start tends to grow into a gigantic doubt followed by expletives. Trust your instinct.
- Groupthink is deadly. Don't be afraid to disagree.
- If something didn't work, don't try exactly the same thing again. Do it differently; more or less power, even a 10 or 20cm different line, different gear.

In aviation we say that "it is better to be down here wishing you were up there, than up there wishing you were down here". In offroad terms that means "it is better to be driving home wishing you were still on the track, than still on the track wishing you were driving home". Discretion is the better part of valour, it's cheaper, and easier to explain to your partner.

This Discovery is definitely out of clearance on the approach angle, and quite probably under the chassis as well. If there was no drag caused by the clearance problem it may be able to move, but given the conditions and the ascent needed to get out of the bog traction may be a problem. That's why sometimes the only option is to winch.

planning!

The next chapter is about specific situations and types of terrain. However, it is important to understand the basic principles of offroad driving, because then you can apply them to any situation.

Before you tackle any obstacle, ask yourself:

- Do I need to go there?
- Can my vehicle and I drive there?
- In any case, what's my recovery plan?

If you answered "yes" to the first question, then you need to think about how you're going to tackle the obstacle. The basic process is:

1. Identify safe locations
2. Plan the approach
3. Plan the recovery

By now it is apparent that offroading requires some thought about where you will end up and how you tackle the obstacle. This is what makes offroading an intellectual as well as a physical challenge.

Do I need to drive this track? Can my vehicle and I make it? What happens if I don't make it? Where is the next location I can safely stop?

1. identify safe locations

Imagine crossing a river by use of stepping stones. Would you take a leap from a stone, and only then look to see if there is somewhere to land? Offroad

driving is the same; for each obstacle, make sure there is somewhere beyond the obstacle you can stop and reassess. This may be on a small patch of flat ground between two bogholes, or at the top of a riverbank.

Water crossings an excellent example of commitment. Once you start, you can't stop until you reach your safe point. Many an offroader has begun a crossing and then shortly regretted not spending a little more time on planning, and I'm no exception. The idea of working out how far you need to go before you're through an obstacle or can safely stop is applicable to all offroad terrains, especially in difficult driving conditions.

2. plan the approach

track forensics

If a track looks tricky, you definitely need to be looking at the line. But make sure you also take a look at the track and see how others have travelled it. Things that tell a tale include:

- **Rocks:** Any evidence of scratching?
- **Ruts:** Are the sides scarred with tyres trying to crawl out?

- **Sides of a mudbog:** Is there evidence of a lot of water flowing out?
- **Between the ruts:** Has anyone dragged a diff along the centre?
- **Trees:** Have any looked like they have been used for winching? (Hopefully this has been done with a tree protector, but even so there may be evidence such as footprints around a likely-looking tree.)

Just take a look around and see what you can find. Learn from the mistakes (and successes) of others.

- **Environment:** Keep to the tracks, don't make new ones.
- **Vehicle damage:** Is the car likely to be scratched, hung up on rocks or slide into something unforgiving?
- **Terrain:** Are there any ruts? Can you – or should you – use them?

Planning the line starts well before you get there. Coming downhill the driver is assessing the climb up, and wouldn't have descended into the dip unless he was sure he'd be able to make it back out one way or the other.

An apparently shallow mudbog, not very long, not very wide. But look at the ground around the track, which shows evidence of water washing over it. There are also scrapes between the wheel ruts leading into the bog, and it's wider than it needs to be. This is all evidence that perhaps it is deeper than it looks. The Prado is properly prepared with a snatch strap ready so if he doesn't make it a recovery vehicle can quickly and easily hook up for a snatch out.

choosing a line

There will often be many lines. Things to consider:

- **Traction and clearance:** As always! Keep all four wheels on the ground. Can you avoid slippery sections?
- **Safety:** What could go wrong? What could you slip into?

The difference 20cm to the left makes. The Jeep's right rear is in the deepest part of the rut, the Patrol's expert driver has straddled it evenly.

1   *If the driver goes to his left, that could be a flatter path. On the other hand, keeping right would avoid the need for a turn (all else being equal, turns should generally be avoided as vehicles generally perform better in straight lines) and that hole could be straddled. There's already a tyre mark showing someone's done that, but was it as wet then as it is now, and what sort of car was it?*

2   *Not a lot of a choice in line here, but the gearing, throttle, use of the swaybar disconnect, lockers and more are still within the driver's control. The line is more than just where you drive; it's how you drive.*

3   *Going straight on straddling the rut could have worked too. However, the track bends and taking this line better sets the car up for the turn.*

4   *Those rocks on the left are slippery, and if the front wheel hits one coming up a steep hill it'll bounce, losing the car a little traction. Best to keep away from them.*

3. plan the recovery

This rule can be thought of as:

- Don't go anywhere you aren't prepared to reverse out of.
- Don't go anywhere you aren't prepared to be stuck in, and have a recovery plan for being stuck in the least convenient place.

If you are crossing a river, what happens if you stall halfway across? What happens if you don't make it through that muddy patch, or get hung up on that rock near the end of that hill climb? A classic example of thinking ahead is the practice of attaching a snatch strap (recovery rope) to a vehicle before it enters a mudbog, which saves considerable time and muckiness if you don't make it. Other examples include removing gear from the vehicle so it's easy to get to and ready, ensuring there are sufficient trees to winch off, or even wondering if it is possible to recover a vehicle at all, given the equipment at your disposal and the situation. Section 3 is devoted to recovery.

That didn't work. A really steep climb failed, the front swung sideways and I'm in trouble. But that was always a distinct possibility so there's another vehicle at the top of the hill with an electric winch, which we knew worked, ready to recover my car. If that wasn't an option I would have needed to back down the hill and from that angle doing so wouldn't have been the safest manoeuvre in the book.

kit list: the basics

Each of the terrain-specific chapters in this section adds to this basic list for any offroad excursion:

recovery gear

- **Recovery points:** The most common method of recovery is using one vehicle to snatch another, using a strap which acts as a giant elastic band. This is very effective but places enormous stress on both vehicles; so you need recovery hooks. These are NOT the tie-downs, but very strong hooks bolted to the chassis. Ask your local 4WD mechanic about them. Recovery points are a non-negotiable, essential fitment. If you need a snatch recovery and do not have any fitted, you are endangering lives

and your vehicle. Chapters 32 and 33 have more detail.

- **Snatch strap:** Snatch strap, joiner magazine (see Chapter 34) and shackles.

- **Tyre pressure gauge.**
- **Jack flat plate:** prevents jacks sinking into soft ground.
- **Gloves:** general hand protection.
- **Plastic box:** safe storage for all your recovery gear.
- **Spade:** Useful in all sorts of situations.
- **Bags:** Because a snatch strap covered in mud should not be lying loose in the vehicle!

communication and navigation

A pair of handheld UHF CB radios are fantastic for keeping in touch with other people, as well as being a good safety measure. They are useful even if you are "spotting" (guiding) from only a few metres away, much easier than shouting.

Maps are essential, and not just of your intended route but of areas bounding it too, as you never know when you need to make a diversion. A GPS receiver is a great addition, but never rely on it alone – you should always know where you are even without its aid.

other gear

See Chapter 32 for more details.

- First-aid kit
- Fire extinguisher
- Air compressor
- All kit stowed in boxes secured to tie-down points (except for the first-aid kit and fire extinguisher which should be secured, but also easily accessible)
- A working jack and wheel brace, a flat plate for jacking on soft surfaces, and knowledge of where the jacking points are. Practice before you go!

personal

clothing

As with any outdoor activity, the weather can turn nasty, and you don't want to be trying to change a tyre in the wet without a raincoat or other clothing.

food and drink

Take more than you think you'll need. Plan for the worst case. Even if you're out on a day trip, take plenty of water and enough food for a day. If you're prepared and travelling in company the chances of needing to use it are remote, but it'll be a comfort to know it's there.

vehicle preparation

before you drive offroad

Remove anything which could be damaged or get hung up, such as towbars.

- Check there are no faults with the vehicle; fluid leaks, damaged tyres, loose batteries, clogged radiators, odd noises or responses.
- Check all fluids are within limits; oil, coolant, brake fluid, power steering and others as per the owner's handbook.
- Start with a full tank of fuel.
- Familiarise yourself with the vehicle. See "What you need to know about your 4WD" at the start of this chapter.

Ask your 4WD workshop what else you should check and how to do it. If they're good, they'll tell you and show you how. Do the check above at the end of every trip, too. That way you have time to get it fixed. It is very, very important to build up a mental picture how your vehicle looks and sounds when it's running normally, under the body and under the bonnet. That means that if you start hearing a "funny noise" you might be able to identify something loose or missing; if you're not familiar with the vehicle that will be much harder. You should also get your vehicle serviced at the arduous-use intervals which are typically half that of the usual service intervals; it'll be a saving in the long term.

Offroading places extra stresses and strains on a vehicle. Find a mechanical shop that specialises in 4WDs, preferably in your particular vehicle or marque, and your vehicle will be far better set up and maintained than if you trust it to a generalised operation. Factory-backed dealers know the vehicle, but are constrained by the manufacturer around what other services and accessories they can offer.

what does what?

You don't need an engineering degree, but you do need to be able to understand the basic engine components and what they do. If nothing else, it'll help you work around any problems, and you'll be able to have a more intelligent conversation with a mechanic than "it doesn't work". People help people that try to help themselves. Also purchase and carry a repair manual for your vehicle. It might help you, or others, repair your vehicle. For example, on one trip I began to hear a knocking noise coming from underneath the vehicle. Concerned, I stopped and investigated. It turned out to be the rear swaybar, which had hit a rock and torn off its mounting. That didn't concern me at all; I knew it wasn't critical, and would actually improve the vehicle offroad. Back on road there would be some extra body roll. The point is that I knew what that part was, and what it did. If I hadn't, we would have spent the rest of the trip being very worried.

insurance

Ensure your insurance covers you for offroad tracks. The various 4WD associations have special insurance for those that use their 4WDs offroad. There are two basic types of policy; agreed value, where you agree with the insurance company about how much your vehicle is worth, and market value, when the value is decided after a write-off. Agreed value is easier and can usually go to 20% beyond whatever the insurance company thinks your vehicle is worth without modifications. Market value is nominally replacement value, but insurance companies typically don't value accessories very highly so you could well be out of pocket unless you're good at arguing the case.

Regardless of policy you must declare absolutely everything you have on the vehicle, with make, model, date fitted, replacement value and preferably photographs to back it up, then keep a very close eye on repairs. If you have an ARB bull bar you may not want a TJM or vice-versa. That said, often insurance companies permit changes if there is no additional expense or you cover the difference. For example, a friend of mine had a front-end crash and used the chance to get a bull bar fitted as it was cheaper than the other parts.

Does your insurance cover you for doing this?

If this happens then you'll be glad of several things; you have a first-aid kit handy, there are others in the convoy, your insurance covers you for offroading, there's plenty of recovery gear and your kit is properly secured. In this case all the above were in order, so while there's no such thing as a nice roll this one was as benign as these things get.

keeping it nice

Offroad driving inevitably means scratches on the paintwork. To minimise these you can buy clear plastic coats to go over the paint, but keeping the car clean and very well waxed helps a lot too. Even so the paint is likely to be damaged in some way, so take the vehicle to a specialist paint repairer (not necessarily the nearest panel shop), who can work wonders with paint jobs, scuffed plastics and everything else required to make the vehicle look brand-new. Frequent washing is a good idea, for example when entering a city after a dusty drive we'll often spend even just a dollar at a manual carwash to rinse the dust off as anything that touches the body panels will grind the dust into the paint.

Special film to temporarily protect a car's bodywork. Takes a few minutes to apply and even less to remove, and mostly saves a clean afterwards too!

Panel with and without a clear plastic coat applied. This protects against scratches but doesn't do much for dents.

Not all tracks are as overgrown as this one, but if you're going offroad you can't expect to keep the bodywork in showroom condition. That said, many touring 4WDs have more damage done in car parks than in the bush!

If you are able to do so without running afoul of water restrictions, leaving a sprinkler under the vehicle is a great way to clean it free of mud and any salty water. The Defender's aftermarket bash plate and diff guard are visible in this photo.

passenger pointers

Passengers new to offroading should be briefed so everyone is safer and enjoys the trip.

Seatbelt: Wear your seatbelt at all times, even when the vehicle is moving slowly. 4WD travel means bumps, unusual attitudes (applies to the vehicle as well) and even a chance of a rollover. It is best to be protected. It is not possible to operate seatbelts at extreme angles, so put them on ahead of time.

Hanging on: In the front passenger seat there is often a "Jesus handle" on the dashboard. You will discover for yourself why it is called the Jesus handle. If there is no handle, simply brace yourself with your feet.

Loose articles: Ensure there are no loose articles. The test; would you want it dropped on your face from the height of a few metres?

Driver: Do not distract the driver. 4WD requires much more concentration and skill than ordinary driving.

Walking: If you are concerned for your safety, you may get out and walk the section instead. It's likely to be quicker than driving anyway.

Convoy procedure: This dictates that each vehicle keep the vehicle behind in sight. You can help by looking behind you for the following vehicle, but remember the idea is they have seen where you have gone so they can follow.

Eating: Be careful about eating on the move. You could bite your tongue over a bump or spill drink.

Mud: Roll windows up before entering mud. Open them before water crossings, in case you need to use them as an exit.

Doors: Be careful when opening doors. You may overstress the hinges if you let the doors bang open if the vehicle is facing downhill. Also, the ground may be a lot further away than normal. It might also be a lot closer than normal, and the door won't open and you need to exit via a window. There may be rocks or earth in the way of an open door. Such is life on a 4WD track.

Environment: Ensure all litter is stored in the vehicle. Keep to marked trails and tracks. Keep away from the wildlife, and do not interfere with plants.

Watch where you watch: If you're outside the vehicle watching, then make sure you cannot possibly get in the way. It's all too easy to slip down into the way of an oncoming vehicle, which has limited manoeuvrability and limited stopping power.

Recoveries: If a vehicle can't move by itself, or can't negotiate an obstacle, it needs a recovery. Keep out of the way unless specifically directed by whoever is leading the recovery to do a given task. Well-meaning novices can be dangerous.

A vehicle on a slope is difficult to get out of. People can get caught in the doors or let them slam shut. Novice passengers can really enjoy offroading, but not if they have an unpleasant experience that could have been avoided with a little warning.

CHAPTER 12

CAR CONTROL

Most of this section deals with terrain-specific techniques, but there are many tips and tricks common to any offroad driving situation.

in the driver's seat

You won't be operating at your best if you aren't comfortable and able to reach the controls easily. Some points to consider:

- **Steering:** Make sure you can reach the steering wheel properly. You should be able to drape your wrist on the top of the wheel while your shoulders are firmly pressed against the seat. Moving slightly further forward than this can help, as you will also need to look out over the bonnet. On the flat everything may feel fine… wait till you're on a really steep hill needing to operate switches and you'll see the benefit of a more forward and upright position than normal.

- **Pedals:** You should be able to fully depress the brake and clutch if necessary without unduly compressing your lower leg into the seat. Brace your left foot against the footwell when it is not otherwise engaged. If your right foot can edge up against the side of the footwell whilst it is on the accelerator that can help with accidental jogging of the foot when you go over rough ground. Ensure pedals are clear of mud and ice to avoid feet slipping off them.

- **Loose articles:** Make sure there aren't any inside the vehicle because they will either damage themselves or the vehicle, be a distraction or worst of all roll under the pedals.

- **Air conditioning:** Air conditioning should generally be turned off during tough sections on low-powered vehicles. It uses additional engine power intermittently which can slightly upset the balance of the car. I have seen a vehicle fail a climb with the air conditioning on, and make it with it off.

- **Sound system:** Turn it off in the hard sections. Listen to your vehicle instead. The note of the engine can tell you a lot, and you need to be listening for any problems, such as sticks caught underneath, or any shouts from bystanders.

- **Windows:** Windows should be either fully up, fully down or just cracked open at the top, depending on the conditions. If they are ¾ down then if your head knocks against the window it'll hit an edge, not solid glass, which can cause a serious injury. If they are fully up you can't hear much outside. If they are any way down you might get slapped in the face by a branch of a tree, or a stick thrown up by the wheels. And on that branch or stick might be a hungry little leech, wanting to be become a big fat leech. Or three. Or a spider. Or a beetle. You get the idea. I speak from personal experience.

- **Controls:** Work out where the wipers, lights etc are before you need them, and even how to select reverse or apply the parkbrake.

Too far away from the steering wheel. At all times your shoulders should be firmly against the seat even when reaching.

Correct position. Her back is resting comfortably against the seat but she can still reach the top of the steering wheel without stretching. Legs can operate the pedals to the full extent without over-reaching, and the seat is as high as possible for the best view.

car control

This section describes some common control techniques used across a variety of terrains. Car control techniques very much depends on the vehicle and the situation. Just because a Formula 1 driver uses a specific technique doesn't mean to say that's applicable to an offroad driver at low range, and similarly offroaders may do things which aren't appropriate for driving large trucks.

general

"Car control" is a term used to describe how a vehicle is accelerated, braked, turned and generally handled. Good car control is essential for any form of

performance driving, and that includes offroading. Different cars and different terrains demand different techniques – sand needs momentum and heavy use of throttle, whereas ice is the exact opposite. However, all cars and terrains have several car control factors in common, which are:

- Plan ahead: Consider the terrain well in advance at a general level, and in detail a few seconds in advance.

- Be smooth: There are very few times when harsh application of any controls is appropriate.

- Car sympathy: Be gentle with the car and it is less likely to fail or lose traction.

Below are some specific techniques that can be used in many situations. The terrain-specific chapters following will refer to these methods.

left foot braking (LFB)

what it is

This refers to operating the footbrake with your left foot when driving automatics, and the technique is also applicable to some manuals in some situations. It is a useful skill because:

- It is a very good technique for any slow-speed manoeuvring, particularly on rocky ground.

- No need to use the park brake for hill starts.

- Can works as a poor man's LSD or locker. When the vehicle is moving and about to come to a halt due to diagonal wheels in the air then maintaining power and momentum with the right foot while braking with the left can in effect send torque from a spinning wheel to the wheel in the air. If on one axle a vehicle has a spinning wheel with no traction and a stationary one with traction, then an open diff will only send the amount of torque to the wheel with traction that it needs to turn the spinning wheel. This not very much, so the vehicle doesn't go anywhere. If you then apply the brakes and drive what happens is that all four wheels become harder to turn, including the spinning wheel, so more torque gets transferred. Even though the stationary wheel is now being braked, the percentage difference between the two wheels has decreased, so the spinning wheel may get enough torque to move. It's not a perfect system and not particularly effective – it would be better to brake just the one wheel in the same way traction control does – but it can sometimes mean the difference between moving or staying where you are.

- Reduces the chances of locking a wheel when descending (see Chapter 22).

how to do it

Your left foot isn't used to braking, so train it! Find somewhere non-public and start to LFB. Accelerating/stopping is a good move, as it'll improve left-right foot coordination. Then try 'driving through' the brakes; chug along in first low, and progressively increase brake pressure by LFB while increasing speed by pressing the accelerator.

Note: this technique is described here for the purposes of offroad driving. Using the left foot to brake for normal onroad use is a question which divides advanced driving instructors who tend to have strong views on the subject both for and against. My view is that left foot braking on the road is not necessary and there are many more important road techniques to learn such as observation.

However, those who wish to learn as a very advanced technique should not be discouraged. Note that left-foot braking should not be used as "poor man's traction control" on ETC equipped vehicles as ETC does a much better job of torque distribution.

Note that some modern vehicles do not permit use of brake while the throttle is applied, and some do but limit the revs you can apply, for example to 1200rpm. This is just a modern vehicle limitation. Fortunately, such vehicles tend to have excellent traction control so you don't need them "poor man's LSD" trick, and excellent engine braking and/or hill descent systems so the need to drive through the brakes downhill is much reduced.

This Hilux has no traction control or lockers, and has run out of suspension articulation on an upslope, leaving the front left and rear right spinning. A second try with some dabbing of the footbrake saw the 'Lux sail through. Of side note here is the good front/rear balance weight of the camper conversion. Many campers, and also utes used for commercial purposes are very rear-heavy which can lead to handling problems.

A rocky descent where the wheel will climb up over a rock and then drop off suddenly, which can lead to unwanted contact with the rocks and bouncing. The solution is to hold the brakes with your left foot such that the car is not moving, then apply the accelerator to move. This forces the wheel to turn slowly and it doesn't drop off the rocks in the same manner.

steering

what it is

How to steer a car is often the start of a holy war, with people arguing strongly for one method or another. The truth is you need to look at the vehicle and the situation before deciding on a steering technique, and there are two basic techniques to choose from:

Push-pull: hold the steering wheel at quarter to three (see photo overleaf) and shuffle it around using small hand movements, keeping the hands at approximately quarter to three.

Fixed-input: hold the steering wheel at quarter to three and turn the wheel, keeping the hands at quarter to three. When the wheel is turned more than about 100 degrees release the lower hand and grab the opposite wheel spoke to continue the wheel turn.

In the case of a 4WD in low-range, offroad terrain the best method is the shuffle because you may well need to operate controls (on either side of the wheel) while the wheel is turned, you'll need both hands firmly on the wheel over rough ground and you'll often need much more than 100 degrees of lock for sustained periods of time, maybe even minutes. The fixed-input method is best for higher-speed work on dirt and bitumen, and has its place in any conditions where you need to control skids or slides, such as ice or shallow mud which require quick spinning of the wheel with a positive return to centre, something not easily done with push-pull. I use both methods and switch between the two from moment to moment.

Whichever method is used remember that in many offroad situations the vehicle will want to steer itself; it will turn down a sideslope, or a rock may knock a wheel unexpectedly, or uneven ground will cause the car to steer in different directions. Positive steering control is essential.

A very common fault with beginners is to be madly steering, ending up wondering whether you have applied two, one or no turns of the steering wheel. Get into the habit of remembering how many you have applied. I once had a student stop a car on a steep hill with a front wheel resting on a rock. He then took both hands off the wheel and looked away. As he did so, the steering spun 360 degrees of its own accord, before he looked back. He hadn't noticed the change which would have been dangerous had he reversed with that lock. The lesson is always to keep a hand on the steering wheel.

When offroad the car will be trying to steer itself as the wheels constantly change traction and resistance, going over rocks, hills, sideslopes and more. These forces can be quite sudden so a two-handed, nine-and-three grip on the steering wheel is essential. This Patrol's driver side front wheel has hit a rock. Fortunately the driver has a good grip on the wheel, otherwise the steering would be spun round.

Even though the Jeep is turning a corner at full lock, there's time to stop and reassess. This is unlike performance car driving, hence different techniques are needed. It is also often not easy to turn a 4WD's steering wheel in difficult situations so two hands are needed for control.

Thumbs out, quarter-to-wheel hold.

how to do it

- Use the shuffle method; hold the wheel at quarter to three and shuffle it through your hands, so your hands do not cross over. This means grasping the steering wheel at nine-and-three (opposite spokes) and more or less keeping your hands there as you feed the wheel through your hands to turn.

- Always keep both hands on the wheel, except when a hand has to do something else, then return that hand to the wheel as soon as possible.

- Remember how many turns of lock you have on so you know when the steering wheel is straight.

- Keep your thumbs out of the steering wheel spokes because if the wheel is suddenly moved then it could break your thumbs. However, this was more of a problem before modern vehicles and power steering which damps the effects of such knocks. Fitting larger and heavier tyres and rims worsens the problem so fitting an aftermarket steering damper may be the solution.

- Ensure you are in the right seating position (see page 162).

reversing with the mirrors

what it is

Reversing using the side, not interior mirrors. Why? Because a fully loaded 4WD will have strictly limited out-the-back visibility out of the rear windows.

how to do it

Just needs practice, but some tips are:

- Fit those small overtaking mirrors to give a wide view of the vehicle.
- Consider angling the mirrors down, especially if you have electrically controlled ones.
- Take a mental note of where the trees, rocks and other obstacles are. You may be meeting them soon!
- Take a good look around before you get in the car and don't be afraid to get out again.

Blind-spot mirrors can show you all sorts of problems that would otherwise be invisible.

wheel placement and visibility

what it is

Wheel placement is putting your wheels exactly where you want them to go. It's not as easy as it sounds. Firstly, you can't see your wheels and secondly, the back wheels don't follow the front.

If you can place your wheels exactly where you want them to go you will go a long way offroad.

how to do it

You have to memorise the road before it disappears under the bonnet. You also need to maintain a picture in your mind of where the wheels are at any given time. If you're turning, the back wheels will take a shorter path than the front.

This skill is definitely one that's easy to understand, but takes a lot longer to master. You can practice this by placing a square of paper on the ground and then attempting to place each wheel on it in turn. A good way to place the front wheels is to remember that your feet are less than a metre away from the centre of the wheel; much less than you may think.

In both cases the driver can just see the stump before it disappears under the bonnet. The driver must memorise the terrain after it can no longer be seen and map that mental image to where the wheels are, while looking ahead to the next obstacles. Despite the slow speeds involved in offroading, the mental work is as great as a racing driver who is constantly reading the track. The difference is that it's easy for the offroader to just stop and take a look around!

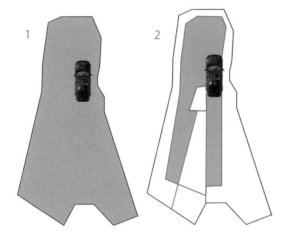

We measured how far the driver could see out of a right hand drive Discovery 4 on flat ground and created these diagrams to scale.

Diagram 1: The shaded area shows the ground hidden to the driver.

Diagram 2: This diagram's shaded area shows how much more you can see by moving around in the seat, craning forwards and looking around, although with the seatbelt always done up. The magenta area on the left is extra visibility from a blind-spot mirror, and the orange is the area visible in the offside wing mirror.

This Ranger has to get its wheel exactly on this wet rock. Either side will see the vehicle hung up on other rocks. This is just one of many situations where precise wheel placement is essential.

controlled momentum

what it is

There are going to be times when you cannot maintain clearance, or ensure that all four wheels are on the ground, or there will be insufficient traction to climb a hill or get over a rock. On these occasions momentum may be the answer, driving fast enough to overcome the obstacle. An example is a rutted, muddy track with a slightly higher section that if you were to drive slowly over would see your clearance disappear and with it your forward motion. Other examples include crossing a ditch at an angle, slightly uphill, or any time when a vehicle has alternate wheels in the air and has no traction aids (and sometimes even when it does), or ascending a large, steep sand dune.

Remember that the differential will direct drive to the wheels in the air, so the vehicle goes nowhere. A little momentum is required in this case too.

Momentum is a dangerous tool, because the greater the speed, the greater the potential for loss of control and damage. Sometimes, however, it is the only solution.

how to do it

When using momentum, a good technique is to start slow, if possible, then back up and try it again slightly quicker. You want to have just enough momentum to complete the obstacle and no more, to save stress on the vehicle and the environment. Consider also if there is another way; maybe a bit of track building (judicious placement of rocks), or lower tyre pressures.

Throttle position; accelerate as required to the obstacle. As you reach it maintain the throttle, or even begin to sightly slacken off. Don't make the classic mistake of approaching relatively slowly and then jumping on the accelerator as soon as the going gets tough. You'll just stress the vehicle and probably wheelspin. There are exceptions to this rule, for example when the front wheels have to climb a ledge and you must smoothly blip the throttle after the front wheels begin to climb and before the rear wheels hit the ledge.

Momentum is often used on soft surfaces such as sand and mud, but has a place in hill ascents and rocks as well. On sand you may accelerate to perhaps even as high as 40km/h to make a dune, on rocks even one to three km/h of momentum could see you through.

This Pajero cannot climb the hill at a crawl, so momentum is required. The trick is to use just enough to make it over the top, and not to apply power once the ascent has begun. Incidentally, the driver cannot see the track ahead, so it was checked on foot before the car was driven over the top. The front driver's side wheel is in the air, but that doesn't matter as the momentum carries the car through.

Sand driving, and dunes in particular, is a common case of needing momentum to ascend. Sand is soft and smooth so speed can be used with minimal vehicle impact.

Momentum works nicely in muddy ruts, but it's so easy to get it wrong. Momentum is always a considered risk.

There is absolutely no point spinning wheels to this extent. The vehicle won't make any progress, but rubber will be wasted, a smell created, an unsightly mark left on the rock and you could snap some transmission components.

stopping a vehicle

Don't just stop anywhere. Consider:

- **Can you get going?** If you can, stop on flat ground or a slight downhill.
- **Will the vehicle stay put?** An apparently secured 4WD can creep down a hill when nobody is looking.
- **Visibility:** Can others see you?
- **Obstruction:** Can others get past, including bikers and walkers? Can the vehicle in front open its rear doors without touching your front?
- **Safety:** It's not unknown for vehicles to stop, doors to be opened, passengers get out and fall down a cliff or plunge into a mud puddle, and that's assuming the doors can even be opened.

Chapter 22 covers stopping on a hill.

The Patrol is stopped in a perfect position. There's enough room for the Santa Fe to make a run up the beach and reverse without worrying about the other car. He can see what's going on, and he's left enough room to get a run-up for his own attempt. Always leave plenty of room between your car and the one in front.

On many hills there will be whoop-de-doos or conservation drains. These temporary flatter spots can be used as stopping places.

wheels in the air

There is nothing wrong with a 4WD having one or more wheels in the air and it happens all the time. In sand, you can have all four wheels in the air and still drive the vehicle afterwards (well, sometimes). However, there is something to consider when wheels leave the ground.

As we know, the differential directs drive to the wheel with least resistance. That means the wheel in the air which, freed of resistance, spins very fast. This is not a problem until the wheel comes back into contact with Mother Earth, then we have the problem of what to do with all that kinetic energy.

If you're lucky, the wheel will simply wheelspin. If you are not, a driveshaft, CV joint or other important component will be broken, or weakened. Put simply, if you spin wheels at high speed and they suddenly gain traction then that is a lot of energy to be dissipated, and sometimes the mechanics just cannot take it.

The solution is never to spin wheels too fast, and to back off before they are likely to come into traction again. An example is crossing a trench. You need momentum to get over the stage where alternate wheels are in the air, but if you keep the power on the wheels will be spinning quickly when you complete the trench crossing and have all four wheels back on the ground on the other side.

The trick is to gather whatever momentum you need first and lift off. This is, in general, a good technique. In the case of the trench, keep the power on until you feel the wheels in the air, then lift off.

Only when you feel the wheels have traction again should you come back on the power, gently. There is no point keeping the power on when you have wheels in the air.

Traction control helps avoid this problem because the vehicle needs less momentum, and when a wheel is lifted the system applies the brakes to that wheel so it doesn't spin up as much. However, don't assume traction control vehicles are immune from transmission damage.

Having one wheel in the air will also destabilise the vehicle, which can lead to a loss of traction and a skid. Bear this in mind and consider a worst-case example, or mitigate the risk by using ruts so you can't slip out.

A comp truck with two wheels in the air. These vehicles typically have large, soft tyres and reinforced drivelines.

Without traction control or lockers, momentum is often needed and that can see wheels in the air as in this case. If the wheel spins up and hits ground, expect problems.

shifting into low-range

Most 4WDs need a little time and distance to get into 4WD and/or low-range. This may be only a few metres, but it is significant because you need to set the vehicle up in the correct gears before you get to the obstacle. The best advice is to take it slowly. Manuals should be shifted into low-range with the clutch down and the vehicle stationary. If it doesn't quite go in, lift the clutch slightly to ease

the vehicle forwards and push the lever home. On some vehicles the transfer case lever can be partially engaged; this is dangerous as it may pop out under load, so make sure the lever is fully engaged.

Automatics typically require neutral for a low-range shift and again slow, deliberate movements give the best results. Vehicles with push-button transfer case systems especially need a measured approach.

using spotters

A spotter is a person outside the vehicle giving you directions. Used properly, this technique can be invaluable. Used improperly, it ends up with damaged vehicles and friendships. Here are some things to consider.

Agree protocols; "turn left" and "turn right" don't mean anything. A common way around this is to use "left hand down" and "right hand down". This means turn the steering wheel anticlockwise and clockwise respectively. Typically, you'd continue the movement, slowly, until told "hold" or "straighten". Agree an emergency "stop" signal, usually holding your palms upwards. Tips:

- Rely on hand signals, not yelling. Agree a raised hand is "stop", regardless of any voice communication.
- The owner of the vehicle makes the ultimate call as the vehicle is their responsibility.
- Use one spotter, and one only.
- The spotter should ideally be a competent driver in their own right

- Either the driver is following the spotter's directions, or doing their own thing. Don't try to mix both.
- Anyone can call a stop if they see something dangerous.

The spotter should stand where they can see the entire vehicle and the track ahead. They should call a stop if they need to look around or at the back, and they should never walk backwards as it's too easy to fall over.

A difficult descent, made easier by an expert spotter who is standing well out of the way, where he can be seen, and where he can see everything. Communication is by hand signal and handheld radio.

other techniques

- **Drive the rear axle:** always consider where the rear wheels will travel. Very often if you do that the front takes care of itself. A good example is turning while straddling a rut; don't be afraid to put the front wheels right on the limit of the gap as that means the rears are more likely to be well away from falling into the rut.

- **Don't turn the steering wheel while stationary:** It places unnecessary stress on the steering systems.
- **Don't fight the car:** Work with it, be smooth, be gentle and anticipate.

No matter how old the vehicle, some techniques are still the same, like picking your line, gear and speed.

skids

how skids are caused

Skids can occur at any speed, on any surface, and as an offroad driver you will encounter them sooner rather than later. Sometimes skids are useful, but most of the time you'll want to avoid them and recover from them if they happen.

A skid is when the traction limit of the tyres has been exceeded. The vehicle may be sliding out of control or ploughing straight on, and the wheel won't necessarily be locked. To correct a skid you first need to understand why it occurred. There's only one basic reason; because the traction limit of the tyre has been exceeded. This may be because of harsh braking, sudden steering input, snatched gear change or jabbing the accelerator. A change of road surface may also reduce the tyre's traction so where a given control input or speed was fine a few metres back it now induces a skid. Speed can be a factor, too, as no matter how smooth you are the quicker you go the more the grip is required to maintain control around the bends.

Skid prevention is all about looking ahead, observing the terrain and being smooth and gentle with the controls while maintaining conditions that don't require the tyres to exceed their traction limit. That traction limit is often represented as a circle or oval called the "circle of traction". The oval represents the limit of adhesion of a tyre – it's oval because the tyre has more traction fore and aft than sideways, and there are concentric ovals because the tyre doesn't break traction instantly. The arrow represents how much traction is being used.

The circle of traction. About half of the tyre's traction is being used to brake. The concentric blue circles represent a progressive loss of traction; modern tyres do not instantly switch from grip to no grip.

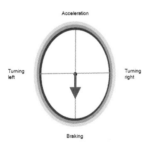

Here the vehicle is braking just as hard as before, but also turning a little. The combination of the two forces is shown, and the resulting arrow is closer to the edge of the circle, or limit of traction. This is what happens when you brake moderately while turning.

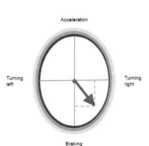

Now the turning force has been increased, but braking remains the same. If it was just the turning or just the braking the tyre would be within its grip limits, but the combination of the two has pushed it past its limit and the tyre is now skidding, with a consequent loss of control.

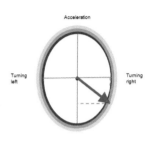

The driver has realised the car is skidding and has a choice of asking for less turning force, or reducing braking. The latter is chosen and now the tyre can turn the car.

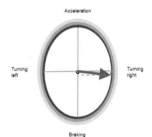

types of skid

So if a skid is caused by the arrow moving outside the circle, skid recovery is all about bringing the arrow back inside the circle, or reducing a car's demands of tyre grip. That means reducing the demand for braking/accelerating or steering. How that is done depends on the type of skid, which falls into two basic types:

- Oversteer
- Understeer.

Oversteer is when the rear end of the vehicle slips more than the front or, in the case of a skid, slides out. Oversteer may be induced by accelerating harshly out of a corner or by braking and turning at the same time, especially on faster corners. On dirt roads a car will oversteer if the front wheels have grip and the rear wheels are on the fine, marbly stones found outside of the usually travelled wheel paths.

Understeer is when you want to turn but the vehicle runs wide. 4WDs naturally understeer a little, but can understeer a lot in some situations, for example when turning hard and then applying the brakes, or when the rear wheels have grip on a dirt road and the fronts are on the marbles. You know a vehicle is understeering when you need to turn the wheel tighter and tighter to get around the corner.

With any type of slide you have a nanosecond to react because it will be sudden. This means you need to know what to do, and be prepared to do it, so driving with both hands on the wheel is appropriate.

Oversteer in a RWD car caused by abrupt power application around a corner.

This Hilux is being expertly driven to demonstrate oversteer. The wheels are pointing where the driver wants the vehicle to go.

Understeer in mud - the wheels are turned but the vehicle ploughs straight on.

An example of oversteer recovery at slow speed offroad. The wheels are pointing where I want the car to go.

recovering from a skid

oversteer

An oversteer recovery:

- Look ahead, to where you want the car to go;
- Turn the steering wheel so the front wheels are pointed in the direction you want the car to go.

What else to do depends on what the vehicle was doing when it began to oversteer.

If you have been accelerating harshly, reduce but do not sharply eliminate the power as the sudden weight shift could destabilise the vehicle.

If you were braking hard, reduce the braking effort and this will place more weight on the rear of the vehicle.

If the car began to oversteer when it was at a constant speed then again steer where you want to go and very gently lift off the accelerator, not quickly as that will unload the rear which is already slipping. Do not accelerate. While acceleration does cause a rearward weight shift, thereby increasing the size of the circle, it's only a very small increase for the average 4WD and you'll need more rear traction anyway (bigger circle) as you're now asking the tyre to accelerate and turn. Any acceleration simply pushes the arrow even further outside of the circle, and since you aren't slowing down either the greater speed will need a greater amount of grip. It is a myth that you can "power out" of an oversteer skid. This myth appears to come from the belief that high-powered racecars power out of skids. In fact, if a high-powered sportscar gets into an oversteer skid, the driver will maintain or perhaps reduce throttle, as suddenly lifting off

the throttle will throw the weight to the front and worsen the skid. This is definitely not the same as suddenly increasing power which will simply worsen the skid as even more is asked of the rear tyres which are already past their traction limit which is why they're skidding.

Changing down while attempting to correct a skid is generally counterproductive. This is because you need to be focusing more on steering and braking, and because the gear change itself will destabilise the vehicle as a lot more engine braking will be quickly applied, which can lead to a loss of traction.

The sequence of images on the following page show a rally car recovering from an oversteer skid. In this case the skid was intentionally initiated (image 1, 2), but that doesn't change the recovery process. Image 3 and the car's rear wheels are sliding, as shown by the extra dirt kicked up by the rear tyres. Notice that the wheels aren't blurred. This is because the driver is not accelerating – the skid is in progress, and he doesn't want to make it worse. He's not braked, either, and the steering wheels are turned in the desired direction of travel. Images 4 and 5 show the skid even further developed, and still no acceleration, steering wheels always turned. Image 6 shows the driver has sensed the skid has been caught, and he's now accelerating. The critical part is that the skid was first caught – then, and only then, was power applied. Image 7 and 8 show the car accelerating, and again those steering wheels are turned in the desired direction of travel. The important point here is that when a car is skidding, you don't recover it by applying a big dose of power, you catch the skid with no acceleration.

1–8 Oversteer recovery. Refer previous page text for captions.

understeer

If the car is sliding in understeer then you have a choice: either turn or slow down. If you want to turn then get off the brakes or accelerator, even quite sharply, and the car will turn. Beware it doesn't grip too quickly and throw you sideways. For example, if you braked at speed then locked the front wheels, then put a lock of turn on you'll find the car keeps going straight. If you then get off the brakes it'll jump sideways as you return grip to the front wheels. This is a standard demonstration on advanced car control courses.

If you want to slow down then stop trying to turn so the tyres have a chance to use their traction for braking.

how to learn

Please note that in no way should the descriptions here be taken to mean that 4WDs can or should be driven quickly, rally style. Also, while stability control (see Chapter 9) may prevent an oversteer or understeer skid, and ABS may allow you to steer while braking; no electronic system can modify the laws of physics and if a tyre is out of grip, it's out of grip. Even the electronic brains can be helped by the correct recovery techniques.

These techniques are not something to practice in your 4WD on a public road. They aren't even something to practice in your 4WD. The best place to learn is on a series of advanced driving courses.

The very best road drivers anticipate road conditions and avoid skids in the first place, and for safety's sake it is better to attend a low-risk driving course which teaches exactly this anticipation and pre-planning. Courses that focus purely on car control tend to instil a false sense of confidence in drivers who assume they can drive out of any situation – they can't, and the safest idea is to avoid the situation in the first place.

If you want to learn these techniques go and rent a rallycar. Remember that a touring 4WD will not handle anything like the rallycar, although the base techniques will translate. Better yet, invest in low-risk driving courses which teach you how to avoid needing these skills in the first place. Again, the wheels are pointing where the driver wants to go, and he's looking where he wants to go.

vehicle-specific techniques

when to engage 4WD

Knowing your vehicle's 4WD systems (Chapter 3) is important for you get the maximum benefit from the traction system.

locking the centre diff, or selecting 4WD

When do you lock the centre diff, or move your part-time 4WD transmission into 4WD? Many answers, but the best is – as soon as you can do so without fear of transmission windup. In practice, that means 4WD should be used on dirt roads but not on bitumen unless it is icy or otherwise slippery. Wet bitumen is generally too grippy for 4WD (although some vehicles, in some situations, can benefit) and unless you're absolutely sure it's better to keep in 2WD and simply slow down – a lot.

The earlier you are in 4WD the better equipped you are to deal with any sudden obstacles, the less likely you are to be stuck and the less damage you'll do to the environment. Don't be one of the "heroes" who tries to drive everything in 2WD.

When offroad, dry, slick rock offers superb traction so any manoeuvring there could easily see windup; you only need to turn through 90 degrees or less to stress the transmission. Consider how grippy the surface is, as opposed to fixed rules such as "offroad is ok for 4WD, on-road is not".

Many people will say you don't need to engage 4WD on dirt roads, and that's true in the sense that the vehicle will still move along the road in 2WD.

It's not like sand where if you're not in 4WD, you're not moving. However, just because it's technically not necessary doesn't mean to say it's not a good idea, and it suddenly becomes a superb idea about half a second after you hit that pothole or take a corner a little too sharply. If the car's not already in 4WD by that time, it's too late.

The Defender is a constant 4WD vehicle, with a simple centre diff. Is there any benefit to locking the centre diff? On flat dirt roads there's no difference, but on hills or cornering the centre diff doesn't distribute torque to where it most needs to go. Going up a hill the front wheels will bounce a little and slightly spin, noticeable by an occasional activation of the traction control light. Lock the centre diff and all that goes away, so constant 4WD vehicles with simple centre diffs do benefit from a lock. Don't forget to unlock when you hit bitumen, which can be done on the fly.

A GU Patrol with a part-time 4WD system. Definitely put it into 4WD and lock the hubs on dirt, but don't forget to take it out of 4WD when you hit the bitumen.

The LC200 has a sophisticated centre coupling, a torsen differential. This behaves far more intelligently than the simple unit in the Defender, and if the LC200 is driven up a dirt-road hill it won't be sending excess torque to the lighter front wheels. Therefore, there's no need to lock the centre diff for normal dirt-road driving. If conditions worsen and it gets slow and slippery, or into low-range territory, that's when the centre diff needs to be locked.

2WD to AWD

Some vehicles, for example the Pajero, can be driven in 2WD or AWD. 2WD offers marginally better fuel economy but AWD offers better grip, making it the preferred choice on winding roads, dirt roads, wet bitumen and even dry bitumen. The tiny fuel economy benefit is cancelled by the improved grip and safety.

when to engage low-range

Generally, as soon as you can, so the vehicle is already prepared for conquering obstacles. That doesn't mean leaping into low as soon as you're on a track if it's likely you won't be travelling slowly enough to warrant it. However, as low-range gives you a set of close-ratio gears I often use it even when it's not strictly needed, just because I have more gear options to choose from while travelling slowly. Like everything else, engage it ahead of time.

know your engine

driveability

Often you'll find yourself needing to idle over obstacles. Does your car have a bit of a surge at a certain RPM range? Find out. Many older turbodiesels have this problem when the turbo cuts in.

When you start it, does it surge then too? The Pajero 3.5L is known for this, it's by design but doesn't make key starts (Chapter 22) any easier. The solution is to start with your foot on the brake to cancel the surge.

A 2004 TD5 and a 2007 TDCi Defender which drive quite differently despite the fact both diesel engines put out a peak power of 90kW. The white '04 model has a 1:45 crawl ratio and five speeds whereas the grey '07 has a 1:62 crawl ratio and six speeds and so is much lower geared. The TDCi also has much more torque and develops it further down the rev range, so it can take obstacles in third low where the TD5 would need second low, and it's got a slightly better traction control. Despite the fact the TDCi is a mere 2.4L it can amble along at low revs like a much larger engine, thanks to its anti-stall control.

fuel

If the vehicle is at an angle the fuel gauge will not read correctly and the engine may not be able to draw fuel from the tank. The solution is to keep the tank as full as possible.

Here's a Discovery 4 at speed in sand. The back end has slipped out. This is where the driver will need to be looking ahead, where they want to go which will be more downhill than up. Lifting off the accelerator quickly will lose lots of momentum and cause a bog, accelerating will just worsen the slip so the correct response with the throttle is a gentle reduction. Assuming of course you want to correct the skid!

Wheels balanced on a log as either side is too deep for the vehicle's clearance. Offroad drivers should be able to do this without getting out to check.

Another wheel placement example.

Here we have a tricky turn. First point is that careful planning ahead even before the stream was crossed makes this manoeuvre a lot easier. Second is that the manoeuvre involves shuffling backwards and forwards. For a manual, simply use low-range, cover the foot brake with the right foot and bring the clutch up with the left foot, smoothly and gently. The car will move in first and reverse low using the engine's anti-stall system to avoid stalling, and this is much easier and safer than using the park brake to do a series of small hillstarts. For autos, much the same technique works; use the left foot to cover the brake lightly, and gentle acceleration to move the vehicle. In fact, it is possible to leave a modern manual in first low and it will climb pretty amazingly steep hills with both feet off the pedals. I do this demonstration for students and they are surprised at just how effective it can be.

Changing gears in this muck is an exceptionally bad idea. Not only are you likely to lose momentum and never regain it, you'll also open the clutch up to mud ingress. Even in automatics, select and hold the gear you need before you reach whatever obstacle it is you'll be driving to.

driving with locked differentials

manual lockers

Driving with locked differentials (which are explained in Chapter 3) requires a little care. The vehicle will still turn, but nowhere near as tightly as before, and there will be more stress on the rear axle. Therefore, the lockers should only be engaged when necessary. When they are engaged the effect can be quite incredible – so much less wheelspin – and especially rocky ascents that needed momentum can now be tackled at a snail's pace. And the pace needs to be slow, because locking a differential places much more stress on the transmission. Imagine a vehicle with a rear locker ascending a steep hill with one front wheel in the air; most of the weight of the vehicle is on the rear axles, and then one rear tyre lifts off the ground. The entire vehicle is being propelled by just the one wheel, with a lot of stress as a result. Lockers and momentum should be combined with caution, and in the example just given, using twin lockers would mean the front wheel still on the ground would be helping pull the vehicle forwards.

While lockers can be truly amazing traction devices, sometimes it's better to use traction control if fitted. Many modern vehicles such as Pajeros, Patrol Y62s and Rangers have optional rear cross-axle lockers and electronic traction control. Unfortunately, for the most part, traction control is disabled on the front axle when the rear locker is engaged. The end result is that in many cases the car is more capable with traction control operating on all four wheels than a locker engaged at the rear with an open front differential. For these vehicles lockers are best used in very slow going with excellent traction at the rear axle, such as dry rocks. For most other situations traction control is better. Even without traction control fitted many owners of lockers tend to over-use them. In tight turns they can be counter-productive, creating wheelspin as the wheels on an axle cannot turn at different speeds so the inside wheel scrubs, and increasing turn radius. In sand they are of very little use and sap engine power by creating inside-wheel wheelspin. On sideslopes they can cause the vehicle to drift (see Chapter 23). Lockers are best used in straight lines when one or more wheels will lift or lose traction when momentum would be lost. The engagement of a rear locker doesn't affect steering as much as engaging the front, or both, so bear this in mind when ascending rocky hills. If your lockers are not instant-acting (and most aren't) then a little forward planning is required.

Lockers are of definite benefit coming downhill (Chapter 22) as you need not lose engine braking on a locked axle.

The G-Class has either an open centre differential with traction control, or a locked centre differential with no traction control. It also has cross-axle lockers on the front and rear axles. In the top photograph the centre differential is unlocked, and the traction control cannot adequately distribute torque front and rear so the front left wheel is spinning and the other three are doing little work – if it was possible to lock the centre diff then the vehicle could progress. In the lower photograph the vehicle is driven in the same line and at the same speed, but centre and both front and cross-axle lockers are engaged so there is no wheelspin and the vehicle easily progresses. The point is that setting up a vehicle is important, and the setup depends on the vehicle's capabilities. In this case lockers win, but in other cases such as level shallow mud the G works better with open differentials and traction control.

Cross-axle lockers and traction control are complementary – one cannot be said to be always better than the other. As a general rule use lockers for slow-speed, high-traction work where wheels are in the air, and traction control elsewhere.

Wrangler Rubicon with twin factory lockers starting a descent. The vehicle's suspension is flexed and the rear left tyre isn't airborne but doesn't have a lot of traction. There is a risk that the tyre will skid, and if it does so engine braking will be lost on that wheel. Applying the rear locker would prevent this. The front can also be applied, provided you don't mind the consequent loss of steering capability, for example if you're using ruts to tramline your descent.

automatic lockers

Driving with automatic mechanical lockers (which are explained in Chapter 3) is all about working around the limitations. Don't apply power around a bend – instead coast around using as little throttle as possible. In a straight line you're always in locked mode and have the same extra stress on the drivetrain in tough situations as manual lockers.

There are also automatic electronic locking differentials, notably in new Land Rovers, and as these lock and unlock automatically they can be driven just like traction control with no need to think about when to engage or disengage. That's mostly convenient, but sometimes you want manual control you cannot have.

Refer to Chapter 9 for an explanation of Electronic Driving Aids.

Utes tend not to have the offroad performance of wagons as they have longer wheelbases, less axle flex, less power, stiffer suspension and the handling isn't as sharp. Most of them come with just a limited-slip differential, so adding twin manual ARB Air Lockers like this one transforms offroad capability. Here the ute is not using either locker as it ascends a right-turn slope and as you can see the front right wheel is spinning as the vehicle struggles to keep enough weight on the tyres. However, if both lockers had been engaged the vehicle would have struggled to make the right turn up the slope. The solution is to engage the rear first, before the turn, and after the vehicle is mostly around the turn, a little before the point in the photo, flick the front in. There will be sufficient steering left even with twin lockers to get the car around the few degrees of turn needed to complete the ascent.

dealing with transmission windup

Windup is explained in Chapter 3. How to recognise it:

- Steering feels heavier,
- The car understeers, you need more steering lock than normal,
- Extra noise from the tyres when corners are turned, especially sharper ones,
- Juddering and vibration that wasn't there before,
- The symptoms above become progressively worse.

Some windup myths:

- Some 4WDs are so strong they can resist windup. Not true; they just go longer before the transmission explodes.
- You need to drive a certain distance before you get windup. Not true; in theory you could drive 1,000km in a straight line and not get windup. In practice there are slight differences between front and rear axle rotation speeds so it'll happen eventually. Otherwise, drive 360 degrees full lock in a car park and you'll feel it straight away, before you have even completed the circle. In fact a friend's son managed to break a driveshaft by trying to turn a 4WD around in a tight circle in low-range on concrete. Words were exchanged after the fact, and the lad's defence that he hadn't realised something was wrong was a little difficult to believe given the squealing from the tyres, a pitiful noise equalled only the subsequent squealing by the driver.
- Windup isn't a problem in the wet. Partially true. It's less of a problem, but don't assume

it cannot happen. I know one experienced offroader who drives his unladen high-capacity ute in 4WD in very wet conditions – that's a judgement call he makes in full knowledge of the situation and it's the right one for him, but that doesn't make it right for everyone else in every situation.

- Tyres slip before an axle will break. True, but not true – the tyres will slip and squeal, but all the while that's stressing the transmission and winding it up. Anyway, why would you want to do that to your tyres? They are expensive safety equipment!
- Windup from turning left can be cancelled by turning right. Not true at all. Whether you turn left or right to get windup doesn't matter, the front is still turning quicker than the rear and that's the cause. If you're talking about the stress created by turning with a cross-axle locker engaged then that is true.

how to deal with it

You must undo the stress in the driveshafts by reversing the process that wound them up in the first place. Do this by allowing or forcing the front axle to turn quicker than the rear. In order, try these fixes:

1. Immediately get the vehicle out of 4WD, or unlock the centre diff by shifting the transfer case into neutral. The main gearbox's neutral will have no effect, the front and rear axles still stay locked together when that one is in neutral. The solutions below get the vehicle to the state when this can be carried out.

2. If that's not possible, as there may be too much stress built up in the transmission, there is another way. Reverse in a circle with full lock on, either clockwise or anti-clockwise (assuming

you've got windup by driving forwards). Reversing straight backwards has no effect as there is negligible difference between front and rear axle speeds. It doesn't matter which direction you reverse in as either direction will cause the front axle to spin quicker than the rear to undo the windup effects, in the same way turning left or right when going forwards increases windup with no left/right cancelling effect.

3. Cross-axle the vehicle gently so diagonal wheels have little weight on them or are in the air, for example by placing a wheel up on a large mound of soil.

Jacking up a wheel works, but is extremely dangerous and not recommended as the sudden release of energy is not to be treated lightly.

The last time I got windup was at a beach. I'd driven on there for a quick photo and not bothered to air down, but had locked the centre diff in my Defender. I then drove straight off the beach, whereas usually I'd stop to air up. After a turn and a roundabout the car felt strange; it didn't want to turn and felt stressed. I looked at the dash for help and saw the 4WD centre diff lock was still in – by breaking my routine I'd forgotten to unlock the centre diff. Fortunately I was able to shift the transfer case lever into neutral and the centre diff unlocked, but only because I recognised the signs early and knew what to do.

driving with freewheeling hubs

manual hubs

There's no need to keep flicking free-wheeling hubs in and out.

As explained in Chapter 3, manual freewheeling hubs entirely disconnect the front wheels from the rest of

the drivetrain. This means that if you have a transfer case lever in 4WD then, unless the hubs are locked, you're not actually driving all four wheels. All you're doing is driving the rear wheels, the front driveshaft, front differential and front axles, but not the front wheels. This is actually useful because if you select low-range then you've got low-range 2WD, which is great for slow-speed work like backing trailers.

If you set the hubs to locked then that doesn't drive all four wheels unless the transfer case lever is also set to a 4WD mode. A common misconception is that vehicles cannot be driven on-road with the hubs locked. They can, so long as the transfer case is set to 2WD. In that case the wheels rotate, the axles rotate as they're connected to the wheels, the front diff rotates and so does the front driveshaft. However, that driveshaft is not connected to anything as the car is in 2WD, so there is no risk of windup – all you're doing is using marginally more fuel by rotating that extra metal. It is a good idea to do this once every month if the vehicle isn't used in 4WD as it splashes oil around the diff. When you're out 4WDing for the day just lock the hubs in and leave them in whether you're in 2WD or not.

If you're moving from dirt roads to bitumen you may as well leave the hubs locked and just shift to and from 4WD as required. There's no need to keep jumping out to change the hubs over.

Most modern part-time 4WDs (if that's not a contradiction in terms) don't have locking hubs and simply disconnect the transfer case from the front driveshaft.

Most LC100s are constant 4WD but the base models beloved of hire companies and corporates are part-time, usually with manual locking hubs.

automatic hubs

Automatic hubs need no driver involvement but they do make a difference offroad as they automatically lock and unlock. The mechanism works by locking when the axle is driven and thus trying to turn faster than the wheel, which will be the case when 4WD is engaged. It unlocks when the wheel wants to turn faster than the axle, which is the case in 2WD, where the axle is not driven.

The problem comes when you want the hubs locked and encounter a situation offroad where the unlocking mechanism is activated. A classic situation is when you're stopped in mudbog and want to reverse; as you do so the hubs will unlock then quickly lock again. It's only about a third to half a wheel revolution, but it's not good, especially if you're trying to reverse out of mud. Rocking the car backwards and forwards can break the hubs too. Another situation where an unlock can momentarily occur is cresting a hill, or descending a hill when the wheel wants to travel faster than it is being driven. For these reasons most serious offroaders use manual locking hubs which are also simpler and much more reliable.

No discussion of hubs could be complete without a reference to the Nissan Patrol, many of which feature an unusual hub that normally operates as an automatic locker, but also has the ability to work as a manually locking hub. Use the wheel brace to turn it to "lock" before going offroad.

the bang! and how to avoid it

4WD vehicles are not unbreakable. It is fairly easy to break transmission components such as CV joints, axles or gearboxes. To make sure you can drive your vehicle home:

- Avoid large throttle openings in low-range.
- Avoid sharp use of brakes and especially throttle.
- Never, ever, let the vehicle sit there, wheelspinning or bouncing up and down without going anywhere. This is a sure-fire way to break something sooner or later.

- When the front wheels are turned the CV joints are also turned and thus weaker than when in their straight-ahead position. Be even gentler on the throttle.
- Avoid reversing against any resistance. The transmission is weaker in reverse.
- Avoid reversing up a hill.
- If your vehicle has variable-height suspension, be very careful with the throttle when the suspension is in the higher modes, as again the CV joints are operating at an angle which will weaken them.
- Follow good offroad practice; correct tyre pressures, lines and track building.
- In manuals, avoid sharp movements of the clutch, for example travelling down a steep hill in neutral before engaging the clutch. You should have the clutch fully up before you start the descent.

Just because it hasn't broken now doesn't mean to say it won't break in the future. The more stress you put on a vehicle the shorter its life. One friend broke a CV joint when accelerating slightly around a bitumen corner. The damage had been done on many a track before and relatively gentle cornering manoeuvre was the straw that broke the camel's back. Not that it really helped with the arguments, but that's the way it is.

what to do it if happens

When a transmission component breaks you tend to hear a loud bang. There may be an instant oil leak, or there may not. The driver is likely to instantly notice a distinct lack of capability as the car will now be in 2WD, or even zero wheel drive. The immediate check is to get the driver to attempt to move the car. At least one wheel on both axles should be turning. If for example one of the rear wheels spins and neither front wheel moves then drive to the front has been lost, which is the most common situation. This could mean anything from a broken front driveshaft to, more likely, a broken CV joint or perhaps the front differential itself is now a bowl of oily soup and cogs. Whatever it is, it's time get the car out of there and back to safety, and that usually means a long recovery operation as the car's capability is much reduced, including its ability to safely descend hills. Mop up any oil to minimise damage to the environment.

Even though a transmission component is broken the vehicle may still be able to move. Part-time 4WDs with manual hubs are at an advantage here as they can isolate the front driveshaft, axles and diff by unlocking the hubs and putting the car in 2WD. Constant 4WD vehicles need to lock the centre diff. If you are lucky it will be a clean break and the car can be driven. If you are not lucky then something will be binding and grinding and whatever it is will need to be removed if the car is immobilised. Either way, take a tow truck home as even if the vehicle appears driveable in 2WD (front or rear), this may change and if something unfortunate happens to the transmission at speed the results will be nasty.

Vehicles with traction control may need the fuse pulling on the system as otherwise the computer will try to brake what appears to be a spinning wheel when in fact only the axle is spinning because it's no longer connected to the wheel.

Beware that pulling this fuse will probably also disable the ABS.

Another common problem is bending steering arms, but those can often be bent back with the aid of a winch. Do what you need to make it out of the bush, but no further than the nearest tow truck point. With enough people, recovery gear and ingenuity most situations can be recovered.

multiple breaks

When a transmission component breaks it puts extra stress on the rest of the vehicle. For example, a vehicle with a front locker breaking a CV joint. With an open diff the broken CV would spin and the other wheel on the axle would not be driven, but with a locker the other wheel is driven.

That's good – 3WD is better than 2WD – but it places the other CV under stress so it usually breaks too. So, stop and assess as soon as you suspect a problem. As stress is placed and removed on any part of a 4WD it slowly fatigues and eventually will fail.

A broken CV joint. This joint actually punctured the rim and caused a flat. We cable-tied the broken end out of the way and the vehicle was able to proceed in 2WD.

The photo shows both the rear wheels spinning and neither front wheel moving. If the vehicle is in 4WD, and this one was, that is impossible. Even if one rear was spinning one of the front wheels should also be rotating. As the vehicle was in 4WD, it indicated there was no drive to the front wheels and indeed this vehicle had suffered a front driveshaft failure. Any vehicle can be broken.

Maximum lock, maximum suspension flex at the front and a lot of throttle. That is a recipe for transmission stress.

CHAPTER 13

THE ENVIRONMENT

The environment is the natural landscape we enjoy exploring by 4WD. It is delicate, and all users, wheeled or otherwise, have a responsibility to take care of it.

Each driving technique will have specific pointers relevant to that technique, but there are many general considerations. One of the best is this:

Before you do something, consider whether you'd want a video of yourself doing it shown on the six o'clock TV news or to the police (in this day of YouTube, this may not be a theoretical question). If the answer is "no", then you probably shouldn't be doing it.

code of ethics

There are many ways to take care of the environment and the 4WD Victoria Code of Ethics is a good place to start:

Code	Meaning
Obey the laws and regulations for Recreational Vehicles that apply to public lands.	Do not drive where not permitted or disobey official signs. Research the area before you go, for example the state's parks service website.
Respect the cultural, heritage and environmental values of public/private land, by obeying restrictions that may apply.	Examples include permits for aboriginal land, permission to cross private land.
Respect our flora and fauna. Stop and look, but never disturb.	Take only photographs, leave only footprints and those in the right place!
Keep to formed vehicle tracks.	Only drive on legal tracks and in conditions which will not damage them.
Keep the environment clean. Carry your own, and any other, rubbish out.	Aim to leave areas as if you had not been there at all.
Keep your vehicle mechanically sound and clean to reduce the environmental impact.	Keep your vehicle maintained and legal.
Adopt minimal impact camping and driving practices.	These include re-using fireplaces, not using generators, taking up no more room than necessary and obeying fire collection laws.
Seek permission before driving on private land. Do not disturb livestock or watering points, leave gates as found.	If a gate is open, leave it so, if it is closed, leave it so. Never leave a gate open for longer than it takes a vehicle to pass through.
Take adequate water, food, fuel, basic spares and a first-aid kit on trips. In remote areas travel with another vehicle and have Royal Flying Doctor Service, or equivalent, radio contact.	Simply, be prepared. You are less likely to have a problem, and any rescuers will be a lot more sympathetic, if you were well-prepared and still got into difficulty.
Enjoy your recreation and respect the rights of others.	You may have a right to party on into the night, but that doesn't mean to say it is socially responsible at a shared campsite.
Plan ahead and lodge trip details with a responsible person.	In case you don't return on time.
Support 4WD touring as a responsible and legitimate family recreational activity. Consider joining an affiliated 4WD club.	Set an example to others and encourage them to do the right thing.

1   *My little 12" chainsaw, properly sharpened, was able to clear this large tree from the track and open up a pristine snow drive nobody else had been through since the tree fell.*

2   *There is no need to drive around this lovely High Country hut. So we haven't. Just because there are no massive concrete bollards and neon signs preventing you from doing something does not mean to say it is permitted, and even if it is permitted that doesn't mean to say it's sensible or environmentally responsible. The soft ground would mean wheelmarks left in the grass which would destroy the area's beauty.*

3   *There are different rules for parks and state forests. It is easy to use the web to find out what you can and cannot do before you go.*

Other environmental care tips:

- Always use a tree trunk protector when winching and only use appropriately sized trees, placing winch points as low as possible to reduce leverage on the tree (Chapter 36).

- Clear fallen trees from tracks whenever practical rather than driving around them.

- Bury your faeces at least 30cm deep. Do not burn toilet paper in dry conditions.

- Respect fire ban days; it's your responsibility to know when one is active and to comply with the regulations, which cover more than open fires. In any case ensure fires are well and truly out, keep them small, use existing fireplaces and have a fire extinguisher.

The bush TV is one of camping's great attractions, but fire is a powerful tool and precautions must be taken, including complying with fire bans.

other bush users

You're not alone out there, especially when you're looking for somewhere to answer a call of nature. Other people have a right to be out there too.

Being out in the bush isn't like being in the city. If you see another group, especially if it's an isolated area, stop and say g'day. Definitely stop if there's any sign of trouble, even a flat tyre. Don't assume they'll be okay, or "someone else" will stop, or you don't have any skills, kit or knowledge. At the very least you can swap knowledge of conditions.

other 4WD groups

It's good to chat and exchange information, but every group wants its own privacy, and huge (10+) convoys are difficult to manage and intimidating to others.

1. This means when the track is wet, which is still some time after the rain finishes.

2. Winching doesn't damage trees provided you use a tree trunk protector to spread the load, and a suitably large tree. If you just wrap the cable around a tree you'll ringbark the tree and may kill it, as the tree carries its life nutrients through layers under the bark. If that's not enough of a reason then you'll also kink and damage your own rope. It should also be pointed out that if you want to change the direction of a pull then use a snatch block, don't just loop the rope around a tree to change the direction of pull. I would not have thought to write this but someone on a trip once tried to do it, so it's worth mentioning.

3. Pay attention to road signs and closures.

4. This is a Management Vehicle Only track, and these are usually also open to walkers. Not all MVO tracks are marked as such on maps, and not all are gated. Always be prepared to turn around or take an alternate route if need be.

5. A convoy of 10 Discovery 3s. With that many cars I had pre-planned the trip and driven the route rather than spearing off into the unknown following the usual "that looks interesting" approach. You want to be arriving at stopping places with plenty of room – turning around that many cars after a dead-end is no fun for anyone.

trailbikers

Many forests are popular with trailbikers. There are many trails that are for motorbikes only, not 4WDs. Don't follow them. If you confront a trailbiker and the path is a little narrow, the best option is just to stop. Trailbikes are far more agile than 4WDs, they'll get around you. Trailbikers, like 4WDers, travel in packs so where you see one it usually means at least two, if not quite a few more. They can't hear you unless they kill their engine. I usually raise a few fingers to indicate how many people are in our convoy. If there are only two vehicles, be careful how you indicate that.

Trailbikers and 4WDers have a fair bit in common. Both are hated by the people who would have nothing motorised in the bush. It's also not unusual for the two groups to help each other. For example, we've provided mechanical assistance to bikers, and they have helped with our recoveries on occasion, after they finish laughing.

bushwalkers

Some bushwalkers tend not to like 4WDs. Bear this in mind. By all means offer a cheery greeting but don't be disappointed if it's not returned. Most walkers will let you by, but some get in your way intentionally. A friend of mine has had people stand in front of his vehicle and refuse to move. At that point, I'm not providing any advice in this book as to how to handle the situation, but remember you're representing yourself, the 4WD movement in general and possibly also your club, so don't bring disrepute to any of the above!

Of course, there are some very friendly bushwalkers who value a chat. They might even appreciate assistance, or a cold drink from your fridge. Many 4WDers are also bushwalkers to some extent and one friend even describes offroading as "bushwalking with wheels". Some of her friends in the local bushwalking club even agree.

horseriders

Only one point, and that's to gently drive by with minimum revs so as not to startle the horses, or otherwise just stop and let them cruise by. Switching the engine off entirely is a nice courtesy.

fauna

Australia has many fascinating animals, only one of which considers humans a food source and that is the saltwater (estuarine) crocodile. That means the threat of animal attack while travelling in Australia is very small. Nobody should consider the apparent dangers of Australian animals a reason to stay home, any more than you'd stay home because of the risk of being killed on the roads.

Native Australian animals are protected which means it is an offence to catch, kill, keep or interfere with them.

Never, ever feed any wild animal, or attempt to tame it. This is an offence and for two excellent reasons:

- Feeding animals leads them to associate humans with food, and they lose their fear of humans. Over time, animals become aggressive in their hunt for food. Emus, kangaroos and large lizards have all been known to try and forcibly take food they see, thinking it's for them. Given the size and strength of these animals that can be disastrous. They may also become entirely dependent on humans. Feeding animals rewards the most aggressive and quickest animals, whereas finding their own food rewards the smartest.

- Human food is rarely suitable for wild animals and could lead to ill health or death.

If you feed a wild animal you are slowly killing it, and your actions could well result in injury or death to other humans later on, just as surely if everyone walking over a rope bridge took a strand out of the rope as they passed.

Snake identification is notoriously difficult. Assume it's deadly. This one cruised through our campsite as we were quietly relaxing. We didn't get excited and present as a potential threat or bother it, so it didn't bother us. I took this shot while sitting in a camp chair.

Goannas aren't dangerous unless they lose their fear of humans through feeding and interaction.

CHAPTER 14

BITUMEN

A 4WD is different to a road car, so it needs different driving techniques even on the blacktop. This is especially true of vehicles modified for touring.

the terrain

Just a normal tarseal road, from the shops to the next state.

preparation and kit list

Before driving a 4WD make sure you know what parts of the 4WD system should and should not be used on-road. Some vehicles cannot be driven in 4WD on-road (Chapter 3 explains this in more detail) while others can be and often various traction aids such as differential locks should never be engaged unless in specific offroad situations. Tyre pressures are an important check as 4WD tyres are expensive and, like all vehicles, the handling can be adversely affected if they are too low.

driving techniques

The handling differences of a loaded 4WD relative to a road car are a direct result of the physical differences. Firstly you have weight. All else being equal, the 4WD will weigh more than a road car. Then you add your accessories and camping gear, which could be another 800kg or more, which means significant additional mass. The tyres are different too; a touring 4WD should have tyres designed for a mix of on-road and offroad performance. Road car tyres are optimised for roads; they will outperform offroad tyres on-road, but won't measure up on the dirt.

4WDs are taller than a road car, and while that can increase body roll there's an advantage because it improves visibility. Out the front, that's excellent, you'll have a much better view of the world from a 4WD. At the rear you'll probably see nothing as it'll be taken up by a full cargo bay. There's also the transmission and the 4WD system. You will have interesting levers to pull and buttons to press, perhaps a centre diff lock, perhaps selectable 4WD. Nothing like that in a road car. Finally there's the power, or in some cases, lack thereof. While you may have a couple of hundred kilowatts under your right foot, all that weight will blunt the performance and fuel economy.

All the differences add up to some different driving techniques to a road car. The first one is speed, as in less of it. A heavily loaded touring 4WD takes longer to stop than a stock vehicle because of the weight and the tyres. It is an excellent idea to find a deserted road and see for yourself, or better yet take the car to an advanced driving school and practice there. It is important to know whether your car is fitted with ABS (Chapter 9) or not, as the braking techniques differ significantly. With ABS vehicles, just brake as hard as you can and let the computers prevent wheel lock. With non-ABS vehicles you'll need to modulate brake pressure to prevent wheel lock. There's no easy way to tell whether a vehicle has ABS fitted, so check with a mechanic. Remember also the offroad tyres fitted will stop you much quicker on the dirt, but not as quickly on-road, especially in the wet. So the first technique is to slow down, and leave plenty of room, at least three seconds between you and the car in front, four in the wet. It's hard to begin with, but when you have it down pat you'll find driving a lot less stressful as you don't need to worry about instantly running up the car in front. Use the advantage of the truck's extra height to look well ahead and anticipate.

The extra weight and height mean more body roll around corners, so you need to slow down there too, especially with a full roof rack. While travelling straight, slow down to the speed you'll take the corner at, select the gear and drive round under gentle power. Extra weight means tyre pressures need increasing, so take advice there too; the manufacturer's recommendation is likely to be too low, especially with offroad tyres fitted.

The extra height has another consequence, and that's parking. A medium 4WD with a roof rack and aftermarket suspension is significantly higher than a standard vehicle, so bear that in mind when entering underground car parks. When parking, consider security. 4WD accessories are expensive and often not that well secured. Driving lights, winch rope and spade holders are easy to detach, so either remove them yourself or pay extra for secured parking.

Drivers with manual 4WDs should adjust their gear changing ideas. Especially compared to a small road car, 4WDs tend to have engines with more torque lower down; in other words they can pull strongly from low revs and don't appreciate being revved nearly to the redline every time. This is especially true of diesels, and in some cases you may as well upshift at a mere 2,000rpm on the flat.

The average touring 4WD has all sorts of traction aids and gears (lockers, low-range and more) which are counterproductive or dangerous to use on-road. If you drive a Pajero, Pathfinder or other vehicle that can run in 2WD or AWD on-road then flick it into AWD mode as this will improve cornering ability and reduce the chance of wheelspin. Do not drive with a centre diff engaged on high-traction surfaces like bitumen, or put part-time 4WD vehicles into 4WD, as transmission damage through windup (Chapter 3) will result. Check the owner's manual if you're not sure. However, if your vehicle has stability control make sure it's switched on whenever you're on the road.

Reversing can be difficult if you can't see out the back, so practice using the mirrors. A couple of blind-spot vision mirrors can be worth way more than the three dollars they cost, and even a reversing camera can pay for itself. Even large 4WDs are more than agile enough for tight spaces, but relative to a small car you need to plan your manoeuvre in advance. If you shuffle back and forth try not to turn the steering wheel until the car is moving, even only just, and remember you'll need very few revs to move the vehicle, unlike a car with a small petrol engine. In manuals you can often just keep your foot lightly on the brake and gently bring the clutch up to reverse. And the tighter the parking bay, the better the reason to reverse into it; it's actually easier than going in forwards, and a lot quicker and safer when you come to leave.

A diesel engine shouldn't be started like a petrol engine. It needs its plugs to warm up before it starts, and this is done when you turn the ignition key to position II. There will be a little light (see image on page 199) which will briefly illuminate. Wait for this to go out – it'll only be a second or two – and then start normally. On the subject of fuel, many 4WDs have two fuel tanks so make sure you know which one to fill and how to use fuel from the other tank. Sometimes there's a pump which transfers fuel from a subtank to the main tank – other times the engine can draw fuel from either tank. Many touring 4WDs have long-range tanks which are 140L or more, compared to around 50L for an average petrol car. Do check that you aren't putting fuel into a water tank inlet! For everyday driving there will not usually be any need to fill any auxiliary fuel tanks as they're only used for long-range touring, but you could fill one of them and then run out of fuel on a main tank if you don't know how to switch them over.

Many touring 4WDs have auxiliary lights fitted. These can be wired in a variety of ways, but mostly are set so that they can turn on and off with the main beam. Be careful, because you can really blind oncoming drivers with four or more sets of lights! Find out how yours work before nightfall.

automatic diesels

Some people who drive automatic turbodiesel 4WDs for the first time are concerned by the sluggish response to the accelerator, often noticing the delay when accelerating into a roundabout or turning right at a T-junction. The problem reported is that the vehicle takes a while to respond, and that is correct, relative to a petrol road car. Several factors contribute to the problem; the weight of the 4WD, the need for a turbodiesel to increase its revs to the point at which the turbo begins to operate, the naturally slower response of a diesel engine than a petrol engine and in some cases the automatic gearbox may be a little slow to select a gear. Sometimes all this is known as "turbo lag"

but that's not usually the case; turbo lag is when you press the accelerator quickly and the turbo takes a while to spin up. The problem is the boost threshold, or the point at which the turbo kicks in sufficiently to make a difference, usually around 1,500rpm.

The solution for dealing with the problem is to change the driver, not the car; look further ahead and anticipate traffic – skills any defensive driving course will teach. There are, however, a few tricks that will help. If you need to make a quick getaway from standstill brake the car with your left foot, bring the revs up to 1,500rpm and then release the brake while accelerating. The turbo will be instantly in its boost threshold. Another one for automatics is to use sport mode, if applicable, as the car will then select lower gears earlier, for quicker acceleration, although fuel economy may suffer. In the same vein manual control over the gearbox can help instead of leaving it in drive. The roundabout entry can be solved too; instead of braking late so that you need to go direct from brake to hard accelerator, brake earlier and approach the roundabout slower, giving you time to choose the entry without braking as hard and keep overall speeds up. Believe it or not this will actually be quicker than a late brake/hard accelerate process and is similar to how racing drivers, chauffeurs and economy experts drive their cars to maintain speed, comfort and efficiency respectively.

environment

No environment to damage, but consider other road users and the fact you are an ambassador for offroaders whenever you drive your vehicle. In particular, consider the effects of your taller vehicle on the visibility of others. If they are behind and complain, that's their problem, not yours, but when alongside you can position your vehicle so they can better see the traffic as the diagram shows.

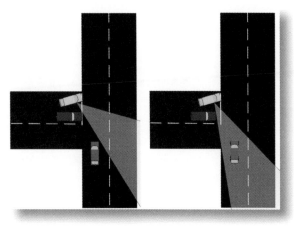

A road car driver can typically see over the bonnet of another road car, but not over the bonnet of a tall 4WD. If the 4WD drops back even a metre then it gives the road car a much better view of the traffic as this example shows.

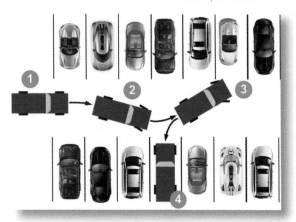

Some people are worried about manoeuvring 4WDs into car park spaces. Here's how to do it – and this technique works well with any vehicle:

1. *Roll down the centre of the car park. This is so that you give those moving out from spaces some room, and it's easier to spot free spaces from a central position.*

2. *When you spot your space, swing in towards it. Take a good look into it to make sure it's clear, and if there are any obstacles you might hit when you reverse.*

3. *Swing out from the space, so the vehicle is angled, ready for the next step. That's the trick in making it easy.*

4. *Reverse into the space. If the space is wide enough to accept your vehicle, then aim to just miss with the inside (driver's side in this case) wheel and the outside part of the car will take care of itself.*

Reversing vehicles are the highest cause of accidents. It is safer to reverse into a spot because you'll be doing so seconds after you've seen it's clear, and there'll be nothing to hit. If you try and reverse out it'll be much longer between when you've checked behind and when you move. Also, reversing in means you can get into tighter spaces with less back-and-forth manoeuvring than if you tried to drive in forwards. A couple of other tips; on flat ground you don't need any revs with a manual, just gently bring the clutch up to move and cover the brake with your right foot. With an auto same sort of deal, no need for extra revs, just foot off brake and the car will move. And in general don't turn the steering wheel when stationary as it stresses the steering system.

completion

Driving a heavily loaded 4WD can be a daunting task, and while this chapter gives some pointers it is no substitute for experience. There are many offroad 4WD courses, but few on-road 4WD courses, so look for an advanced low-risk course and take your 4WD, loaded to the hilt on it, so you build confidence.

This means a constant 4WD's centre diff is locked. In general, the presence of any such icon means offroad systems are engaged, and using offroad systems on the road is not good for the vehicles and can be dangerous.

4WDs, with a high centre of gravity and long-travel suspension tend to have more body roll than road cars. They need to be gently eased into corners, not thrown in with abrupt steering movements. It also helps to ease smoothly off the brakes as you begin entering the corner and winding on steering lock so you're off the brakes before the tightest part of the corner.

Blind-spot mirrors are especially handy, because your mirrors will be higher than a road car's bonnet.

A standard five-speed gearshift with a small transfer case lever below. You won't need the crawler gears on bitumen.

The 4WD won't handle the bends like a road car, so drive it slower. You can see in this photo how much better visibility the 4WD has over the road car due to the higher driving position.

When loaded, you can't see anything out the back of a 4WD.

When starting a diesel 4WD, turn the ignition key to position II, wait for this light to go out, then start the engine.

1   Unloaded softroaders handle just as well as road cars, and sometimes better given their all-wheel-drive grip, especially on lower-traction surfaces.

2   Different vehicles, different driving styles.

3   Offroad tyres are far tougher than road tyres, grip much better on dirt roads but are noisier and less grippy than road tyres on the bitumen, and less again in the wet.

4   A LC200 with a lift, mud tyres and lots of accessories. This vehicle has quite different handling characteristics to a road car, but is a powerful diesel automatic so doesn't lack power and its AWD grip means it is easy to drive. But just because it can accelerate quickly doesn't mean to say it can manoeuvre as well or stop as quickly as a roadcar.

CHAPTER 15

DIRT ROADS

There is a saying in nautical circles, born of painful experience. "The sea is not inherently dangerous, it is just terribly unforgiving of carelessness." You can say the same about dirt road driving.

the terrain

Compared to tarseal, dirt is looser and softer. Importantly, it can change nature in a matter of metres. There could be loose gravelly sections, dust, mud, corrugations or a surface so smooth and hard you can squeal tyres on it.

preparation and kit list

The softer and looser surface means traction is less than on the bitumen, which means special tyres are preferred. The best are all-terrain or mud tyres which grip the dirt significantly better than the road-pattern tyres seen on showroom 4WDs. Because dirt is soft and loose, let a little air out of the tyres – say 20% down from manufacturer's recommended. This increases the tyre's contact patch, which is good for grip on loose surfaces, and the softer tyre is more able to absorb the little irregularities in the road, bouncing less, which further increases grip and improves ride comfort. Lower pressures also reduce the chance of punctures, and as the tyres are softer you must drive slower which again improves safety and further reduces puncture risk. However, sometimes the dirt roads are so hard and well graded you can drive almost at highway speeds, so pressures shouldn't be reduced if you're not going to slow down.

Other preparation includes making sure the washer bottle is full as things get dusty, and knowing how the 4WD system works. Take sunglasses as whiter roads can produce eye-damaging glare. If you have it, always engage stability control. Secure everything in and outside the vehicle as you really don't want anything moving around, if for no other reason than it is a driver distraction.

Part-time 4WDs should engage 4WD for dirt roads to reduce wheelspin and improve handling; unlike bitumen roads, dirt roads don't present a risk of transmission windup. AWDs don't need to lock centre diffs unless it gets particularly chopped up or slippery. Refer to the section on brake bias in Chapter 8 for a technical explanation of the effects of locking the centre diff or engaging 4WD on a dirt road.

driving techniques

Most drivers cruise around with one hand on the wheel. This is bad practice in any case but potentially fatal on dirt roads. Both hands should be on the wheel, both eyes on the road. You have to be ready to react instantly, because dirt roads are unpredictable. You could drive from Sydney to Melbourne and never worry about any change in the road surface, but the dirt will lull you into a false sense of security with a nice long smooth patch, only to hit a washout or rock that caught you unawares, leading at the very least to a nasty jolt, at worst a crash.

So for safety slow down, which ties in nicely with dropping a bit of air out the tyres, as the lower the pressures you run the slower you must drive. You also need to learn to do something you don't do on bitumen, which is to vary your speed to the conditions. On the tarseal, if it says 80, that's generally the speed you drive at. On the dirt, the safe speed could vary from 10 to 100 and back again, with no signs to tell you. As the terrain varies, so must your speed. Bulldust, corrugations, blind corners mean slowing; straight, dry, smooth patches mean you can speed up.

Sooner or later you'll make a mistake and find some huge pothole coming up out of apparently nowhere. Don't swerve sharply to avoid it. If you go straight over it there may be one hell of a thud, but you're less likely to roll or lose control than if you swerve. Secondly, brake hard but get off the brakes just before the problem. If you brake hard into a hole you'll enter it with the suspension already compressed so the hit will be worse. Your wheels may well lock and control could be lost. Thirdly, this is when you're happy everything is tied down and you've already got two hands on the wheel. Still, it can all go wrong and that's where you need the skid recovery techniques described in Chapter 12.

If you need to brake on a dirt road then how you do it depends on whether you have ABS or not. With ABS (Chapter 9) just slam the brakes on as hard as you can. You may feel a pulse through the pedals and hear noises, but that's just the system working. You may also feel the brakes aren't working, which is a limitation of some ABS systems on some loose surfaces, but keep the pedal pressed hard. Steer if you need to, but gently, remembering that when you steer you are using some traction for steering so less is available for braking, thus you take longer to stop.

If you are driving a car without ABS then if you stamp on the brakes you are likely to lock at the least the front, possibly all four wheels. This may well be the quickest way to stop the car as the wheels dig in, but it will not be the safest as when a wheel locks steering is lost. That means any slight sideways movement – common under braking especially on cambered roads – cannot be corrected and could lead to a sideways skid which quickly leads to a roll. The correct technique is to brake progressively, building up to hard, and quickly, briefly, release the pressure if a wheel locks. This takes a lot of practice to get right but is well worth the effort.

Animal strike is an ever-present possibility. Small ones like snakes aren't going to damage the car, but please don't aim for them. Don't avoid them either, they'll often just double back at the last second. Just brake and drive straight, and that applies to larger animals like roos and cows too. It's never nice to hit any animal, but put it this way; if you swerve to avoid an animal you may well hit it anyway but with your roof.

Flying stones from oncoming vehicles can crack a windscreen, but that's easy to avoid. The oncoming car will flick the stone up, but how hard it hits your vehicle is dependent on how fast you are going, not the other car. So, if you slow down to 30km/h, the chances of damage are much smaller than at 80km/h. Slowing down as you pass other cars on dirt roads is a good safety idea anyway, and in some cases where the road is narrow it is required. If that's the case then slow down and put two wheels on the verge (in that order) well before you pass the other car. If the other car is a roadtrain then stop entirely and pull well out of the way, leave the engine running, windows up.

Dust is a major problem on dirt roads. When a vehicle is oncoming and kicking up a big dust storm you must slow down, because you'll effectively be blinded for seconds to a minute as it passes you. Put the air conditioning on recirculation, crank up the fan speed to minimise dust ingress, and keep headlights on low beam.

When following someone you need to have clear visibility of least two to three times your stopping distance behind them; in other words, about a four-second gap. You never know when they'll slow down or hit a much dustier patch. Inexperienced drivers almost always drive far too close. If the road's that bad you're not likely to be left behind at the lights, and at 70km/h you could be as much as one kilometre behind, but less than 60 seconds in time. Dust can often herald the approach of an oncoming vehicle, but don't assume that no dust means no vehicle. They could be just pulling away from a halt. Driving with low beam on means you are far, far more easily seen.

On dirt roads there are no dividing lines, so you pick your own route. The surface will not be consistent across the width of the road; there may be parts with fine-grained gravel or with little loose material. Keep your wheels out of the loose stuff, which is usually achieved by following existing tyre marks. Bear in mind that if you need to move out of those tyre tracks then traction will be suddenly reduced – hopefully only suddenly and not dramatically.

The lack of dividing lines also means that others may be where you don't expect them. On some wide, long roads you may drive on the wrong side if there is visibility. Many drivers do not consider oncoming traffic and drift too far over to the wrong side. They also may not consider crests. So, you have to. That often means moving your vehicle away from the best part of the surface so as to reduce the chance of collision. If you aren't in the best surface then you need to reduce speed. Once you see the way is clear then you can accelerate again.

This constant variation in speed, to account for hazards, oncoming vehicles and generally react to the changing surface, is probably the hardest thing for road drivers to get used to; they generally drive at the one speed unless there's a sharp corner or limit change. On dirt roads, you must use your intelligence to determine the safe limit which varies from moment to moment. A tip – it is easier to reduce acceleration coming out of a corner than to try and increase braking going into it, so err on the side of caution when braking.

Corrugations are unpleasant for occupants, and wreck vehicles. You can drive so fast you fly over the top of them, but good luck trying to brake or control your car at that speed. Best to drop pressures further and drive at a speed that still gives you control over steering and braking.

Gear choices are a little different on dirt roads too. In general, use lower gears; where you may have changed to fifth, leave it in fourth. On descents use the gears to slow the car, fourth, third, even as low as first on steep hills. This applies to automatics too. The reason for the use of lower gears is because the lower the gear you are in when you begin braking, the quicker you'll stop and the less likelihood there is of a skid.

1   Crests are dangerous. This driver will need to slow down and move off the best line over the top, just in case.

2   Dirt roads change continually. Here is a marked change shown by different surface colours. What that change means for the driver is probably unknown unless you've seen that change just before, but in any case be alert.

3   A little water masked a fairly deep hole. This car coped, because it had good tyres and suspension, the driver was alert, in the right gear and holding the steering wheel correctly. Going slower in the first place would have been a good idea as the stream could be (and clearly was) masking a pothole, but this photo was specifically set up for demonstration after we crossed it first time and I thought it would be ideal for illustrating this point.

4   Know which roads are open and which are not. Some are formally closed and open, others are merely marked "Dry Weather Only". Unlike bitumen roads, the condition of dirt roads cannot be guaranteed. Even when they are open travel times can vary. For example, one April I made four trips up and down half of the Peninsula Development Road in Cape York. The last one was much quicker than the first as there were far fewer water crossings and the road crews had graded much of the road. The fact that I knew the road better made little difference as it is always best to drive without assuming you know what's around the corner.

5   Another little stream; but what's underneath it? What we do know is there's an oncoming car, mainly visible by its headlights.

1-2 If you hit this rock at speed expect at least a puncture if not worse. The driver has noticed the rock and decided to straddle it, even with the trailer around the corner. Swerving to one side or the other is generally more dangerous than a straight-on approach. Of course, the slower you go, the less of a problem there is with such unexpected hazards. This is not the sort of thing you see on a bitumen road, but on dirt it's a matter of when, not if. While the rock was already there when we stopped for the photo, we did move it after we'd finished.

3 Clearly visible are the existing wheel tracks, which have much less gravel in them. Keep to these tracks. Moving out onto the "marbles" (tiny pebbles on hard dirt roads) will be like trying to ice skate in shoes.

4 In a few seconds we will be blinded by dust so we have to slow down, especially as we're likely to move to the centre over the water crossing. Low beam would help too. Imagine if you were following close behind – you'd have no idea what was in front.

environment

Many dirt roads are dry weather only, which means you shouldn't use them when you'll make ruts. That also means not driving on them immediately after heavy rain. There are heavy fines for doing so.

completion

When back on the tarseal, air up and pay attention to your car; handling problems or odd noises may have been masked by the rough, noisy dirt roads. Finally, if there's one thing to take away from this chapter it is this – don't take dirt roads for granted. They will bite you. That's not a "maybe", that's a "definitely".

The sure grip of AWD (or engaged 4WD for part-timers) pays dividends around corners.

Dust can hang in the air and obscure the road for quite a distance behind the original vehicle.

No divider lines, so be wary of oncoming traffic – if you have to move off line you're also likely to lose traction.

Slow down to avoid wildlife but only at a safe and controllable rate of deceleration. Never swerve to avoid animals. Kangaroos are most active at dawn and dusk so avoid travelling around these times if possible.

You don't need a sign to tell you the surface is loose.

Another view of the differing traction across a road surface. The area most travelled has the least loose stones and the most grip, as well as the least chance of punctures. Unfortunately, oncoming traffic may like that line, too, and there's a corner coming up.

Twisty, steep roads need 4WD for best traction. The Discoverys are constant 4WD so that's taken care of, but the drivers are using low gears to assist with braking and control around the corners. Automatics can be slow to select the right gear going uphill in these conditions so selecting Sport or a manumatic (Chapter 4) mode can help. These vehicles have advanced ABS which is much better than older systems on dirt.

A pre-cleaner on a snorkel definitely collects a lot of dirt which would otherwise make its way through to filter, so the less work the filter has to do the better. We didn't notice any adverse effects on performance or economy but some drivers do.

The wind is helpfully blowing the dust away from the road, but if the road bends to the left it'll blow it straight back at us.

A daily clean of the air filter by removing it and giving it a tap or blow with compressed air is a good idea for engine longevity and performance.

This bend shows the camber of the road – the slope towards the inside of the bend. This camber greatly contributed to keeping the vehicle on the road. If we moved out to the left onto the flat or even worse onto the negative camber then a slide would be the result. Also, the area of hard dirt with few fine stones is much less defined around a corner as the four wheels take different paths. You will also often find corrugations on the bends, as this is where vehicles shift weight, brake and accelerate. All these are reasons to treat dirt road corners with more respect than those you find on bitumen.

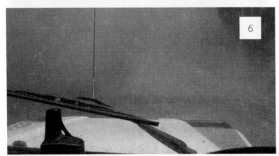

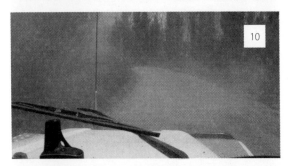

A dusty road in the High Country. We saw an oncoming vehicle and, as it was clearly very dusty, stopped.

The first shot is just as the vehicle passed us. There is no safe way to be driving through that.

The second shot was taken six seconds later – hazy but still not safe.

The third is after 10 seconds, and the fourth after 12 seconds: safe to proceed.

Tips; stop if you see a massive dust cloud coming towards you, and if you're following another vehicle, keep a safe distance behind their dust cloud rather than their vehicle. Expect the dust cloud distance to change as conditions change; state of the road, sidewinds and speed.

Dirt road driving is not for the inattentive – which is why it's so much fun.

Be careful accelerating out of dirt-road corners at low speeds in 2WD. Running part-time 4WD vehicles in 4WD reduces the chances of oversteer, and means you can accelerate quicker. Any acceleration tends to push the car wider, so accelerate only as you are unwinding lock and do so smoothly.

CHAPTER 16

MUD

Many touring offroaders hate mud, others do nothing else but drive in it. Sooner or later you'll need to try it.

the terrain

Mud, mud, glorious mud. Nothing quite like it for getting stuck. Mud comes in a huge variety of flavours from thin, slippery clay to thick, sticky peat and everything in between, sometimes in the space of a few metres. But all of it is low traction, some very low, and it's all soft. If you had to break it down into just two types it would be these:

- **Shallow mud:** where the terrain is simply muddy all over, but no or little standing water and there is a relatively hard surface underneath so the vehicle does not run out of clearance.
- **Deep mudbogs:** holes with mud and water in them where vehicle may sink in and lose clearance.

preparation and kit list

Lower tyre pressures to around 40-60% of the manufacturer's recommendations to increase the contact patch, maximise traction and reduce rolling resistance. It is a myth that high pressures "cut through" down to good traction, and even if they did the increase in rolling resistance would cancel out any traction gain. Expect to get dirty, and have your recovery gear handy. If you have a set of mud tyres, use them; open treads are far superior in the mud. Many roads are closed when wet, so be aware of those.

Lock centre diffs and disable stability control as in this low-speed situation where you're sliding around it will not help – instead it will hinder you when it wrongly thinks you are about to crash, and even if you are about to crash stability control is unlikely to be any help at low-range speeds. Front and rear lockers could well be useful, but generally only use them in a straight line so turning is easier. Also, given the choice between cross-axle lockers and traction control it is usually better to choose the latter as it permits more directional control.

Most people find putting the windows up a good idea, and make sure the windscreen washer bottle is full.

Snatching and winching are often done in mud driving recoveries. Take bags for muddy equipment and water for washing hands and the like.

If you know it's going to be muddy, then prepare the interior of the vehicle. Thick, rubber mud mats with raised sides are a great investment. Low tyre pressures work really well, so a compressor is very useful. A tarp for the deeper mudbogs is a good idea too. A winch, several snatch straps and a joiner rope may be handy, and make sure people know where your recovery points are. These may be under muddy water when you need to get to them and there tends not be a surfeit of volunteers to do some underwater exploration.

driving techniques

shallow mud

For thin mud on the flat or downhill which is slippery but in which you aren't sinking, the key to success is finessing the car with a delicate touch and planning ahead to pick ruts and lines, as last-minute direction changes are difficult. Use the highest gear you can and the minimum revs, in either high- or low-range. This is to avoid wheelspin, because when the wheels spin they lose traction. Use the engine to slow down rather than the brakes, and be very gentle with the steering – steer under slight power, never braking. A light sprinkling of rain can have a surprising effect on grip, for example if you've driven in, had lunch and seen rain you can expect a different drive on the way out.

If there are ruts, use them – they act as very effective tramlines. If the ruts are too deep to use you'll either need to build a track with rocks to make up the clearance, or straddle the rut, which is high-risk as you may slide in, possibly getting yourself cross-rutted with a front wheel and a diagonal rear in the same rut. Building tracks with wood can work but muddy wood has little traction – for that reason you should also steer clear of tree roots. Rocks are best.

If the vehicle's rear end slides out; look well ahead in the direction you wish to go, turn the steering wheel in that direction, accelerate slightly and do not brake. In all offroad driving it is very important to know where your wheels are pointing, especially with mud. It is very easy to wind on lock, not have the car respond for a while and then suddenly turn when it regains traction. Watch for this, particularly when following ruts.

Going uphill will often require momentum, lots of power and could result in wheelspin. The risk is if you do not make it you will just slide back down the hill; very risky, so consider winching or

an alternate path. If you do try, use a high gear, probably third low or even fourth, and don't let off the throttle. The "fatal hesitation" is the single biggest cause of people coming to grief in the mud. There are times for utter commitment and a slippery climb is one of them.

deep mudbogs

A mudbog is usually relatively small, perhaps a few metres long, but could be many car lengths, and some are as deep as they are long! It'll be covered with water, and you need to get across. First off, we need to review the dangers. Water is not a good idea to immerse your vehicle in, and mud is even worse as the dirt particles are ground into your precious mechanical components. A deep mudbath may see you replacing alternators, starter motors and more. Believe me, I've been there and done that. Quote from a friend who drove his 100 Series into a deep mudbog (following me, I must admit), after we extracted him; "My dashboard is lit up like a Christmas tree!" Obviously you'll try to drive it, but if you don't then recovery needs to be quick and decisive.

As per the general principle, stop the vehicle a few metres away from the bog entrance, not right at the start. Switch the engine off, which allows everything to cool. That way the vehicle won't be quite so hot when it meets the cold water. When the vehicle is hot, gaps open as metal expands, and water can get in the gaps. Moreover, the hotter the vehicle the greater the stress when it is suddenly cooled.

Track forensics again. Study the entry and exit lines. If the entry is steep, then the entry speed will need to be gentle. If the exit is steep, it is possible you may not be able to climb out. Even if the exit is not very steep, it may have tree roots or other axle-twisters in the way. Remember that the vehicle will have its tyres full of mud, so traction will be much reduced, and it'll be struggling through water, too.

Probably the most important part of the inspection is the actual bog itself. Find a long stick and poke the bottom of the bog. You're looking for two things; how deep it is and how firm the base. Where you poke is also important. Ideally, you should poke all the way along the proposed route, on both wheel tracks, and in the middle to see if there is any possibility of bottoming out, which is when the vehicle comes to an ignominious halt, resting on its belly instead of the wheels. Checking all these aspects isn't always possible, but at the very least check both sides of the track because it is very often the case that one side of the bog is deeper than the other.

Experience will tell you whether you are likely to get through or not. Unfortunately, experience is only gained by trying it or persuading someone else to have a go. Every vehicle and driver is different, but generally speaking the limiting factor tends to be the state of the bottom. If your stick hits the bottom and you can continue pushing and pushing, chances are your vehicle will just sink. The water level is less of a problem. Given a firm base, most 4WDs can manage over-bonnet water quite easily, provided they don't stop and the engine doesn't ingest any liquid.

So you have decided to give it a go. Remember that mudbogs are essentially a risk. Because you aren't going to spend hours creating a 3D map of the thing with sonar, even the most diligent

stick-pokers may miss a crucial hump under the water which will bring them to a halt, which is why recovery preparation is important (see Chapter 32).

If you drive into a mudbog and get stuck, your mates will be too busy photographing you and laughing to launch a recovery. Even if they do get their act into gear it'll be a while before you're recovered, and all this time you're sitting there, slowly sinking, and muddy water is finding its way into your nice clean vehicle. Not pleasant, I can assure you.

Preparing to drive the bog

1. Set up a snatch strap, or other recovery device. If you're first through, attach the strap to the rear recovery point, put the rest in through a window (NOT the door!) and get a passenger to hold it. Pull the strap tight so it doesn't interfere with anything. That way if you get stuck all you need do is throw the strap out of the window, and it's already attached. Nobody needs to wade into the mud (try finding a volunteer for that) to try and work out where your recovery point is, which is now probably underwater.

2. Designate a recovery vehicle and driver. Make sure they get into an appropriate position after you go for it.

3. Designate a recovery controller, someone to take the snatch strap from you or your passenger, connect it to the recovery vehicle and control the recovery. Make sure the recovery controller knows where and how to attach the strap to the recovery vehicle. Mistakes are often made in the heat of the moment.

4. Agree a method for calling for a recovery. A blast on the horn, use of the CB, or when the only part of the vehicle that can be seen is the snorkel.

If you do all of that, then if you do get stuck you'll be spending the minimum of time possible in the goo. And that's a good thing.

Other preparation points

1. As per water crossings, a tarp may be appropriate (Chapter 21).

2. Spray the engine with WD-40 or similar.

3. Put the windows up.

Trying to skirt around the outside of a mudbog doesn't often work as the resulting momentum loss because of the turn does more to stop you than the deeper mud if you ploughed straight through. The uphill wheels have less weight on them than the downhills, and so are far more likely to spin. People have rolled their cars trying this before now, and you are also likely to slip into the ruts anyway. Never say never, but the technique is certainly not an automatically great way to drive deep bogs.

driving the mudbog

Of course, you're not going to get stuck if you have properly assessed the bog and are driving it correctly.

The correct driving technique is dictated by the terrain. Mudbogs involve water and mud, both of which cause a lot of driving resistance. Therefore, idling through in a high gear isn't an option. Reasonably high revs are needed. The best gear varies, but second low or first high is pretty good.

The way to do it is to enter firmly but not too quick. As the resistance builds up smoothly increase the power to match. Do not change gear, as momentum will be lost. Do not make sudden throttle movements. If the vehicle slows, gently increase power, and whip the steering wheel from side to side by about a ¼ turn each way as this lets the tyre lugs bite into the side of the track, and changes the relative difficulty of the diff turning each wheel, so one wheel is less likely to end up spinning madly because the diff has decided that's the one easiest to turn. For that reason this technique is less effective with traction control and lockers, but it can still work. Don't overdo it to the stage where you're rocking the vehicle so much you're losing momentum that way.

Consider also driving through the brakes (Chapter 12) but if you do, be very gentle with the brakes because stamping on the brakes with the wheels spinning fast will shockload the transmission, and that's not good. If you have either traction control or lockers don't bother with that technique as either will do a better job of torque distribution than you can by adding some braking.

Whatever you do, as long as the vehicle is moving forwards, do not give up, do not get off the throttle. Hang in there.

If you get out the other side, do remember to slack off the throttle as you come out, and ensure the steering wheel is straight. You don't want to ruin a good mudbog drive by spearing off the track at high speed.

If it all goes wrong and you come to a halt, do NOT attempt to go any further. Once stopped, you are going backwards. And that's what you have to do, immediately. Whip it into reverse and drive backwards, but don't do a Grand Prix getaway. Your only hope is to gently bring the power on. Increase rpm to a high level by all means, but if you drop the clutch and floor it you have a good chance of staying where you are as the vehicle simply digs a hole.

This is where high-range is an advantage, because low-range is likely to be too low for the mudbog.

Wheel waving and overdriving the brakes work in reverse, too, so try them.

If you do manage to go backwards, you can have another go forwards but this is not usually successful and is only likely to provide more photographic opportunities.

Don't spend a lot of time revving around in the bog trying to get further in or out. Generally speaking, if you didn't get through first time you won't get through without another clear go from the beginning. Spending time in the bog will only rip it up, making subsequent attempts harder, and you're increasing the risk of mud damaging the vehicles components.

summary

1. Stop a few metres back, switch the engine off.

2. Inspect entry and exit lines.

3. Poke a stick in several places to ascertain depth of water and the state of the bottom.

4. Prepare your snatch strap, recovery driver and controller.

5. Drive it, don't be afraid to use the right pedal, remember wheel-waving.

6. As long as you're moving, no matter how slow, don't give up hope.

7. Abandon hope as soon as you stop moving and get out immediately.

As you exit the bog, smile thankfully and reduce revs before you shoot off into the undergrowth. Left-foot-brake to clean your brakes as they may be ineffective.

environment

Don't drive around mudbogs, drive through them, if indeed you need to drive them at all. If a track will be damaged because it's too wet then don't use it.

completion

Thoroughly clean the vehicle underneath as mud bakes on and corrodes. Mud on rims will throw wheels out of balance. Clean mirrors and lights, check brakes. If tyres fail to keep pressure, break the bead and check to see if debris has got between the bead and the rim. Make sure the radiator isn't blocked with mud as this leads to overheating; use CT-18 and a high-pressure wash to clean, it's a dirty job.

1   *If you are going to drive these bogs, assume you will not make it. My passenger is not impressed.*

2   *Mud often requires a fair bit of power and momentum. Don't stop till you're through!*

3   *A Hummer with tyres full of sticky, sticky mud although neither clearance nor axle flex is a problem. When that happens there is very little grip available. Mud tyres would be much better, but even they can get filled. The solution is to drive very gently and carefully, and where possible give the wheels a spin to try and clear them. Lower pressures are a definite bonus in these situations.*

4   *This is tricky mud driving. The mud is shallow, but very slippery and with undulations so the weight is not constant on each wheel. The keys to success here are good anticipation, using the contours to slide the vehicle, being very gentle with the controls, and on occasion a little judicious momentum to get up and over. The ute is shown about to descend slightly; the driver should not attempt to brake while doing this as the wheels would only lock, but simply accept the descent and slip at whatever speed the car ends up at.*

Clean your recovery gear, especially straps, as mud works into the fibre and weakens it. Winches may require lube, as will the car, because mud works its way in everywhere. Many experienced offroaders hate mud with a passion, as while it is great fun it can result in some very expensive maintenance bills and nobody enjoys the subsequent cleaning process.

If you spend time sunk in a deep boghole, this is what your car will look like.

Not treading lightly. There is absolutely no need to drive this fast through mud unless you are in a competition.

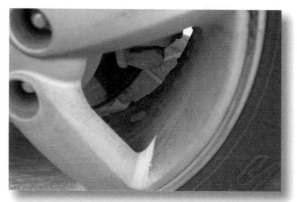

After you finish mud driving you may well find mud has stuck to the inside of the rim. This will throw it off balance, and you'll notice a vibration, usually above 60km/h. Before you panic, clean the wheels and the rest of the vehicle whilst you're at it.

1   First vehicle through. A thorough examination followed by a committed drive in second low. Note the winch controller is already fitted, and though out of sight there is a tree trunk protector waiting around a tree just in case. The entry is steep so you can't rush in. The technique is to enter slowly and then as soon as the car starts to level out smoothly apply the power and keep it going! The Discovery ended up winching out of the hole, but this was anticipated by the driver who organised his recovery crew across the other side, ready to leap into action.

2   Too much momentum and the Pajero jumped out of the ruts.

3   A shallow downhill, but wet and slippery. First low, finesse the controls, low tyre pressure, lots of forward thinking and worst case – if I slip off where am I going to end up and how shall I recover? Don't assume you will be able to stop the car part-way down, even on a gentle slope.

Get in the ruts carefully and early. Use first low and don't brake. You can see a gouge mark made by someone's diff on entry, a useful indication of conditions.

Slippery uphills need power, momentum, commitment and confidence to control the inevitable sideways actions without easing off on the accelerator. Aim for the line that least robs you of momentum, i.e. the smoothest way up.

Mud tyres are so named because they do well in mud; despite the stickiness, the STTs aren't quite jammed up. A 20psi pressure greatly aids traction.

A covering of mud over a hard surface. Maybe no clear tracks through the mud. Expect slides, correct but don't overcorrect, and always steady momentum. Watch for the deep ones!

1   Slippery mud with wheels in the air. Good car control is essential – smooth but quick inputs, coordinated throttle and steering.

2   Find a stick and work out if it's driveable. It's time well invested.

3   Very slippery mud, with running water in a rut. All you can do here is use the ruts to tramline and go where they go. Before descending, make sure you don't need to back up as it'll be difficult.

4   A snatch strap is on as this is the second car through, and this owner has sensibly opted for a tarp. The strap is either held by a passenger, or passed in through the window and the window closed to keep it in place. The amount of water displaced means there is significant resistance to the vehicle and that, combined with a soft bottom and the turn, means power is required. Second low in this case and some revs, and a lot of commitment.

5   You can never tell what lies underneath muddy water. Here our D3 leans a little to one side exiting some ruts. The driver has kept her steering wheel straight as she has both hands on it with a firm grip, and not altered the throttle. No problem in this case, but you don't want to be sliding off the track and colliding with trees like the one on the left.

6   The ascent will be made harder by the newly muddied tyres. Momentum must be gathered before the climb.

1   Mud is very hard on vehicles. My old Pajero had a low-mounted alternator that was prone to filling with mud. I kept a reconditioned unit as a spare and swapped it in when required. At the same time the radiator was removed, CT-18 truckwash applied (a very effective mud cleaning agent) and then hosed off.

2   Use ruts where you can, and steer with them, never against them. Again, steady momentum and third low with the D3's torquey diesel. There is a significant side angle, but because the driver had checked it out before he entered this was not a surprise. The D3 is in Mud/Ruts mode, raised suspension and the stability control is off as it would otherwise surely intervene in these slippery conditions.

3   Stability control off, 4WD lock on, first gear, following the ruts with steady momentum. Softies do well in the mud as long as they don't bottom out.

CHAPTER 17

ROCKS

Perhaps the most technically challenging terrain, rocks are a favourite of many because you don't need to clean the car afterwards – just maybe repair it!

the terrain

Rocky terrain varies from pebble-sized stones to boulders to loose shale to huge expanses of smooth, slick rock.

Rocks can be bare, or covered with loose material, mud or water. Tyre grip is not normally an issue on bare rocks – the bigger problems are clearance and articulation, as traction will be lost if a wheel is in the air or has little weight on it.

Clearance is a problem if you run out of angles, usually ramp angle but often approach or departure too. Finding the limits of clearance means you are likely to be stuck, lose momentum and possibly damage the sills or other parts of your vehicle. Rocks are hard and unforgiving. Hit a rock at speed, even low speed, and put it this way – in the ongoing war of attrition between rocks and 4WDs the rocks are well ahead.

preparation and kit list

Lower tyre pressures to around 40-60% of the vehicle manufacturer's recommended to increase the contact patch (assuming you have tyres of approximately standard size) to maximise traction and articulation. There is a school of thought that tyre pressures should be kept high to minimise problems with the tyre bagging out and puncturing on rocks. That's just wrong – see

Chapter 7 for why. Lower them so you bounce around less and they mould to the shape of the rock.

Rocks can bend things, so alloy sidesteps need to come off and steel ones on. Open tyre treads do better than closed ones. A winch is useful, as is a jacking system in case you get hung up. Rocks are also the terrain where cross-axle differential locks make the biggest difference. Expect scrapes, so fit decent bash plates. The most useful accessory is one, repeat one, mate who knows what they're doing who can spot you (Chapter 12), acting as a guide outside the vehicle with radio or pre-arranged hand signals.

driving techniques

More than any other surface, rocks are all about slow control and planning your line. Essentially, you are trying to do three things. In order; have only the tyres touching the rocks, as many tyres as possible in contact with the ground, and the vehicle level. A skilled rock driver can make a tough track look easy by just cruising up on the right line; less skilled drivers in more capable cars could end up needing to winch. However, sometimes one or more of those three objectives need to be compromised, for example you may opt to take a line that lifts wheels in the air as it will set you up better slightly further ahead. And rock driving does require careful thinking ahead. You are constantly thinking of a 3D model of where the car's wheels and sills will be, and planning what to do. You can stack the odds in your favour sometimes by some moving of rocks to build the track, or taking some large loose ones out of the way, but don't throw them downhill! With rocks you can often get out and review the situation, then continue.

As ever: as slow as possible, as fast as necessary, as Land Rover instructors like to say. Usually that means pretty slowly, but if the wheels need to clamber over largish rocks, then the engine needs to be developing some decent torque. That's where very low gears come in, and why specialist rock crawlers have crawl ratios (Chapter 4) of 1:100, as opposed to a normal 4WD's 1:35 to 1:45. Automatics are better than manuals as they can go infinitely slowly, although automatics are not a substitute for low gears. The faster you go, the more you'll bounce around and the less traction you'll have.

Don't change gear in the middle of a particularly tricky section. No matter how fast you do it, you'll lose valuable momentum and stress the drivetrain. Automatics should be fixed in single gear, as should manuals, and if you need to change pick an area where the car is not under stress.

Don't be afraid to get a wheel right up on top of a rock. In this way the rest of the car is raised up, and often that's just what you want, rather than trying to straddle a rock. But do make sure the rock in question is solid and won't move as your wheel rides up on it. Many a vehicle (and person) has been damaged by a wheel flicking a large rock backwards. Don't necessarily be afraid of side angles either; crawling on your side may be preferable to a mighty leap straight forwards.

Low-range is what you want for rocks and all your lockers should be in. Automatic drivers can hold the car on the brakes with their left foot and edge forward by increasing the accelerator; this gives

great speed control once mastered. Keep a firm hold on the steering wheel, thumbs out, as the rocks will try to steer the car for you, and lean forwards for best visibility.

In general for rocks the speed should be slow but steady. You will need to vary the throttle constantly as the car goes up and over rocks – ease on the power just before you need it, not as the car starts to struggle – but try not to stop. If you do stop, back up as far as you can without going back into the previous problem (that's where your mate comes in), and retry.

Sometimes you cannot proceed unless you do use a bit of momentum. Again, back up and give it a shot, but beware that higher speed means that the suspension will compress and your clearances will decrease. Chances are when you do use a bit of speed one or more wheels will be in the air, spinning madly as they leave the ground. If they are still under power when they return to earth they generate a shockload through the transmission, which could easily break something. So select the highest gear you can, minimum power and back off as soon as you're through. In general, anything more than brief and intermittent wheelspin on rocks is to be avoided as it probably means you won't make it, but break it. Lockers avoid this, but create their own problem; all the torque could be going on just the one wheel in a twin-locked vehicle, and that's a lot of stress on that axle. If you use lockers, go slow or not at all.

It is possible to drive many rocky sections by placing one's brain in neutral and one's foot to the floor. That is success, in the same way using a machine gun as a target rifle is success. Even if the car doesn't break, it will be weakened for next time, to say nothing of the danger to others and damage to the track.

If you fail to proceed, work out why. It could well be you've managed to get hung up on a rock – which could weigh several tons and isn't about to move – so the car literally needs to be jacked up over it, or winched sideways.

Rocky terrain is definitely a problem for vehicles without low-range. This is because these vehicles simply move too quickly in first gear. Imagine driving up a series of kerbs with the clutch fully up. As the speed is high, the stress placed on the vehicle (and occupants!) is greater. In addition, the wheels begin to bounce, which means they are no longer stably in contact with the ground, so traction is lost. The problem is compounded by the fact that you probably need a couple of thousand rpm, which further increases the speed.

Why not slip the clutch? Two reasons; firstly because if you do the air will shortly be filled with a burning smell. Clutches are not designed to be slipped for anything other than changing gear, and continuous slipping to reduce speed will greatly increase clutch wear.

The other reason not to slip the clutch is because the vehicle is likely to stop when the wheels meet an obstacle. The engine is connected to the wheels via a driveshaft. The driveshaft is not solid, but cut into two. At each end there is a flat plate, and that is the clutch. When the clutch is up the two plates are pressed hard against each other, effectively forming a solid axle. When the clutch is down the two plates are apart and the engine cannot drive the wheels. When the clutch is partially up the two plates are touching, but the engine's plate can spin faster than the wheel's plate. What this means is that when the wheels meet an obstacle, there is suddenly an increased force required to turn the wheels. It is quite possible that the clutch plates may not be sufficiently close together to transmit this extra force, and instead the wheel plate stops turning and the engine plate continues to rotate. The vehicle stops, losing valuable momentum.

You can experiment with this for yourself. Find a high kerb, but one your vehicle can mount. Place your vehicle in second gear, at idle, and lift the clutch so the vehicle is just moving. You will probably find that the vehicle is stopped by the kerb.

Keep a firm hold of the steering wheel and be prepared to be bounced around. Often with rocks you can stop, get out and reassess, but be sure the vehicle is well secured before you leap out of the door.

Every so often vehicles break transmission components, usually those such as constant-velocity (CV) joints or axles. This happens more often on rocky terrain than anywhere else because rocks are so hard and unforgiving. See Chapter 12 for details on how to avoid the expensive "bang".

environment

Rocky terrain isn't as fragile as mud so can be driven in most conditions. Don't smoke up tyres on rocks as apart from potentially breaking something and ruining a tyre the smell and stain lasts a while. If you can't drive a track without major roadwork then don't bother, come back another time.

completion

Check for damage to bodywork, tie rods, control arms and the like. If any are damaged handling deficiencies may not be apparent until you drive on. But you'll be back, because conquering a difficult rock ledge is a great thrill.

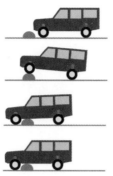

Diagram showing what happens when you go over a rock. The faster you go, the more the suspension compresses and the less clearance you get. A wheel will naturally roll off a rock and that is where low gearing and techniques like driving through the brakes come into their own.

A steepish descent. Not particularly tall rocks but with a loose surface and often with a dirt covering means traction may be a problem, particularly in the wet.

Careful wheel placement is essential. The rocks are dusty, and thus slippery, but there aren't too many loose rocks. A crawl will work well. If the car runs out of suspension travel lockers could keep it going.

Putting a wheel right up on the rocks helps with the clearance; all four wheels are level and thus traction is maintained. In rocks, an expert spotter is worth their weight in engine oil.

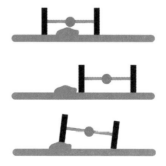

One rock, three lines. Straddling it works as long as you have clearance. You can try to avoid it but that often requires a sharp turn which is generally to be avoided. If the wheels are put up on the rock then you can raise the entire vehicle up, which is always a bonus in rocky terrain.

Rocks can be used to build a track. Use flattish ones wedged in so they aren't spun out by the wheels. This was enough to get a car over a difficult section.

A spinning wheel that will stress the transmission when it returns to earth. On the left, a loose rock flies through the air looking for something to damage.

More than enough momentum to get over the ledge, which is dusty and loose. Despite the LC100 having excellent front-

end suspension travel the front axle hasn't really twisted to flex to the terrain. This is because most of the vehicle's weight is on the back. The fact the vehicle is accelerating slightly also moves some weight to the rear – another reason not to accelerate on hills.

Many lines, some of which could damage sills. First low, slow but steady speed. Note the metal rock sliders in case it goes wrong.

We drove a standard JK Wrangler up after this modified Jeep, but we did need to place a few rocks in strategic locations. If in doubt about a line, take the option that is straightest.

The rear tyre is balanced on a loose rock, but the other three have good traction. The front left will shortly fall off the rock. If the car is driven through the brakes this will not cause a sudden lurch.

Slick rock – giant slabs of rock – is not common in Australia. Slick rock offers phenomenal traction, when it's dry, and not covered with leaves, dust or moss.

Creek beds are often level with many medium sized loose rocks. Low-range, steady, firm grip on the wheel and even trailers can be dragged. Minimise wheelspin, as moving a large, loose rock can be disastrous. On the upside, rocks are often easy to move and the terrain is generally flat.

Some rocky tracks are full of large but loose stones. These are difficult to drive as the wheels constantly slip on the loose material, but momentum cannot be used as there is too much bouncing and a danger of throwing large rocks back towards vulnerable parts of the vehicle. The slower you go, the less bouncing and the more traction, but the faster you go the more able the car is to move from rock to rock. Every track has a middle speed, which will constantly vary. If in doubt go slower, drop pressures and move a couple of rocks, but never throw a rock downhill. They tend not to stop.

1   Even a tiny rock like this can be enough to stop a 4WD if it's on the limit of traction. It was in this case for the Triton, so a tiny bit more momentum and the vehicle was able to clear it. Anticipating momentum-sapping obstacles like these is a major part of rock driving. It is better to anticipate and build a little momentum than come to a stop against the rock and then rev your way past.

2   Gradient-located rocks set in a bed of lightly-moistened earth drizzled with a topping of light dust, presented in an attractive corner location. Many lines to choose from and this Patrol has opted not to drive around the rock it has its wheel on, but to go straight, which has the advantage of needing to turn less. However, the front left has lifted and thus isn't doing much to help. As the rock is dry traction is good; if it were wet it would be another matter. The Patrol's strong LSD (Chapter 3) is keeping both wheels providing traction and the driver has just the right amount of momentum to pass through the moment the wheel lifted, then the right front came off the rock, right rear up over its rock and all four wheels were back on the ground with traction restored.

Discovery 4 keeping wheels level and on the rocks, raising the chassis clear. When the steering is turned large throttle openings should be avoided to reduce risk of breaking the CV joints.

1   The rear wheel of this 80 Series is about to drop off a ledge which will temporarily speed the car's descent and possibly also see the vehicle running out of departure angle with the consequent possibility of damage. The solution is anticipating the problem and coming down as slowly as possible. The rock sliders shown protect the sills from damage.

2-3 This 76 Series was initially hung up by this rock on his rear differential. A slightly different line cleared the diff but hit the spring hanger. If it were a tyre against the rock momentum would have worked, and indeed sufficient momentum here would also have worked – but not without damaging the vehicle. The solution is to drive around or over the problem, and the prevention is to notice it in the first place and remember where your low points are. In the case of this vehicle that rock could have passed between the left rear wheel and the diff, but not between the right rear and diff.

Smooth expanses of hard rock (slickrock) usually offer excellent traction, and that can lure drivers into attempting extremely steep or off-camber obstacles that other surfaces would make impossible. Keeping all four wheels on the ground and the vehicle level can be a challenge. The keys to success are very slow, measured control, excellent articulation, cross-axle lockers, low gearing and excellent wheel placement to maintain weight distribution.

Image courtesy Barlow Jeep School, www.barlows.us

CHAPTER 18

FORESTS & RUTS

The nearest offroading for many of us is the local state forest or national park. It's an excellent way to enjoy a day out or try out some new gear. Forests may be local, but don't get complacent. While you may only be 20 minutes drive from a town, this can start to look like a long way if you're lost or immobilised.

the terrain

This chapter is about any wooded area, typically a state forest. They may not be particularly large, but can have every form of terrain imaginable. The one thing in common is trees and a maze of tracks so that is the focus of these techniques.

preparation and kit list

As ever, preparation is the key and that starts with researching where you're going. All national parks and state forests are controlled by some authority, and these days that'll mean a website. There you can see which tracks are open and which are closed, as well as lots of interesting information that will add an extra dimension to your visit; you can learn about the history, flora, fauna, attractions and scenic walks. Some areas may be national parks, others state forests and the difference is important, typically camping and pets are restricted in national parks, and some parks require an entry fee. While you're on the web check out the weather forecast, and whether or not it is a fire ban day. You may not be intending to start a fire,

but you don't want to be in the middle of a long recovery and seeing smoke nearby either.

Forests can present challenging navigation with many tracks, not all of which may be marked or aligned with the map. For this sort of driving you need 1:50,000 or 1:25,000 topographic maps, backed up with the ranger's park notes and maps which often add useful information. A GPS receiver is no bad idea either.

Forests have trees, and trees fall down on tracks. These can often bar your way, and you are usually allowed to remove them; this is preferable to creating a new track around the tree. At the very least take gloves, a bowsaw, an axe and eye protection. A set of drag chains and a tree-trunk protector mean you can drag things out of the way, and best of all is a chainsaw, where permitted. A winch and snatch block is useful for dragging logs off the track as opposed to alongside it. On summer days forests can be flammable, and while you hope it'll never happen, a fire extinguisher could save your life or the environment.

Many forest tracks are narrow and scratchy. "Beauty marks" are just part of offroading and a professional can often do a wonderful restoration job come resale time, but you can get clear plastic covers for your bodywork or metal protection bars for some models, plus some quality waxing beforehand works wonders. However, most people stop wincing after the first few marks. If your snorkel has a reversible head consider turning it to avoid ingesting overhanging twigs or damaging the intake.

You probably will – and should – have more than one car in the group so UHF radio is an ideal way to communicate. Bear in mind that range is limited in forests because of the undergrowth and more particularly the hilly terrain. Mobiles may not work at all; satellite phones will but may require moving to higher ground. While company is a good idea, most authorities either ask or mandate groups of 10 vehicles or less. Any more than this is often difficult to work with in a tight forest anyway.

Forests can run the full gamut of terrain from mud to rocks to hills and even sand, so all your recovery gear could be needed. One advantage is that there will be no shortage of trees to winch from. Given the relatively short distances involved, lowering tyre pressures to around 20psi-25psi for a mid-size 4WD is a good idea as the traction improvement is dramatic on all loose surfaces, from dirt to rocks to thick mud, and it reduces the chances of a puncture as well as improving ride comfort.

A full tank of fuel is also a wise precaution, even if you don't think you'll need it for the short distances, as low-range work uses much more fuel than high-range cruising. Nobody ever finished a trip feeling inconvenienced by extra fuel in the tank. At extreme angles fuel pickups can have difficulty with near-empty tanks, you may not know about diversions during the trip or on the way back, you may want to get home quickly and sometimes a day trip turns into a night trip. For these reasons take plenty of provisions and clothing. The bottom line about preparation is you prepare for the worst and it won't happen. On one occasion a group I was leading exited the forest and while we were airing up a young bloke in an old Range Rover turned up and asked directions. He was going to retrieve his mates (wasn't sure

how many) who had taken a car (he wasn't sure which) somewhere into the forest (they hadn't said where exactly). He had no map nor any recovery gear but good intentions. We turned around, located the group and spent the next couple of hours winching their Hilux out of trouble. It is so easy for a simple day trip to go wrong.

Gloves, axe, bowsaw, drag chain and tree trunk protector to extend the chain, plus a shackle to help connect things. With this kit you will be able to move a surprising number of fallen trees and most of it can be used for other duties such as firewood collection (where permitted).

driving techniques

The main feature of a forest is of course trees, and there will be lots of sticks and logs on the tracks. These can be dangerous. If you hit a branch the wrong way you could easily rip a tyre apart, or flick it up into the bodywork, causing a dent, or into the vehicle's chassis to be dragged along as a "traveller". In the latter case you may well hear it as you drive; stop immediately and remove the offender, checking for damage such as torn lines. Occasionally the stick won't want to come out, which is where your bowsaw comes in handy. To avoid stick problems slow down, and either straddle them or drive on a side that won't cause it to fly up. Imagine standing on the end of a rake which flicks up; it's the same principle with sticks.

On one occasion I had to take a chainsaw to a log which had managed to lodge itself between the bulbar and the bodywork.

Other things that can enter your car are twigs on trees you drive by, bushes on narrow tracks and everything that lives on them like spiders and other insects, so driving with your windows open is not necessarily a good idea. Plenty of people have had eye injuries caused by objects coming in through the window, even with sunnies on, so keep the windows all the way up. When you drive over a stick on the ground it may be thrown up by the wheel and it is possible that it could even come in through an open window. If you do put the windows down put them all the way down so your head will not be cracked on the glass edge.

Eventually you will find a tree across the track that will need removing using the kit you prepared earlier. A chainsaw course is an excellent investment, as is the proper safety gear. Even without a saw you can do a lot with a bowsaw and drag chain. Trim the log as best you can, then attach the chain at one end of the log and pull it backwards. Pass the hook end of the chain around the log, then through the eye end and pull tight. The chain will bite into the wood and not move. A strap won't be anywhere near as effective and will be damaged. Often you'll need to extend the chain with a tree trunk protector and shackles for extra length – otherwise you may pull the log back onto your own car, especially if pointed downhill. If you can drag it down the track then you can use a few guys to roll it out of the way. With the right gear and a bit of practice even large tree falls can be cleared by a group working together, and you'll be

doing a good deed for all the other bush users and the emergency services. If you do cut through a fallen tree please cut the gap a bit wider than what you need, as others may have larger vehicles! See Chapter 38 for more on drag chains.

driving over a tree

Although it is best to move them, sometimes you need to drive across sizeable logs on the track. The best way is to approach such that one wheel goes across at a time, with all your lockers engaged, in your lowest gear. Do not stop, expect a bit of a bump as the car moves across and hold the steering wheel straight as it will kick a little as the front wheels move over the log. Be careful with large logs as you may get the front wheel over only to get hung on up on the chassis or diff. Engage lockers if you have them and if not, try overdriving the brakes. Larger logs can be driven over by piling rocks and smaller logs up to make a ramp. Observe; is the tree trunk slippery? Are there any branches that the vehicle may slide in to? Will the tree slip as the vehicle moves over it? What effect will that have on things? Consider chocking the tree, or removing the odd branch. Can the tree be shifted slightly, making it easier to climb? A wheel can in theory climb a vertical obstacle a little under half its height. In practice, it tends to be less than that.

An option is to build a little ramp out of smaller logs, rocks and soil. This also helps stabilise the tree.

If you drive off the track and around the tree you are guaranteed to become unpopular with environmentalists, forest rangers and everyone else. If you can't remove the tree or drive over it, find another track.

ruts, gullies and ditches

Crossing ditches

Sometimes you will need to cross a ditch or gully. Approach these in the same way as a log – diagonally and one wheel in at a time so as to reduce the chance of running out of approach, departure or even ramp angles. A little burst of momentum may be required to ease the vehicle through the point at which it has diagonal wheels with little weight on them, but ease off just before you have traction again to reduce transmission stress of a spinning wheel hitting the ground. Keep the steering wheel straight – as the vehicle's weight shifts from wheel to wheel it will want to turn of its own accord. Second or third low is best, first is usually too slow and gives too much wheelspin.

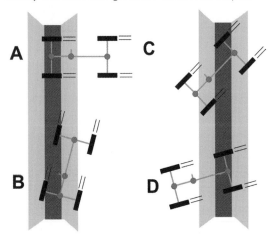

If possible, cross ditches at an angle to maximize approach, departure and ramp angles.

A: Straight on. Sometimes this is the only possible line, and it can work fine provided there is clearance.

B: Extreme angle. This approach maximises the uses of approach/departure angles but it also means the vehicle is

at a significant side (tip) angle as both right wheels in the lowest part of the ditch, and the vehicle also has to climb up out of the ditch. There is a risk of running out of rampover angle. On entry a rear wheel may lift, but gravity helps with the momentum.

C: Reducing the angle the ditch is taken at starts to level the vehicle. Front left again likely to spin up on exit.

D: This is usually the best angle to take for ditches. The car remains level, never drops down into the ditch, approach/ ramp/departure angles are maximised. However, it is likely that the vehicle will momentarily balance on two wheels, so some momentum will be required to carry the vehicle past the balance point, or use of traction control or cross-axle lockers.

Patrol crossing a ditch downhill and uphill at an angle. A wheel lift is normal and no real issue.

Sometimes direct into the ditch is all you can do.

Ruts

Ruts are something you will definitely encounter in forests. If possible, drive in them rather than avoid as that will widen the track. In slippery conditions, following ruts can help keep the car on the track too. What you don't want to do is end up cross-rutted, with diagonal wheels in the same rut.

Clearance no issue, slippery and would just widen the track so staying in the ruts.

Diagonal wheels in ruts, usually caused by slipping in at an angle, sometimes accompanied by a tyre parting from the rim. Can be tricky to recover from.

Clever use of ruts on one side to keep the car straight during a slippery climb.

If the ruts are too deep to drive in then one option is to fill them. Wood can work, but when wet it provides very little traction. Rocks are much better, and traction ramps better yet (see Chapter 37 for an example picture).

If the ruts can't be driven or filled they must be straddled. Straight-line straddling is easy enough – just pick a line that centres the rut under the vehicle. But most of the time ruts are curved, so the vehicle must turn. This means that you need a very good appreciation of exactly where your wheels will be (emphasis on *will be*, for forward planning) at all times, which means understanding the basic rule that each of the four wheels will describe its own arc. Most of the time you're aiming to "drive the back axle", as you can change the direction of the fronts more easily. You're also looking to keep one of the rear wheels just on the edge of tipping into the rut, because that way the opposite rear is taken care of, and you've usually also given the front wheels the best chance of staying out too. Which wheel depends on the nature of the rut – most of the time it'll be the rear outer wheel (see diagram 1), but sometimes you need to think ahead (diagram 2).

If the rut is rocky then you can get your tyre right up to the edge of the rut, and sometimes even halfway over. If, however, the rut is earthen then it may give way, and you need to allow for that possibility. Deep rut straddling should be done at a dead slow pace with smooth control inputs (particularly no harsh brake application), and ideally you should be "spotted" from outside by someone who is looking at the intended and actual path of all four wheels. If you make a positioning mistake then very carefully think through the remedy as it is

not unusual for people to panic, shuffle around and end up in a worse situation than they started with. It doesn't hurt to stop, assess, and move on only a half metre or less.

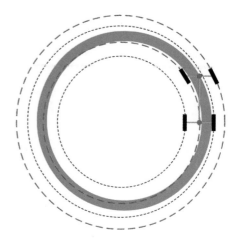

Diagram 1: Perfect arcs are rare, but the diagram illustrates the fact that centring the rut between the front wheels is not usually a good idea.

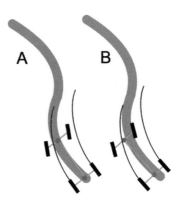

Diagram 2: If you start off centred (A) the left rear wheel will end up in the rut. As the first turn is to the right both inside wheels can be close to the rut as the turn will take them away. By the time B's left rear is near the rut it will be time to turn left which will take the left rear away from the rut again.

On rutted tracks you often need to drive at side angles. If you do this, ideally have the lower tyres hard up against the side of a rut (page 238).

The two front wheels are out of the ruts, but the rear left is well and truly in, so had this been an enormous chasm it would have been disastrous. What's wrong here is that the driver has not "driven the back axle", but focused on the front wheels. A much later turn in to the corner would have worked, and the right front wheel should be on the verge of tipping into the rut. This is demonstrated graphically:

1   This is a good line. Notice how the car is still going straight, and will for another half-metre or so. The right front wheel is on a huge rock, which offers excellent traction. Going straight until the last minute will give the rear left most room to clear the rut, and of course the front left will have plenty of space, and rear right will be inside front right so no concerns there. But if any wheel fell into that rut we'd be looking at panel damage, and a recovery as there'd be no driving out of it.

2   *Same obstacle as (1), previous page. Here we see a wheel on course to land in a big hole, caused by incorrect lining up to begin with, and then turning too early. When doing this sort of straddle a good spotter is a great aid, as long as they check all four wheels! It is also important to consider the nature of the terrain, as tyres can get very close to the edge of deep ruts, even in extreme cases hanging on by half the tread width. On dry rocks that should be fine, but on sandy soil or wet clay you'll have traction problems or concerns about the rut wall simply disintegrating. A little work with a shovel can go a long way to improving things.*

environment

Forests are where you are likely to find other users; motorbikes, mountainbikers, walkers, horseriders, rogainers, hunters and more. There is no reason why we can't all share the environment, so be courteous and don't assume you will have the tracks to yourself. If you do see others abusing the privilege of being out in the forest you can always report them to the authorities using the Dob in a Hoon hotline, or via your state 4WD club association.

If it is not a fire ban day and you want a campfire then respect the firewood collection protocols; this usually means going outside national parks and only in specific areas for state forests.

Clear fallen trees and don't use tracks when they will be damaged.

completion

Air up and check the vehicle over for damage, branches lodged in the chassis and so on. Clean your car as soon as you can – it is possible for 4WDs to move environmental contaminants from one area to another. Take only memories, leave only tyre marks – and those only on legal tracks!

Seasonal road closures are common. You can see in advance which tracks are closed on the authorities' websites. There are typical start and end dates, but these are modified as required to account for unusual weather. It is your responsibility to know the difference.

1   There are usually, but not always signs warning of logging activity. Drive as if there were a truck around each corner anyway.

2   This car caught on fire for no apparent reason. Lucky we had an extinguisher. I have no images of other vehicle fires as in those situations photography tends not to be top of mind.

3   Approach ditches and logs at an angle. Crawl over logs in your lowest gear, but ditches may require a little momentum as the vehicle may be temporarily cross-axled (diagonal wheels in the air, or with little weight on them). Keep the steering wheel straight.

4   You very often find significant ruts in forests. Here the vehicle has to cross into the ruts and a log has been placed to help the car through. The right wheel needs to stay just on the top ditch, with the left picking up the protective rut seen on the right, which will tram-track the vehicle. This is where a spotter is useful. If the vehicle does fall in it won't roll, but recovery could be tricky and panels may be damaged.

5   Trees and cars lean at angles, so be aware of where all parts of your vehicle are.

1   Large logs can be ramped over with smaller logs.

2   Even small bits of wood can rip a tyre apart or damage the vehicle. Slowing down and picking your line is the best defence.

3   Chainsawing a fallen tree and using a drag chain to pull it backwards. For extra pull length you can add a tree trunk protector.

4   Cross logs at an angle and without stopping. This little one is no problem, but larger ones can be, especially when they're wet.

1   Don't expect all tracks to be wide open. Leaves aren't a problem, but branches can leave a nasty mark on the paint.

2   Often tracks are closed, and those signs must be respected. Contacting the authorities beforehand is a good idea, and sometimes, as here, there is a UHF channel to contact the workers on.

3   Two minutes with a bowsaw means no risk of panel damage.

4   Multiple vehicles mean safety. Note the spacing, so if one vehicle is in trouble the others can see it before they also become stuck.

5   This Pajero is inching down the hill…but is about to drop hard onto the left front wheel which will give the driver a shock if he's not expecting it. The important thing to do is not brake hard, which will just further add to the risk of a roll.

When following ruts it can be impossible for the vehicle to leave the ruts, which is often why you're in them. But it also means that you may be able to wind on lots of steering lock and still tramline in the ruts. But then when the ruts end, the car suddenly jumps out of the ruts and into a tree. So, ensure you always know how much steering lock you have on at any given time. Chapter 12 has more details on steering techniques.

CHAPTER 19

GRASS

Grass often looks lovely, but hides dangers.

the terrain

Grass driving is any terrain overgrown with grass, from a close-mown lawn to grass so tall the vehicle is hidden.

preparation and kit list

Grass doesn't need any specific preparation except for avoiding one very important risk, and that's fire. Dry grass such as Spinifex can and does collect under a vehicle, coming into contact with the hot parts like the exhaust, and more than one vehicle has been lost to fire as a result. A hooked piece of wire is great for removing the grass as you don't want to touch hot exhausts and may not be able to reach in all the places grass collects. For longer grass watch for a build up of debris in around the radiator. Take a couple of fire extinguishers too.

driving techniques

short grass

Wet grass on a hard soil can be incredibly slippery, second only to ice, and the same techniques apply – lower tyre pressures, very gentle on the controls, use the engine to brake and high- or low-range as required but keep it smooth. Dry, short grass typically has good traction as it prevents the ground from shearing under the torque of the tyre, but if there is wheelspin the grass is removed and the soft, loose ground is exposed, which has considerably less traction.

axle-height grass

Longer grass generally has worse traction than short because once a wheel presses it down it becomes slippery (but nowhere near as much as ice). However, long grass is extremely dangerous because, like snow, it does a great job of hiding the terrain and problems like large logs. Many a 4WD has been manoeuvring around a grassy campsite and inadvertently discovered a hole which, if you're lucky, will just give you a fright and if you're moving at anything other than walking pace may damage the vehicle or the occupants if they aren't wearing seatbelts. Longer grass often becomes a little tussocky which is an excellent indication to keep speeds low.

bonnet-high grass

If the grass is that high usually you shouldn't be there, but now visibility is a real problem so you need to go very slowly as you're feeling your way along – driving blind – and remember the fire danger. Check you're on the right track as wheel marks will be difficult or impossible to see.

environment

Grass is easily damaged, and even flattened grass doesn't look good, so avoid driving on it where you can and don't turn tightly in 4WD or with lockers as the tyres will scrub and slightly rip the grass. If the going is easy and traction good drive it in 2WD or with the centre diff unlocked to avoid this problem. Airing down helps too. Aggressive tyres can really dig into grass and chew it up – simply driving an aggressive tyre over grass can result in more damage than a wheelspinning road tyre. Follow

in other's wheel tracks where possible. Remember that snakes are often found in long grass and are difficult to spot.

completion

Check for any grass, twigs or debris caught in the vehicle and move on.

1   There is actually a track in this grass, but it's overgrown either side and in the middle. That presents a fire risk as it's very dry so we check for grass build up in the underside of the vehicle.

2   A grassy incline. Good traction when it's dry, very slippery in the wet.

3   In this case the wet grass is slippery, and the mud is very slippery! Plan ahead, gentle on the controls, use the engine to brake and low tyre pressures..

4   Campsites often have longish grass, and if you fall into a hole at even two km/h you'll regret it. Be very careful as grass does a very good job of hiding nasty problems.

5   This paddock is wet, and thus slippery. The grass is also long to hide all sorts of problems.

SAND

There are several types of sand driving, such as beaches and dunes, but all sand has a few factors in common and the most important of those is that it's just plain fun.

the terrain

Sand is often very soft, and it's very loose, with little traction. It's also the only surface that becomes easier to drive on when wet. Sand can be flat, like beaches, or swept into steep dunes. It can be found everywhere from the coast to the central deserts, it can have a hard base or be bottomless and can vary from fine particles to coarse, almost gravelly stones. Desert sand driving is covered in Chapter 25.

preparation and kit list

Softness means the car sinks into the sand and if that happens the wheels can't get out of the resulting hole – instead they spin, which digs you in further. To avoid sinking you need flotation, which means increasing the tyre's contact patch to spread the weight over a wider area. This is done by reducing tyre pressures (Chapter 7) to around 40-50% of the manufacturer's recommendation, and for a 4WD weighing 3,000kg that means around 15psi. Even then you'll be sinking, which means the vehicle will be working hard as it is in effect driving up a hill even on the flat, and lower tyre pressures increase rolling resistance anyway. All this means high fuel consumption, so always start with a full tank. It also means the cooling system will work overtime, as will automatic transmissions. Watch temperatures, especially on long downwind runs where there is very little airflow cooling.

Sand driving often involves dunes, and you cannot see what's coming over the top before you hit it. So fit a tall – three metres or higher – sand flag (see Chapter 25, Desert Dune Driving).

Mud tyres do not perform as well as road patterns in sand. The open muddies dig in, when what you really need is overall flotation. That said, a well-driven vehicle on muddies at the right pressure will drive anywhere a road tyred vehicle can go.

A shovel is an absolute essential, as is a flat plate for your jack. If you get bogged, dig all around the car, almost to underneath the tyres, and create a shallow ramp for the car to drive up and out. Deflate the tyres to eight psi and then very carefully idle the car out of trouble, using minimum throttle and never wheelspinning. This is far safer and often more effective than trying to snatch or tow out. Once out, re-inflate the tyres using a compressor back to 15psi or so and continue. Bring a tyre repair kit in case a tyre comes off a rim, which is a possibility with low pressures but is mostly caused by coarse driving techniques. Winches are rarely of use, but traction aids (Chapter 37) are worth their weight in gold when you're sand driving. You'll certainly need a tyre pressure gauge as low tyre pressures are critical to sand driving.

Disable stability control systems, even if it means also killing traction control. Momentum is the key in sand, and you don't want an overactive computer braking the wheels and destroying precious momentum if the car jiggles a little bit. However, traction control itself is only a bonus in sand. Some say it doesn't help, but I think they're mostly confusing traction control with stability control, and in years of sand driving in many, many different vehicles I've only ever found traction control to be useful. Make sure you lock the centre diff, but cross-axle lockers do not help much in sand and should mostly be left disengaged. Remove weight from the vehicle, especially from the roof rack. Take tide charts if there is any chance of going anywhere near the water.

driving techniques

general

Sand is all about controlled momentum. Some element of wheelspin in sand is always the case, but if it gets excessive the wheels will rapidly dig in, which promotes more wheelspin, which in turn means more digging in. It is quite possible to see a 4WD stop and then move vertically downwards as a driver spins the wheels. To avoid this, instantly back off the throttle at the first sign of excess wheelspin – excess is defined as when the vehicle requires rapidly increasing amounts of throttle to maintain speed. Back up and use more momentum, dig out or drop tyre pressures.

Sand requires more engine power than normal, as the rolling resistance is many times greater, and therefore possibly a lower gear than usual. Don't be afraid to keep the revs up.

Beaches can provide sand so hard-packed it is easy to speed. Don't. There will be hidden dangers, for example Fraser Island is well-known for streams across the beach. Turning at speed is dangerous too. When a vehicle turns it puts weight onto the outside wheels and rolls a little. As sand is soft the outside wheels sink in, and this increases the roll effect, which adds effective weight, which makes the outside wheels sink further in…and you're over. A heavy roof rack only worsens the problem.

If you need to turn around on sand try and do so by working your way up the beach and then turning slowly towards the water. This will be downhill and towards (hopefully) harder sand. Assume the turning circle will be much larger than normal due to the soft surface and remember that as the vehicle turns the rear wheels no longer follow the compressed sand ruts of the fronts, so rolling resistance is greatly increased for the duration of the turn (another reason to do it downhill so gravity helps). Beware of sticks and flotsam above the high tide mark which can mean punctures. However, sometimes sand is so saturated with water it becomes like a bog, and you need to avoid that sort at all costs. As always, never drive anywhere until you're confident about the surface.

If you need to stop, just lift off the throttle and avoid using the brakes as the rolling resistance of sand is an effective brake. Once stopped, gently reverse back a metre or so to leave a "ramp" of sand packed down by the tyres for an easier takeoff. Try to stop on the top of dunes, ideally facing slightly downhill.

Sand dunes are great fun, but potentially dangerous. Firstly, be sure you know the dunes' layout. The windward side of a dune is often a shallower gradient, so there may be a significant dropoff on the other side, or another vehicle. Always drive directly up and down dunes (see above regarding turning on sand for the reasons why, as once you start getting sideways it just gets much worse, much more quickly than a hard surface). Coming down a dune you are unlikely to need first low, or even to brake as the sand will retard progress. Ideally you would be in a gear that requires a few revs to progress downhill. Do not use electronic hill descent systems as these rely on brakes – first high will often be sufficient. Avoid side angles at all times as the vehicle will rapidly roll sideways.

Drivers of automatics may wish to manually control gearshifts as slow-shifting autos can lose momentum at critical moments. Using a sport mode, if available, usefully keeps the revs up. Manual drivers need to change up at higher revs than usual and be aware the car will quickly slow down as soon as the clutch is depressed. Don't change gears when going up or down dunes.

The decision to use high- or low-range depends on average speed of the track. For example, a petrol Pajero 3.5 will do 60km/h or more in low-range fifth gear. On a winding, soft inland track you're unlikely to get close to that, so if you're more likely to spend all your time between 0 and 30km/h, low-range gives you five gears to choose from. In high-range, there'd be just two, just first and second, so low-range becomes in effect a close-ratio gearbox. Remember that fifth gears aren't particularly strong so fifth low should be avoided on sand unless it's hard-packed, in which case high-range is usually the way to go anyway. Much depends on the vehicle, too, for example a powerful six-speed diesel could cruise in high where a low-powered petrol engine may be revving hard in low.

accelerating on soft sand or up a slope

This is difficult, but sometimes you need to do it, for example to crest a dune. Start off in no lower than second gear, low-range, and initially feather the throttle to get the car moving with little wheelspin.

If possible, continue feeding on the power to accelerate, minimising wheelspin. Sometimes that's not possible and you need to feed in more power, accepting a higher rate of wheelspin for greater acceleration. This can work but while the power used is great and the vehicle may be close to the redline, that doesn't mean to say the application of power cannot be smooth, consistent and gentle, squeezing the throttle rather than jabbing it. If that approach doesn't work you'll know because the car will start to slow down despite the power increase. If that happens and you clearly aren't going to crest your hill then give up – gently ease back off the power to come to a halt, don't just come right off as that can produce a shock load, and you definitely must not sit there spinning your way into a deep hole. Lower tyre pressures, smooth the way, reduce weight and maybe even wait till evening when it is cooler, as then the sand won't be so fine and the engine will have cooler air.

deliberate digging

This is an advanced technique for use on hills. Let's say you're on a slope and you can't quite make it up, and you can't or don't want to reverse back down. What you can do is deliberately wheelspin the wheels into the sand, just a touch. Then, very carefully, reverse back onto the mound of sand you've just created. You now have a tiny ramp to roll down, so off you go again – down the micro-ramp, and do another wheelspin. Except this time you'll have moved forwards by maybe 15-30cm, and your new mound will be further up the hill. Back up onto the new mound, and repeat the process. Takes a while, but it's worked for me and only techniques known to work are in this book!

ruts and coming off the beach

Often on a beach you need to track parallel to the sea in a straight line, which sounds easy – and it is when the sand is hard-packed. However, when it's soft and the beach has a slope it's a lot harder, as sand offers little lateral grip. All you can do is keep in the ruts and keep a constant speed, making sure that as much as possible of the tyre's grip is going towards stopping the vehicle sliding down the slope. That means no, or very gentle, acceleration and braking, a slowish speed – 20km/h may be about right – and gentle steering, anticipating any slight changes ahead of time. This is one time when you'll want to leave a long distance between vehicles in case one gets into trouble.

Eventually the tracks will turn up off the beach and then you're faced with a difficult task; how to turn up the beach and negotiate an incline at the same time. The trick is to be smooth and steady. Keep in the ruts, as coming out will destabilise the car and you'll lose momentum. If you find yourself running wide around the corner, needing to add more lock, then you've entered it too fast. You should get the feeling that the car is just about to run wide, but hasn't, and as the car completes the turn then gently feed in more power to maintain momentum. Sometimes even all that doesn't work, and then it's spade time, usually to make a decent set of ruts that you can tramline around and not lose the momentum you need to make it up and out.

environment

Make sure you know where the prohibited areas are, for example dunes where vegetation is growing, or areas at the top of beaches where birds are nesting. The tide will erase any vehicle tracks but it can't reach inland so stick to defined tracks.

Pass other vehicles as you would on public roads, i.e. keep them to your right. Consider indicating well in advance, as that tells the other driver that they have been seen, and on which side you intend to pass them. If you're going to have the other vehicle between you and the water and the beach is narrow, edge up as far as you can so there is enough room for the other to pass without going into the water.

Slow down for people on the beach. Remember you can't swerve as you can on bitumen.

Headlights can be good, too, as beaches often have a lot of glare and two vehicles two kilometres apart (barely visible) travelling at 60km/h each will meet in 60 seconds.

completion

If your car has been in, or come anywhere near, salt water (even a beach drive) hose it down and underneath thoroughly with fresh water. Make sure the tyres are reinflated before travel on the roads as it is very bad for the tyres, and generally dangerous to travel on-road at sand pressures.

How far your heel sinks into the sand is an indication of how far the tyre will sink in. It doesn't hurt to get out and stamp around to see what the surface is like. This is wettish sand, as the tyre print is very distinct, and relatively firm.

1   Driving around a sharp corner then up a hill can be tricky. If it doesn't work, move the sand around so the vehicle stays in one set of ruts all the way around. Use the highest gear you can. Turn the car in under slight power and accelerate gently rather than trying to get to the maximum speed you can before entering the turn. Definitely don't go understeering around the corner, losing momentum. The final solution to sand problems is usually more digging, a drop of pressures or a combination of both.

2   As soon as the wheels start spinning, the car digs in and shortly afterwards is bellied out. Experienced drivers recognise this and back off before they're stuck.

3,4,5   Too high a pressure, into the soft stuff and sunk. Recovering using a snatch strap is problematic as the beach is sloped and the sand all around the vehicle is soft. Instead, we just let the tyres down to eight psi, dug out underneath the wheels and the driver was able to easily reverse out back to safety. Notice how far under the tyre sand has been removed (4).

On ascents if there are defined tyre marks then that means there's been no wheelspin, which means traction is good and the sand firm so you don't need much momentum.

1   This Cruiser has stopped in soft sand. It's a slight upslope and there's no way that car is moving forwards from there. If it reverses back a metre or so it'll have a packed wheeltrack to get a little momentum and stands a chance.

2   Just a few metres away the sand is so hard packed this Cruiser doesn't even sink in at road pressures.

3   Beaches can vary from hard-packed sand to super-soft. Generally, wetter sand near the water is harder. Beware debris at the watermark and be aware of environmental restrictions like nesting birds. It's best to keep vehicles well spaced out so they don't all get into trouble.

4   Always drive dunes straight up or straight down.

5   This X-Trail drove along a beach, downwind, at road pressures. That meant the car had to work hard, had no cooling airflow at all and boiled the radiator dry.

Traction aids (Chapter 37) can be essential to avoid a salty bath.

Ran out of power halfway through, but didn't dig the car in so was able to back it out, very slowly.

chapter 20 sand   **253**

Coming off a soft beach can be difficult due to the direction change and increased gradient.

A long-handled shovel is essential for sand recoveries.

Soft beaches with a slope, close to the water…if we came out of the ruts there would be trouble.

Sand flag, shovel on the back, traction aids on the roof and a compressor under the bonnet and a flat plate for the jack. Sand driving essentials.

Trailers can be towed in sand but this magnifies the difficulty and they are near-impossible to reverse down dunes as the tow car's rear wheels slide. This Tvan's tyres are at eight psi which is about right for the average camper in soft sand.

The Saharan Desert varies from firm sand to power sand. Don't assume all sand in the same area is equally easy to drive on.

1   Water crossings on beaches should always be checked first. Some hide soft sand, others are unexpectedly deep.

2   Dunes like this cannot be ascended without momentum. The fastest speed should be at the base of the dune, then gently feed, feed, feed in the power as you ascend, without changing gear. Lift off smoothly as you crest, not quickly as otherwise excess momentum will be lost and you risk a bogging.

3-4 Once you start going sideways in sand it's easy to go too far. The key is a good line and confident momentum, but you don't want wheelspin as that reduces lateral traction and increases the chances of slipping off sideways. No gear changes on the hill.

5   Sand is often very soft and turning the vehicle about doubles rolling resistance as each of the four tyres now ploughs their own furrow instead of the rears following the ruts of the fronts. Only turn when you have sufficient momentum and try to do so downhill. Use existing ruts if possible.

Great fun, but a little too fast. Sand's not so soft it can't damage vehicles.

CHAPTER 21

WATER

There are people who specialise in sand driving, mud racing and rock crawling. Few people specialise in water crossings, but it's an essential 4WD skill.

the terrain

Shallow crossings, which are those up to around hub height (half the wheel height), don't pose any problem – at least none due to the depth of the water. Even if stuck the vehicle is unlikely to be washed away, won't be drowned and the doors can often be opened even if immobilised mid-stream. However, anything beyond hub height is classified as deep and requires some analysis, preferably before you enter. Some mudbogs (Chapter 16) have elements in common with water crossings.

preparation and kit list

Planning the crossing starts with reading the water to determine the best path through, which is not necessarily direct from entry to exit. There is a trade off to be made between depth of water, speed of flow, the underlying terrain and where the entry and exit points are.

The depth of the water is a limiting factor and what that limit is depends on your vehicle, how well it is prepared and particularly the speed of the flow. A properly set up 4WD can often ford water above its wheel height or above bonnet height, so you should not automatically choose the shallowest path if it is not the easiest. However, depth combined with flowing water is definitely a problem. If you come to a stop in deep, calm water your car will be damaged but it is unlikely to be a life and death problem. In fast-flowing water it could be washed downstream and that presents a serious risk of rolling, injury and much more damage potential. Water flowing under the car's bodywork is usually fine, but as soon as it's deep enough to hit the panels the sideways force greatly increases and that presents a risk. If you have difficulty standing in the water chances are the car will also struggle. Remember that one cubic metre block of water weighs one tonne, which is probably $1/3$ to $1/2$ of your vehicle weight.

The underlying terrain needs to be considered. There is no point trying to drive a relatively shallow section if the bottom is so soft you sink in, or if it is full of boulders that are difficult to see or would stop the car. In the former case marking the problem points with sticks or positioning people as markers can help you remember where things are when you start to drive. One thing you learn about offroading is that the terrain looks very different once you're behind the wheel compared to how it looked when you were walking around.

There may or may not be a choice of entry or exit points. Even if there is no choice, there will be a choice of angle of approach and again that is a trade off.

So the ideal water crossing line is one which is as shallow as possible, with the easiest underlying terrain, lowest flow rate, easiest entry and exit points and shortest time spent in the water. Out of that lot the shortest path is the least important. The underlying terrain is critical; you need to be certain you can drive it, and that along with the flow/depth factor are the two main factors that should influence your choice of line across the water.

An understanding of the flow, depth and terrain can only really be achieved by getting in the water and seeing for yourself. A good thing to do is decide how deep you want to take the car, mark it against your leg and then go for a wade. However, you can make some assessments just by looking at the water. The amount of water flowing at any point in a river at a certain time is constant, irrespective of the depth or width of the river. Let's say the river is X deep and Y wide. If the river narrows to half X and is still as deep as Y, then it'll need to speed up to maintain the flow rate, so in general, faster water is shallower water. Beware of rivers that narrow and flow at the same speed; it'll be deeper, and in general as the saying goes, "still waters run deep". An exception is water around a bend which is typically narrow and deep on the outside and shallow, with possibly a softer bed, on the inside of the bend – slower-flowing water is more likely to drop its load of sediment. Faster-flowing water is less likely to have a soft bottom or loose rocks, but if rocks are there they are likely to be big.

Of course, there are exceptions to all these generalisations. Don't forget that water crossings do vary in depth; not only due to rains, which may still affect rivers days after they stop, but also due to the periodic release of water for environmental reasons in rivers downstream of major dams. Never assume the crossing will be exactly the same as the last time you drove it. There are also crossings which vary in depth according to the tide.

When you get to a crossing the first thing to do is switch off the engine and assess the situation. Turning the engine off allows the car to cool, which means metal that has expanded, leaving gaps water can enter, will start to contract and there will be less stress of hot metal meeting cold water. Switch lights off too. In days gone by you needed to loosen the fanbelts to avoid problems with water hitting the blades and pushing the fan into the radiator. This is no longer advisable for modern vehicles because the fan operates through a thermal coupling only when the engine is hot, and in any case a single belt may also drive other components. So just make sure the engine is cool before you start by leaving it off for a few minutes.

The manufacturer may provide a wading depth. This will be in ideal conditions for still water with a level and flat bottom. In reality, that's almost never the case so you need to err on the safe side as water ingestion usually means a new engine and these days that's far from cheap.

Water crossings are all about stacking the odds so you do get out the other side and being able to recover if you don't.

the crossing process

Identify the likely entry and exit points for your crossing.

- **Walk the course:**
  - Put marker sticks or people at appropriate intervals, if required, as you are unlikely to be able to memorise the terrain exactly.
  - Exit and entry points. At the exit you'll have soaking wet tyres and poor traction. Can you make it out?
- **Prepare the vehicle:**
  - Put a tarp on the front of the car.
  - Open a downstream window.
  - Ensure all doors are unlocked.

- Place anything that might be damaged by water up out of the way.
- Spray water repellent (WD-40, etc.) on your electrics under the bonnet.
- Prepare the recovery strategy. That might be having a winch point set up on the far stream, or connecting a snatch strap to the back of your vehicle. The recovery strategy always involves a signal for it to be invoked, e.g. radio. However, don't rely on the in-car radio, because if you get into trouble it might not work. Use a handheld radio or a hand signal. Don't assume your electric winch will work under water or that the engine will continue to run. The best recovery may be to pull the vehicle backwards, so attach a strap to the back before you enter and have another car, facing back to the water, ready to recover as well as people briefed about their jobs in the event. People may not be keen to run into the water.

walking the course

The reason you walk the course you intend to drive is to see if there are any nasty surprises in store. For example, rocks, soft, sandy sections, garbage and so on. You may end up taking a rather indirect route across the water. There are several methods to walking a course, and some of them are:

- Walk up one proposed wheel track and down the other.
- Zigzag between both of them.
- Walk in the middle.

It doesn't matter which one you choose. The point is you need to become familiar with the terrain you're going to drive over.

driving techniques

Water crossings can combine every other terrain; mud, sand, rocks and hills, plus the water itself. Use the other techniques for the underlying surface in the same way even though the terrain is under water.

Diagram showing the still water level compared to the bow wave and trough around the vehicle.

The correct speed for a water crossing is one which creates a bow wave that reduces the effective water depth of the car so it is in a "valley" of water. In other words, the car pushes a wave of water ahead of it, which means the engine bay and wheels are in water less deep than what they would be if the car were stationary. This also means that there is less lateral force against the car pushing it sideways. If the water is at hub height or below don't bother with a bow wave as there won't be sufficient frontal area to create one. As the water gets deeper the wave becomes more important, and you can judge it by looking out the side and seeing if you have created yourself a "valley" of water around the car that is lower than the surrounding water. The speed will typically be around a brisk walking pace, but it is a speed relative to the water, not the ground. That means go slower (relative to the ground) heading upstream, and faster downstream. Bear in mind that while the depth of water is reduced around the car, it is increased in front of the car so don't be surprised if water that you measured as a little above wheel height turns out to be bonnet height when the wave is factored in; it could be anywhere from 10 to 50% higher depending on speed.

If the water is flowing fast enough to be a concern then angle your crossing so the flow is not at right angles to the vehicle, thereby reducing its lateral force. If you angle downstream then the car is helped to move by the water, as opposed to using its grip to move over the terrain as well as push the water. Also, remember that the "valley" on the upstream side will be shallower than that on the downstream side.

Pushing water needs a huge amount of force – water is 800 times denser than air – so you need a lower gear than normal to overcome the resistance, generally second or first for deep crossings. Err on the side of the lower gear, especially in deeper water, because a gear change means you will stop and, once you've stopped, starting again could be a problem. Automatics should not use drive but restrict gears to low first or second for the same reason.

As ever, maintain a constant speed and do not stop if the water gets deeper. Once you start you are committed all the way through whether you like it or not, and that's where you regret not doing a more thorough recce. Look at the bow wave to see if you need to vary speed. If you see the revs dropping and your foot is flat to the floor, you have selected too high a gear and need to change. Do so as quickly as you can, revving high and slipping the clutch to keep momentum, minimising water ingress between the clutch plates.

if it goes wrong

If the car starts to slide downstream, turn upstream or downstream immediately – if the car moves sideways and catches a rock you could roll. If you get stuck put your recovery plan into action, and if you are stuck and stationary with the car beginning to drift you must sink it by opening a downstream door. Anything is preferable to the danger of being washed downstream and rolling. If the water is still, exit through a window. There is some hope in (most) modern vehicles that water will not enter the interior unless a door is opened.

If you come to a halt in the water, and the level is over (or close to being over) the bonnet, thus presenting a risk of the engine sipping some liquid, then you have a problem. It would be time to put into action the recovery plan you worked out before.

Switch the engine off. When the vehicle moves, less water will enter the engine compartment due to the bow wave effect. When the vehicle stops, the engine compartment will be flooded. That won't do anything any good. Switching the engine off also shuts down the electronics which is important as you do not want them shorted – water is an electrical conductor, especially salt water (by the way – never, ever immerse your vehicle in saltwater or drive in surf unless you want to ruin it in short order).

If the vehicle begins to move of its own accord, for example being washed downstream, open a downstream door. This will let water in and weight the vehicle. Bad, but not as bad as being upside down. You will not be able to open an upstream door.

If you come to a halt in fast-flowing water with a soft base and the vehicle seems safe, don't assume it'll stay that way. Have you ever stood on a beach and let the waves wash over your feet? Remember how the waves eroded the sand under your feet?

Fun, wasn't it? Not so much fun now the same thing is happening to your vehicle.

If the water is not so deep that there is a risk of the engine ingesting any liquid then there is no need to switch the engine off, and don't worry about the exhaust; as long as the engine is running there's no way water can enter and it can bubble away safely.

If you're driving a manual and it stalls in water and the engine won't restart, you may be able to get it out on the starter motor by cranking it over in first low a few times. This worked for me once in New Zealand, but needs a strong battery – even then you'll only be able to move perhaps a few tens of metres. However, I must warn that this technique does not impress any passengers who become prone to starting unhelpful sentences with "I told you so".

If a vehicle with electronic systems has been submerged then all may not be lost. Dry it out carefully; after the vehicle is recovered remove as many parts as you can and dry or warm (not cook) them over several hours. This technique works best if the vehicle has been immediately switched off before the water has had a chance to work itself into the circuits while the engine is running

and the electrics are live. Make sure everything is thoroughly dried before any restart attempt is made. The problem areas are where water can get in through tiny cavities where it can resist any drying out attempts. If it's all gone wrong I take the view you can't make it any worse.

environment

After a successful crossing, stop, if practical, and let the water drain from the vehicle. Don't make repeated crossings in areas that have sensitive water life or campers.

completion

When you move off do a little left-foot braking to dry the brakes and leave plenty of room for the following cars before running back with your camera. Remove any tarps or covers as these inhibit engine air cooling. Wet belts may whine until they are dry again, as may any passengers you used during the crossing. If you have done many crossings get your vehicle's fluids checked ahead of the next service as even with proper preparation they may been contaminated.

Same car, same line. Image 1 is too slow; notice how the water level doesn't change around the car, and the water is up to the sills. Image 2 at the correct speed the bow wave means the water level is below the sills, but when we go too fast (image 3) all that is lost and we no longer have a water level reduction around the sills.

Never trust water depth gauges. Both of these are incorrect.

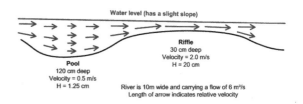

Assuming the river is of a constant width, the slower the water, the deeper it is. Shallow water is preferable, but whether you can actually drive the terrain or not is more important. Happily, faster-flowing, shallower water usually has a harder base, but there are exceptions to every rule.

All is going well on the crossing…then the car dips and water starts to move up the bonnet. You're now committed, so the response is to gently increase the throttle so the car maintains momentum against the greater water resistance. Do not stop. Celebrate when you finish.

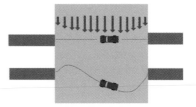

Two crossings, same river. Most people would drive directly across, and that may well be the best path as following where other vehicles have been is often best. However, if the river is fast-flowing then you want to present as little side angle to it as possible. A 4WD can handle a much greater water flow head-on than it can side-on. This is where the line in the lower part of the diagram can make sense. Where the water flow is shallow and slow, angle downstream; this allows you to cross the deepest and faster part of the river at an angle, greatly reducing the tendency to be pushed downstream. If you are pushed downstream it'll probably be the back end being pushed to face the car upstream, which is a lot safer than the car being pushed to face downstream, as may happen in the first instance. Once you are through the deep and fast part you can turn downstream to meet the exit. This isn't just theoretical, I've done it and it works (otherwise it wouldn't be included in this book), but every situation is different. The point is that thinking about the crossing can stack the odds in your favour.

This water was around one metre deep, over wheel height; definitely snorkel territory. Not visible is a cover for the bonnet, sprayed electrics and an experienced driver. The gear is first low; second wouldn't provide enough torque to shift the mountain of water out of the way, at least in this vehicle.

A standard car can ford deep water if prepared and driven correctly as this bow wave shows. This crossing was on a normal dirt road, and deepened rapidly. Note the side angle - be prepared for the unexpected!

If the water can comfortably pass under your chassis the crossing won't be a problem and if you get stuck the engine and interior is out of the way...but any higher and you need to use the correct crossing techniques. You still need to check for hidden obstacles on any crossing.

Near the car the water is turbulent and the bottom can be seen. It is fast-flowing, shallow and has a rocky base. Near the exit the water is still, and much deeper. The car can be driven to the right of the rock in the centre, but imagine if the water were a little higher and you found the rock with your diff. Not many people will ever see this crossing as they typically get to the summit and turn around, but we like to explore.

Sometimes the direct way isn't best. This Pajero angles off downstream in search of shallower water. The exit is in the top-left corner.

Too fast is fun and looks good, but car control is more difficult and it doesn't do the vehicle any good.

Water crossing techniques apply to deep mudbogs as well. There you won't have a problem with water flow, but you will have a problem with a soft bottom. Camper conversions can still be capable offroaders too!

Hummer H3 pushing a wall of water ahead of it but not smashing through - about the right speed.

Take heed of these signs. The authority's website will usually give flow conditions; watch for annual releases for environmental reasons.

A few years ago I was setting up a nav comp at night which involved driving the Thomson River just downstream of the dam. I'd been through the previous week and the water was deep, but nothing problematic, so that night we carried on down to the river. However, our path was blocked by a tent which had been literally set up on the track. The campers were most surprised to see us at 2am and after moving their tent couldn't believe we were going to drive the river. "But it's really deep" they warned. "No worries there," I said, full of local knowledge. But not local enough because I'd missed the sign saying the seasonal flow had been released in the last three days. I began to notice something was amiss as the water climbed beyond the headlights, onto the bonnet and moved up the windscreen. Nothing for it but to floor the throttle before the revs dropped and aim upstream, so we finished the crossing somewhat sideways, lucky and chastened. I have had a new respect for river signs ever since.

A water blind is a widely used device to minimise water flow into the engine compartment. Its value comes mainly from ensuring any water that does get in isn't high-pressure, and its large blunt area does a better job of creating a bow wave than a plain bull bar or front end. This MSA bra is purpose-made for the job, but bodging up a cheap tarp with ocky straps can work although not as well and we've seen these attempts come loose mid-crossing.

If possible, stop after a crossing to let the water drain out. This Rangie Sport has also raised its air suspension before the crossing began.

CHAPTER 22

HILLS

The most dangerous offroading terrain is a hill. Gravity is not your friend.

the terrain

The difficulty with hills isn't so much the gradient as the terrain in combination with the gradient. Hills can be rocky, sandy, muddy...the techniques for those terrains need to be applied to hills too, but the gradient amplifies the challenge as you need more traction than on the flat. Appropriate tyres, lockers and good articulation become even more important, and so does a strong engine, not for its top-end power, but because it can precisely meter out low-end torque.

percents and grades

Ever see those signs saying a hill is a certain percentage? That just means the ratio of the run to the rise. The run is the horizontal distance travelled, the rise is the vertical. At 45 degrees they are equal, so that's 100%. The following table shows the percentage grade, the equivalent angle in degrees, the rise, and the actual distance travelled.

The reason percentages are used is because it's easy to tell how far vertically you have travelled. If you descending a 9% grade and have travelled 2km, then you have lost about 180m in elevation (approximately 560ft).

In an ideal world where it has the traction, the surface is smooth and the vehicle is lightly loaded, a 4WD will generally climb a 45 degree hill. In the real world this isn't likely, so the maximum hill climb is likely to be closer to 30-40 degrees, and anything near 30 degrees looks pretty steep.

Percentage	Angle	Rise (km)	Distance (km)
100%	45	10.000	14.142
84%	40	8.391	13.054
70%	35	7.002	12.208
58%	30	5.774	11.547
47%	25	4.663	11.034
36%	20	3.640	10.642
27%	15	2.679	10.353
18%	10	1.763	10.154
9%	5	0.875	10.038
7%	4	0.699	10.024
5%	3	0.524	10.014
3%	2	0.349	10.006
2%	1	0.175	10.002

weight shift on hills

When a vehicle is on a gradient the uphill wheels have much less weight on them than the downhill wheels. As an example, take a 3,000kg 4WD with a 2,970mm wheelbase and assume each axle supports half the load, or 1,500kg. (This is never the case in practice but for the purposes of demonstration it will work.) On a 30 degree slope the uphill wheels now only handle around 1,270kg, but the downhills are up around 1,730kg.

This is an important point for offroaders. As the weight on the uphill wheels is much less, their grip is correspondingly decreased, and if the vehicle is nose-up then steering ability is decreased because of this grip loss. The suspension is designed for 1,500kg per axle, and with less weight the front suspension is too hard so the uphill wheels are prone to bounce, further reducing grip. At the rear the suspension is compressed, lowering the vehicle, possibly leading to clearance issues. The situation is worsened by acceleration.

The amount of weight shift depends on the position of the centre of gravity, both horizontal and vertical. Most people understand intuitively that raising the centre of gravity reduces the sideslope angle which the vehicle can negotiate, but it also increases weight transfer on gradients and thus becomes a limiting factor there, too. If the vehicle in the above example raises its centre of gravity from 800 to 1,000mm, and also changes the level weight distribution to 1,600kg on the rear axle and 1,400kg on the front, then the front axle on a 30 degree gradient now has only 1,050kg on it – about 500kg per tyre – while the rears are now up to 1,950kg or nearly a tonne per tyre.

The ideal tyre pressure varies with weight on the tyre but it is clearly impractical to vary for each climb, although in difficult situations it's no bad idea. Dropping the front pressures for an uphill climb would restore the contact patch and reduce the bouncing. This is also where low-profile tyres have a significant disadvantage as the extra weight on the downhill tyres means there's very little rubber between the rim and the ground. In fact, with some low profile tyres (Chapter 7) I do not air down at all in hilly country for this reason, which is a significant handicap.

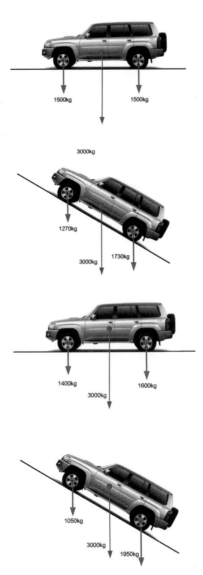

Diagrams showing weight shift on hills. The arrows representing weight are in proportion.

preparation and kit list

Your car will work hard at low speed, so it needs to be in good mechanical order. Your park brake should be working well and a wheel chock is a good idea, as is a bulldog clip for your seatbelt to stop it retracting when on a hill. Walking to the top of a hill is recommended so you aren't surprised by something around the corner and to check that the vehicle's ramp angle can deal with the crest. In convoys, let the first car get all the way to the top and then call the second in turn. If multiple cars are on a hill space them widely. Disable stability control if it will rob you of precious momentum as you ascend, but consider leaving it on for downhills as should you need to correct a slide it could be of great assistance. Leave it on if disabling it also disables electronic traction control (Chapter 9). If you have an adaptive terrain system (Chapter 9) and your centre diff cannot be locked then choose a Rock Crawl mode for hills. This is because you really want the centre diff to be locked up as much as possible so when ascending a hill the front wheels don't start to spin and the rears have little torque. Rock Crawl modes typically pre-load the centre diff, reducing this risk. Other preparation should be as per whatever terrain you're driving in.

If you drive up a hill you can drive down it. If you drive down a hill and have to turn around and come back up – or worse, reverse back up – things can be a lot closer to impossible and you run the risk of transmission damage. So an exploratory walk can be time well-invested, and you should only send one car down at a time. With many hills you can't see down the hill until you start – another reason to get out, have a look and line up properly.

Tie everything down, as steep inclines have a habit of dislodging things and a drinks bottle under the brake isn't a good idea. As ever, have a failure plan and especially for slippery hills; where is your runoff area? Will you run out of approach, ramp or departure angles?

Bulldog clips at the ready should they be needed to stop seatbelts retracting if the passenger or driver needs to exit the vehicle. This should be avoided if possible, but if you do get out and back in you definitely want your seatbelt attached again.

driving techniques

ascending

Select the gear you'll use to get to the top, as changing gear on the hill is best avoided. This is because any gear change involves a temporary loss of drive, causing the vehicle to lose momentum quickly. The problem with offroad hills is that when the vehicle is travelling quite slowly there is not much momentum to lose before it rolls backwards and since the hill is steep the loss is quick. Therefore, when a gear is changed, chances are the vehicle has lost so much speed it can no longer take a higher gear, or if you're going for a lower gear then the sudden shockload will damage the transmission. It is possible in manuals, but it's not easy and you risk damaging the gearbox. Automatics can change with less risk, but even so best select a gear there too, maybe by pulling the shifter back to "2" instead of "D" (Chapter 4 has more on automatic gearboxes). Only use first low up a hill if it is very steep or you can go very slowly. Otherwise second is better, or even third or fourth. The higher the gear, the less the wheelspin and better control. The old credo of "second low up a hill" may be too low a gear in today's world of strong engines and six-speed gearboxes.

Keep a constant momentum up the hill, go as straight up as possible, especially if it's soft, because any side angle means the car sinks in on the downhill side, which starts a vicious circle. Don't get onto the hill and apply the loud pedal, apply the power before you start the climb and keep the throttle steady, but ease off over the top. All else being equal, more momentum is required on a hill than on the flat, and if the front starts to bounce around it is very important that you are pointing straight up. Steering capacity in general will be reduced as there's less weight on the front wheels and therefore less traction.

Hills are often rutted; if you can, stay in the ruts. If you can't, you'll need to straddle and that requires a careful line which is risky in the wet. Extremely steep and short hills can be conquered by momentum alone, but anything much higher than a few metres will usually need sustained traction or an appetite for risk that will later get lots of views on YouTube.

The big problem with hills is when you need to stop and go back down again. Don't even think about turning around on a steep hill; you'll only try it once in your life.

If you absolutely need to change down a gear on a hill in a manual it can be done. I had to do this to get my fully-loaded Defender over a very hot Big Red sand dune. You need to start off in the higher gear (in this case second high) and as soon as the revs drop, very quickly dip the clutch fully, slide the shifter into first and then (the tricky bit) smoothly bring the clutch up while setting the revs at the point they should be for the gear and speed. You need to be very quick, smooth and confident, but in general you should avoid the need to do this at all.

You can't necessarily see what's in front of you as you crest a hill. It pays to get out and look first.

A slippery descent; first low, no brakes, using what little ruts there are.

This Prado hasn't quite crested a short, steep hill because the front wheel hit the hole dug out by previous drivers. If the line had been a little away from the hole it would have worked, or alternatively a touch more momentum would have seen the car through. However, the momentum approach runs the risk of the wheel bouncing out of the hole, having no traction as a result and the car going sideways. Avoiding the hole means not tackling the hill square on, which again has a risk of sliding sideways. There is no single answer, just tradeoffs. Incidentally, with the wheel in the hole as it is now the car is well secured from sliding sideways as the driver begins preparation to bring the car back down the hill.

A wet, rocky, muddy climb with a bend. Doesn't get much more difficult than that, so be prepared to back out.

failing a hill climb

The technique varies depending on whether you are driving an automatic or a manual, but all the methods have this first step in common:

recognise you've failed

If you need to abort a climb, do so before you actually grind to a spinning halt, especially on slippery or soft surfaces. If forward progress has stopped, or it's clear it will stop, you have failed the climb. In some cases you might decide to fail the climb before you actually stop (and that is often a wise idea), for example if it's harder going than you thought or if you haven't walked the track and have decided it would have been a good idea after all. Whatever you do, don't end up with wheels spinning, as if wheels spin they lose lateral traction, which means you are likely to slip sideways, and if you slip sideways you're likely to end up side-on to the hill, and risk a rollover.

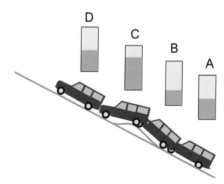

On some hills you find mounds made for drainage. Often they temporarily steepen then reduce the gradient. To deal with them (green bar shows relative throttle position):

A: Approach as quickly as the terrain allows.

B: Just before the front wheels crest reduce the power but do not come off the throttle entirely. This is to avoid jumping the front over the crest and risking damage as well as lost momentum.

C: As the back wheels crest ensure you smoothly apply power to regain momentum, using more throttle than you would to maintain the climb so you accelerate.

D: Smoothly reduce throttle back to the appropriate setting for the climb.

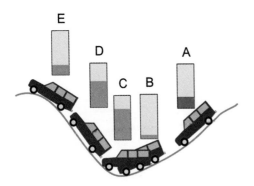

How to apply throttle on an upslope:

A: Use descent techniques (see later in this chapter).

B: As the vehicle levels, use a little throttle to maintain momentum. You want to be going as fast as you can, which is likely to be quite slow, otherwise you'll compress the front suspension and bounce the front wheels.

C: As the front starts to rise smoothly apply a lot of power. The car is now rotating so the power won't destabilise the vehicle, and you need to get as much benefit as you can from the fact the rears are still coming downhill or not on the main slope.

D: Maintain throttle. At this point don't increase power as that is likely to result in wheelspin.

E: As the front wheels begin to crest smoothly reduce power. In most situations you're looking to bring the car to a near halt simply by judging power reduction and not using brakes. This is best for any subsequent descent, safety, and car sympathy as the front wheels are then less likely to be in the air.

quick and slow fails

There are two ways to abort a hill climb and come back down again.

- Slow fail
- Quick fail

The first way is the safest and easiest, and should be used wherever possible.

The slow fail involves stopping the vehicle and carefully preparing to reverse back down. It's the preferred technique because it's easier to execute and less stress on the vehicle. However, it assumes that you have sufficient traction to be able to hold the vehicle when the climb fails, and if you don't, you wouldn't have attempted the climb.

The quick fail is riskier, harder to execute, harder on the vehicle and should only be used in situations where there is insufficient traction to hold the vehicle on the hill. You really need to be asking yourself whether it is safe or advisable to tackle such a hill.

In all the descriptions below, keep at least one hand on the wheel at all times.

manuals

Low-rangers: Slow fail

1. Brake firmly (but don't stab) and stall the vehicle in gear. Don't touch the clutch. Throughout this process keep at least one hand on the steering wheel at all times.

2. Apply the park brake firmly. Keep your foot on the footbrake.

3. Turn the ignition off. The engine is already off, because you stalled it. This is done so if the vehicle does roll backwards it does not bump-start.

4. The vehicle is now secured. The next part is when you want to reverse back down the slope.

5. Cautiously put the clutch down and put the vehicle into reverse. Bring the clutch up. Keep your foot on the brake. The vehicle may groan a little as by dipping the clutch you have (temporarily) removed one of the mechanisms holding it on the hill.

6. Prepare. In a moment you'll reverse back the way you came, so you need to check:
   - The path backwards. Is it clear?
   - Are the front wheels straight, or do you at least know where they're pointing?
   - What's going to happen when I move backwards?
   - Do you need anyone to give you directions? How will they do it – by radio or by shouting? If the latter, consider opening the windows. Remember the "hand down" direction style (e.g. "right hand down" to rotate the steering wheel clockwise).

7. Slowly release the park brake.

8. Very gently, release the footbrake pressure. In some vehicles the engine will hold the vehicle on the hill. With others you'll need some light pressure on the brake pedal.

9. Get ready to switch the engine on. When you do, the vehicle will start in gear and move backwards.

10. Start the engine, with the vehicle still in gear. As the vehicle moves, reduce the pressure on the brake pedal if you needed your foot on it. In any case, keep it covered with light pressure. Return your hand to the steering wheel immediately.

11. Reverse down the hill. Reverse is usually slightly higher than first low. Try not to brake hard, and if you do need to brake do so smoothly, don't jab. Remember where the steering wheel is pointing. Directions from outside will help.

12. Keep going backwards until you're well down the hill. Then reconsider your approach.

If you are descending too fast then press the brake, even quite hard, rather than dip the clutch. If you need to stop again, simply switch the engine off and apply the brakes then go through the process again.

This technique has been used for decades and is recommended by most manufacturers. It does not stress the vehicle. Some petrol engines have a surge on startup so require extra brake pressure when the engine is started, otherwise you'll leap down the hill.

Low-rangers: Quick fail

This is not a preferred method, but if it is clear it would not be safe to stop the vehicle on the hill then it can be used. Notice that there is no step to check behind before descending because it all happens so fast there is no time. So it's a good idea to have thought about a possible descent before you even ascend.

1. Stop the vehicle by braking quickly but smoothly. Dip the clutch at the same time and keep the engine running.

2. Immediately change into reverse.

3. Bring the clutch up, right foot over the brake, applying gentle pressure as required and back you go.

Softroaders: Slow Fail

Manual softroaders do not have the low gearing required to use the same technique as low-rangers, and if the clutch is up these vehicles will come down hills far too fast to be safely controlled in real-world situations. Even a key-on-off-on-off technique where you start and stop the engine in quick cycles is too fast, and some vehicles cannot be started with the clutch up. Instead, use this method:

1. Brake firmly (but don't stab) and stall the vehicle in gear. Don't touch the clutch. Throughout this process keep at least one hand on the steering wheel at all times.

2. Apply the park brake firmly. Keep your foot on the footbrake.

3. Put the clutch down and start the engine. While the clutch is down, put the vehicle into reverse. Keep your foot on the brake. The vehicle may groan a little as by dipping the clutch you have removed one of the mechanisms holding it on the hill.

4. Prepare. In a moment you'll reverse back the way you came, so you need to check:

   - The path backwards. Is it clear?

   - Are the front wheels straight?

   - What's going to happen when I move backwards?

   - Do you need anyone to give you directions? How will they do it – by radio or by shouting? If the latter, consider opening the windows. Remember the "hand down" direction format (e.g. "left hand down" to rotate the steering wheel anti-clockwise).

5. To move off, slowly release the park brake. There may be a little groan from the vehicle as it takes the strain.

6. Cautiously release the brake pressure until the vehicle is just about to move backwards, then hold that pressure constant.

7. Bring the clutch up, maintaining that brake pressure, and the vehicle will move backwards, slowly. You are forcing the vehicle to rotate

the wheels against the brakes, which is good because rotating a wheel at a slow speed means it is less likely to skid than if you just applied the brakes with the clutch fully down.

8. Keep going backwards until you're well down the hill. Then reconsider your approach.

If you are descending too fast then dip the clutch or increase the brake pressure. If you need to stop again, simply increase the brake pressure, switch the engine off (it may not stall as it's going downhill) and go from step 1.

This is not as good a technique as the low-range version, but you do what you can and not having low-range in a manual is a definite limitation on the hills. You know you've got the throttle and clutch balance right if you dip the clutch and the car stops without you varying the brake pressure.

Softroaders: Quick fail

1. Stop the vehicle by braking quickly but smoothly. Dip the clutch at the same time and keep the engine running.

2. Immediately change into reverse.

3. Keeping the right foot over the brake, bring the clutch up to move the car (but not fully up) and reduce the brake pressure without coming off the brake entirely. Be prepared to go backwards quickly. This is a quicker version of steps 7 and 8 above.

automatics

Both these techniques are for low-rangers and softroaders. The slow fail is preferable:

Slow fail

1. Stop the vehicle with your left foot by braking quickly but smoothly. Note: you can use your right foot instead and swap feet when swapped.

2. Apply the park brake. Leave the vehicle in the forwards gear it is in.

3. Prepare. In a moment you'll reverse back the way you came, so you need to check:

   - The path backwards. Is it clear?
   - Are the front wheels straight?
   - What's going to happen when I move backwards?
   - Do you need anyone to give you directions? How will they do it – by radio or by shouting? If the latter, consider opening the windows. Remember the "hand down" direction format. (e.g. "right hand down" to rotate the steering wheel clockwise).

4. Place the vehicle into reverse. Keep your foot on the brake. The vehicle may 'groan' as the transmission now wants to take it back down the hill, not drive it up. Additional footbrake pressure may therefore be required.

5. Slowly release the park brake.

6. Cautiously release the brake pressure until the vehicle is just about to move backwards, then hold that pressure.

7. Now increase the revs until the vehicle moves backwards. Keep your foot on the brake. This is driving through the brakes.

8. Keep going backwards until you're well down the hill. Then reconsider your approach.

If you need to stop simply take your foot smoothly off the accelerator.

As the slope incline changes you will need to modulate throttle and brake to maintain speed. You know you've got the balance right if when you lift off the accelerator the vehicle gently stops without you varying the brake pressure.

The advantage of this method is that you are forcing the wheels to turn slowly as opposed to braking them to a set speed, which is stopping them from turning fast. This reduces the chance of a wheel locking and losing traction as the wheels are always turning. It should only be used where necessary, not for long distances, and it works well with softroader autos.

Quick fail

Again, not an ideal technique but if you need to get down in a hurry:

1. Stop the vehicle with your left foot.

2. Immediately shift into reverse, keeping footbrake pressure. Do not release the footbrake until the transmission is shifted into reverse.

3. Immediately accelerate, keeping your foot on the brake to drive through the brakes.

This is more or less the same as the slow fail without the park brake, except that you do it a lot quicker!

hill starts

manuals

The classic hill start is to hold the car on the park brake, clutch down, into gear, revs up, bring the clutch up to biting point and release the park brake as you move off. That works, but runs a risk of wheelspin on takeoff and relies upon the park brake being strong enough to hold you.

Another way, which works with many modern cars with anti-stall controls, is simply to put your right foot on the brake, park brake off, clutch down, select first low and bring the clutch up without touching the accelerator. As you get to the clutch biting point just ease off the foot brake as you bring the clutch the rest of the way up. That way it doesn't rely on the park brake and there is little chance of wheelspin, although it does mean you start in first low.

Another technique is heel and toe. Here you apply the foot brake, yet also depress the accelerator for revs with the same foot. Then bring the clutch up to move off. This is borrowed from racing cars, and it's a lot easier in those cars as they have pedals especially designed to do it. In some 4WDs it may not be possible at all.

Hand throttles, for the few cars that have them now, are another option, and so is just reversing back to flatter ground!

automatics

Easy. Just hold the car with your left foot on the footbrake, then release the brake pressure till the car is just about to move. Then hold that pressure. Next, using your right foot, simply increase the revs till you move off, and as you pull away smoothly come off the brake entirely.

electronic aids

Refer to Chapter 9 for:

- Hill Start Assist
- Hill Descent Control systems
- Gradient Release Control, Gradient Acceleration Control

Keep in the ruts if you can, especially where it's slippery.

Quite a number of lines to take up this hill; the correct one will vary depending on your vehicle's characteristics. Often it may be better to opt for a harder line first that becomes easier, than vice-versa.

1   It is very common for one wheel to lift during a hill climb, and often both at the same time. Obviously air has little traction so this is best avoided, or done only if the car is pointing straight up the hill. Even then it risks mechanical damage.

2   Sometimes you can't drive it and you need to winch.

3   One wheel in the air but both rears firmly on the ground keep the H3 moving. It has just come out of a water crossing so the wet tyres aren't gripping as well as they would if they were dry, especially if previous vehicles have dumped water all over the track instead of stopping to let it drain first.

Very often hills need momentum, in the highest gear the engine will comfortably pull. This is usually second, or third low.

Only a small incline, but with road tyres and no ruts the back end slid in. Reversing all the way out and trying an entirely different line did the trick.

If this were flat ground this Patrol wouldn't be stopped, but it's not flat and it's out of axle flex so it's going nowhere. The solution is a slightly different line to keep the wheels in contact with the earth, or more momentum to carry the car through. Either way, backing up for a fair distance is going to be in order.

A Jeep Wrangler Rubicon climbing a steep, rutless hill whose surface is also a little loose. The combination of the gradient, lack of ruts to tramline and the loose, damp surface mean this is the most dangerous type of slope to ascend.

descents

Select a low gear, usually first low. Go straight down at a constant speed, picking a line that keeps all four wheels on the ground. Reduce speed as far as possible before you start the descent. If a wheel loses traction, for example lifting in the air

or coming close to doing so, you will lose engine braking on that axle, the car will lurch forwards, you'll hit the brakes and perhaps induce a skid. For that reason you should engage cross-axle lockers if you have them, but be aware of the effect of this on steering. In any event read the terrain and don't over-react if there is the occasional slight skid.

If it all goes wrong and you go too fast, avoid rolling at all costs. Better to smack into a tree head-on than roll avoiding it. If the back slides out, look well ahead to where you want the car to go, reduce brake pressure if applied (or accelerate slightly if you weren't braking) and keep the steering wheels pointed in your desired direction of travel.

If there are ruts, use them, and certainly do so in the wet. Be very careful to keep the steering wheel straight in the ruts; it is possible to descend straight in ruts with a turn of lock on, then as the ruts lessen, traction is regained and the car jumps out sideways into a tree.

Never, ever descend in neutral. You are almost guaranteed to lock wheels. If first low with some extra braking is too fast then you or the car are not capable of the descent. If you take a bad line and feel the car tipping then you can halt to stop it getting worse, but remember that jabbing the brakes could be enough to send you over whereas letting it roll may not. Sound scary? That's why we recommend walking the track first to plan the descent.

Few hills have a consistent slope and traction all the way down. Sometimes there will be spots where you'll need to accept the car will travel quickly, other times you can slow it right down. Look for variations in slope and traction and use the easier parts to get the speed right off so the next tough part is negotiated more slowly.

This Pajero is descending a short but slippery downhill. It cannot get square-on to the hill and there are no real ruts to assist. The driver absolutely must not brake otherwise the wheels will lock and the vehicle will go sideways.

There's nowhere near enough traction so you're glad if the belly rubs to act as a brake, keep in the ruts and steer within

them, lowest gear you can and walk (slide?) it first to check you don't need to turn around and drive up!

avoiding locking a wheel

If a wheel is locked sometimes it will brake better in loose surfaces, sometimes worse. What will certainly happen is that you will lose steering ability and on a hill that means potentially going sideways, which leads to a roll. Therefore, preventing a wheel locking is of paramount importance. If a vehicle is proceeding down a hill at five km/h, under brakes, then when traction is lost, let's say it goes to seven km/h. As brakes were applied, the wheels are no longer rotating. A loss of traction, no steering and we have ourselves a sledge.

If the same vehicle were proceeding down the same hill at five km/h, but under engine braking only (Chapter 3), and traction was lost, it would again go to seven km/h. However, the wheels would still be rotating at five km/h. That means you have a measure of steering control. Hardly sports car handling, but perhaps enough to avoid a tree. Engine braking also helps loss of traction in the first place, as the brakes need to be applied less hard.

It also helps to accelerate, gently, or reduce braking pressure if applied. Now this really is against all instincts. Why do it? Because it helps the wheels to grip. Remember driven wheels are better able to bite and pull, idling wheels are more likely to just stop rotating, and the more of a tyre's grip you use for braking the less there is for lateral grip and steering.

low-ranger manuals: descents

Manual descents start with gear selection. This should be the lowest gear the car has that will not lock the wheels. Mostly this is first low, but in some cases, like very slippery descents, a higher gear like second low is better to avoid a wheel slipping, even if it doesn't lock. It leads to a higher descent speed, but the laws of physics dictate slippery slopes can't be descended at crawl pace so if you try by braking you'll just slide. Better to accept a faster pace and some control, or find another way.

Another situation where a higher gear than the lowest may be applicable is a dune descent, where there may be more than sufficient retardation from the vehicle sinking into the sand and a low gear would cause further sinking, risking a loss of control. It could also be that the hill simply isn't very steep, so there's no point crawling down it.

However, for most hills you'll want the lowest possible gear. Simply come off the pedals and let the engine do the work of slowing the car. If it's too fast, gently modulate the brakes without dipping the clutch. The chances of stalling are small as gravity is helping the car move, and you can slow the vehicle quite significantly this way with a lot of brake pressure. However, if you dip the clutch the wheels are likely to lock, but if you just press the brake the engine will continue to turn the wheels and not lock. Use variations in hill slope, such as washouts, to slow the vehicle down more than you would like so you are then going as slowly as possible as you enter the next steep part.

If the wheels do lock release the brake pressure just a little, hold it and then gently reapply. Reduce any steering lock if any was applied.

softroader manuals: descents

The best gear for descending in a softroader is always going to be first gear. Very often that will be too high, and the low-ranger technique of pressing the brake while the clutch is up isn't as effective as you may stall and in any case you may be going too quickly. An alternative is to start off stationary, clutch down, brake on, before simply lifting the clutch up to move the vehicle, keeping as much brake pressure on as possible without stalling and not using the accelerator at all. This is the same technique described above with regard to failing a hill climb. Again, this technique forces the wheel to turn. This is nowhere near as good as low-range, and thus manual softroaders are limited on hills compared to low-rangers.

low-ranger and softroader automatics: descents

Many modern automatics with five, six or even eight speeds can be driven like a manual downhill; first low and just let the engine brake for you. However, softroaders and older automatics without a really low first gear will simply descend too quickly for many situations with that technique, and eventually even modern automatics may be going a little fast. If traction is good you simply apply the brakes a little, but if it is marginal you run the risk of locking the wheels and coming to a halt, unlike in a manual where there's a direct connection from the engine to the wheels and you can apply lots of brake pressure provided the clutch is up. The solution for automatics, both for low-rangers and softroaders, is driving through the brakes. This is how to do it:

1. At the top of the descent hold the car with your left foot on the brake such that the car isn't moving. Select first low.

2. Increase the revs till the car starts to move and begins the descent so that you are only moving because of the extra revs. If you have the ratio of brake pressure to revs right you should be able to gently remove your foot from the accelerator and the car should stop.

3. You will need to increase the brake pressure as the gradient increases, for example as you go over the top of the crest.

This technique has the advantage of forcing the wheels to turn slowly as opposed to braking them, which is stopping them from turning. In other words it reduces the chance of a slide. Use this technique for short distances only, a few tens of metres here and there. In other places simply braking gently will be sufficient, for example where all four wheels are on the ground and the track is not too uneven.

Note that some modern vehicles will either not permit throttle and brake to be used at the same time, or limit the throttle you can apply. In this case do the best you can, and also consider electronic hill descent systems (Chapter 9).

changing gear downhill

In a manual vehicle you will need to change gear, sometimes when you are heading downhill. For on-road driving you would simply make the gear change and not worry about it, but consider the case of driving downhill and changing from first low to second low. Under first low you have excellent engine braking. Under second, still a fair amount of engine braking. But during the change? The clutch is down, no drive to the wheels, no engine braking. The solution is not to rush the change, as that could induce wheelspin, but to gently brake throughout the gear change. If it is too slippery to consider braking, then you probably should not be changing gear either!

Automatics can use the same technique of covering the brake as while their shifts are quick, there will be a momentary loss of engine braking.

stopping downhill

Manuals

To stop a manual on a downhill:

1. Turn the engine off. Turbo timers need to be disabled if fitted.

2. Apply the footbrake smoothly to stall the car in gear. Then apply the park brake.

3. To restart, release the park brake and start the car in gear, never having touched the clutch. This avoids braking which reduces the chance of a slip.

You will need to switch the engine off, otherwise it may be impossible, or very difficult to stall the vehicle. The entire stopping process should take perhaps three seconds.

Automatics

To stop an automatic on a downhill.

1. Drive through the brakes (as described in section: low ranger and softranger: descents starting on pg 273), then smoothly release

the accelerator to stop the car which should equally smoothly come to a halt.

2. Apply the park brake, gently release the footbrake and the vehicle settle on the park brake. Shift the transmission into P.

3. To restart, apply footbrake, shift the transmission into first low.

4. Park brake off, hold vehicle on footbrake so it's just about to move.

5. Increase revs to move off to drive through the brakes. Then continue as is, or just brake normally.

ABS

ABS is not a substitute for engine braking but may complement it. It may or may not stop a wheel locking at very low speeds, depending on how it is calibrated. What will certainly help is using the lowest gear possible, as this means there is less braking effort required, which means less chance of a braking-induced wheel lock. If your ABS works in low-range then you have more ability to brake hard without fear of inducing a skid, although you should still use the most appropriate gear (which will usually be the lowest).

parking on a hill

In general, try not to, it's not unknown for parked vehicles to become un-parked by themselves or just creep backwards. 4WD park brakes may not reliably hold the vehicle on a hill, especially those that act on the rear brakes. If the vehicle is in 4WD (centre diff locked, hubs in etc.) then although the brakes act on the rear wheels all four will in effect

be locked. Try to stop in an area as flat as possible, use logs or rocks as chocks and make sure all four wheels are on the ground. Don't stop too close to another vehicle. If you get out, use a bulldog clip to prevent the seatbelt retracting as you will not be able to pull it out again.

Beware vehicles with "clever" centre diffs or couplings; some of these unlock when stationary, so park brakes only work on the rear wheels.

All vehicles parked on hills should be in low range and any centre diffs locked, manual hubs engaged.

Manuals

1. Gear in first low (usually a lower gear than reverse).

2. Ignition off to prevent an accidental roll-start.

3. Park brake on hard.

4. Chock the wheels.

Automatics

Automatics are special. They have a pin inside the park brake mechanism and if you simply put it in park on a steep hill you may well not be able to shift it back into drive. The only way to do it is to move the car a forwards a few centimetres; easier said than done. To park an automatic on the hill:

1. Come to a smooth stop, footbrake on.

2. Pull the park brake on hard.

3. Shift into neutral, with the foot still hard on the brake.

4. Very gently release the footbrake so the car rocks back against the park brake – it may hold, if not you'll need a chock.

5. Once it holds and doesn't rock back any further then put the shifter into park and switch the engine off – using this method you shouldn't have any difficulty moving the car out of park when you drive off.

Try this technique on a shallow hill and see how much easier it is to move the shifter in and out of park.

vehicles without a lockable centre diff

Some vehicles are AWD but cannot lock their centre couplings or differentials. **Such vehicles are dangerous on steep hills.**

Road vehicles are set up with a front brake bias, which means the front wheels get more braking effort than the rear. This is because the front wheels do most of the braking work, but also because if you're going to lock wheels when braking, better the front than the rear so you slide straight on, as opposed to spinning around with the rear locked (Chapter 8 has more detail in the section on brake bias).

When a vehicle is facing up a steep hill most of the weight, and therefore traction, is on the rear wheels, but all that braking effort still goes to the front wheels, so it is very easy to lock the front wheels into a skid and still keep the rears rolling. If the fronts are sliding, you can't steer and very soon you have problems which marry the words "sideways" and "hill" – never a good combination.

However, if you have a locked centre diff or similar then that can't happen, because it is then impossible to lock both front wheels without also locking the rears. Another way to look at it; the huge additional traction of the downhill, rear wheels with weight on them forces the lighter uphill fronts to continue turning at the same speed, thus you retain control. You can get into a four-wheel skid if you find the right hill, but with a locked centre diff the point is that the front wheels must turn as long as the rears also turn, meaning you will have control. This is the ideal situation for backing down a hill.

What is not ideal is having some form of centre diff system which disengages, allowing the front wheels to lock (which they do easily) and the rears to still rotate. This is exactly what happens with some vehicles and that is the safety problem. Hill Descent Control (Chapter 9) would solve the problem as it brakes each wheel individually, thus permitting steering control, but most HDC systems work far too fast for a safe descent backwards in many real-world situations, especially without low-range. In any case, assume you've stopped on a hill and are holding the car on the brake. Without a locked centre diff it could still slide backwards with the rears rotating and the fronts locked.

The best solution is that if the centre diff cannot be locked, or does not automatically lock itself, then avoid steep or slippery hills in that vehicle.

environment

As per the type of terrain you are driving in. Remember that hills can very easily be chewed up when driven in the wet, more so than level ground.

completion

Check everything is still where it should be as often things move around. Allow brakes time to cool after steep and prolonged descents and beware engine overheating after prolonged climbs at low speed. Give it a couple of minutes to cool down at the top of a descent before you switch it off, but prolonged idling doesn't do any good. Apart from that, check as per the terrain you've driven; for example hose the vehicle free of salt if you're been on the dunes.

1   *This hill is totally blind to the driver. The front left is about to drop into a rut, there may be a clearance problem over the crest, it's pretty steep and there's some loose material too. Once over the top you are committed so it pays to plan ahead. You can accept some scraping on the way down, keeping a direct line, as gravity will assist you. Coming back up any scraping over the top will rob you of valuable momentum so it is best avoided, which is easier said than done and may mean a line that isn't square to the hill and thus more risky.*

2   *Braking on three wheels as one rear is in the air, but Hill Descent Control is still ensuring a controlled descent on this steep, but smooth hill. With engine braking alone there would be no braking on the rear axle at this point. The hill is smooth so the relatively quick descent of Hill Descent Control isn't a problem. However, as in this case ABS works at low speed you may as well brake yourself to permit a more controlled descent.*

3   *It's dry so the ruts can be straddled on this hill. Be careful you don't drive yourself into a situation you can't get out of; could be you'll need to cross the ruts before they finish. It is easier to straddle ruts coming down than going up.*

4   *It's a good idea to think about a hill before you drive it and a training course is a great way to explore your vehicles capabilities.*

5   *A rocky descent; extremely low gearing, slowest possible speed and a careful line. Rock sliders as fitted here are invaluable.*

1   Steep, but dry, good traction and all four wheels on the ground so not difficult. Lowest gear, straight down, modulate brake, enjoy.

2   A very steep descent. There is no point trying to stop the car, once you're committed you are committed. Before the car goes over the edge it must be absolutely square to the hill, clutch fully up and in gear. Brakes are covered but not locked hard on the descent. Not for the faint of heart or those with poor approach angles, and you must accept a fairly quick return to earth.

3   A steepish and slippery mud descent. Look where you want to go, keep the steering wheel pointed where you want to go, use first low (maybe second), centre diff locked if applicable, use electronic hill descent systems if possible but not cross-axle lockers as they restrict steering. Use smooth control inputs, but if the wheels lock, relax the brake pressure slightly – but don't jump off the brakes. If you turn the steering wheel and the car doesn't respond then wait; if you really need to turn then jam the brakes on, wind on full lock and then release the brakes. If that worked then prepare to do lots of quick opposite-lock correction, if not, prepare for impact. The Freelander is a little sideways already. The worst part is easily visible in the middle where the ruts widen, so don't be expecting to slow down in that patch, do it before or after.

4   Steep, loose rocks, uneven surface. Typical situation for the occasional wheel lock as traction changes across the four wheels. Anticipate, steer straight and go gently.

1   It may look like a Patrol, but it's really a toboggan. Shallow hill, but very slippery so ruts are a must. You're going to the bottom whether you like it or not.

2   Get square on to the hill before you start the descent, and think about where the rear and front wheels will go.

3   Thinking about the hill. What is at the top? What will happen if we can't make it? What is the best gear, and what revs? Should I attempt to crawl upwards slowly, or do I need momentum? Will I run out of clearance? Is anyone close behind me? In this case the hill is fairly smooth – often they are corrugated as drivers run up with too high a pressure and then boot the throttle, causing wheelspin. The track is fairly straight so there will be minimal loss of speed due to turns or shimmying, and traction is reasonably good. It was a straightforward climb in third low for that vehicle.

4   A lack of axle flex and a less than ideal line means the Pathfinder has only three wheels on the ground. Still, this temporary situation may be preferable to having to go sideways to keep four wheels on the ground. On this hill there is actually a little choice in line despite the track being narrow, but the traction is good, tyres grip well so it's fine to lift a wheel. The driver should anticipate this and be ready with additional brake pressure or to let the vehicle go a little because as soon as one wheel on an axle loses traction the differential in effect moves all engine braking to that wheel. This is why engaging rear and sometimes front differential locks is a good idea downhill, it means that you'll still get engine braking even when a wheel on an axle is in the air or has otherwise lost traction.

CHAPTER 23

SIDESLOPES

A sideslope is crossing a hill at an angle, as opposed to straight up or down. Nobody likes sideslopes, but sometimes there's no option.

the terrain

Sideslopes are dangerous because the vehicle can tip over, but that's nowhere near as likely as it feels from inside the vehicle. Unladen, your 4WD might be able to handle a sideslope of up to 45 degrees. That is frighteningly steep! Even a mere 15 degree tip makes people nervous, at 20 they're desperate and by 25 degrees they're terrified into rigor mortis, worried that moving a finger will destabilise the vehicle. Nobody has been conscious long enough for me to discover the reaction to anything over 35 degrees. Sideslopes do feel worse if you are on the lower side of the vehicle.

However, the fear is actually well-founded. What's more likely to happen at significant sideslope angles is that the vehicle will slide sideways, catch something and then tip. Any way you look at it, sideslopes are something to avoid.

The ground may also be soft on the downward slope. As the majority of the vehicle's weight will be on the lower wheels, they will sink further into any soft terrain. This again increases the roll angle.

Diagram showing an example of weight shift for a 3,000kg 4WD on a 25 degree hill. The weight shift is dependent on the centre of gravity's location, both horizontal and, especially, vertical. Few 4WDs are loaded so the weight on the left and right wheels are equal. The theoretical tipping point of the average 4WD is well beyond where drivers feel comfortable, and rightly so, as usually the vehicle will slide sideways before it tips, and once it slides sideways it may

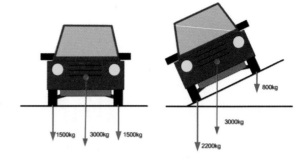

well "trip" and that momentum is often enough to cause a roll. If there is even the slightest rut, use it to increase resistance to sliding sideways.

preparation and kit list

Ensure nothing is loose in the vehicle – this is especially important with sideslopes as a moving load has a greater effect on vehicle stability than the same load secured. If there is even a small rock the upside (or downside) wheels need to go over, remove it. See what you can do about creating or improving ruts for the downhill wheels, which helps prevent the vehicle slipping down the slope. However, the unfortunate side effect is that lower ruts also increase the side angle, so creating a rut for the top wheels is better as that has dual effect of lowering the effective side angle and, importantly, helping prevent the vehicle slipping down the hill. You only need a little rut for the downward wheels – usually even a couple of centimetres is much better than nothing.

Extra air pressure (from say 20 to 40) in the downhill wheels and less on the uphill (20 to 12) can seem like too much trouble at the start, but a superb idea about 15 seconds into it. This not only lowers the effective sideslope but reduces the chances of a lower tyre parting company with the rim. On a sideslope there is always an increased risk of a lower tyre coming off the rim, because there is a great sideways force on it, and more weight, so more air helps there too. Losing a tyre could be enough for a rollover by itself. Remove any weight that is high up on the vehicle, if possible, for example jerry cans and spare tyres. Passengers need to be sitting on the higher side of the vehicle, especially those that are of generous proportions.

driving techniques

Get into gear and select your speed before you start the slope. The correct speed is somewhere between very, very slow and extremely slow. Brace yourself against the seat, as gravity will slide you in your seat.

No sudden movements. Resist the temptation to speed up, as any unevenness will be magnified as the higher side of the vehicle bounces rather than flexes over undulations. This is because the suspension is designed for a certain amount of weight on it, and when the vehicle is on its side the suspension is much stiffer than it needs to be as the up-side weight is now much reduced. Go as absolutely slowly as you possibly can, which also means the tyre is using as much of its grip as possible for lateral traction rather than accelerating or steering. Do not jab the brakes. This will destabilise the vehicle. Be smooth and gentle, so as not to destabilise the vehicle.

If you're picking up a pattern about not destabilising the vehicle, then good!

If the vehicle begins to tip you have about a nanosecond to recover it, if you even decide to try. The only way to do it is to turn downhill and

accelerate rapidly, or uphill. In general, downhill is more likely to work as you're turning in a way that uses centripetal force to counter the roll, but uphill is preferred as that way you don't end up hurtling downhill. Uphill is only really an option if the back end also slides so that you're already pointing uphill. However, it may be worth simply locking the brakes and accepting the roll at a slower speed and not making it worse; the worst-case option is something you should work out before you start. Often a roll is just a tip onto the side; nobody is hurt, the vehicle is repairable, driveable and it's not a huge disaster. Consider spectators before you do anything like attempt to drive out of a potential roll.

Avoid use of locking differentials as these restrict steering and can cause the vehicle to slip down the slope or turn up it. When on a sideslope the vehicle has significantly more weight on the downwards wheels than the upward wheel and, as traction is related to the weight on a wheel, most of the vehicle's traction is now coming from the lower half of the vehicle. This creates a skid-steer effect, but an open diff permits the top and bottom wheels to slip at different rates, countering the effect. A difflock does not.

If a vehicle does roll it is usually easy to right. Simply winch or tow from the top of the chassis rail. It doesn't require vast forces to right a vehicle, so a hand winch can do the job and has the advantage of being able to be easily set up to direct force exactly where it's needed, unlike an electric winch which is attached to a vehicle and may need a set of blocks to get the line in the right direction.

environment

As per the type of terrain you're driving in. You don't do much in the way of sideslopes on sand; it's rocks and forests driving where you'll see them the most.

completion

Most people breathe a huge sigh of relief after a serious sideslope session. The only specific point is to check everything is still in its place and hasn't slid around. Apart from that, complete as per the terrain you've driven in, for example clean mud off, check for rock damage and so on.

1   Sideslope in a Sport. Note the vehicle's body has rolled a little relative to the hill, as expected. The slope is not dramatic but does require an off-camber turn (to the driver's left) which if taken at any speed would increase the effective angle, unlike a turn to the right where you'd get an effect similar to racing cars taking banked corners on an oval. Another consideration is the very woody terrain which means there are loose sticks, leaves and other items on the ground on which the wheel could slip.

2   Taking an intentional sideslope around a corner to get the best line.

3   A sideslope can be any side angle, even a temporary one like this as the Defender 130 eases into the rut. This vehicle has a very wide turning circle so it was difficult to get to the rut crossing at the correct angle.

4   It is amazing how far a vehicle will go before it rolls when there are ruts to help stabilise it.

1   I said "drive to the left a bit". I never said "drive up the bank and see how close you can get to rolling it". When the argument finished we recovered the car by digging out the top wheels and gently moving it forwards by starting the engine, holding it on the brake and gently lifting the clutch up to move the car into the little holes we'd created for the topmost wheels.

2   The LC100's body is tilted, compressing the downward suspension and flattening the lower tyre which increases the risk of the tyre parting company from the rim. The ground is loose dirt on hard dirt so there's a risk of slipping. There's also ruts which will increase the side angle and if taken at any speed will make the car slip downslope. This is time for very slow, measured control in low-range.

3   It's actually better to straddle this one but for the purposes of demonstration a side angle can be achieved. The car is unlikely to roll, and if it does it certainly won't go all the way over so it's quite safe, if not particularly good for the panels in the event of a slip. We drove out of this one without a problem.

4   More ot a rut than a sideslope but it does demonstrate the technique of jamming a wheel against a rut. If you can do that then the angles you can safely negotiate are quite impressive.

5   Not much of a side angle, but it's not the angle so much as the combination of grip and angle. And there's not much grip. The only reason the Hilux is not sliding sideways is because the lower wheels are in a rut.

This vehicle is at a reasonable side angle, but the bigger issue is there's nothing to stop the rear end sliding down that little dirt slope (2). If that happens the momentum and extra tip angle would probably see it on its side. So we dug a little terrace for the downhill rear tyre (1) which fixed that problem. The driver was extremely careful to move very, very slowly – he held the car on the brake and just lifted the clutch gently to move the car, foot never leaving the brake, no jerky movements so the tyre's grip could be dedicated to stopping the slide.

Wider view of the vehicle (3), needing to move up to the left. The front right wheel is doing well in a rut (for the moment), but the right rear has no rut and can slide downhill. Not good. The vehicle has twin lockers but cannot use them as it needs all the steering capability it can get.

CHAPTER 24

SNOW & ICE

There are some offroad experiences that should be on your do-before-you-die list. Close to the top would be a scenic drive in virgin snow.

the terrain

Snow can fall anywhere and combine with other terrains, and wherever there is snow you're very likely to find mud and ice too. Snow can range from a gentle sprinkling, under which the track is still visible, to a deep blanket, metres deep. Snow cover can cover up ruts and undulations, leading the driver to believe all is flat when it is not, and the wind can build up banks of snow on flattish ground. All this means that the terrain underlying snow is difficult to read. Like sand, snow can vary in consistency. You can find anything from fragile flakes to thick, well-compressed surfaces.

Ice is the slipperiest surface you'll ever drive across – or slide across to be more accurate. Normal tyres are no good, and no amount of skilful car control or electronic aids will change the laws of physics. The good news is that ice is relatively rare. It's not like you'll be needing to drive across sheets of the stuff, at least in Australia.

The bad news is that because ice is more or less transparent, you often can't see it, or at least not until it's too late. That means learning to anticipate ice. Clues to ice on the road include shaded spots where the sun hasn't been able to shine or anywhere where water could collect, especially shallow water, such as puddles on the road or slight depressions. Deep puddles tend to be fine as if they ice over the car breaks through, but shallow puddles may be ice all the way through and that's where the danger lies.

preparation and kit list

Snow only forms in the cold, and that's the major factor to consider when preparing for a trip. You'll need gloves, a change of clothes, a tarp to kneel on in case you need to change tyres or fit chains (Chapter 35) and to generally be well prepared for the weather. Use the layer principle of a thin body garment with several outer layers, finishing with a waterproof jacket and warm headgear. Not only is this the most effective way to retain warmth, it also allows you to shed layers selectively to match the temperature. You won't regret any investment. As sun glare can be a real problem with the highly reflective snow, worse than sand, a pair of sunglasses is important.

Recovery equipment you'll find useful will be a spade (not a wide shovel, as snow is often difficult to dig), a winch, gloves and a flat plate for jacking. Mud tyres are best, and take chains if you have them. Winter tyres (Chapter 7) are also ideal for cold conditions. Studs for ice driving may be fitted to some tyres, if legally permitted, and there will be little running on surfaces that will wear them. Snowfalls also cause trees to topple, so don't be surprised to find fallen timber blocking your track, requiring use of a chainsaw, winch and drag chain to remove.

For an up-and-down day trip you don't need much special preparation, but if you are staying overnight in sub-zero conditions there are a range of precautions to take. The first item is fuel. Petrol engines can use their normal fuel, but diesels require alpine diesel – which is available only at service stations close to the mountains.

Best idea is to fill up in the mountains rather than carry a load of non-alpine mix into the cold, but there's no need to swap back when you're off the mountain. Snow driving, like sand, increases fuel consumption because of greatly increased rolling resistance, although there is less of a problem with overheating as the climate is colder.

Fuel isn't the only fluid to worry about – you'll need an anti-freeze mix in your coolant and washer fluid too. These can be purchased at any auto parts shop. Any fluid is subject to freezing, but in Australian conditions you are unlikely to freeze your oils. However, any water in the oils may freeze, so check lubricants for contaminants before you leave. Hoses and belts can become brittle and prone to breaking in cold weather too, so again replace any that are close to end of life. In short, the vehicle needs to be in good mechanical conditions, as with every offroading situation.

If you stay overnight your windscreen may frost over. Prevent this by covering it with a tarp or even newspaper – the water vapour will condense and freeze onto that instead of the glass. Condensation occurs when temperatures drop as cooler air cannot hold as much water vapour as warmer air, so you can find windscreen frost forming as temperature drops.

Never use hot water to clear it as the sudden temperature change will crack the screen. A credit card can work, but if your windscreen doesn't accept credit cards best of all is specialist defroster fluid. Starting the engine and using the air conditioning also works but idling a vehicle for prolonged periods of time is not good for it. Still, it's better than driving off with restricted visibility.

Move wipers away from the windscreen so they don't freeze on. Battery performance reduces in the cold and the engine is harder to turn over so it is important to have a good battery and not run accessories with the engine off, and don't forget high-performance jumper cables. Don't apply the park brake as it may freeze on – use chocks instead. Use a heat blanket over the engine to preserve warmth and run it late in the evening. Never build a fire under an engine to warm it, but using exhaust gases from other vehicles can work, as can the sun in the morning so consider that when choosing a night-time parking spot. If fluids have frozen that could cause damage, but sometimes a little defrosting is all that is required. If you open doors with a key, you may need to heat the key with a cigarette lighter first. Also remember that tyre pressures will naturally decrease as the air gets colder.

driving techniques

Winter driving starts with the trip up the mountain. The cool air will make your car engine feel like a new one, but slow down. It's likely to be icy, and the particular enemy is black ice, so named because it looks black. Actually, it's a transparent layer of ice over the road surface, and it is pure evil. It could be anywhere, but in particular places where water could stagnate, or that haven't been dried out by the sun, maybe under a thin dusting of innocent looking snow – look for particularly flat patches. Just slow down, engine brake on the straights before corners and be gentle.

When to engage 4WD or lock the centre diff – the usual rule applies which is as soon as the terrain is sufficiently slippery that there is no risk of windup, for example if the bitumen is covered with snow. At high-range speed leave stability control on, and disable it for very slow, low-range work. Don't expect your ABS to be effective. Some automatics have a snow mode which just reduces throttle sensitivity; it doesn't turn your car into the automotive equivalent of Santa Claus' sledge and it's still bound by the laws of physics, particularly the tyre traction. Some automatics (Chapter 4) have a second-gear start mode to reduce off-the-line torque and thus chance of wheelspin.

Like with slick mud, drive as gently as possible in shallow snow; careful turning, gentle acceleration, plenty of braking distance. Choose between accelerating and braking, or turning. Try and keep all turns to a constant speed – minimal braking or acceleration, so all the available traction is being used for turning. As the vehicle will be colder for longer than normal, this softly-softly approach also helps with wear and tear on the vehicle.

Shallow snow only a few centimetres deep requires caution, not because it's hard to drive on, but because of what it hides. Snow has a terrible habit of hiding stakes, drops, bogs, ice patches, potholes and everything else. Proceed with care, with reduced tyre pressures (approx 60% placard), use engine braking (lower gears to slow down, Chapter 3) and generally treat the controls with a feather touch. Keep a long way between vehicles. Once you've experienced the utter helplessness of a slide on ice you'll see why. The only way to deal with ice is to be going so slowly that when you find it there is no problem. If you do slide on ice, you're in a toboggan.

Consider low-range ahead of time as it has better engine braking options at low speeds, but use

minimum throttle at all times, which often means pulling away in third low. The reason engine braking works is because you are forcing the wheels to turn at a slower speed, rather than pure braking which attempts to lock them up.

Mud tyres grip snow better than all-terrains, winter tyres are even better, but chains or studs are best of all. With chains (Chapter 36) your speed will be limited, but they are definitely the best option for icy conditions as they dig into ice and grip, a capability not even the most aggressive rubber can match. Fit chains early and when directed. The laws for when to fit or carry them vary from state to state.

Keep to the centre of the track, especially when cambered as you run a risk of sliding into gutters and a covering of snow will make this more likely. Bear in mind that navigation will be harder as signs may be obscured and it can be difficult to tell where a track starts, stops or turns off or even where it is as there won't be any road markings to see.

As the snow gets deeper the car will start to work harder to push the snow out of the way; to some extent this is like sand but snow is generally softer so you're more likely to have to push through it rather than float on top. You can now become more aggressive with the throttle as momentum will be needed to counter the increased rolling resistance, and the vehicle will make or follow ruts which will reduce the tendency to slide in unwanted directions. However, if you are in virgin snow following a cambered road then you can easily end up making a lovely set of ruts leading straight off the road, and then you have the more difficult job of reversing and trying to make a better set that does follow the road properly.

Always look ahead in snow and try to work out where the vehicle is likely to go. In some cases a little preparatory spadework to create a rut to tramline in can work wonders.

If the depth is such that the car still has under-body clearance progress can usually be made on the flat, but as soon as the front of the vehicle is doing a snowplough impression or climbing it is much harder to continue. Backing up and slamming into a wall of snow can sort of work for a short distance, but it's not great for your car. You're also likely to ride up onto the snow, sink down and become very stuck. This may be as far as many wish to go, but if you're game you can press on.

The trick in really deep snow is to float on top of it, and that is like sand driving, except it's trickier because snow is softer and you don't use momentum anywhere near as much because any wheelspin tends to dig you in. What you do is drop pressures right down to eight psi or so for a medium 4WD and float. If you do drop in don't even try and drive out. You'll need to winch up out onto the top again, using only the winch to move the car, not driving the wheels, and if you have no winch, it'll be a long dig. You can also use a traction aid (Chapter 37). It helps to have a light car with high-profile tyres. If you need to recover in snow you'll be glad of a few spades, and often cars slip so winches are useful. If you need to build up a ramp remember that icy, wet wood has next to no traction and, like sand, removing snow out of the way of a vehicle greatly reduces the recovery force required. Don't underestimate how difficult it can be to shift snow, it is typically a harder job than sand as snow doesn't fall away as you dig a hole.

Following in wheel tracks is a good idea as this reduces the chances of slipping off the track and is generally easier. However, compressed snow may turn to ice, and ice is by far the most slippery surface known to offroaders.

environment

The snow does a good job of insulating the vehicle from the track, but even so tracks may be damaged if driven on when wet. As it is winter time there will be seasonal closures so respect those. Make sure you don't venture off-track as the vehicle's wheels will often dig through the snow to leave ruts apparent after the snow melts.

completion

Air up, remembering tyre pressures in cold air at slow speed will increase with speed and heat. Snow can mask handling problems, so take it easy, and ice on cold brakes isn't good for stopping. Remove snow cover from lights, and warm up on the way back!

A smooth patch, with dark undertones. This is a shallow puddle iced over; black ice.

where to find your snow

There are places in Australia where you can drive in the snow, and pretty much have a winter playground. Look for tracks that rise above 800-1,000m, and – this is the kicker – are open in the winter, which you can check by looking at the website of the relevant authority. Mere height is no guarantee of snow. Big dumps can come at any time, and often disappear suddenly. It's best to be able to drop everything at a moment's notice and just go, but if you can't then plan a few days in mid winter, but have a backup plan in case you don't get lucky. A good place to look for conditions is the ski resort reports at www.ski.com.au and www.vicsnowreport.com.au; look for the resorts closest to where you're going. Bear in mind the resorts can make their own snow, and you won't quite reach their heights.

1   Ice in Australia is extremely unlikely to support the weight of a vehicle, so you'll break through. Standard mud-driving precautions apply, but go slow because chunks of ice can damage your vehicle.

2   The Defender has sufficient clearance for the track. The limiting factor will be traction, which is where the chains come in.

3   Deeper snow and it builds up to an impassable wall very quickly. The only option here is a lot of digging, or to deflate the tyres right down to less than 10psi and try and float on top.

4   Keep in the ruts where possible. Stability control tends to interfere too much in slippery conditions so disable and then be gentle.

Even snow chains can be overwhelmed. Clearing snow away from this car would have been a big job, harder than sand.

Following in wheel ruts is a good idea, but the compressed snow can turn to ice, especially overnight. Not real good for traction.

Navigation is more difficult in snow because everything looks different and tracks can be entirely hidden. This is actually a defined track.

Where there be snow, there be mud…be prepared.

1   A servo with a pump marked alpine diesel. All pumps in the mountain regions should dispense alpine diesel whether marked or not. It's not really a problem unless you are staying overnight. During the day stopping for a few hours shouldn't cause any problem, but best to be on the safe side.

2   Deeper snow needs low range and higher revs, but if you start to spin, back off the power. For deep snow the best Terrain Response mode is not Snow, but Mud/Ruts, Normal or even Rock Crawl.

3   We add a cap, scarf, carrot and gloves to our kit list for snow trips. Our long-term tester Santa Fe carried us up the mountain to our play area for the day.

4   If you're going to the snow…you can find it in the air too, and that can be unpleasant. Be prepared.

5   Snowfall often pushes trees over, and when on the ground they become wet and icy making crossing more difficult than usual. Approach at an angle, one wheel at a time, and do not stop. Better yet, clear them out of the way.

6   It's a special feeling to be first though a track after snowfall!

CHAPTER 25

DESERT DUNES

As an offroader exploring the outback you're going to have to deal with dunes sooner or later, even if you never go sand driving just for the sake of it.

the terrain

Many areas, like the Simpson Desert, Border Track and Googs Track comprise hundreds of sand dunes which you need to get your heavy vehicle up and over, time after time. It's not difficult, once you know the tricks. General sand driving is covered in Chapter 20.

Deserts are rarely completely barren. The title photo for this section was taken on the Border Track in the Little Desert National Park. Nevertheless, the sort of vegetation you find is unlikely to make good winch anchor points.

preparation and kit list

Sand is soft, so to avoid the vehicle sinking in you need to lower tyre pressures. That often doesn't mean 25psi, but for the average medium-large 4WD weighing 3,000-3,500kg when loaded, a maximum of 20psi and probably more like 15psi. The difference in flotation between 15psi and 20psi is far greater than between 20psi and 25psi (Chapter 7), so those last few psi make a big difference. In fact dropping two psi out of the tyres at around the 25psi mark can result in a noticeable improvement. It also helps smooth out the corrugations. How low to go? In general, keep reducing until you can drive up the dunes using the techniques described below, without having to resort to uncomfortable momentum.

But isn't that too low? What about a tyre coming off the rim? Well, it's always a possibility, but in the outback you're usually just driving straight, quite slowly, in sand ruts. The chances of a rim leaving a tyre in those conditions are small. Punctures are another concern, specifically with the sidewalls bagging out where they are vulnerable. It's not much of a problem (Chapter 7) because the lower a tyre's pressure the more puncture-resistant it becomes, and in sand you may be able to spot any potential sidewall-ripping objects before you run them over.

However, there are downsides to low pressures. Decreasing pressures runs the risk of heat build up in a tyre which leads to failure, but in desert dune driving the amount of braking/accelerating will be minimal, speeds will be very low, stops frequent and so heat stress isn't a problem in these conditions. However, these pressures are too low for highway dirt road driving, so do carry a compressor.

An apparent downside is that softer tyres do mean greater fuel consumption, but only on hard surfaces like bitumen. In sand this rule is reversed, as the extra effort required to rotate a soft tyre is more than outweighed by the fact you aren't sinking in to the soft stuff anywhere near as much. Also remember that deserts become very cold at night and very hot in the day, which means your tyre pressure will vary accordingly. Setting 15psi as you set off in the morning could be around 20psi by the time you've driven on it and the sun has warmed everything, and 15psi in the day could become 10psi by morning. Check before you set off, and again after an hour or so, perhaps at morning tea.

Reducing tyre pressures by a couple of psi will solve a lot of dune-driving problems. It won't hurt.

One important safety item you'll need is a sand flag, and that should go on the bull bar or roof rack so it's at a relatively high point on the vehicle as it crests the dune. Attaching to the spare tyre is the worst position because it's 5m or so behind the front, and much lower down as you crest a dune compared to the front. Mount the flag as high as you can without getting it caught in the trees where it could break. Carry a UHF radio too, and have it on scan to pick up approaching traffic. Recovery gear should be the sand kit; flat plate for the jack, shovels, air jack. Winches are unlikely to be of much use due to a lack of anchor points – there aren't many large trees or rocks in the desert – and the other kit listed is likely to be more effective in a sand recovery anyway. The best recovery gear will be traction devices like sand mats (Chapter 37), followed by a snatch strap. Use them in that order, for safety.

driving techniques

So with low pressures and flag you head for the first dune. Get into 4WD and lock the centre diff if applicable. There is no glory in forcing a vehicle over a dune in 2WD, because all you're doing is chewing the track up, stressing the car, making corrugations worse and using extra fuel. Also, disable stability control if you have it as it won't help at low speeds and may well work against you. Cross-axle lockers won't assist much unless the dune is scalloped, but leaving them in won't hurt. Use those traction aids, because that's what you paid for. There is no risk of transmission windup in sand.

Low- or high-range? Mostly high. With the pressures down it's amazing how easily you can idle up dunes in first, second, even third high. Our Defender did the entire Simpson in high-range,

never above 1,200rpm (well, with the exception of Big Red) and returned slightly better than 10L/100km at 16psi. The higher the gear, the better the fuel consumption and less damage to the track. Of course, if you need low-range don't be afraid to use it, but maximum revs in low-range usually signals a need to lower pressures further. Sand driving will use extra fuel so plan for this.

You can never be quite sure what's lurking over the side of a dune, so try to arrive at the top at walking pace, especially if you're the lead vehicle. There could be a maniac without a sand flag, an interesting animal, a mallee root ready to stake a tyre, a bad washout or the track may not go straight down the dune. However, don't idle up to the start of the dune and then plant the foot as you begin to climb (refer to Chapter 22 for a diagram on slope/throttle use). Whatever momentum you need (and it shouldn't be much) should be acquired by accelerating slightly down the previous dune if it's smooth, or on the flat, when you can clearly see in front. As with any hill, select whatever gear you're going to use before the base of the dune and lock it in. This applies to automatics too, as even their downshifts take time and lose a tiny bit of momentum. You can gently depress the accelerator as you begin to ascend the dune if required, but do let the speed wash off as you crest, so you use minimum fuel and cause minimal track erosion, arriving at the top as slow as possible.

When descending a dune there's usually no need to use first low or sometimes even first high, but do drive the car down gently rather than descend under brakes for control and to avoid creating washouts. Always be smooth and gentle. It is possible to change down on a sandy upslope in both automatics and manuals if you're quick and smooth, but this is not recommended due to risk of transmission damage.

Tune a UHF radio to whatever the designated channel is for travellers in the area, or have one on channel scan. But trying to determine the exact location of another group is very difficult, and it's easy to have a long and pointless conversation about precisely how many klicks one is away from somewhere. Just keep a good lookout over the dunes. When you meet the convoy tell them how many vehicles there are in your group and what the last one is, and agree whose convoy will give way to whose. If it's a narrow track, when you think you're getting close send the lead vehicle out further from the main group so passing negotiations can be made.

Don't follow another vehicle too closely; you should be no closer than a few car lengths away from the bottom of a dune as they crest it, in case they stop or retry. If you do need to stop on a dune try to do so just over the crest but still on top, for maximum visibility and an easy restart.

Conditions change the difficulty of the dunes. Hot, dry weather makes the sand finer and you sink in so it's more difficult, and hot air reduces engine efficiency. Overnight wind can blow fine sand over the top of dunes, so the first vehicle through has the hardest time.

You are unlikely to run into a patch of really soft sand and sink in, as you do on beaches. Most boggings are near the top of dunes, and due to a combination of the driver running pressures too high, attempting dunes in too low a gear and, most of all, continuing to try and power through when it should have been clear all hope was lost and the only option was to

back down. It's simple; if the wheels spin and speed washes off, you've lost it – back it back down, drop pressures even by two psi and try again. Maybe try a higher gear, perhaps third low instead of first high. Trust your engine's torque – you don't always need 3,000rpm plus. You can also flick the air conditioning off and throw a passenger out for that last little bit of power to weight ratio, and in fact passengers should be out digging anyway, earning their keep. If you do need to recover over a dune, dig out the wheels to dramatically reduce the recovery load.

All these tips apply to trailer drivers too, but remember to deflate the trailer's tyres even lower than the tow car. If the tow car is running 18psi and weighs 3,000kg that's 750kg per wheel, or more likely 1,700 on the rear and 1,300 on the front, and there's a rearwards weight shift as you ascend the dunes.

If the trailer weighs 1,000kg, and has a towball mass of 120kg then that's 440kg on each of the trailer's wheel, much less. So if the tyre/rim combo is approximately the same the tyre pressures can be much less on the trailer; work them out by looking at the length of the contact patch. We've used 14psi front, 18psi rear and 10psi on the trailer in deep sand with success. Trailer reversing in sand on a hill can be very difficult, so if you aren't going to make it give up early and come back down in low-range. If there are non-trailer cars in the convoy let them go first as they will compress the sand for you, can warn of difficult terrain and assist with a tow from the front.

environment

Desert dunes are almost certainly going to be in a national park and so should be treated with due respect. There are places in Australia you can romp on the dunes to your heart's content, but no desert is such a place so keep to marked tracks, no matter how tempting the dunes. The authorities cannot afford to put gates up everywhere, and that would ruin the place, so don't take the view that you can drive anywhere simply because there is no sign specifically saying "don't drive there". And driving trailers over dunes is not always permitted or advisable - check the local rules.

completion

Make sure those tyres are re-inflated and drop sand flags once out of the dunes. Outback desert driving should be a lot of fun, but it should also be easy on the environment and the vehicle. Nobody enjoys corrugations or the scalloping caused by wheelspin on the dunes, so drop the pressures, drive gently and enjoy!

why sand flags are important

If two vehicles are travelling at just 10km/h each then they have a closing speed of 5.6 metres/second – more than a full vehicle length covered every second. In the scale diagram two two-metre tall Defenders are climbing at the same time a 30 degree dune with a five metre long flat section (and that is a relatively long flat section). Diagram A shows without flags the drivers will spot each other when they are two metres apart, giving 0.34 seconds to stop. Given a reaction time of 0.5 seconds (and that's quick), impact is certain.

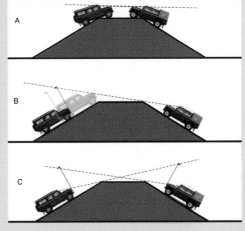

Diagram B adds one four metre flag, which increases the visibility to 11m, giving the unflagged vehicle only two seconds to stop. Just sufficient time, if you're really alert. Diagram B also shows a shadow Defender with the flag on the back; on a 30 degree dune the top of the bonnet is actually visible before the four metre flag on the back.

Diagram C has two four metre flags. The distance the first driver can see the other car is still 11m, but both drivers can see the other's flag at the same time. This means the chances of averting a crash are greatly increased as both can apply brakes instead of relying on the driver without a flag, and given they're driving dunes sans flag you wouldn't want to be relying on them for anything.

The diagrams also show the importance of using a tall flag, especially as wind drag reduces effective height still further by bending it, and why you should crest dunes as slowly as possible. Tying a red rag to a radio antenna is a nice try, but almost pointless and not a device to place trust in.

LC100 with a four metre sand flag on the back of a dune. And, what it looks like as you approach the dune from the other side, the flag won't necessarily be in the middle of the track.

Vehicles with sand flags mounted in the ideal location – on the bull bar, and on the right so if there is any undergrowth to negotiate the flag is less likely to catch in the trees.

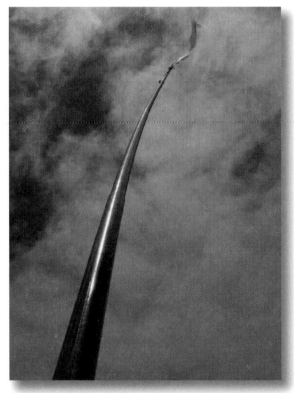

Flags often bend in the wind, reducing height significantly. Ensure your mounting point is robust. Cheap nudgebars are unlikely to be up to the job.

Lower tyre pressures to really bag the tyres out for flotation.

You never know what's on the other side of the dune.

A rugged offroad trailer can be towed over desert dunes too, where permitted, but it's a lot harder than a solo car. We ran 14psi, 18psi and 10psi on the three axles to get through Googs Track and had no problems, even as first car through after the wind had swept loose sand to the top of the dunes.

If you need to stop on a dune, stop on the crest where you can get going again and where others can see you. Err on the side of the downhill rather than the uphill part.

If this dune were ascended with stability control engaged the slight curves would see the system kick in and kill valuable momentum.

1,2 Corrugations and scallops on a dune, caused by too many revs at too
high a tyre pressure. Don't make it worse.

3 There's generally no need to crawl down desert dunes in first low.
Second, third or first high is usually all that's needed, but select a gear
that doesn't require very much braking effort.

4 The secret of dune ascent success – correct pressures, steady momentum
acquired before you get onto the slope, going straight up and a gear so
that you just about feel like changing down but you don't quite have to.
Ease over the top as you don't know what's on the other side.

1-2 *The famed Big Red. There is no need to take a run up the likes of which could see a 747 take off. If you don't get over simply drop the tyre pressures by another two psi out and try again. That's what we did with this Escape and it sailed through. We saw a group of a Cherokee, Pajero and LC100 try increasingly large run ups which eventually worked, but there was no need for a 60km/h approach. By using pressures of 14psi and 16psi on the Defender we were able to amble up in second low after performing a u-turn at the bottom.*

3 *Some desert tracks, like Googs, are quite overgrown so passing convoys is more difficult. Send the lead car a distance ahead so a passing place can be worked out.*

4 *Softroaders can attach sand flags to good-quality nudge bars, like this Ford Escape in the Simpson.*

CHAPTER 26

NIGHT DRIVES

Some people drive at night for fun. Some because they have to, others are victims of circumstance.

the terrain

The terrain at night is not very much different than in the daytime, so all the other driving techniques apply. In some cases there are slight changes, such as the lower night temperatures meaning sand may not be as fine as in the day. The cooler air will be appreciated by your engine, but that's counteracted to some degree by the extra work it has to do powering your lights and various other electrics. Some animals are more active at night or at dawn or dusk.

preparation and kit list

While the terrain is the same, offroad driving at night is quite different to road driving at night. Firstly, you're unlikely to have streetlights on the average track, or cat's eyes. Secondly, the track may be overgrown and is likely to have sharp corners, steep rises, drops and situations where the car is at an angle, so the headlights aren't pointing exactly where you want them. For all these reasons your standard headlights won't cut it in low-range at night, and you need auxiliary lighting. Even a cheap but workable set of halogen lights can be had for a couple of hundred dollars, and they make a difference. Upgrading to a set of HIDs almost turns night into day.

Normal headlights vs HID in a paddock.

It's not just headlights you need to be concerned about. Many people mount lights on their roof as well, but check your state laws before doing this. A work light at the back can be very useful when reversing, and don't forget your personal lights. I find a quality LED headband light an invaluable asset in the dark, plus another couple of backup lights. A high-powered spotlight is no bad idea either. Inside the car a set of aftermarket LED interior lights make a huge difference as well.

High-mounted spotlights can improve the view, but beware bonnet glare – this is why the bonnet is black. Lights mounted this high cannot be used on-road.

Night can be cold, so take extra clothing, working on the layer principle (Chapter 24). Something reflective always seems more hassle than it's worth until it saves your life. If you break down on an unlit road or need to change a tyre you'll be glad of a triangular reflective hazard marker, something compulsory in Europe but not in Australia. Also watch for fatigue, particularly between midnight and 6am, especially if you're already tired.

Navigation definitely doesn't get any easier at night, so good preparation with a GPS receiver and topographic map will go a long way to making sure you don't become lost. Stow lights (and everything else) where you can find them easily, as searching for a torch in the dark is ironic but not fun.

"Night vision" is the acclimatisation of your eyes to darker conditions. It takes a few seconds for your eyes to move from dark to light conditions, but over half an hour for full night vision to be developed. Your eyes adapt much more quickly to changes when they go from dark back to light, and younger eyes are significantly better at night vision than older ones. An offroad environment is a difficult condition for human eyes, blending a mix of very bright lights and very dark terrain. To make it easier, avoid bright interior lights and never look at headlights. Most vehicles have instrumentation dimming, so use that and also turn the brightness down on computers and PDAs. Some software, like OziExplorer, even has a night-vision mode as do some GPS receivers. Choose a green option, if there is one, over red; as research indicates this is the best colour at night, and always choose the dimmest possible light inside the vehicle. Preparation works here too, if you're printing notes use a larger font than normal and generally try to reduce the time you'll need to pore over small details in the field. Also remember that in

rural areas fuel and other shops may not be available at night.

A head torch can be invaluable. Get one that is switchable to LED and spot mode.

driving techniques

Dusk, dawn and night time are when you're most likely to hit animals such as kangaroos, so be aware of the possibilities. Wombats are also active around these times and they are not to be argued with.

It has been said that driving in low-range territory at night is easier than driving in the day, as you can't see anything to be scared of. That's a weak joke, but it has some truth to it. There are two problems when driving offroad in the dark; firstly the general lack of light and secondly perception of obstacles that are partially lit. Even the best lighting setup won't illuminate the way ahead like the sun, so you cannot necessarily see all the obstacles and the risk of driving into a problem increases. Your light source is also coming from only one direction, so for example if you approach a gully you may be able to see the track to the start of the dip, and after the dip, but not see down into the gully. In contrast, sunlight comes from three directions; direct from the sun, diffused through the atmosphere and reflected on various surfaces. The reflected light you get from headlights is of less use as the light source is located close to the viewing point.

For these reasons it is recommended that your first low-range night drives are in areas you know reasonably well, so you can experience the difference between night and day. A good way to start is to drive a track in the day, then go back at night and do it again. The experience is, one may say, illuminating. To overcome the lack of lighting you can obviously just add more lights, but there are other techniques too. You can use the vehicle(s) behind you to shine light where you can't. You may need to get out of the car and use the high-powered torches you brought to see where things are at. And you will need to look further ahead, taking advantage of when your light is shining in the right direction to assess the track condition. For example if you're driving a steep downhill followed immediately by an uphill then as you ease from the flat down the slope your lights will illuminate the forthcoming uphill. Take the time there to look at it, as you may not be able to see the uphill properly when you begin it from the bottom. You

can even take different lines as you drive to get your headlights pointing in more useful directions, maybe putting a wheel up on a rock you don't need to, or swinging wide or tight around a corner.

On higher-speed dirt roads you may find oncoming traffic – dip early if you have high-powered auxiliary lights. Drivers may also be further into the middle of the road than usual, so slow down more than you normally would when passing. As when driving low-range, even long-distance lights may not illuminate dips, so use extra caution on hills. In general, I recommend at least one spread beam rather than all pencils as there is little point lighting the road two kilometres ahead. It's rare you'll find a road so straight and flat, and a good spread beam, especially in the newer and more effective HID type (Chapter 40), throws light a long way and also helps show you the edges of the road and any problems in the next 300-400m. Those running HIDs should be aware of the significant glare caused by those lights from road signs. As a courtesy, try and keep noise, revs and speed down to a minimum in rural towns. 4WDs don't need a lot of revs to move off the line and mud tyres can be noisy, producing a din that carries a long way at night. You also probably don't need your auxiliary lights in town and can go back to just the standard high beams.

Often you need to illuminate areas that your car is not actually pointing towards. This isn't a posed photo, my car is actually stuck on a wet rock ledge and so the winch comes out plus the operator brought along for that purpose. The camera's flash has illuminated a greater area than the headlights.

environment

Just because it's dark doesn't mean to say you shouldn't follow all the usual rules. In addition, be particularly careful of nocturnal wildlife and avoid noise anywhere near campsites or buildings. Signs in the likes of forests will be more difficult to read at night as most of them are not reflective, but they still need to be complied with.

completion

In daylight check your vehicle over for any damage you've missed, and don't forget to sleep!

A 60m long winch rope. Recoveries of this nature are difficult enough in the day. The dark adds an extra dimension of difficulty, and there is the risk of fatigue especially after midnight.

Rear spotlights. Five is probably sufficient.

If you don't clean your lights they won't perform.

Dipping hot lights into water is not a great idea. The HID lights run cooler, so another advantage there.

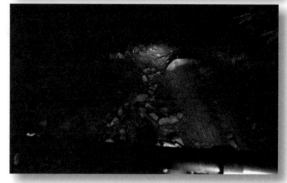

With and without HID spotlights, using exactly the same exposure settings on the camera. Definitely worth the money, even before you damage a panel on a rock, and it's easy to transfer the lights from car to car so the investment is not wasted.

The camera flash has illuminated terrain not possible to discern from the driver's seat using headlights (1 and 2).

CHAPTER 27

DISTANCE DRIVING

A couple of week's holiday. A long distance to cover, but you can do it. But can you do it safely?

the terrain

Offroad touring can involve some very long distances, which mean long hours behind the wheel, something the average driver is not accustomed to. Lengthy driving stints mean the risk of fatigue is very real, and fatigue is one of the biggest killers on our roads. Depending on which survey you read, around 20% of crashes involve fatigue, and that's even higher in rural areas.

You don't really want to hit this at any speed, let alone a closing rate of 200km/h.

preparation and kit list

Fatigue is a problem because it significantly reduces a driver's ability to safely handle the car. Roadsafe Victoria determined that being awake for 17 hours has the same effect on your driving ability as a blood alcohol level of 0.05, the legal limit. Simply, you won't notice hazards as quickly, if at all (leading to a false sense of security), and when you do notice your reaction times will be slower, and you may make the wrong call. You may also microsleep; at 100km/h you cover over 27m in a second so could be off the road into a tree in the blink of an eye. Fatigue is a very serious problem and nobody should consider themselves immune.

Like everything else in 4WD, a successful long trip starts with planning. Know your route well so that you aren't stressed by navigating or need to make up time. Don't commit to specific times, so you don't need to rush to meet someone. Prepare the vehicle well ahead of time and in particular increase tyre pressures as you'll be at high speed for a long time, and probably heavily loaded. Plan several stop points along the way, more than needed as you don't need to use all of them. Get a good night's sleep, after everything is prepared, and avoid stimulants like caffeine and any alcohol.

Plan your route to avoid driving between midnight and 6am, and between about 2pm and 4pm. The reason is your circadian rhythm, or daily pattern of alertness. Those who teach have long-lamented the slot immediately after lunch when attention wanders, and for good reason. Humans do indeed have reduced alertness around these hours, and crash researchers have noticed there is a disproportionate amount of accidents – twice to six times more – at these times. Another rule is don't drive when you'd normally be sleeping, and remember that you suffer from fatigue on the road instantly if you start off tired.

Have a backup plan too. Attempting a long drive runs the risk of not making it, and you'll be under less pressure if there's a Plan B.

driving techniques

The first technique is posture. The correct driving position is one where your feet can operate the pedals fully without overstretching the leg, and where you are close enough to the steering wheel to drape your wrist over the top of the wheel with your shoulders hard back against the seat (Chapter 11). Don't forget sunglasses to protect your eyes, and wear loose, open, comfortable clothes.

Drive smoothly and steadily as opposed to trying to eke out the last couple of km/h. Don't stress about having to slow down a couple of km behind a slow vehicle. If you drove for 500km at 105km/h it'd take 4.75 hours, but 5 hours at 100km – only 15 minutes longer. Even that little less speed is a lot less stress, not to mention disproportionately greater fuel economy and less chance of speeding tickets. Drink water, and lots of it, never alcohol. Caffeine drinks can feel good, but like a sugar hit once the high wears off you're worse off than before. Frequent consumption of caffeine can lead to dependency and a tolerance to its stimulating effects so you need more and more of it to get the hit. Take snacks, but go for fruits and cereals, nothing sugary or fatty.

Stop every two hours or so, perhaps a little longer, perhaps a little shorter, but listen to your body. If you aren't going to use the stop time properly you may as well not bother, it's more about what you do once stopped than the act of stopping itself. Don't just sit down and veg out, make sure you get up, go for a walk, do something moderately active. Consider parking the car some distance from whatever facility you've stopped at, just to stretch yourself. A few smaller breaks are better than one

big one with longer stints. You'll need to eat, but take light meals. Pigging out on pasta is a bad move, a salad is much more easily digested and is the better choice.

This photo was taken at 0730 in the morning on the Cape York Peninsula Development Road. I had a 250km dirt-road drive to do that morning after an overnight stop, and had originally planned to do it in one go after starting at 0630. The drive started really well – I love early starts, a good car, a clear road and I was feeling very alert and enthusiastic. But less than an hour into the trip I suddenly felt tired, so I pulled over and power-napped for 15 minutes, then got out and walked around, put the car back on the road and took the photo. That stop made all the difference, and I was still on time at the end as the arrival time I'd given was conservative. On the way back I drove for three hours without a break as I was feeling fine. The human body is unpredictable so you just need to monitor yourself for signs of fatigue and deal with them quickly.

Something else to consider when stopping is a power nap. Research at Flinders University has shown that subjects waking from a 10-minute nap demonstrate an immediate significant increase in alertness that lasts for at least an hour afterwards. However, a 30-minute nap doesn't have such an immediate effect, producing its alertness improvement about half an hour after the nap ends. Power naps are not, however, a substitute for proper sleep. Use them when you feel drowsy, before it's too late, and keep them to no more than 15 minutes. A tip; humans like to sleep reclined, and not even laying your car seat flat will really do the trick. So, if you, can, put the front wheels up a steep slope for a little extra comfort. Crack a window a little open, and settle in. Signs you need a power nap are yawning, over-correcting, noticing you're taking longer to react, not caring about things as much, not remembering the last few minutes, sore eyes or blurred vision and to be honest you'll pretty much feel it anyway, but most people kid themselves into just keeping going. Don't be that foolish.

Stopping at a playground allows the kids to get some exercise. Put them back in the car tired!

Offroaders generally have a UHF radio fitted, and outside of the small-minded idiots that pollute the channel in the cities you can find many genuinely friendly people with lots of useful information. Set yours on scan, or listen to channel 40 and don't be afraid to say hello – we've met many a fellow

traveller who has provided delightful company along the way and at the next stop. This is all part of keeping the mind active as you drive. That's active, but not distracted. Fresh air and a cool but not cold temperature also help.

While it may be anathema to some, sharing the driving does work, allowing extra relaxation time. However, merely being a passenger can be fatiguing, so it's not really a case of double the drivers, double the distance.

Some kit for distance driving – water bottle that's easy to open, GPS receiver for navigation, atlas, sunnies and non-sugary snacks.

children

Small children do not like long distance driving, but there are techniques to manage this too. If we have a big day we'll prepare the car the night before, get up early with the kids asleep, and bundle them straight into the car. A leisurely breakfast is an hour or two down the road with some significant distance already covered, then it's playground time to take the edge off the energy. Don't fill them with red cordial and sugar either! In the car we play games like I Spy, or Car Bingo. DVDs and handheld games can be a lifesaver too, or you could just try good old-fashioned talking. There are plenty of in-car game suggestions on the web. By this time we've put another couple of hours in, and lunchtime is approaching. Again it's playground time, and everyone gets involved including the adults. Quite often we won't even feed them during the stop as they're too excited and busy playing, especially if we're travelling with friends. Once under way again they munch on sandwiches which again keeps them occupied for a while as the kilometres slip by, then maybe a post-lunch snooze. Afternoon tea is the same sort of routine, and on we go. If we need to, we can drive on in the night after dinner and the kids sleep in their seats. This sort of pace isn't ideal, but sometimes you need to cover the kilometres and that's one way to do it. It helps that our kids have been on 4WD trips ever since they were four weeks old so are well used to travelling and camping, having seen friends try the same with their kids who are used to no more than an hour's drive hasn't been as successful.

environment

If you're stopping by the roadside take your rubbish with you. In small towns make sure you do a little to support the locals, rather than just stop and use the community's playground, rest area or other facilities – see if there's a local shop you can buy refreshments from. This way you'll build up your own supplies and support the community – do you really care that the prices are a few dollars higher, isn't it a rather mean victory to save such a tiny amount? You never know who you may meet or what you might find out, either. And fuel up. The time to play Scrooge on fuel prices is in the city, not in the Outback.

completion

Park up and congratulate yourself on a successful trip. If you had a near miss, think back to what might have avoided it – perhaps a longer rest the night before?

Not really a distance driving problem per se, but seeing as we constantly forget about cross-border fruit zones and have to do quite a lot of last-minute scoffing – here's a reminder.

Long distances on the bitumen at high speed and heavily loaded demand more air in the tyre than running around town lightly loaded. If you run pressures too low the tyre will disintegrate due to heat build up.

Tea can be refreshing, but avoid overdosing on caffeine.

CHAPTER 28

SOFTROADERS

No low-range doesn't necessarily mean no 4WD tracks. This chapter isn't about a terrain but a specific type of vehicle, the softroader.

preparation and kit list

A softroader is a 4WD without low-range and built for light-duty offroading. This means, relative to low-range 4WDs, limited clearance, suspension travel, lighter and less robust components and not having little touches such as air intakes and engines set as high as possible, and probably no recovery points. Softroaders may be more agile due to being lighter, but typically lack aftermarket accessory support.

There are now some very capable offroaders that lack low-range, such as variants of VW's Amarok and some Range Rover Sport versions, so the lack of low-range is no longer a particularly defining characteristic but exceptions do not disprove the rule. Eventually, low-range will disappear, probably supplanted by electric drive which provides superb low-speed torque control. All this means a different driving style for those used to low-rangers, which starts with the setup. Although there's no low-range, most softroaders do need some preparation for offroading. Most of them use an "on-demand" 4WD system, which typically means the front axle is driven and the rear trails (Chapter 3), only being driven when required, great (well, better) for fuel consumption but by the time the computer decides to engage the rear axle it's often a bit late. Therefore, many softies have a 4WD lock mode which pre-emptively locks the centre clutch and sends drive to the rear axle, too. If your vehicle has such a lock, be sure to engage it for any offroad work. However, lock modes often unlock at speed, or when the engine is switched off. Even when activated, in some vehicles the centre clutch which "locks" the 4WD system is not designed for prolonged use, so it may give up and need a cooling-off period, for example in sand driving where it is constantly working. In such situations consider unlocking it where you can in order to rest the system. If it does overheat, stop the car with the engine running for a few minutes, then switch off, then on – that usually allows the system to cool and then reset. Such are the joys of softroaders. And in some cases the lock is not a true 50/50 front/rear lock, it just increases torque to the other axle more than usual. Either way, if there's a lock it'll be worth engaging for the rough stuff. Don't use lock modes on high-traction surfaces like bitumen, as there may be a risk of transmission damage.

Consider disabling stability control for low-speed work, as this hinders progress in situations where the car slips or slides, such as muddy ruts or sand. However, some vehicles also disable traction control at the same time and for offroad work you really want traction control working for you. If your vehicle falls into this category keep stability control engaged unless it restricts progress; you'll know when it does as you'll feel the car's brakes being engaged, the throttle may not respond and there will be dash warning lights and possibly a warning sound too.

Very few softies have recovery points, so get a square-hitch towbar fitted which will solve the problem at the back, and if you have to rely on those feeble screw-ins at the front, fit two if possible, use a bridle (Chapter 33) and avoid any front recovery work.

driving techniques

With the vehicle set up, the first technique is to slow down. While a softie may be able to get over spoon drains and the like, clearance is reduced which means you need to go slower. This means transit times are longer, but you still get there. The limited clearance also means you may often need to stop to shift rocks or logs out of the way, especially combined with the usual lack of under-body protection. The lack of axle flex will mean wheels lift more frequently, but all modern softroaders have traction control so a little extra revving can wake up the electronics and pull through. That said, try not to come to a halt then rev your way through, but anticipate the obstruction and use judicious amounts of momentum to avoid coming to a halt. On the flip side, lack of flex is in some cases an advantage, because as suspension flexes, the chassis becomes lower to the ground and side angles are more achievable with less body roll and a lower centre of gravity. This means looking at lines differently; where a low-ranger might go straight up a hill with wheels in washouts, a softie may need to skirt the edges to avoid running out of clearance, relying on its manoeuvrability to take a more indirect route. Or you may just go for more side angles, anything to not run out of clearance (the softie's biggest drawback), and secondly keep wheels on the ground – less of an issue as that can be solved to some degree by traction control and momentum.

The lack of low-range gearing is a real problem in rocky and hilly terrain, especially for manuals where the clutch will need to be slipped. It is at this point you need to consider whether you really want to drive the terrain with the vehicle, considering safety and also the effects on vehicle longevity. The difference between a softroader and a low-ranger is often not that one can drive the terrain and the other can't, it's how easily it's done; the margin of safety and the repair bills now or later. If you decide to proceed, rocky or steep descents that are too rough for clutch-up speeds can be negotiated in a manual by holding the vehicle lightly on the brake, then bringing the clutch up gently to move the car. This forces the wheels to turn slowly as opposed to relying on braking adhesion, but it's nowhere near as good as a low-range clutch-up descent. Use the same technique to reverse down a hill, as the usual key-start technique to get a manual low-ranger down a hill will be far too quick with a softie (see Chapter 22).

Automatic softies are far, far better offroad than manual softies because they can easily slip their torque convertors (Chapter 4) and thus inch through obstacles under good control, although doing that for a long time may overheat the transmission and cause excess wear. Diesel softroaders tend to work better than petrol engines as the diesel engine delivers more torque lower in the rev range, and has slightly better engine braking. However, the automatics are no substitute for low-range and it is possible to get into situations where the car simply cannot deliver enough torque to the wheels to move, for example on steep sand or rocky ascents. The only solution there is to reduce weight, increase momentum and try a different line. Coming downhill the engine braking will be poor but the technique there is to drive through the brakes (Chapter 12). Hold the vehicle in first with your left foot on the brake and increase the revs to move the car. Again, this forces the wheels to turn slowly rather than be braked, decreasing the chance of a skid.

Electronic Hill Descent Control systems are often fitted to softroaders, but their big problem is that they have the vehicle thundering down the hill, far too fast for many real-world conditions. They can also be jerky and if the ABS works at low speeds you may as well just brake yourself to achieve the same effect. They are in no way a substitute for low-range, despite the claims of the marketing material.

Another common softie option is electronic Hill Start Assist; the computers hold the vehicle on the brakes while your foot moves from brake to accelerator. If you drive an automatic forget this feature and learn to hold the car on the brakes using your left foot – it's much safer and smoother. For manual transmission drivers it may well be useful, but don't assume it'll always work as advertised. The left-foot-braking technique for automatics also works well in rocky terrain; when you increase revs to get over an obstacle the vehicle can shoot forwards as it clears, and if your foot is already on the brake reaction times are cut.

Some terrains are more softroader-friendly than others. Slogging up and down steep, rocky hills is to be avoided, as are deep ruts and large rocks. Aside from that most other 4WD terrain can be driven, and softies do well in slippery mud and shallow snow, though less well in ruts and bogholes, where you may need to straddle deeper sections. They also do well in sand, but be careful to back off as soon as the wheels start to spin because the vehicle will ground very quickly, and certainly disable stability control in sand regardless of whether traction control is also disabled. The

lack of clearance is a constant problem, so learn to approach crests at a slight angle, choose your line carefully over the top of sharp hills and again go over at a slight angle. Sometimes just a few centimetres away from the low-ranger line, or just a few degrees angled off, can make the difference between a scrape and a clear run, and the slower you go, the less suspension compression and the less clearance is lost as a result.

If you can, have a look at the obstacle first. That will mean securing the vehicle, so do that on the flat if you can as there's no low-range to help immobile the car and it is entirely possible the 4WD system may disengage when stopped, which means the park brake may only work on two wheels.

Most of a softroader's offroad work will be done in first gear, and often it makes sense to lock the automatic transmission into first to avoid any unwanted upchanges. Beware of fords, as softroader wading depth may be shallow and it is unlikely a snorkel will be available. Short of avoiding the crossing using a blind across the front and a careful bow wave are your only options, but do check the location of the air intake – some softies have them positioned almost as water scoops.

Don't let any of this put you off. A well-prepared and driven softroader can go far beyond the limits of a normal car, so get out there and explore, low-range or not. Once you've learned to drive a softroader on rough terrain a low-ranger will be much easier!

environment

As per whatever terrain you've been driving in.

completion

Softroaders are more likely to lose the odd bit of trim and often under-body protection is just plastic, so keep an eye out for damage.

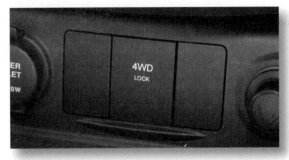

If your car can lock the transmission to distribute torque equally front and rear, do so.

On-demand 4WD softies without a centre lock system are prone to front-wheel-drive wheelspin. There's no clearance or power problem here, just traction caused by the system not driving the rear wheels properly. The only solution is momentum – or, maybe turn around! A low-ranger would have idled up this slope.

Lack of axle flex is a disadvantage…but the ability to handle side angles is an advantage.

Softies can be quite agile – drive to this strength.

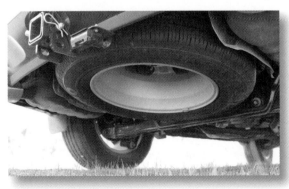

Take a full-sized spare (Chapter 7).

Softies easily ground if you don't back off quickly when you start to sink. This vehicle was crippled to begin with as the pressures were too high at 22psi. The 235/65/17 mud tyres, two-tonne weight and soft sand means that 15psi would have worked a lot better, giving a far larger contact patch and better flotation.

A typical softroader engine is sunk as low in the engine bay as possible, in order to lower the centre of gravity for improved handling. This Kluger has a noticeable gap between the bonnet and the top of the engine. In contrast, a low-ranger's engine will be as high as possible to keep the engine away from the likes of water and mud.

The Subaru Club would be happy to explain how to explore Australia without the benefit of low-range.

Jeep Patriot manual in a state forest. The manuals work well enough on flattish ground, but on the hills the gearing is too high and that's where automatic softroaders have a huge advantage over manuals.

Slippery surfaces where clearance is not challenged are a softroader strong point.

Softroaders lack suspension flex, which is sometimes a good thing, sometimes a bad thing. Either way, good traction control, as shown on this Freelander, can pull the vehicle through when wheel(s) leave the ground.

Sand is another terrain made for softroaders, provided they can move at a speed which allows the engine to develop useful amounts of torque in first gear. This Escape handled the dunes without a problem, but got into trouble later during a very slow, twisty section. The problem was it simply could not move up the slight slope as first gear was too high. The engine's revs simply didn't come up enough to turn the wheels. If it was a manual the clutch could have been slipped, but that's not an option in an automatic. What is an option is throwing the passengers out and dropping another two psi, and that's what worked. This vehicle is a four-speed automatic, and the five and six speeds are much better in those situations as their first gears are lower. The companion low-range vehicles had no difficulty going through in second low.

Softroaders are often clearance-challenged, so up straddling the ruts is the answer. This works in the dry, but even so it was hard to get the car up out of the ruts. The small-diameter tyres and lack of suspension flex do not help.

A Jeep Patriot with a typical dash icon display when stability control is disabled, a "4WD" sign to say the centre coupling is locked, and even a tyre pressure monitor.

Somewhere in a Victorian desert. Softroaders can generally roam free in these areas. They may not be able to move as quickly as a low-ranger, but they get there. As always, be prepared to turn around.

Beautifully driven Escape using just enough momentum to get up over a rock. The driver made the track look easy and had less trouble than many of the low-rangers. The driver makes a difference.

Lacking the clearance to go straight across this dip, the Santy angles off to one side instead but gets cross-axled. Momentum and traction control pull it through, but it takes some judgement. If you drive softroaders offroad, you really drive them.

Out of approach angle, and the small diameter tyre doesn't help. If we try to drive it there'll be a crunch, and two diagonal wheels in the air…not going to work. The solution was to dodge sideways, not the ideal line on a track like this, but it worked us the Santa Fe is quite agile. If tracks like this are where you intend driving on a regular basis then buy a low-ranger.

CHAPTER 29

DRIVING FOR FUEL ECONOMY

If you find yourself desperately short of fuel with a long way to go, there are ways to eke out as much mileage as you possibly can. Or maybe you just want to reduce the fuel bill.

There's quite a lot you can do, and after following my own advice I managed a 36% improvement in my fuel economy. Sound good? Read on.

To improve economy you need to understand where the energy needed to drive a vehicle goes. In order, the main factors are:

Overcoming inertia: Just getting the big thing moving or accelerating it. The heavier the vehicle, the more energy required to shift it, and the quicker the acceleration, the more power is needed.

Drag: Aerodynamic resistance through the air. There are various types, but it's all drag. Drag is very, very important because it doesn't increase proportionally to speed; it increases according to the speed-squared law. So if you increase speed from 30km/h to 60km/h, drag quadruples, rather than doubles. A tripling from 30km/h to 90km/h sees a ninefold increase in drag. Above about 30km/h the major source of friction to a vehicle is drag, so reduce it where you can.

Tyre rolling resistance: This is split out as turning a tyre uses a surprisingly large amount of energy as it deforms every rotation.

Driveline friction: Energy wasted turning all those cogs and shafts in things like the engine, gearbox and differentials.

on the vehicle

You can go outside right now and make some changes which will improve economy.

Tyre pressures: We all know about lowering them for offroad work. Now what about raising them to reduce rolling resistance? While the manufacturer has recommended pressures and any deviation from these is at your own risk, there are a few things to consider. Firstly, the recommended pressures are for a stock vehicle. Yours probably has heavy accessories, and the heavier a vehicle, the higher the tyre pressure required, but never, ever, exceed the maximum inflation pressure which will be embossed on the tyre. Look for a difference of about four psi from hot to cold pressures and check them weekly because all tyres do lose pressure over time. Chapter 7 has more information on pressures.

Weight: When I go offroad I carry a hand winch, winch accessories, a drag chain, various tools, a compressor, an axe/shovel holder...the list goes on and the kit totals around 150kgs. It's pretty easy to remove the weight, which improves fuel economy by reducing rolling resistance and lessening the energy needed to overcome inertia. Do you have twin spare wheels? Lose one unless you go out into the country, and reduce the attractiveness of your vehicle to thieves too. Put your vehicle on a diet, effective immediately.

Drag: Got a roof rack? Ditch it if you aren't using it. Not only will you save between 25kg and 70kg, but you'll also significantly reduce air resistance (drag). Same goes for any aerials, anything that creates drag.

Air filter: Clean it, replace it – just make sure the engine is sucking air efficiently.

Transmission options: If you've got free-wheeling hubs, free them. That helps with driveline friction. If you own something like a Pajero or Pathfinder which has options for constant 4WD or 2WD, consider selecting 2WD. However, if the road is wet or loose, I'd want all four wheels driving regardless of the fuel cost.

driving style

Acceleration, braking: Driving style can make a huge difference to fuel economy and this is definitely where the biggest gains can be made. Start by looking ahead as far as you can in order to minimise the need to brake and accelerate, anticipate traffic situations and react in plenty of time. If you ever drive a car with an instant fuel-consumption display, take note of what the consumption looks like when you accelerate as it's easy to get 4WDs, even diesels, into 50-60L/100km, and it doesn't take really harsh acceleration to run off the scale with 99L/100km plus. The moral of the story is twofold; firstly, reduce the times when you do accelerate, and when you must, do so gently. Try short-shifting manuals – most 4WD diesel engines are pretty torquey and don't need to go beyond 2,000rpm. Get into the highest gear you can, quickly, without labouring the engine. Use your overdrive in automatics if you have one.

Even in a turbodiesel you can easily hit a consumption of 100L/100km or worse under harsh acceleration. The solution is…avoid accelerating by avoiding braking in the first place, which means very good road reading and anticipation. If you need to accelerate, do so gently.

Cruising speed: Given the effect of drag on vehicles and how quickly it builds up, it pays to drop your cruising speed. Try 90km/h or 95km/h instead of 100km/h or 105km/h. Not only will you reduce drag and use less fuel, you'll also not accelerate as long, reduce the revs the engine spins at and your slightly slower speed will allow you to better anticipate what's coming up. Now, what about the time you'll lose? Travelling at 90km/h you'll take 13 minutes to travel 20km. At 100km/h it'll take 12 minutes. After 100km you'll be seven minutes behind, which you'll begin to make up by less-frequent refilling at the bowser anyway.

This scenario assumes the quicker driver is actually averaging 100km/h, which is unlikely on a busy road, where the slower driver has a better chance of maintaining the reduced cruising speed. Some organisations claim a 10% improvement in economy by cruising at 90km/h rather than 100km/h.

Drop cruise speeds from 105km/h to 95km/h and get a fuel consumption benefit

Accurate navigation helps with economy, and that often starts before you leave your destination.

Cruise control: This doesn't necessarily help unless you are particularly inattentive because it cannot anticipate anything. For example, on a hill it doesn't know when to back off and accept a loss of speed but will continue accelerating hard right up until the crest before backing off. A better approach would be to accept a slight speed loss over the top and regain momentum on the downhill. The next generation of intelligent cruise control systems linked to detailed topographic maps and forwards-sensing radar will overcome this problem.

Navigation: Carefully plan where you're going to go, to avoid u-turns and mistakes because when you're running late and stressed you'll definitely use more fuel. Try and make trips well outside rush hour.

Idling: Switch off at railway lines and other extended waits. Owners of turbodiesels should refer to their vehicle handbook about idling periods after use. Don't start the engine and idle it – drive off straight away.

Select neutral at lights: Every little bit helps and for automatic drivers disconnecting the transmission entirely not only saves fuel but also the transmission wear.

Avoid short trips: Most of the wear and tear on a vehicle occurs when the engine is cold and fuel consumption is highest at this point. Combine several short trips into one if you can.

Accessories and air conditioning: Avoid! Don't wind the windows down either, as that is a pretty big source of drag and at higher speeds it will be more efficient to use the air conditioning. All accessories draw power from the alternator, which is driven by the engine.

long-term

There are a few things to do for the long term, too:

Servicing: You know a properly serviced car uses less fuel. It also looks better at trade-in and is less likely to let you down in the bush. Don't skimp; find a reputable 4WD shop and make sure they see your vehicle frequently. This is the best way to reduce driveline friction. Regular servicing also takes care of things like spark plugs, fuel and oil filters, which all affect consumption.

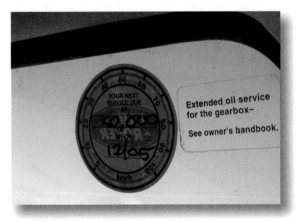

Regular servicing means good fuel economy or, more precisely, often avoiding problems that result in poor economy. One bill caused by poor servicing can wipe out years of fuel-efficient driving.

Road tyres: If you own a set, use them. Passenger construction tyres are lighter than light-truck (LT) tyres, and as that's rotating mass, that's good. The closer tread construction means less resistance and noise, too. Anything that generates noise (including tyres) means it uses energy, or another way of thinking – your cash at the bowser. For the same reason going back to alloy rims is a good idea. I measured mine to be four kilograms per wheel lighter than the steelies. While on the subject of tyres, a balance and wheel alignment reduces energy loss and is good for handling and tyre life.

Freewheeling hubs exist to improve fuel economy, so use them – it's not as if you could put the vehicle into 4WD on the bitumen anyway. However, like the AWD mode on some vehicles, it's not worth trying to save the fractions you get by using 2WD on dirt roads. Neither is it worthwhile stopping at the end of every track and switching them to free, then back to locked shortly afterwards. The fuel used in the stop/start and a minute's idling simply won't make it worthwhile.

in practice

So there's quite a lot you can do to reduce fuel consumption, and that's not even an exhaustive list. For example, you could polish your vehicle to reduce a type of drag called skin friction!

Now back to my experiment. I ran my Defender in bush mode, full of gear, with the tyre pressures at the manufacturer's recommended of 28psi in front and 48psi at the rear. Driving conservatively I returned 10.3L/100km. Less-conservative driving typically sees 11-11.5L/100km. By "conservative"

testing pressures

To see what effect tyre pressures had on rolling resistance we tried a simple test: drive the Defender at precisely 15km/h measured on the GPSR, drop the clutch when the front wheel went over a plank of wood and see how far it rolled.

Starting point, into neutral at 15km/h.

28psi front, 48psi rear, manufacturer's recommendations and 52m was the base result. Dropping to 25/35psi saw a reduction of around four percent or two metres.

50psi front, 60psi rear, well above recommendations (for the weight carried) and 61 metres, or 17% above the base result.

20 psi front and rear, 46 metres and 13% below the base. There are many factors which dictate overall fuel consumption but making sure your tyres are correctly inflated will definitely help consumption, handling and tyre wear.

larger-diameter tyres

Don't forget that larger tyres will cause your odometer to under-read relative to what the manufacturer intended, so unless you compensate for this error you'll be thinking economy has suddenly worsened when it hasn't.

Larger tyres also increase the effective gearing which helps with highway cruising. On the downside, they weigh more and create more drag, especially if they're wider than standard.

On a related note, pretty much every car's speedo under-reads so the manufacturer doesn't get sued for speeding fines, which means larger tyres may eliminate that error. Check your speed with a GPS receiver when you're travelling at a steady speed, on the flat in a straight line.

I mean cruising at 90-95km/h, short-shifting at 2,000rpm or so unless traffic conditions demand otherwise, generally following all the advice in this article and not hooning around.

Roof racks are great for loads, but the extra weight and especially drag doesn't do you any favours at the bowser.

Then I dumped all 150kg of my bush gear, including the roof rack, and upped the pressures, keeping the same driving style over the same roads, all urban, much of it freeway. Consumption dropped to 8.4L/100km, or 22% better. That was

all long (50km+) trips, no air conditioning. If I kept it up for a month's worth of driving, say 2,500km, I'd save myself over $120, with fuel at $1.70/L. If I compared my previous non-economical driving style then I've improved fuel use by about 36%.

My bush kit. Hand winch, winch kit, tyre repair kit, tools…it all adds up and just means I'm burning money having it in the truck when I'm in suburbia.

Now there's a common Internet saying of "YMMV" which means Your Mileage May Vary, and this is never more true than in the above example. Exactly how much fuel you save will depend on how serious you are about saving it, but certainly the potential is there if you try as many of these tips as you can, especially the one about driving style.

are mods worth it?

There are quite a few modifications that could potentially improve fuel consumption. Performance exhausts, ECU chips, intercoolers… the list goes on. The economics aren't all that flash though; assuming fuel costs $1.70 a litre, a $600 modification that improves 1L/100km (if you can find such a thing) will see you driving 35,000km to pay it off. And that's assuming it's not a performance modification which is tempting you to use that extra grunt, in which case you might see worse consumption!

extending range

Saving fuel to save money is one thing, but many offroaders are more interested in extending range. Adding a long range tank (Chapter 40) is one way, but you can also get more out of your existing tank using the techniques above, plus:

- **Brim full:** The fuel bowser will click shut, but there'll be more fuel you can fit in. This could be anywhere from five to 15 litres, a significant amount. However, there's a reason so much space is left and that's safety, because fuel can expand and you will need that room. So if you're going to trickle-fill, and it takes a while, don't do so unless you will immediately drive enough to use a few litres and free up that expansion space.

Trickle-filling to the brim takes a while, but you get quite a bit of extra fuel in the tank. However, you must use it immediately.

- **Minimise stops and overnights:** The more times you stop, let the engine cool and restart, the more fuel you'll use. However, you may need the stops to rest, and safety comes first. Don't leave the engine idling during a stop as that uses more fuel than a restart.

- **Use other vehicles:** In a convoy in sand, don't be the leader, follow in the wheel ruts which are compressed before you get there. Let them go down u-turns and report back.

It should be said that if you're relying on any of the above then you really need to take more fuel or a different route, so they're more tips in case things get desperate, or as an extra safeguard.

You can save a little fuel by running the likes of Pajero and Pathfinder in 2WD rather than 4WD on the road. However, try measuring the difference…it's negligible, unlike the improvement you get in safety and handling with AWD. Not all fuel efficiency gains are worth the tradeoff.

Every 4WD should have at least two (one spare) of these in the vehicle at all times. Use it frequently.

Economy driving means a smooth, flowing style that not only saves fuel but is easy on the car and sets it up well for unexpected situations like this drift of bulldust. But while you may be saving fuel, never miss a chance to fill up as conditions thus far are not necessarily indicative of conditions to come, which could be heavier on fuel again, like this – slower, heavier going in deep dust. Also, the next place may not even have fuel available.

OFFROAD TOWING

Your camper trailer may spend most of its life on bitumen or dirt roads, but with the right techniques it can follow your 4WD pretty much anywhere.

This chapter discusses towing a trailer on the sort of terrain that you'd normally consider driving in at least low-range, i.e. more difficult than just a dirt road. A trailer, for these purposes, is a specialist offroad trailer, the same width as the towcar, with two wheels. Before attempting offroad towing you need to be very comfortable driving your 4WD without a trailer in all sorts of offroad conditions (this chapter builds on the information in the other chapters in this section). You also need to be very skilled in the art of trailer manoeuvring in tight situations. This is because the difficulty of trailer towing is much magnified by mud, ruts, camber and rather unyielding trees.

Like any form of driving the key to success is preparation. This starts with understanding the forces involved in a vehicle and trailer (collectively known as a 'rig'), and adjusting your driving techniques accordingly.

For an overview of trailer weights such as ATM, GCM and GVM refer to Chapter 6.

trailer dynamics

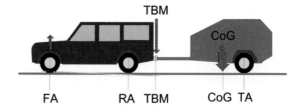

This diagram shows the centre of gravity (CoG) of the trailer ahead of the trailer axle (TA). This means the trailer exerts a downward force on the towball, known as the TBM or Tow Ball Mass. The size of the towball mass and location of the centre of gravity relative to the trailer axle are critical to trailer handling. Factors affecting both are the weight of the trailer, the distance from the trailer's axle (TA) to the CoG, and the distance from the CoG to the TBM.

On the towcar two important measures affecting handling are the overhang, which is the distance between the rear axle (RA) and the TBM, and the wheelbase, which is the distance between the towcar's front axle (FA) and rear axle. The shorter the overhang and the longer the wheelbase, the more stable the tow. Balancing the TBM is a smaller but corresponding upwards force on the front axle – the greater the overhang and shorter the wheelbase, the greater the upwards force on the front wheels.

A typical offroad camper trailer weighs between 700 and 1500kg when loaded, and should have a TBM of around 10% of the trailer's mass, so 70-150kg. Due to leverage (distance between RA and TBM), the force exerted on the towball is greater than the trailer's drawbar weight. As an example, an overhang of 1200mm, 130kg TBM, and wheelbase of 2750mm means a weight increase of 187kg on the rear axle and a reduction in front axle weight of

57kg. If the concept of increasing weight on the rear axle beyond the TBM doesn't make any sense, think about what would happen if the front wheels were removed and so much force was put on the towball the car balanced on the rear wheels only.

Inertia – the resistance of an object to changes in its direction – has a lot to do with trailer handling. The trailer will resist any turning force, so the towcar must overcome inertia.

Rig 1 in the diagram on the right has the towcar turning left, producing a turning force at point TBM to turn the trailer. Because the trailer CoG is ahead of its axle the force is resisted by the moment (rotational force) between CoG and TA. The greater the distance between CoG and TA, the bigger the moment and the more stable the trailer in a straight line, which is why moving the load forwards stabilises a trailer at speed albeit at the cost of manoeuvrability. As the distance between CoG and TA is much greater than between TBM and TA, less force is needed at TBM to overcome the moment of CoG and TA, which is why a longer drawbar also means improved stability but again at the cost of manoeuvrability. A shorter overhang is better for stability as it means the trailer's leverage to sway the front wheels is limited.

The happy medium with trailers is to find a centre of gravity location that has sufficient stability without compromising manoeuvrability. In practice this is done by adjusting load distribution, mostly on the trailer, and then testing the handling.

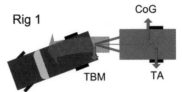

Rig 2 shows the centre of gravity a long way forwards. This gives very good stability, but you can have too much of a good thing and you can get to a point where the towcar has difficulty making the trailer deviate from its current trajectory, for example going around a corner. This configuration also increases the TBM, and that increases the upforce on the front wheels, which reduces their grip, particularly on steep uphills.

Rig 3 has the centre of gravity very close to the trailer's wheels. Now there is no problem with manoeuvrability – the trailer follows the towcar, but the rig is unstable. The slightest of forces will move the trailer offline, for example a bump in the road or a wind gust. There's very little self-centring effect, so the trailer is now prone to every tower's nightmare, 'sway' – ever-increasing oscillations that can end up in a crash.

Rig 4 is dynamically unstable as it has the centre of gravity behind the axle, so movement can't be damped out. There will also be an upward force on the towball. Not recommended!

Towing offroad can see significant forces on the trailer and towcar. The force required to move a 2500kg 4X4 on flat bitumen is around 3% of its mass, so only 75kg, and a 1000kg trailer adds only 35kg or 40% more effort. However, that force rises dramatically with gradients, and whenever the trailer needs to be dragged over rocks, logs or anything other than the flat. As an example, on a 15-degree slope a 2500kg 4WD needs around 700kg of force to move off, but with the trailer that rises 40% to 980kg, the same sort of force needed for the towcar alone to overcome gravity on a 22-degree hill. In short, the trailer may be easy to tow on a hard, relatively level, high-traction bitumen surface but once you move away from the easy terrain these forces start to make themselves felt. This is why you can't tow a 3500kg trailer offroad but you can do so onroad.

selecting a rig

trailer selection

Because driving a trailer exerts all sorts of mostly unwanted extra forces on the towcar, and those forces may be the difference between moving or not moving, the setup and choice of both towcar and trailer is critical.

design

First off, the trailer must be strong enough for the job which means it must be especially designed for offroading. Standard trailers do not last long in low-range territory or on high-speed dirt corrugations, and a good way to check the manufacturer's faith in their product is to ask if there are any warranty restrictions based on where the trailer can be towed.

It is important that the trailer follows exactly in the towcar's wheelmarks in a straight line so rolling resistance is minimised in soft ground, and it stays in the same ruts as the towcar which contributes to stability. This means the trailer's track (distance between the centre of the tyres on an axle) must be very close to that of the towcar – within half a tyre width is a reasonable rule, as it is not always possible to match tracks exactly. Good offroad trailers permit you to change parameters such as the track, rim offset or stub axle length to line the trailer wheels up exactly with the towcar, although changing rim offset may mean you cannot swap trailer and towcar wheels. This is important as it is best practice to use exactly the same tyre and wheels on towcar and trailer so you have more spare tyre options.

The hitch connecting trailer to towcar absolutely must be an offroad coupling, not a standard ball hitch. This is so that the trailer can be at any angle relative to the towcar, and if the trailer or towcar rolls it won't necessarily take the other part of the rig with it.

suspension

Suspension is much overlooked on trailers but makes a big difference to towability. The more the trailer bounces around the greater the energy and traction required to tow it and the more it destabilises the towcar, which again has an effect on traction. The tougher the terrain, the more noticeable the effect.

What's important with suspension is the quality of the design and the tuning, not so much a specific type of suspension. There's a lot to be said for independent coil suspension with shock absorbers and the results can be superb if done well, but you're simply wasting money if it's done poorly. Conversely, leaf springs and a live axle are cheaper and if set up right, tow very well indeed and are less expensive to produce, simpler and easier to repair – always important qualities in the bush.

The advantages of coils for trailers are exactly the same as for vehicles; the coils compress and extend with virtually no built-in damping, so all the damping can be precisely controlled by the finely tuned shock absorbers which offer much finer control of suspension movement than leaf springs. Independent suspension permits one wheel to move independently of the other, which is a bonus, even with a trailer that is a tripod and so nominally has both wheels on the ground at the same time. Another advantage of independent suspension is the excellent ground clearance. For trailers this is important as the towcar must choose the best line for itself and sacrifice the trailer's clearance.

The trailer should also follow the towcar exactly so as to minimise the corrective force the towcar needs to exert on the trailer. One not so apparent advantage of independent trailer suspension is the ability to set the wheels up with camber, caster and toe wheel alignment settings that help keep the trailer tracking behind the towcar.

Offroad trailers must also have recovery points. Sooner or later you'll need to pull the trailer backwards, perhaps even with the towcar attached, so there must be at least one point to do that. Two on the end of the chassis rails are preferred so one can be used to impart a rotating effect to the trailer if needed, or both used with a bridle for a straight-back pull.

trailer setup

Any trailer used offroad should be braked, regardless of whether brakes are required by law

onroad. You may be legally allowed to tow up to 750kg without brakes depending on your vehicle, but you won't want to when you're sliding down a hill. Make sure to get electric brakes, not overruns. Electric brakes allow you to vary when the brake force comes in, and by how much relative to the towcar brakes, and also to apply the trailer brakes independently of the towcar – all essential features in the rough. Overrun trailer brakes are automatically applied when the trailer tries to go faster than the towcar and so can come on when you don't want them to; for example, as you reverse with any significant resistance – mud, sand, or a rock – the overrun triggers and the brake activates.

For onroad use you'd typically set the trailer's centre of gravity forwards to promote stability and reduce the chance of trailer sway. That comes with the disadvantage of reducing manoeuvrability, as the trailer is more reluctant to change direction, and increasing towball mass which means more forces for towcar to stabilise. That's fine, because the towcar has sufficient grip to overcome the trailer. However, for low-speed offroad work a centre of gravity further back is preferable to reduce TBM. At low speeds trailer sway will not be an issue but it is desirable to maximise manoeuvrability and minimise the trailer's effect on the towcar. Changing the centre of gravity isn't easy or in some cases possible, but relocating jerrycans is one way to shift quite a bit of weight around. As ever with trailers, try and locate the weight as centrally as possible. Achieving a low TBM by balancing a heavy weight at one extremity of the trailer with a weight at the other end simply makes the trailer balanced, but unwieldy.

tyre pressures

The trailer tyres are also very important. While they may not be driven, they will need to grip laterally and provide braking traction. They must also be tough enough to air down and withstand the usual offroad abuse. Pressures on trailer tyres can go a long way below that of towcar tyres, assuming the tyres are identical. As an example, if we have a towcar weighing 3000kg we might assume for the sake of argument that the weight is split equally over each axle, 1500kg apiece, or 750kg per tyre. We then add a trailer of 1000kg. Each of the tyres on the trailer supports 500kg – but actually less because the towball mass is say 100kg, so it's more like 450kg a tyre, and the rear tyres are now up around 800kg. The pressure a tyre requires is proportional to the weight borne, so the less weight a tyre has to bear, the less pressure required in it. As trailer tyres take less weight than those on the towcar their pressure should be correspondingly lower. The way to set pressures is simply to keep lowering the trailer tyres until they reach the same contact patch length as the towcar. As an example, photos of a Defender and Tvan in this chapter ran tyre pressures as follows: 16, 18 and 12psi across the three axles which used Cooper light-truck construction tyres on 16" rims. This worked fine.

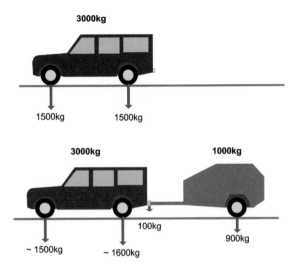

Arrow lengths are drawn to relative scale.

towcar selection and setup

The car itself needs some setup work, and anything that improves its offroad capability is to be welcomed. Low-range is a must, given the slow-speed work and extra torque required. Mud tyres and locking differentials are two easy improvements, and suspension could typically benefit from an upgrade unless it is self-levelling air suspension. A small but valuable addition is clean mirrors with blind-spot sub-mirrors on each so you can see what the trailer's wheels are doing. The ideal towcar will be a torquey automatic with a tight turning circle and excellent offroad capability.

The towcar should be rated to tow considerably more than the trailer weight as the towing ratings are for onroad use, not offroad. For the offroad rating dividing by about three is a good rule, for example low-range Land Rovers can usually tow 3500kg onroad but are recommended for 1000kg offroad.

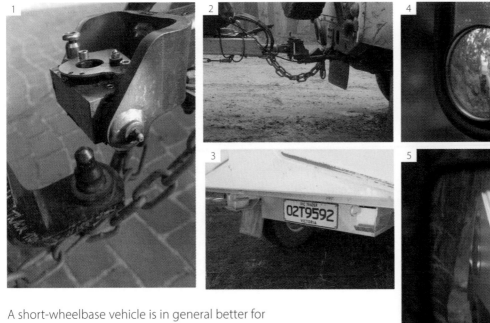

A short-wheelbase vehicle is in general better for towing offroad than a long wheelbase. The shortie will have a tighter turning circle, and is of course physically shorter. The overhang (distance between the rear axle and tow hitch) is also shorter, which is important in order to minimise the forces described earlier.

Fuel consumption will be dramatically increased in rough terrain. On the flat, often all you'll need is enough energy to maintain speed, and drivers may be used to small increases when towing below freeway speeds on flattish dirt roads. But offroad it is all hills, stopping and starting and that means energy required to move several hundred kilos of trailer up, down and around. We found our fuel consumption offroad increased by between 50 and 70% for a diesel compared to without a trailer, far more than the onroad increase of 10-30%.

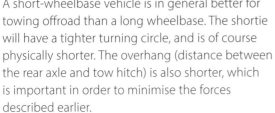

1 *A good offroad hitch permits 360 degrees of lateral rotation, and 90 degrees up and down. It is also important that it is very easy to hook up, as lining things up is difficult when offroad.*

2 *Make sure all your chains and leads are well out of the way. Cross over chains, and shorten if you can.*

3 *Two recovery points are important so the trailer can be pulled backwards, or sideways.*

4-5 *A blind-spot mirror proving its worth – the driver can see the trailer is going to miss the cut log, and the main mirror shows the van will just clear the tree.*

1 This is why is it is not a good idea to carry much on the rear door when in difficult offroad situations – it'll get squashed!

2 Here the trailer can be used to help lower the towcar down over the rock, by adjusting the electric brake controller to increase the trailer's brake sensitivity relative to the towcar.

3 This is why you need an offroad hitch.

4 If the towcar can drive there, the trailer can follow!

5 Trailer tyres need to be just as tough and grippy as that of the towcar. They need to provide lateral grip and braking grip.

6 The trailer is pushing the Discovery's rear end around the corner as the rig negotiates a sideslope, a corner and a muddy area. Careful use of the ruts avoided a problem.

driving techniques

the basics

All offroad drivers soon learn they must form a visual model of where the vehicle's wheels are at any point in time. Offroad trailer drivers must extend that model to include the trailer; they need to know where the wheels are, whether the trailer will cut in to a corner, and what forces it is likely to exert on the towcar. For example, if you're ascending a rock ledge you know you'll need a squeeze on the throttle to get the front wheels up and over, and another for the rear axle, but now you'll need a third for the trailer.

The line through an obstacle is important, but not as critical as it may first seem. The rule is to drive the towcar. Just as without a trailer, keep four wheels level and give priority to the towcar's line for good traction and clearance over that of the trailer. The ideal line is far less important for the trailer as it is a tripod with both wheels on the ground at all times, and its wheels are not driving. You can pretty much pull a trailer over anything if the towcar has traction, but you're going nowhere if the trailer is looking good but the towcar is in strife. Assuming you have a decent trailer, if it is canted over at a steep angle it is almost as easy to pull as if it were level – a good offroad trailer should have even better clearance than the average towcar. It will also be more tolerant of sideangles than the towcar, and less likely to slip into deep ruts as it is lighter and more stable.

hills

ascents

Look at all hill ascents as a potential problem. Not only do you have to drag a weight up the hill, but there will be even less weight on the front wheels due to the TBM. Expect reduced steering control and more front-wheel lifting, a critical point if you are using cross-axle differential locks for the ascent which already reduce steering capability. A lower gear may well be needed to account for the extra weight. Remember that the hill doesn't end until the trailer, not towcar, is over the top (Diagram 3).

The real problem with hills, and perhaps the biggest issue with offroad trailer driving, is what happens when you need to fail the climb. You will need to back the trailer down, but it may be at an odd angle, with the towcar unable to go forwards, or otherwise unable to get the lock on needed to manoeuvre the trailer. Unhooking the trailer may not be much use if the towcar cannot then ascend the hill from where it is. The solution may be winching forwards, so consider that before you start the ascent. If going forwards isn't possible then the trailer may need to be unhooked and pulled backwards. A handwinch (Chapter 36) can be used for this, with a flat plate for the jockey wheel to stop it sinking in. Handwinches can also be used to pull vehicles sideways. Once the trailer is out of the way you can focus on recovering the towcar. If that sounds difficult – you're not wrong!

If you do need to reverse down a hill it is very likely you'll be quite hard on the towcar's brakes. If the trailer's brakes are also on then the trailer will want to jacknife, so reduce the trailer's brake sensitivity such that when the towcar brakes are applied the trailer's brakes are not immediately activated. However, don't go too far with the desensitivity, because if you need to stop the rig then you need to be able to apply further brake pressure and activate brakes on all six wheels.

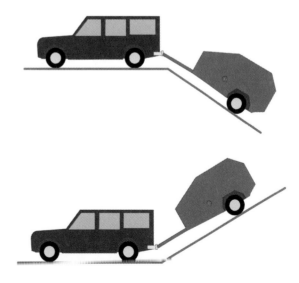

descents

It can be hard enough to descend a hill without a trailer pushing the car downslope, so to fix that you need to apply the trailer brakes – but not so much that the wheels lock, or the towcar is over-braked. The solution is an electric brake controller. This invaluable tool allows you to change the sensitivity so that gentle braking on the towcar means a greater braking force on the trailer. As the towcar has the advantage of engine braking this would about equalise the retardation forces and mean a controlled hill descent.

The towball downforce is increased, which is a good thing as the gradient naturally shifts towcar weight to the front, so the increased TBM restores some weight to the towcar's rear axle. When completing the descent the descending trailer can help push the towcar along the ground or up the next hill.

When starting a sharp descent from flat the trailer will retard the towcar until it too comes over the crest, after which you can expect the descent to become more interesting! As ever when descending, use ruts and make sure the trailer and towcar use the same ruts. This may require some extra lining up before the descent. If things go wrong there should be little chance of the trailer overtaking the towcar because the trailer is lighter, assuming it has appropriately aired-down tyres of the same type as the much heavier towcar. Therefore, the trailer is better able to brake itself on a hill. If the brakes are released, the trailer will continue to push the towcar as long as it is descending, and that can be used to advantage where a descent turns immediately into an ascent.

side slopes

Side slopes are more difficult with trailers. The diagrams below show the rig on a side slope. Here the trailer is exerting a force trying to move the back wheels of the towcar down the slope, and thus pivot the front wheels up. That is why, on side slopes, the rear tyres do a lot of work and it's easy to have the back end slide downwards.

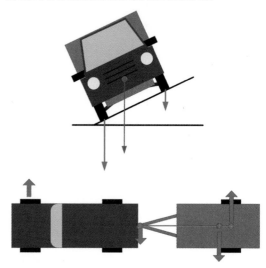

soft ground

Soft-ground driving in mud, sand and snow is straightforward – literally. The key here is minimising resistance, so the trailer follows the towcar's wheels as closely as possible. The extra weight and resistance will mean more momentum or a possibly a lower gear. Avoid turning, because then instead of all six wheels following in the same rut you now have all six wheels making their own ruts which increases rolling resistance. Remember that backing a trailer in slippery or soft conditions may not be possible, so again consider recovery options carefully.

Sand driving with a trailer is entirely possible, but drop tyre pressures even further in this case. The big problem with sand and trailers is any form of side slope, for example on beaches. When on a slope, the trailer exerts a sideways force on the towcar, and the sand might not offer enough lateral traction to resist, so you end up with the towcar back end sliding downslope. That problem quickly becomes worse as the six wheels cut their own ruts. In sand with the average camper you will be looking at 10-15psi maximum, and certainly less than the towcar. Reduce pressures to match the towcar's contact patch.

The other big risk with sand driving is ascending. Firstly, any slight side angle will again see the trailer pulling the back of the towcar sideways. Secondly, reversing a trailer down a sandy slope is often next to impossible because sand offers so little lateral traction, meaning the trailer easily jacknifes. It is also very difficult to drive uphill in sand to reposition the towcar. Even worse, how do you get out of it? In sandy country there's not usually a conveniently placed tree to act as a winch anchor. The answer is digging, traction ramps and other vehicles. And as with any soft conditions, avoid turning as you'll be creating six, not four wheel tracks which all contribute to drag.

water

Water crossings need a bit more torque, so that means lower gears and more revs, despite the fact the towcar largely forces water out of the way of the trailer. Again, any change of direction rapidly starts to increase trailer resistance as the trailer's front starts to drag. Backing a trailer out of deep water isn't easy, especially if there is any appreciable flow.

Any offroad trailer worthy of the name will be at least as waterproof as the average 4WD.

manoeuvring

A trailer decreases a vehicle's manoeuvrability, but not the outside turning circle – any offroad trailer should still allow you to turn at full lock. What does change is the inside turning circle, as the trailer wheels cut inside those of the towcar (Diagram 5), and the shorter the drawbar, the better. The loss of inside radius can be anywhere from 500 to 1000mm depending on the trailer/towcar setup, but that's only after turning both through 120 degrees or so. Most of the time you don't need to turn that amount so the trailer cut-in may be 300mm or less. Swinging out wide with the towcar helps to get around. When towing you need to be thinking and planning ahead, much, much more than you do without a trailer; if you only react to a tight spot when you get to it, chances are you won't make it through.

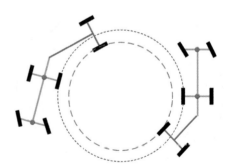

When you drive a trailer in a circle there are six ruts, not four, so much more drag than a towcar. The trailer's wheels describe the shortest arc, but shorter trailers more closely follow the towcar.

If you do attempt a full-lock turn and don't make it then you have a problem. The diagrams show two common situations you may drive into, or slide into.

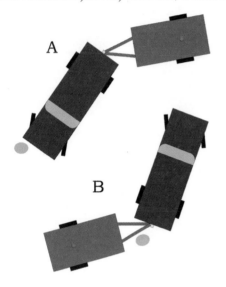

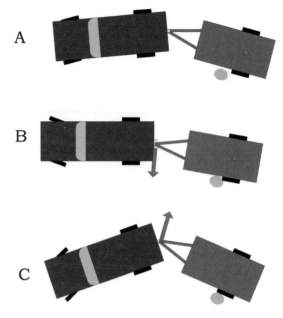

Two common problems. Rig A has run out of lock. The trick here is to anticipate this early, and shuffle the trailer. You can also, at this stage, back up with maximum opposite lock and try again, intentionally jacknifing the trailer. That had better work, because if it doesn't you will be unable to go further backwards. Winching the nose around works too, as does a pull from the back. Rig B has a different problem, usually caused by lack of planning and not understanding the obstacle-avoidance technique of turning to swing the drawbar away from a problem (Diagram 3). The best solution here is to unhitch, pull the trailer free and then hitch again. The trailer's nose may be pulled around by use of winch if need be.

The top rig (A) shows a common problem: the trailer is about to hit an obstacle. The instinct of most drivers is to turn away from the problem (B). This moves the drawbar towards the problem, and the trailer will hit the obstacle. However, if you override instinct and turn sharper (C) then that swings the drawbar wider, and the trailer has a chance of clearing the obstacle.

One tip which works with many vehicles is to unlock the centre diff to reduce the turning circle, or if conditions permit, slip into 2WD. Drivers of modern manuals can simply use low-range, leaving one foot covering the brake and using the other to bring the clutch up and down to manoeuvre the trailer. The vehicle's anti-stall will kick in, so you can manoeuvre the rig and for the most part not need any extra revs beyond idle. This is much safer, easier and more controllable than the classic method of applying the parkbrake and quickly moving your foot from brake to throttle and back again. The technique also works as a hill start; come to a halt, select first low with clutch down, right foot on brake, reduce brake pressure so the car is about to roll backwards but not quite, gently bring the clutch up to biting point and when the car moves forwards progressively release the footbrake. I have started on steep hills with 1500kg trailers using this method.

Even on the road, backing a trailer at full lock may mean a jacknife, and offroad the chances of trouble increase. One solution is to reverse the towcar slightly at full opposite lock, intentionally jacknifing the trailer to squeeze a little more turning circle. This works well, provided you don't run out of lock.

It is quite easy to become wedged between the jacknifed trailer and whatever it is you're trying not to hit with the front of the towcar. One solution is ruts, which tramline the trailer quite nicely, another is to unhook, and a third is to use a winch to literally drag the front of the towcar around. You can also get creative with intentional skids. For example, manually applying the trailer brake and then driving the towcar may induce enough of a skid or slip to move the towcar just enough to make it through – or, if you have the option, place the towcar in 2WD and do something similar to move the rear wheels sideways. You should use these techniques with caution (in fact, that advice summarises the entire approach to offroad trailer driving!), but once you master them you'll be amazed where you can drag your trailer.

The towcar's line has been prioritised so it keeps all four wheels on the ground. The trailer dropped in the rut, but that doesn't matter as it is easy for the towcar, on a good line, to pull it out.

1-2 Handy hint: For an easy hookup, connect the tongue to the hitch, and then manoeuvre the towcar onto the tongue, then slot in the pin.

3 Tricky, muddy, rutted hill descent, so use the ruts to tramline the vehicle. Set electric brakes so the trailer is retarding the rig with gentle towcar brake pressure, and focus on the towcar's stability – the trailer is better able to handle the ruts and much less likely to slip in. But don't drive it unless you're sure you can get all the way out, as turning around would be very, very difficult!

4 Mudbog driving is the same as always – low pressures, momentum, but even more importantly take a straight line so you have two wheel ruts, not six.

5 Notice how much the Patrol's body is rolling, but the trailer sits flat to the road. This is because the trailer weighs far less and has a much lower centre of gravity. Its tyres can use all their traction for lateral grip, sparing none for driving forwards.

6 Some perfectly judged momentum to carry the rig through.

7 Focus on the towcar's traction. A good offroad trailer can be dragged anywhere, provided the towcar keeps moving.

2 Will the trailer's wheels hit the rock?

1   Sometimes you can't ascend at a crawl. But if you use speed to crest a hill then consider what you'd do if you don't actually make the crest, because backing down is not necessarily possible.

2   When ascending hills with a trailer there is reduced weight on the front axle, which leads to less steering control.

3   The left trailer wheel has just been pulled over a rock, and now the right wheel is over a different one. The driver must remember those rocks, even though the towcar is now well down the track, as well as thinking about the towcar itself and what's coming up.

4   It doesn't take much for the towbar to come close to touching. Make sure chains and cables are tidy.

5   The trailer is trying to pull the towcar sideways, a force the rear wheels must counteract.

6   An intentional jacknife (reverse at opposite lock) to tighten turning circle. Make sure it'll work, otherwise you really will be stuck. And don't reverse too far into the trailer and bend something!

7   Sometimes the trailer downforce can assist with stability.

1   Trailers usually work well on sand. However, avoid turning so that only one set of ruts is made, use lots of momentum and be prepared for recoveries!

2   A rutted, and somewhat slippery ascent requiring momentum. This sort of marginal-traction situation is where a trailer that is easy to tow is the difference between making the hill or a recovery.

3   It is important to keep in these ruts for this descent, so the trailer track must be the same as that of the towcar, and some early lining up is essential. A light touch on the towcar brakes should activate the trailer brakes.

4   Ideally you'd take this ditch at an angle, but it's not always possible. Hence the need for good clearance!

5   Expect drawbars to scrape.

6   Spotters are always useful, but even more so with six wheels to consider.

7   The towcar has completed the turn, but the trailer is some way behind. Trailer drivers need to be thinking about the trailer all the time.

8   Momentum is needed more often with trailers, and it carries a higher risk. The driver must have worked out 'what if' for both towcar and trailer.

CHAPTER 31

UNFAMILIAR VEHICLES

It used to be simple – just a few 4WDs on the market, and they all worked the same way with simple mechanicals. Now there's a vast array of models, most with complicated electronic controls, so it's no longer easy to work out what sort of 4WD you're dealing with and how best to drive it.

What you need is a very, very thorough understanding of offroad vehicle operating principles, some general knowledge, some intelligent deduction based on that understanding and knowledge, and then some careful experimentation.

The principles include truly understanding the concept of windup and the main solutions, the difference between two types of traction control and stability control, LSDs, lockers, the various effects of differentials in both cross-axle and centre applications, the basics of adaptive terrain systems, ABS and what various dash symbols look like. General vehicle knowledge includes knowing that any vehicle with stability control must, logically, also have traction control and ABS, as those two are part of stability control.

The owner's handbook – assuming it is actually available – will have a section describing what the vehicle's controls are, and how to operate them. But be warned, it won't really tell you in which circumstances to use, disable or enable features, and to properly understand it you'll definitely need that base understanding of vehicle principles. The handbook will also cover all models, not just the one you're driving, and it won't cover everything you need to know. In some cases its advice about techniques may even be questionable – I just read one which specifically advises against creating a bow wave in water, for example.

So if you want to drive an unfamiliar vehicle, read on to learn how to do it. You start by gathering as much information as you can about the car.

step 1: look outside

Before you even get close to the vehicle you can start learning about it.

- **Is it in fact 4WD?** Some vehicles, particularly softroaders and utes may be only 2WD and look identical to the 4WD versions. Check for '4X4' badges, but remember that the absence of such a badge doesn't mean it isn't 4X4.

- **What do the badges tell you?** As well as the 4X4 badge, sometimes there's a hint to whether it's an all wheel drive, diesel or petrol, auto or manual.

- **Are the hubs freewheeling, automatic, or neither?** If the hubs are either freewheeling or automatic you're dealing with a part-time 4WD. But, if you don't see the hubs that doesn't mean to say it's not a part-timer. See Chapter 4 for more details.

- **What are the angles and clearances?** From the outside you can assess the approach, ramp and departure angles. Are there any problems with towbars, or loose mudflaps, or is there any bar protection fitted? What's the lowest point of the vehicle?

- **What accessories are fitted?** Perhaps a winch, driving lights, a heavy roofrack, or a suspension lift.

- **Do recovery points exist?** This is important enough to warrant a specific mention, so check they exist. Very often on new vehicles they may be hidden behind plastic covers.

- **What tyres are fitted?** Check what condition the tyres are they in, whether they are low or high profile, whether there is a spare and whether it matches the rest of the tyres. Check the spare to see if it is a space-saver.

- **What about load?** If there's a roofrank tent, a cargo bay chock full and two spares on the back you know you're dealing with a vehicle that isn't nimble.

step 2: Look inside

This is where you learn more about what the car's got, and also how to operate it.

control locations

There are four main locations for car controls. For a right-hand drive car these will be, in order of probability of finding controls: in the centre console around the shifter and parkbrake area, on the centre dashboard, on the right of the steering wheel, and in the roof. You must carefully scan all these areas for buttons, levers, switches and toggles to learn what the car can and can't do. If there's anything you don't recognise, work out what it means, as it may be important to either switch it on or off. You're looking for things such as:

As you approach a vehicle check out the angles. They're not bad in the case of this Jeep, but there's a mudguard or two in the way. Look at the tyres, which are road pattern and low profile. It's also clear the rear windows are tinted, which combined with dirt and a cloudy day means restricted visibility. It's clearly a modern car, so we can expect traction control, an auto and decent amounts of power. Plenty to be learned at a glance!

Start looking for controls around the centre area between the seats (1), then above in the lower dash (2). The area to the left and right of the steering wheel (3, 4) is a favourite. Any controls on the steering wheel (5) are usually duplicated elsewhere. Some vehicles now have controls in the roof (not shown).

Subaru's EyeSight system of hazard detection has its controls located in the roof. This needs to be disabled when offroad, like many advanced safety features.

- **Gearshift:** The obvious control will be the gearshift. Now you can see if the vehicle is automatic or manual, and how many ratios the gearbox has if manual or an older automatic. On an automatic vehicle you can also see if the gears can be selected manually, as there will be +/- symbols, but not whether it is a maximum-select or gear-select automatic (Chapter 4). Also note the up/down shift pattern which will be either left/right, forwards/backwards or backwards/forwards. Look for a Sport mode too. Some automatics have selector dials instead of shifters, and look also for paddle shifts around the steering wheel, and note whether they move with the wheel or are fixed. The presence of a 2nd start button is a sure sign the automatic box is a maximum select or conventional – selecting '3', for example, means the box will use gears 1, 2, and 3 at its discretion whereas a gear-select system uses 3 as best it can without changing (Chapter 4). Take a note of where reverse is, and whether it needs to be selected

via detent or not. You want to find this out before you get onto the hills.

- **Dash lights:** Turn the key to ignition 1 and take a look at the dash. There will be an array of lights which tell you all sorts of things about the car. If it is a diesel there'll be a glowplug lamp. If there is stability control there'll be an icon there too, and much more. But the lights only tell you what the car can do, not where the controls are.

- **4WD selector:** Any part-time 4WD vehicle will have a 2WD and 4WD selector system. This may be a button, or a lever. In general, utes tend to be part-time, as do very old wagons. There are very few new part-time wagons, but three are the Patrol GU, Toyota FJ Cruiser and the Colorado 7/Isuzu MU-X twins. Some softroaders may have a 4WD lock button. This will be designed to distribute torque 50/50 front and rear (well, kind of) and probably disables at speeds over around 40km/h.

Tip – a selector that has 2H will be a part-time 4WD. A selector that has 4H, 4HL and 4LL is all-wheel-drive with a lockable centre diff which locks in low-range. A selector that has 4H and 2L does not lock the centre diff in low-range – look for a separate button for that (as for many new Toyotas, for example).

The H-N-L transfer case (1) doesn't have a lock option, so look for it elsewhere (3), in contrast to the 2H-4H-N-4L transfer case lever (2) which clearly means 2WD and no centre diff lock.

- **Park brake:** This may be a conventional large lever between the seats, a foot-operated brake (softroaders), a pull-handle system (often on utes) or a finger-operated electronic brake (modern wagons). The latter may even be on the right side of the steering wheel (Subaru) or on the end of a stalk (Mercedes) or on the gearlever itself (Range Rover).

- **ABS, traction control and stability control:** There is no easy way to tell whether a vehicle has ABS other than looking at the dash warning lights. However:

  - all vehicles with stability control also have traction control.

  - all vehicles with traction control also have ABS.

  - the reverse of the above points is not true, for example not all vehicles with ABS have traction control.

Most offroad vehicles with stability control have a disable switch. This may be marked with a vehicle skid symbol (newer vehicles) or it may be marked with the manufacturer's acronym such as DSC or VDC (older vehicles). Some vehicles do not have this switch, notably some Toyotas, and disable stability control by locking the centre diff.

You have to know what all these mean – RSCA is Roll Sensing Collision Airbags, Toyota's system of disabling side airbag sensors when offroad. 4Lo means you're in low-range, the green ascend icon is Crawl Control activated, and the other two refer to stability control being deactivated.

- **Lockable centre diffs:** Obviously part-time 4WDs won't have a manually lockable centre diff, but some constant 4WDs won't have one either, relying on computers or mechanical devices to do the job automatically. Modern Land Rovers are an example. Some vehicles, such as the Prado and LC200, have both a centre diff and a 50/50 front/rear lock mode. If there is a lock mode it'll be a button or a lever. The button typically is a stylised 4X4 transmission with an X in the centre.

- **Cross-axle lockers:** Manually operated cross-axle lockers will always have a switch somewhere, usually a stylised 4X4 transmission with an X through the rear axle. Note that enabling factory-fit lockers typically disables traction control. There is no easy to way to determine whether a vehicle has a mechanical auto-locker, or an electronic auto-locker such as those found in some modern Land Rovers. However, for the latter, switch the centre console screen (if fitted) to 4X4 display mode when driving in Rock Crawl – the rear locker, if fitted, will soon activate.

- **Hill descent control systems:** If fitted, there will be a switch somewhere, unless one of the few that activates automatically. The speed of descent can sometimes be controlled by the cruise control switches (Land Rovers and others) or the gearshift (Jeeps). Ensure the icon you're looking at is a car descending, not ascending – the ascent icon is for hill start systems or similar.

- **Suspension:** If the suspension is variable-height then there will certainly be a control to adjust it.

- **Adaptive terrain systems:** All adaptive terrain systems will have some sort of selector system – this may be a series of buttons or a dial. In the case of some Toyotas the dial does double duty as a Crawl Control (Chapter 9) selector. The control will be prominently placed somewhere close to the driver.

- **Petrol or diesel:** The easy way to tell, if there's no badge, is to look at the rev counter. Diesels won't go much above 5,000 rpm, petrols will. You can also switch the ignition on and look for the presence of the glowplug symbol, which on modern diesels barely illuminates even on cold start.

- **Safety systems:** Some vehicles have switches to disable deployment of side airbags (e.g. late model LC200s, RSCA), others may have parking sensors that should be deactivated, or autonomous braking systems (i.e. the car decides when it should slam the brakes on) that need switching off.

From left to right – high/low-range, crawl control which also acts as hill descent control, variable height suspension and suspension firmness controls in an LX570.

Turn a vehicle's ignition on and you'll see a set of warning lights test-illuminate. You can use these to determine some of the features. This is a Discovery 3, and it is clear the car has ABS (centre), hill descent control (green icon on left), to the left of that a variable-height suspension system, and to the right a stability control icon.

Sometimes vehicles have features which are difficult to find. The Discovery 3 and 4 have an emergency park brake release, shown here in the D4, and the Y62 Patrol has a hidden method to disengage the centre diff lock.

That's a 4WD, right? Well, this one is. But there's also a 2WD Hi Rider variant that looks identical, with the same ride height, and without the '4X4' badge. Many softroaders are also available in 2WD and 4X4 configurations.

step 3: drive

You've now worked out as much as possible about the vehicle, so it's time to drive. On the flat, assess the throttle response, and how low the gears are if you're in low-range. Check the turning circle, and the visibility. Try an offroad obstacle, and see how well the suspension flexes and/or the traction control works, if fitted. When selecting a mode – low-range, for example – look for confirmatory dash lights and check the vehicle feels appropriate to the selection you think you've made.

Check the theories you developed about how the car works. If it seems to struggle where it shouldn't, check everything is as it should be. For example, Defenders can be driven in low-range without the centre diff locked, which catches out those used to the centre locking automatically in low-range, and with modern cars it's easy to forget to be in low-range and wonder why things seem harder.

golden rules

1. **Take it easy first.** Get to know the vehicle before you attempt that super-steep rock climb.

2. **Don't assume.** Just because the last 1000 Prados you drove always locked the centre diff in low-range doesn't mean to say this one does too.

3. **There are exceptions to every rule.** There may be aftermarket mods, or a car's systems may not be fully functional.

4. **Go back to first principles.** There is absolutely no substitute for understanding the basic 4WD design principles listed earlier in this chapter. Even when you discover what a vehicle has you'll still need to work out how effective it is and how it should be driven.

how to drive

In general, you need to ease gently into each type of vehicle, especially if you're not used to the type. The driving techniques described in this book are applicable to all types of 4WD vehicle, but each type of 4WD has some specific techniques. For example, a lightly loaded petrol manual Pajero needs revs due to its engine characteristics and not very low range, whereas a fully loaded Defender 130 just chugs everywhere. Identical vehicles with traction control can be driven differently as ETC means you can go slower, as do cross-axle lockers. Some specific types of vehicle are covered below:

manuals vs autos

Anywhere a manual can go the auto can follow, and vice versa. Overall, autos are easier and more capable. The modern ones now have excellent engine braking which was a weakness in the past.

While manuals need their gear selected, modern automatics can mostly be left in drive. Yet for best effect they often benefit from specific gear selection, particularly for ascents and descents and if their downshift logic tends to be late and jerky. Autos are very good at inching forwards using the driving through the brakes technique (Chapter 22). Manuals have the advantage of a direct connection from engine to wheels so you're less likely to come to a complete halt – to do so would mean the engine has stalled. Manuals can also be left in gear on a hill, whereas autos need a special parking technique (Chapter 22).

Modern manuals have an anti-stall mode; put the car in first low, and see where it can go at idle, clutch up, no accelerator. Often the car will run out

of traction before it runs out of torque. This facility is also useful when manoeuvring, as you can simply modulate the clutch to move in first or reverse, with the right foot always covering the brake instead of jumping the right foot from accelerate to brake and back again. See Chapter 22 for details of different hill techniques.

petrols vs diesels

Anywhere a diesel can go, the petrol can follow, until it runs out of fuel. Both engine types have ample torque and power, especially with modern gearboxes, and good engine braking. The petrol is still a little revvier, easier to gather momentum quickly in sand or mud compared to the slightly more sluggish diesel. Diesels need less revs to maximum torque and can use higher gears as a result, which can be handy in slippery conditions. Small engines of both types often need quite a few revs.

loaded vs unloaded

A heavily loaded 4WD handles very differently to a lightly loaded one; more power will be needed in any given situation, braking distances will be increased, the vehicle will be more unstable, particularly if the suspension is worn, the suspension will be compressed (unless height-adjustable) which will reduce clearance, and the centre of gravity may be affected so the vehicle doesn't balance on diagonal wheels but rocks back onto the rear wheels. For any given tyre pressure the contact patch will be increased, and you can't lower pressures on a heavy vehicle as far as you can on a lighter one, for fear of rim damage or tyre debeading. The differences between light and heavy can be quite dramatic, so consider the vehicle's capability on and offroad to be much reduced when fully loaded. This is another reason to choose a vehicle that has much more carrying capacity than you need.

long wheelbase vs short wheelbase

In general, the short wheelbase (SWB) vehicles are better offroad than long wheelbase (LWB) due to better departure and ramp angles, lighter weight and smaller turning circles. That said, LWBs hold a stability advantage on very steep hills, and sometimes their extra length helps them put one set of wheels beyond a slippery patch. Onroad, SWBs can be a little jumpy and nervous compared to LWBs, especially over corrugations. Often SWBs have smaller fuel tanks, translating to less range, and certainly less cargo room.

large vs small

The large 4WD is big and heavy. It doesn't have a lot of choice in the line through an obstacle, but it should have good clearance and traction. Once moving, it has momentum, and usually has a powerful engine capable of lugging through obstacles in a relatively high gear. The smaller 4WD is narrower and shorter, so it can dart around obstacles – which it needs to do because of its relatively small wheels and clearances. It may be narrow, and not tolerant of sideslopes, and the engine is likely to only develop useful torque at higher revs.

For more information about the following vehicle features, see the relevant chapter:

- Electronic driving aids – Chapter 9
- Cross-axle differential locks – Chapter 4
- Terrains – Section 2
- Choosing a 4WD – Chapter 39

The Defender 90 is a light, nimble offroader. But when it's heavily modified, and then even more heavily loaded, it loses its manoeuvrability. You then can't lower tyre pressures as far as you normally would, the vehicle sinks in more, the engine must produce more power, clearances are reduced as the suspension compresses, side slopes become a problem and fuel consumption shoots up. Loaded 4WDs are very different from unloaded ones!

Seven vehicles, seven different driving styles – even the two LC200s on the left are petrol and diesel. As an example, the LC76 and Defender either side of the yellow H3 are ostensibly the same – old, live-axle designs. But the Defender has a modern 6-speed manual mated to a small engine fitted with electronic anti-stall, and very low gearing with traction control. The Toyota has an older, but much larger engine, 5 speeds, higher gearing but front and rear cross-axle differentials. So the Defender might require more gear changes, and would need more momentum over rocky terrain where the LC76 could cruise with lockers. The Defender is likely to do better in slippery terrain with its excellent axle flex and traction control.

SECTION 3
RECOVERY

CHAPTER 32

RECOVERY PLANNING

If you drive offroad then sooner or later you will be in a situation you can't drive out of. That's when you need recovering.

Vehicles need to be recovered any time they cannot move where you want them to go, which may be immobilised bonnet-deep in mud, or able to move but not quite able to get over something like a sand dune. If you have the knowledge and even some basic gear then recoveries aren't an issue. If you have neither then recoveries are extremely dangerous.

the dangers

4WD vehicles are heavy. A typical touring 4WD weighs, with a normal load, between 2,300kg and 3,500kg. By definition, when a vehicle is stuck (becomes a casualty) it cannot move of its own accord, so sufficient force must be exerted to move the vehicle, and those forces are more than enough to be dangerous; deaths or injuries are not unknown. Every so often there is a tragic accident and someone is killed, but injuries tend not to make the news and neither does damage to vehicles.

4WD recovery is an inherently dangerous activity which is made safe by careful planning and execution. The same is true of skiing, skydiving, scuba diving and many more sports; even just driving a normal car on the road or using power tools. All these activities can hurt if you don't take basic precautions.

Enough doom and gloom. The rest of this chapter explains how to recover.

Even a stock-standard vehicle weighs around 2,500kg these days (this D3 doesn't weight 3,000kg, as often reported). The forces are considerable. Here there are two ways of recovering the vehicle, forwards and backwards. Which is the safest? Consider all the options.

the method

Every recovery is subtly different. Many are straightforward, other involve hours of work. Sometimes getting stuck is predictable, while at other times people can be left scratching their heads wondering how the hell that happened. I remember leading a trip along a perfectly innocuous little track that a road car could have handled. Suddenly the call came that a Patrol in our convoy was stuck. I returned, wondering just how on earth they could possibly be stuck. The answer? The vehicle had stopped. The driver and her husband discussed something. Then they started again, but the vehicle wasn't pointing quite down the track. The front wheel went up over a rock. Hubby said to keep going. Wife was worried, but followed the advice. Down came the front wheel over the other side of the rock, and the vehicle was then resting on three wheels and its front sidestep. Oh dear.

No matter how bizarrely you are stuck, a good old method works. Like the first-aider's method of DRABC (Danger, Response, Airways, Breathing, Circulation) we can make one for 4WD recoveries too.

Danger

Why?

Options

Plan

Execution

Completion

danger

As stressed earlier, 4WD recovery is a dangerous activity made safe. So don't go rushing in close to a stricken vehicle. It may not be able to make progress, but that doesn't mean to say it can't move. Approach with caution. Calm everyone down and move them out of the way, then agree on one leader. There is NO RUSH, and if a vehicle is balanced precariously, even less rush. Get the coffee out, have an impromptu break.

My fault for simply being careless on a track I knew well – can't even use the snow as an excuse. The Defender isn't stuck as such, but it couldn't drive out and there's a drop to one side. The solution was to whip the spade off the back, dig the snow out, engage the rear locker and very slowly inch the vehicle out onto the track. Winching was an option too.

why?

Before you do anything, figure out why the vehicle can't move. Is it obvious? Are you sure? Sometimes it looks like a vehicle is hung up somewhere, but in reality the problem is elsewhere. Sometimes the problem is obvious, but there's another hangup just waiting to happen next. You can also save on the effort by checking the simple things like hubs being locked, pressures down, centre diff engaged and so on. I was once driving a friend's truck in a winch competition and I'd got the car up onto a rock ledge but no further, so we winched. And winched. But the car didn't move, and against our better judgement we kept going. Then the cable broke and the snatch block came hurtling back towards the car, ripping the wing mirror off. Had it been a little closer this book wouldn't have been written. The problem was the car was hung up on a rock ledge and no amount of winching was ever going to work. But we didn't check and I nearly paid for that mistake with my life.

options

So the danger has been assessed, and we know why it's stuck. Now we can consider options for recovery. And do consider them all. It's all too common for everyone to start working towards a recovery, even if it's not the best solution. And at the end everyone says "well we should have done it that other way…."!!!

Options might include:

- Snatching forwards
- Snatching backwards
- Winching forwards
- Winching backwards
- Digging out
- Airing down further
- Jacking up and filling under, or using a traction ramp
- Driving out using a different technique

or a combination thereof. A sign of your preparedness is the amount of options you have available to you. The more the safer. On one trip we negotiated a slippery downhill with a large rock in the middle. A Prado got hung up on the rock by its rear diff, with no way to go backwards or forwards. It was the last vehicle in the convoy, too. So we used an air jack to lift the back end and it simply drove forwards once the back was lifted. Another time we needed to recover a red Pajero at an odd angle in mud (see photo); to spin it around to make the recovery easier one experienced old hand put it in 2WD, spun up the rear wheels which slipped, the back end moved half a metre and the recovery was much easier from then on.

On the other hand, I was once out on a two-car photoshoot with highly experienced offroaders. All was going well till we bogged both vehicles within thirty metres of each other. That left this group slightly more experienced and considerably more embarrassed. My excuse was as photographer I expected them to bring the recovery gear, but it seems nobody thought it was really needed. That's just tempting fate, and of course it bit hard.

The red Pajero stuck in mud.

This is far from an easy hill, fairly steep, slippery and no ruts. Hence the LC100 didn't make it first time and ended up in the dozerpush. We got it out by dropping pressures a little, building up with stones to equalise weights on wheels and increase traction, and a little muddy spadework. Winching was an option, but it was going to be difficult to get a vehicle in position.

Another unexpected recovery…I'd said "swing out wide to take the sharp bend" but neglected to say "don't drive your car into the hole". Apparently, that'd be my fault then.

plan

So you've decided on an option.

Think through what will happen from the word go to the vehicle being recovered. Play the situation in your mind. Let's say you decide on a snatch recovery.

- Is there enough room for a snatch? Will the recovery vehicle be able to stop in time? Will it be at the right angle?

- Are the recovery points available?

- Is the casualty likely to hit anything?

- Can the recovery vehicle provide enough traction? Should we level a mound or let a bit more air out of the tyres?

- Is the vehicle likely to slide sideways? Do we need to dig it a bit of a wheel rut?

- If the strap breaks, what will happen?

- If it doesn't work, will the situation become worse? Watch for that especially in mud where cars can slide off tracks, a moment's impatience can turn into a long afternoon.

- Have the drivers done this before?

Good planning and a recce means you may be able to avoid recovery in the first place.

This Pajero was in danger of slipping sideways into the rut, so we chocked the front wheel with stones and dug out the rear upside wheel so as soon as the vehicle moved backwards it reduced the roll angle. From there it was relatively easy. There were only two of us to recover the vehicle (the two occupants remained inside), both experienced, so teamwork was no problem. However, a larger group can easily end up with members working against each other, so there you need control for safety and effectiveness.

This Defender 130 backed onto this large rock and got hung up. We winched it forwards to recover. You can get stuck when you're least expecting it.

There are other things to plan too:

- Roles: Who does what? Who'll drive and who is recovery controller, the ONE person in charge?

- Preparation: What do we need to do first? Clear anything out the way?

- Execution: How do we know when to start, when to do what? Signals?

- Emergency: If X event happens, what do we do?

- Marshals: Do we need to stop anyone hurtling around the corner? Trailbikers and winch ropes don't mix.

Pre-planning helps prevent recoveries in the first place.

Bogged Outback, tyres at road pressures. Down to 25psi, one minute with the shovel and out it drove. Bogged caused by stopping too harshly.

Really not the best place to carry anything, especially recovery gear that you'll need when bogged to your axles.

Why "two lengths back" is a bad idea

The diagram below shows a snatch recovery, but it could be a winch recovery or anything else that involves force. The accepted practice is simply to keep two lengths or so of strap away. But that ignores the likely path of projectiles. Coroner's reports have indicated that broken snatch straps can launch things over 100m, so the diagram reflects this scale and the likely path of projectiles. In summary, stand at right angles to the recovery, nowhere near in-line.

execution

All planned. Everyone knows what should happen, and their role. They also know what might happen, and what to do.

So you do it, or rather try it. Perhaps the plan doesn't work or another option becomes available. Don't persist with any plan that isn't working, and remember the definition of insanity is trying the same thing again and again but expecting a different result. By that definition, quite a few offroaders are insane. I think perhaps it's something to do with groupthink. If it doesn't work first time, and chances are it won't, then try something slightly or entirely different.

On one occasion we were trying to get a ute up a steep, off camber hill in the wet. There wasn't quite enough traction, but we did a few things right. Firstly the driver was told to back off early, before he'd lost traction entirely and slid right off the track. Secondly every time he failed we improved the situation; another two psi out of the tyres, a little bit of rut building…and we could see he wasn't far off. Eventually he made it after all this patient work. Perhaps the gung-ho approach would have made it first time, but had it not worked we'd have had the second major winch job of the day on our

1 *This Pajero has slipped into a hole. The recovery must be carefully angled such that it moves the vehicle forwards and stabilises it at the same time. In some snatch recoveries it's a good idea for the casualty to spin its wheels before the recovery vehicle starts moving, but in this case it would be a bad idea as any wheelspin is likely to skew the vehicle sideways further into trouble. Therefore, very little or no throttle should be applied, which will work because the vehicle is not so much bogged as precariously balanced and unable to safely move. The snatch recovery will be more of a tow.*

2 *This bogged Pajero is in no danger of slipping anywhere, so can happily get its wheels spinning before the recovery vehicle moves. This ensures the recovery vehicle is always pulling a casualty that is trying to move of its own accord, and a couple of seconds wheelspin is worth it, although there's no need to go crazy with the throttle.*

hands and that would have meant me backing my car down this slope into a winch position, quite a risky proposition.

Supervise people, for example well-meaning helpers may join things together incorrectly by simply thinking they know how.

communication

Communication is an important part of many recoveries, particularly winching and snatching. The driver, recovery controller and possibly others must be able to communicate effectively and quickly. There is no one way to achieve this, but some ideas are:

- UHF radios: Great for talking, but only one person can speak at a time, and so these are prone to others butting in. Requires everyone to have a radio.

- Hand signals: Require people to look in a given direction, or directions, and the controller to be visible to everyone. This may be impossible on an overgrown track.

- Vehicle horns: May be difficult to hear, and you need to agree on what a horn blast means.

- Lights: Really only effective in the dark, and what does a flash mean?

- Whistle: Very easy to hear, can be operated by mouth while the hands do something else.

In my experience using a UHF radio and controlling excess conversation works very well, however there is a time and place for all of the methods.

completion

Don't forget to:

- Check all the recovery gear for damage and stow it away. It's surprising how much is left around.
- Move vehicles to a safe place.
- Check vehicles for damage.
- Learn from the experience!

So that's the method. It is not an official method or formally accredited. It's just a mixture of common sense and experience, which most offroaders who have been around a while do naturally.

Deep mudbog in Tasmania. Bogging was always a risk, so the plan was to winch if the Hilux didn't make it, using the Hilux's own winch. If that failed, my car was behind rear to execute a snatch recovery from the rear. You don't want to be starting the plan after the failure, particularly in deep Tassie mud!

vehicle setup

recovery points

Remember those tremendous forces? Your vehicle is going to be pulled, and hard. There needs to be a suitable mounting point for that force.

Don't assume that any old hook on the vehicle will do. Many hooks are simply tie-downs, designed to stop the vehicle moving when being transported, or for bitumen towing. The forces involved in a recovery are much, much greater and can rip tie-downs right off the vehicle with catastrophic consequences.

The safest way is to check with a 4WD mechanic, and that means a 4WD shop where the staff live, eat and breathe 4WD. The average car dealership is unlikely to have that specialist knowledge.

Towbars are fine to use as recovery points, provided that they are secured to the chassis of the vehicle and the towball itself is never used.

Some say that you can bend the tow hitch. You can, but tests show it takes around 10 tonnes of effort, by which time you'll have broken something else, like the snatch strap.

This is not described by the manufacturer as a recovery point, but it's generally used as one.

This is definitely not a recovery point. It is a tie-down point. Unfortunately, that's all many softroaders have, so if you're in that position all you can do is avoid front recovery, and if you need to and the car will allow it, fit two eyes and use a long bridle (Chapter 33) to reduce (but not halve) the load to each eye. Not recommended at all.

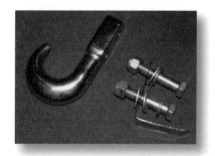

Aftermarket recovery point designed to be bolted to the chassis rails.

using a towhitch as a recovery point

There are many ways to attach straps to vehicles with towbars. Here are some of the wrong and right ways.

right ways

Insert the pin through the eye of the strap. You'll need about ten tonnes of force to bend the pin, and by that time something else will have broken or the vehicle will have been recovered. However, do not use this method if there will be significant side pull on the strap as it may damage the strap eye against the hitch.

This is the best method for recovery.
You can use a special device which fits in the towhitch and allows a shackle to be threaded through. The best ones can rotate to horizontal or vertical – choose based on how the strap is likely to be angled. Extended recoveries can see significant wear of the strap against the shackle if the shackle cannot move so it is in-line with the recovery.

wrong ways

This is very, very dangerous because the strap might rip the towball off and turn it into a lethal projectile. Also, the strap itself may slip off under tension and snap back – think a little mud, water, angle and then maybe an accidental slack/tension cycle. But how come it's so dangerous if the tow system is rated to tow 3,500kg? Firstly, recovery loads can exceed 3,500kg (see next chapter). Secondly, towing 3,500kg doesn't involve 3,500kg of force. The rolling resistance on flat bitumen of a 3,500kg trailer is around 90kg. On a 30-degree slope – and that is a VERY steep slope – the total force required rises to around 1,850kg. Acceleration is never going to be particularly stressful with a 3,500kg load, and any trailer that heavy will need brakes. So, towing 3,500kg doesn't put anything like 3,500kg of strain on a towball, therefore it's not rated for 3,500kg of load. So as recovery loads of 4WDs can exceed that amount, and are often shock (snatch) loads then those recovery loads can break towballs and kill people.

This has been seen in the wild. It does not make the situation any better. In fact, it makes it worse as you've just made the projectile bigger.

Using a standard towhitch with a shackle through the towball hole avoids use of the towball, but leaves the recovery reliant on a tongue which is welded together and does not have a large surface area for the weld. In addition, the pulling forces are not aligned with the chassis: firstly, the force is not vertically in-line with the hitch even in this example, let alone drop hitches where the shackle would be at a different height to the hitch; secondly, any lateral pull will exert significant sideways forces on the tongue and hitch, especially with longer hitches. Contrast the construction of the tongue with the one-piece recovery point above, which also aligns forces with the pin.

jacking points

Know where you can and cannot jack the vehicle before you go out. Discovery 3s and 4s, for example, are often jacked up on the air compressor instead of the chassis, which damages the compressor.

waiting

Time can make a difference. In even an hour a track can dry out, and the cool of an evening both gives the engine denser air to breathe and makes sand easier to drive on, and a lot of work can be done in an hour. Perhaps the biggest effect of time is on the people, giving them time to think and then to act.

vehicle-specific tricks

Sometimes the trick to recovering a vehicle is hidden somewhere in the controls. Vehicles with variable-height suspension (Chapter 5) may be able to raise themselves and drive out, and perhaps switching off stability control (Chapter 9) may work, or even switching it on if switching it off disables traction control. Swaybars may be connected or disconnected, lockers engaged or disengaged. People have even died as a result of not understanding the operation of free-wheeling hubs.

One tip for vehicles with self-levelling suspension that need a bit more clearance: put your heaviest people in the back of the car, close all doors and allow it to self-level. Open doors, remove people but do not fully close doors. The vehicle will have raised but won't level until the doors are closed. This trick may provide sufficient clearance to get going again.

recovery kit care and maintenance

Each of the following chapters has specific advice for the recovery gear being discussed, but there are some general rules.

practice

The first rule with recovery kit is to use it before you need to. That means a lazy Sunday afternoon with your kit in the backyard, checking you know how it works, and that it does in fact work.

I have a friend who bought a Tirfor winch and carted it all the way around Australia. He never needed it. When he got back he sold it. A day later the guy he sold it to came back and complained

the wire rope was the wrong size. So had my friend ever needed to use his winch he'd have been very disappointed. I have seen air jacks bought and unwrapped in the field only to find they do not fit the vehicle's exhaust. On more than one occasion a new owner has unwrapped a snatch strap, gone to attach it to a vehicle and either not had a shackle to fit into the closed-loop recovery point, or one the wrong size. Many a time a winch rope has been pulled out only to discover the winch does not, in fact, work, or the controller cable has been mislaid.

know what's in there

It's easy to buy so much kit you forget what you have. You'll remember the big stuff like a winch, but what about the smaller items like the 4.7t rated shackle or even drag chains? Easy to forget in the heat of the moment.

paint it

Losing kit is easy. Put it down when in the forest and shackles just blend into the background. So paint everything something garish, bright and non-natural, like orange. It also identifies it as yours in the case of a mix up with other people's kit.

maintain it

Every now and again get all the kit out, wash it, clean it, oil it, paint it and use it. That way you remember what you have and where it is, and it stays ready for use.

renew it

You're trusting this stuff with at the very least something expensive, and at the most the lives of you and others. So don't take chances – replace things that look worn, frayed or damaged. For example, snatch straps do not last forever and should be replaced after every five or six hard recoveries.

Washing synthetic rope after a muddy recovery.

the most important recovery gear of all

The most effective bit of recovery gear is the human brain. Where there's a will, there's a way. Common mistakes:

- Going with the first option you think of.
- Groupthink – ending up with a plan nobody really wanted or the most forcibly argued plan.
- Not checking to see exactly how the vehicle is stuck.
- Forgetting what recovery gear the group has available to it.
- Trying the same thing again and again and expecting a different result.
- Focusing only on plans which can be executed in less than five minutes, whereas some recoveries take longer to set up – for example complex winching, significant road building.
- Blindly following all the rules!

They're not pretty, but they are effective. Knowledgeable and skilful friends are the best recovery devices of all.

A typical atypical recovery. The Pajero has managed to impale itself on a tree root on a steep hill and slight sideangle, on a corner, such that it cannot drive forwards or backwards, bending the rim and deflating the tyre in the process. The solution was to chainsaw the offending root, roll the car down the hill and fit the spare tyre.

important: ratings

There is an important point to understand about 4WD recovery gear ratings and that is that most equipment is "rated" to its breaking strain. For example, an 8,000kg snatch strap may break at

8,001kg, or higher. It may even break at lower loads if it is not manufactured correctly, or is worn, kinked or otherwise less than perfect.

Some gear used in 4WD recoveries is also gear for hoisting, and as such has a WLL or Working Load Limit. The most common example is shackles (Chapter 33) which have ratings of Grade M or S, meaning they are designed to break at loads beyond 4 and 6 times the load stamped on body – for example, a 3.5t Grade M would withstand at least 14t of load. Drag chains (Chapter 39) are usually rated to 3,800kg LC, which is lashing capacity and is not the same as hoisting capacity. The lashing capacity is usually half the maximum breaking load, so a 3,800kg chain would be designed to break at 8,000kg.

You may also hear talk of "rated" recovery points. No manufacturer is going to write you a letter saying the points (hooks or loops) on their vehicle are good for a given strength rating or suitable for recovery, unlike for example shackles which have load ratings stamped on them. However, ARB have released a range of integrated recovery point

kits for some popular vehicles which are indeed rated to specific loads. You can also buy generic aftermarket points with high-tensile bolts, but then it is up to you to work out how and where to attach them. Advice from an 4WD specialist mechanic familiar with your vehicle is highly recommended.

the rest of this section

The next chapter is all about recovery loads. The chapters after that describe the most common recovery tools as follows:

- What it is
- When to use
- When not to use
- How to use
- Care and maintenance.

Hung up on the chassis and a bent alloy sidestep. Solutions here include; winching backwards or forwards, jacking up the front left wheel and putting rocks under it, or a gentle snatch. A more or less acute approach angle would have seen the car through the ruts.

Who needs winches when you've got a group of blokes?

CHAPTER 33

RECOVERY LOADS

Recovery often involves dangerous
forces, but how much force?

about recovery loads

This chapter takes a look at some of the forces
involved in recovery. The forces are not exact; just
because we found that it took 300kg to move a
given vehicle in a given situation doesn't mean to
say that it'll always take 300kg; the sand changes,
the vehicle could weigh slightly more or less, tyre
pressure will vary…so many variables. Therefore,
the figures are very much indicative, not absolute.
That's another reason to be very conservative
when estimating. The most important point about
recovery forces is that it is best to follow the
example of the hoisting industry and over-rate
everything.

To estimate a recovery load and whether it's safe
you need to know:

- The weight of the casualty
- The force required to move it (nature of terrain
  and gradient)
- The load limits of the recovery gear

Important – just because the loads have been
estimated to be within the equipment limits does
not mean the recovery is actually safe. However,
any load likely to exceed the limits or come even
remotely close is definitely unsafe.

recovery load examples

The examples here are just that; examples which
roughly represent a load. Make sure you err well on
the side of safety.

The vehicles shown in this chapter, and their
weights as tested, are:

- Land Rover Defender 110 TD5: 2,600kg
- Toyota LC100: 3,180kg
- Land Rover 90 (not a Defender): 1,980kg
- Patrol GU 4.2 tdi: 3,160kg and Kimberley
  Kamper: 1,000kg (total 4,160kg).

Testing was carried out by using a load cell which
indicated maximum pulls. Multiple runs were made
the results averaged and no vehicle assisted in any
recovery by driving its wheels.

*The load cell in use. It registers a maximum load and can be
reset between tests.*

flat bitumen

The force required to move the Defender on flat
bitumen was 2.6% of the vehicle's weight, or 60kg
when at road pressures. Dropping the pressures to
20psi saw that rise to 80kg, or 3.4%. This is the basic
rolling resistance of a typical 4WD.

flat sand

Sand varies greatly in consistency. This sand was relatively hard-packed, but still sufficiently soft for the vehicles to sink in – a 2WD would not have coped. Powdery sand would require a much greater recovery force.

At road pressures the vehicles needed a force equivalent to 10% of their mass to move. At 20psi this dropped to 7%. While the bitumen example proved that lower tyre pressures increase the tyre's rolling resistance, that effect is more than countered by the fact the increased contact patch means the vehicle does not sink in as far.

When existing tracks were used, as opposed to deliberately roughing up the sand after each run, the effort required was reduced by 50%. That meant the vehicles, with sand-driving pressure, required little extra force to move them on packed sand than on bitumen. It also highlights the importance of following in wheel tracks.

Adding the 1,000kg camper to the Patrol, with all tyres at sand pressure, meant another 50kg of force required for the combination over the Patrol by itself.

The sand forces are for vehicles moving in a straight line so the rear wheels follow the front wheels in ruts. Should the vehicle turn then forces would increase again as all four wheels now have increased rolling resistance.

The Patrol being pulled on flat sand, but with no ruts to follow.

dips

A very small dip (see below), barely noticeable but you can see the LC100's suspension is flexed, although it still has weight on all four wheels. However, that was up to treble the load required when compared to a dead flat test, up to around 30% of mass, or around 300kg for the larger vehicles.

bogged to the axles

The LC100 (3,180kg) was placed into these holes and recovered with no engine assistance, via a winch. The force required was 3,450kg, or 108% of the mass. We then recovered the vehicle using the Patrol to snatch it out. The first attempt failed and registered 2,850kg. The second attempt, which was one of the more violent snatches I've seen, was successful and registered 4,850kg. The important point here is that winches can measure out precisely the force required to move a vehicle. In this case, if we had first tried at 3,300kg the LC100 wouldn't have moved, and it's not possible to be so precise as to increase the effort in increment of 100kg. Therefore, snatching typically places higher loads on the casualty than winching. This is also apparent from the acceleration; when a vehicle is snatched out it accelerates out quickly and clearly more force is required to do that than to bring it out very slowly.

Of note during this recovery; the allegedly 8,000kg snatch strap tore but did not quite fail, while the allegedly 10,000lb (4,536kg) rated hydraulic winch could not move the vehicle could not move the vehicle at all, so we used my electric winch but the Defender moved at 1,500kg and had to be re-chocked (see bottom right pic).

the effect of digging out

The 90 (see page 384) was bogged and no attempt made to dig the front wheels out. The recovery force required was 1,610kg, or 80% of its weight. However, five minutes effort with a shovel and the picture looked quite different – the vehicle needed only 730kg of force, or 36% of its weight. The point there is that we were very easily able to remove around 1,000kg of recovery force. Digging out is always worth it.

hill: 16 degrees, hard dirt

mounds

The 90 was pulled over the little mound as shown. The force required varied from 10% to 30% of vehicle weight, or 200kg to 600kg. The point there is that it is worth making any path for the casualty as flat as possible.

All the vehicles were winched up this hill and the average was 35% of the weight required, so in the case of the 3,180kg LC100, that was 1,100kg, and 1,460kg for the Patrol/camper combination.

At a load of 920kg the Defender was pulled downhill (no chocks used, just brakes), so it was secured to a tree further up the hill.

Winching over the top so the rope touched the ground added another four percent to those loads. Usually it would better to let the casualty winch so the rope only touches but does not drag on the ground, but this casualty had no winch and we wanted to conduct the test.

The diagram is provided so a 16 degree hill can be easily visualised. It is reasonably steep and most hills of this nature would be ascended in low-range.

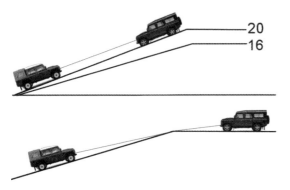

hill: 20 degrees, hard dirt

Λ 20 degree hill was found and the exercise repeated with some vehicles. This time 42% of the weight was required, so 840kg for the 1,980kg

shortie Land Rover. There was a four percent increase in load between the effort required to hold the vehicle statically and to actually start moving it. This is definite low-range territory and would be classed as a steep, but not impossible hill.

The next section is theoretical and compares the results of the testing against the results found by maths.

calculating loads

The force required to move a vehicle is made up of three main components:

1. **Vehicle rolling resistance:** Energy required to overcome friction in the transmission and the constant changing of the tyres' shape as they deform and reform to create the flat contact patch.

2. **Coefficient of rolling resistance:** Energy required to move the vehicle through the terrain, for example due to sinking into soft ground.

3. **Incline:** The slope, both the general gradient and any small incline such as the mound in the example above.

There is a fourth component, which is the force required to accelerate the vehicle. However, in most recoveries that force is quite low as the recovery force is ideally just a little more than that required to overcome the three factors above.

There are widely accepted figures for the coefficient of resistance of 4WDs in different terrain which incorporate points 1 and 2 above, and these are:

Terrain	Coefficient of rolling resistance (percentage of vehicle weight)
Bitumen	4%
Grass	13%
Hard-packed or wet sand	17%
Sand	28%
Shallow mud	34%
Clayey mud	58%

These figures are close to what we discovered in our tests. Of course, grass can vary from hard-packed close-mown to soft, long and tussocky, and how deep is shallow? Nevertheless, the figures do provide an approximate indication of recovery loads for terrain.

The incline figure can be calculated approximately as follows:

- slope in degrees x (weight/60) = force required to recover

To this is added a percentage from the table above to cover the rolling resistance. As an example we can use the LC100 on a 16 degree hill:

Slope	16 degrees
LC100 weight	3180 kg
Incline resistance	848 kg
Rolling resistance	6% (190kg)
Total force required	1038 kg

Our tests showed 1,100kg was required, so the result is close to theory. Still a few factors could throw it out – the theoretical load is just to balance the vehicle on the slope, not actually move it.

It would move with a force of 1068kg, just one kilogram more than that required to keep it at rest, but in practice more force would be required as the winch accelerates the vehicle from standstill even if only to a slow speed. We noted this as around an additional four percent, and how smoothly that force is applied is another factor. More importantly, the state of the ground, which was not perfectly flat, and the mounds example above shows how much extra load even a small mound, rock or rut can add. Then you have measurement errors. We calculated the slope at 16 degrees, but we could well be two or three degrees out and in any case it isn't precisely even all the way.

This formula given above is not perfectly accurate but is pretty close up until about 35 degrees and that is an extremely steep hill. After that point the formula overestimates the pull so has a safety factor. The correct formula is:

- sin(slope in degrees) x weight = force (due only to the incline) required to recover

If you try this in Microsoft Excel remember that Excel expects the argument for sin to be in radians, so to convert from degrees to radians multiply by pi()/180, and if pi is not available as a constant use 3.14.

conclusion

The point of all this is that while the theory is great, you're best off at least doubling if not tripling the calculated loads to allow for safety factors. In this case, if the load was calculated at 899kg then you'd want kit capable of withstanding around 2,500kg, which is more than double our measured load. Chapter 34 has an explanation of shock loads which are another good reason to be generous with your force calculations, and even after all the calculations are done and everything is within limits, remember the recovery is not necessarily made safe.

A Nissan Patrol, estimated weight 2,700kg, needing to ascend a slope of around 15 degrees which gives a basic load of 675kg. Add 40% for the mud and we have close to 1,000kg. However, the vehicle's wheels are able to drive which considerably reduces the load.

Testing with the camper hooked up to the Patrol. That's in excess of 4,000kg there to move.

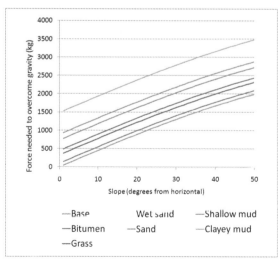

Approximate effort required to move a 2,600kg vehicle on slopes up to 50 degrees and in varying terrains. Assume real-life loads to be at least 30% more than this, and factor safety beyond this.

A snatch strap has been broken while trying to get this 4Runner out of its predicament. There is a significant upslope, mud, and the vehicle is hung up on its diff. Snatching typically applies a force well beyond that required to move the casualty, which is why the strap broke. Using the winch may well have been a safer option.

CHAPTER 34

SNATCH STRAPS

The snatch strap is one of the cheapest and most useful items of recovery gear, but too often people just blindly use it without considering other options which are often safer and more appropriate.

what it is

A snatch strap is basically a giant elastic band made of nylon, which can stretch between 20 and 30%. One end is attached to the stuck vehicle, one end to the recovering vehicle which uses momentum to jerk the stuck vehicle free. Yes, it's as dangerous as it sounds. It's also known as a kinetic recovery rope or snatch-um strap.

ratings

Snatch straps come in a variety of ratings. The rating is the load at which it is designed to break, not a hoist rating with a 4X safety factor. Common ratings vary between 6,000kg and 12,000kg.

That rating is under ideal conditions. All of the following will lower the limit of a strap:

- Damp or wet, as nylon absorbs water, leading to a loss of strength of up to 20%.
- Not perfectly straight, any twists.
- A strap that hasn't been kept in a perfect condition.
- Any frays, especially at the stitching.
- A shock load.

Basically, any strap that isn't fresh out of its wrapper may not live up to its rated strength, and even then

it might not make it. So be warned. There is no safety factor in these ratings, so a strap may break before its rated load.

Which strength strap to use is an interesting question. There are two factors to consider; firstly you don't want to break the strap, but more importantly if anything does break, you do want it to be the strap. For example it is far safer for a nylon strap to break than to rip off a metal recovery point (it's been known) which becomes a high-speed projectile. Chapter 33 covers recovery loads so you can make your own mind up based on your vehicle's total weight. My view is to keep recovery loads to a minimum so you never get close to anything breaking in the first place.

Straps also take a little time (5 minutes or so) to return to their original length, and over time never quite return to the original length. For these reasons straps should be discarded after 5 or so heavy (more than a simple tow) recoveries.

This strap is overstressed and can no longer be used. It is an 8,000kg rated strap, and we did that to it with a load of 4,200kg, measured on a load cell.

when to use

Any time a vehicle is stuck, you have a recovery vehicle and sufficient space for the operation. Snatches can be very quick to set up, which is why they are often used.

The Pathfinder didn't make it all the way through, so we turned the Pajero around and set up a quick snatch. In mud, snatching the casualty backwards tends to work better than forwards as the casualty has created ruts and moved mud out of the way. However, it is not unknown for the casualty to slide over a rock on the way in, only to have that same rock catch an axle on the way out. Never persist with a recovery, simply applying more force, if it isn't working.

when not to use

Snatch recoveries can be anything from a gentle tug to a high-energy, relatively high speed operation. Avoid their use when the vehicle is hung up by rocks, or needs to be very carefully moved.

You also need a fair bit of room and a near-straight line for recovery. Non-straight recoveries don't work all that well as they stress both vehicles and are inefficient.

A very light vehicle recovering a heavy vehicle is not ideal although it can work.

how to use

preparation

The recovering vehicle should position itself for the snatch. A snatch can recover the casualty either backwards or forwards. Either way the recovering vehicle should recover while moving forwards because:

- 4WD differentials are stronger going forwards than in reverse because of the way the gears are cut.

- The rear differential is stronger than the front.

- The driver can more easily see where the recovering vehicle is going and control it better (I managed to reverse into a tree by attempting my first ever snatch going backwards on my first ever 4WD trip in New Zealand – much of the advice in this book comes from my own mistakes, and the rest comes from watching others).

The strap should be attached to the recovery vehicle and the casualty, without using shackles if possible, and at the last minute so it is 'live' for the minimum amount of time. **The strap is now live and nobody should walk over it.** All slack should be close to the recovery vehicle and laid out to the driver's side because:

- It is then visible to the casualty's driver and the recovery vehicle's driver via the wing mirror.

- As the strap tightens it will drag on the ground, and with the slack away from the casualty that dragging is minimised.

Check there is no debris that will damage the strap when it pulls straight.

As with all recovery procedures, ensure spectators are well out of the way, generally three times the length of the total snatch strap and not in-line with the vehicles.

Some people place a dampener over the strap. This is a large, heavy piece of fabric or cloth such as heavy overcoat. The idea is that if the strap breaks the dampener will stop the strap flying through the air. Unfortunately, the theory doesn't often hold true and sometimes the danger involved in locating and relocating the dampener is more trouble than it's worth, and it may give people a false sense of security. They are worth placing over items like shackles through recovery point loops as if a strap fails it is most likely to fail at the eyes and stitching as this should give way gradually, or relatively gradually compared to an instant failure in the centre. In any case the best advice is reduce recovery loads and keep everyone out of the way.

A snatch strap set up. The principle of operation needs some slack between the casualty and the recovery vehicle. That slack should be collected at the recovery vehicle end of the strap (see text).

The strap is attached on the passenger side of the vehicle so should it break the chances of it hitting the driver is reduced. The slack is at the recovery car end, laid out so it is easily visible to both drivers.

This driver had actually connected his strap before he entered this hole, but as his recovery point was an open hook it fell off. Fortunately, his kind friend was there to reattach it. We recovered the vehicle forwards as Pajeros had already driven the obstacle and we knew the way to be clear.

the snatching operation

By means of signal (see Chapter 32 for signals) the stuck vehicle now spins its wheels. Technically the stuck vehicle should use a lower gear than the recovery vehicle (e.g. first low instead of second low) in order to avoid the stuck vehicle running into the back of the recovery vehicle. However, if that is likely to be an issue lengthen the strap instead (by joining a second strap, see later in this chapter) and use whatever gear is appropriate to move the vehicle off. The "crash into the back" is more of an issue when the drivers aren't clear when to stop or go than the gear they use, so brief carefully.

The recovery vehicle then moves off, at first using a very light pull; just a few revs above idle in first low. The strap tightens and hopefully the casualty is assisted to drive out of its predicament. If that doesn't work try again a little faster, but only a little, and when you need more than around 1,500rpm, change to second low. The laws of physics says that kinetic energy is proportional to velocity squared, so double the speed gives four times the energy and treble the speed gives nine times. In other words, little increments of snatch speed are best.

If the recovery vehicle has a manual gearbox, then the clutch should be up before the snatch's slack is taken up.

If the recovery is successful both vehicles should continue moving until the casualty is on firm ground. This is where your pre-planning comes into its own – you don't want one vehicle stopping before the other. Make sure the ex-casualty does not drive over the strap.

If it is not successful then the recovering vehicle stops the attempt as soon as it comes to a halt or begins to wheelspin, or as instructed by the controller in charge of the execution, even if the casualty is moving slowly.

When a stop is called both vehicles stop and the recovery is re-attempted. If the casualty moved, then the same amount of force can be applied and repeated until the vehicle is recovered. Better a few small pulls than one large one.

If the casualty does not move at all then a harder pull may be required. Pulls up to a fast walking pace may be required. If those do not work then it is recommended the recovery load be lessened, for example by jacking the stuck vehicle and placing rocks under the tyres, digging it out, recovering in a different direction, removing weight from the vehicle or some other combination. Snatching accidents happen as the forces build up.

The drivers of the casualty and recovery vehicles need to work together for the recovery to be successful, which means communication. The exact method of communication will vary according to the situation. Which method is chosen does not matter as long as it is clear and all parties understand what the signals mean. It is important that signals are established for:

- Indicating that each of the vehicles is ready
- Indicating that the recovery will begin
- An agreed abort signal
- A stop signal.

Examples of communication methods are:

Radio: The controller counts down 3, 2, 1, GO. On "1" the stuck vehicle slowly spins its wheels. On "GO" the recovering vehicle moves off to complete the recovery. Anyone can shout "STOP".

Horn: Stuck vehicle sounds one note to begin recovery. Recovery vehicle begins recovery. Sound a continuous note or two short notes to stop.

Lights: Stuck vehicle flashes lights once to begin. Sustained flashing from either vehicle indicates to stop.

Hand signals - third person: Third person controlling to be visible to both drivers, and the start and finish. Controller raises both arms. When one arm drops the stuck vehicle spins its wheels. When the second arm drops the recovering vehicle recovers. Both arms raised stops the recovery.

Hand signals - drivers only: Recovering driver places arm outside window. When the arm is taken inside stuck vehicle spins wheels, recovering vehicle recovers. Stop signal; either driver places arm outside window (note; arms outside the window is risky, consider obstructions when choosing this method).

A Santa Fe weighing around 2,200kg recovering a Patrol weighing around 2,800kg. Didn't need a lot of effort as the Patrol wasn't really stuck, just unable to get over the sideslope. The snatch strap pull helped keep the nose pointing where it should be. The driver applied sufficient power to help move the vehicle, but had he applied too much the Patrol would simply have shifted sideway due to wheelspin. Other options were to air down from the 15psi that the Patrol was running to 8psi; or use a traction aid (Chapter 38). The Patrol has a recovery point on the front, and we put the strap through the Santa Fe's towbar, secured with the pin.

Part-way through recovering a Discovery that took an ill-advised leap over the dune. This was one of several pulls, and after each one the recovery controller (on the left) approached to inspect progress before talking to the drivers again. It was a windy day so controlling the recovery with a radio worked very well. Bystanders can be seen too, and they constantly had to be shooed away!

This LC100 slipped into the ditch. A simple tug with the Pajero and all was well.

lengthening a snatch strap

You can't literally lengthen a snatch strap but you can join other straps to it. The options are:

- Another snatch strap,
- A winch extension strap (see following),
- Tree trunk protectors (see note following).

You can join as many of these together as you need. There are two things to consider:

- **The elasticity of the combination:** The elasticity of a strap is how far it can stretch as a percentage of its length. This percentage remains constant if you join two or more together, but each strap means more stretch and thus distance to drive before any real force is applied to the casualty. One snatch strap and a winch extension strap will stretch just as far as a single snatch strap.

- **Ratings:** You may have a 12,000kg rated snatch strap. You can use this with a 4,000kg tree protector if you remember you now have a 4,000kg line.

Never attempt to use a snatch strap where you'd use a winch extension strap as the winch will simply elongate the strap for no good effect – just a dangerous build up of tension. Similarly, never use a winch extension strap as a snatch strap as it doesn't have the required elasticity.

Note: a snatch strap is designed to be elastic. Tree trunk protectors and winch extension straps are not, although when joined to a strap the combination becomes elastic. However, even though that's the case, when a shock load is applied (and snatching is a shock load) both straps are shock-loaded. Therefore, for high-stress snatch recoveries it is best to use only snatch straps. High stress may be those recoveries where you take off quickly in second low and keep the revs up.

joining two straps

There are dangerous ways and safe ways:

Dangerous 1

Using a shackle is dangerous, but not because the shackle will break. If it's a rated shackle any snatch strap will give way long before the shackle. The danger comes from the strap breaking and launching the shackle. What we have here is a nine metre elastic band being pulled by a 2.5 tonne vehicle launching a 0.5kg projectile. That doesn't hurt, it just kills outright.

Dangerous 2

Tying the two straps together. There is no way you'll be able to get them apart again and tying anything reduces the overall strength by around 50%.

Safe

Better still, join the two as per the images and slide a thick magazine in between. That way if the magazine slips out the two straps just join. OK, you'll never get them apart again but that's better than having the strap effectively fail.

This example uses two tree-trunk protectors purely because they are short and thus easier to photograph. The same principle applies to snatch straps.

Step 1: Lay the straps out side-by-side.

Step 2: Thread the end of one through the eye of the other, and vice-versa at the other end.

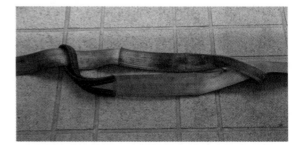

Step 3: Pull tight.

Step 4: Insert a rolled-up magazine to stop the straps binding under load. The straps are now securely joined, the magazine won't hurt anyone, the strength of the straps is maintained through the join and if the magazine comes out you've just got a long strap, not a deadly projectile. This technique works for joining any two straps. Do not use a newspaper or thin pamphlet because that will not stop the straps binding. You can also use a cut-up part of an old strap, or even a car footmat

load splitting

If a vehicle has two recovery points, use them both with a bridle. This spreads the load evenly on the chassis but a little more than half the load is placed on each point. Chapter 33 goes into the physics of a bridle.

Bridle used to split loads on an LC100. The load on each recovery point is less than the total force needed to move the casualty, but more than half the force. Do not use a shackle to connect a strap to a bridle.

double pulls

Sometimes you need more than one vehicle to recover another. The forces can be immense, so before you opt for this approach try everything else. An example of where it may be needed is an extremely slippery recovery where one vehicle cannot gain enough traction. In any case, use less momentum than with a single vehicle.

There are two ways to dual-pull:

- **Side by side:** Use straps of unequal length so the recovery vehicles do not slide into each other. Use two recovery points on the casualty, and both recovering cars move off, slowly, aiming to snatch the stuck vehicle together.
- **In-line:** Have one vehicle take up the slack and then, as it's stationary with its wheels spinning trying to move the casualty, gently snatch it. Has to be gently as it's already got a lot of stress on it to begin with.

A double-pull is really a last resort and not recommended. It is most appropriate where a single vehicle is in very slippery conditions and cannot get sufficient traction to generate the force required, as opposed to merely adding more and more vehicles because the casualty is difficult to move. If one vehicle can't shift the casualty then consider alternatives, in order:

- Digging it out or jacking it up and placing stuff under the tyres.
- Lightening the casualty – nobody should be in apart from the driver anyway.
- Winching.
- Letting more air out of tyres of both vehicles for extra traction.

towing with a snatch strap

In this context towing means moving a casualty that isn't stuck but cannot move of its own accord. A snatch strap can be an excellent way to tow a casualty over rough ground as it has built-in elasticity, so as the distance between casualty and tow car varies the strap absorbs some of what would have been a shock load. However, this constant stress on the strap quickly robs it of its elasticity, and of course towing on what amounts to a giant rubber band can mean the distance between tow car and casualty can close up rather quickly. It is for those reasons that the general advice is never to tow with a snatch strap, but like most rules, there are times when it can be broken for good reason as long as you know the pros and cons of doing so.

care and maintenance

Snatch straps are webbing, and webbing care applies. Little particles of dirt can build up and rub against the fibres, so clean your straps. Recommended methods for doing so are bunging it in the washing machine (after you hose off the dirt, obviously) or just using a hose. Always allow the strap to fully dry before you store it, but not in direct sunlight.

- Store your straps dry and coiled, away from excessive heat and sunlight.
- Inspect them for fraying and wear, especially around the eyes, and replace as required.
- Check for the presence of overload indicators, which are small labels near the eyes. They are exposed if the strap is overloaded. Discard if the label is visible. The normal label describing the strap is not an overload indicator.

Discard snatch straps after five to eight recoveries regardless of condition as they lose their elasticity even if correctly used. Cut them so they cannot to be used by anyone else.

You can knot a snatch strap, but be aware it'll then have 50% of its strength, at best. And remember its "strength" is not likely to be its rated strength. This strap is perhaps rated at 8,000kg, but it's wet, dirty and twisted so what it'd actually break at is anyone's guess, except I wouldn't put any money on it still being whole by the time you get to a load of 8,000kg. So whatever the new breaking strain is, it'll be half that at best after that knot. Basically, throw it away – the best idea is to carry a spare strap at all times.

Perfect conditions for a snatch – the recovery vehicle (turned around so it's moving forwards) is on flat dry ground and there's plenty of room in a straight line. Before the Defender driver attempted the crossing potential recoveries were discussed and turned out to be needed sooner rather than later. The Defender driver was wise to give up early rather than wheelspin the vehicle in deeper.

These two vehicles have different weights which has an effect on the recovery. In an extreme example, I once saw an F250 recover a Suzuki Samurai with some enthusiasm, and the little Zook was last seen orbiting Saturn. Similarly, a RAV4 trying to de-bog a LC100 was like a little yappy dog on the end of a leash attached to a lamp post. Consider relative weights before you execute the recovery, and use the heaviest vehicle you can as the recovery car.

Another view of a damaged strap. Discard immediately and, even better, cut it up so nobody finds it by accident and decides to use it.

CHAPTER 35

JACKS

Every vehicle should carry a jack as standard equipment, so there's one built-in recovery tool you have at all times. There are several other types of jack but all have some operations in common.

The first step before any jacking commences is securing the vehicle. All jacking operations involve lifting one or more wheels and therefore destabilising the vehicle. On bitumen the vehicle is likely to be stable; offroad it is likely to be unstable as it may be on a gradient, a soft surface, loose surface, slippery with mud or snow or some other combination. Many vehicles have fallen off jacks with disastrous consequences.

Jacks are used in recovery to raise a wheel so something can be put underneath it to improve traction, clearance or both. That "something" varies. It may be a rock, or dry wood, but generally not wet wood. It could just be loose earth, or a traction aid (Chapter 38), whatever it takes. It is a good idea to jam the material into the ground by scraping a slight trench as opposed to just laying it on flat ground. Even a little indentation in the ground will help stop the material shooting backwards as the tyre begins to rotate.

When using any form of jack assume the vehicle will fall off it, so don't put your hand under the wheel, and don't work under the vehicle or anywhere it could crush you if it fell off.

Jacks are also used to raise a wheel so it can be removed, and that operation is covered at the end of the chapter.

securing the vehicle

Stop it moving: While the vehicle may be stable, if it's at an angle when it's jacked it may slip off the jack. You may need to secure it with a winch or two, dig out the upside wheels or move it to a different location. A good idea is to dig little ruts for each wheel and roll the car into them; a 4WD can drive a short way slowly with a tyre off the rim or entirely deflated. If you're careful it won't damage the tyre any further, and is preferable to a dangerous jacking operation. Also, think about how high you'll need to jack the vehicle. It's at this point some forward-planning can pay off, for example digging out where the damaged tyre will be so you get some extra clearance when it's jacked up. Obviously everyone should be out of the vehicle. On an extreme slope consider increasing the tyre pressures on the lower side and decreasing upwards to get the vehicle a little more stable.

Secure the wheels: Park brake on, 4WD low-range first, centre diff locked. If the centre diff isn't locked then not all four wheels will be braked. This is very important for vehicles with transmission park brakes like Land Rovers.

Always assume the vehicle can and will fall off the jack.

Check the owner's manual: Some newer vehicles have odd requirements for being jacked. The previous tip mentioned locking centre diffs; especially any vehicles with height-adjustable suspension.

With any vehicle that has variable-height suspension check the owner's manual for jacking instructions. You don't want the vehicle deciding it needs to move halfway through the operation.

Prado 150 variable-height suspension jack warning.

This Discovery rolled a tyre off its rim while on a sideslope. If it had been jacked up where it was it would have slipped off the jack. To level the vehicle we dug shallow trenches for the uphill wheels, reversed it back into the trenches and put the rear downhill wheel onto a log. That levelled the vehicle, and the trenches prevented the vehicle slipping. It's usually fine to move a vehicle a metre or so with the tyre off the rim.

car jack

what it is

Your humble jack that is standard equipment can help you out. Often jacking up a wheel, removing an obstruction, or strategic placing of something can see you drive out of a tricky situation.

when to use

If necessary raise a wheel to put something under it, or remove something from under the vehicle. This may be on rocks for clearance or soft ground for flotation.

when not to use

Car jacks are designed to raise a single wheel on a given vehicle on flat, hard ground. Offroad, you might need to raise a wheel a lot higher than that, and the ground might not be hard. Alternatives such as the air jack or possibly high-lift would be appropriate in this case. Another idea is to carry blocks of wood to increase the lift height, although this creates a destabilising problem. Entirely replacing the jack with a larger, better model is another option and some manufacturers do skimp on their jack design and quality.

Do not use a car jack designed for a light vehicle on a heavy vehicle, especially if the heavy vehicle has a downhill wheel to be lifted.

It is not unknown for people to fit suspension lifts and/or larger tyres, then as a result be unable to change wheels as the standard jack will no longer lift the wheel off the ground.

how to use

Follow the manufacturer's instructions, in particular those about jacking points. Some jacks can only be fitted into specific slots in the chassis. All are designed to lift vertically, so if the jack is not perfectly level as it takes the strain then expect problems. Make sure any screws or gears are clean of debris or mud.

Using a standard scissor jack on soft earth. Ready and waiting are rocks to go under the wheel for clearance and traction. The Pathfinder doesn't have a lot of suspension travel so we're jacking under the chassis and in this case it's more convenient to place the jack there. Jacking in mud is messy, and if the vehicle is not in ruts it can slide once jacked up. Not fun.

air jack

what it is

An air jack is basically a big balloon. You put the deflated air jack underneath your vehicle, connect its input hose to your exhaust and this inflates the bag and lifts the vehicle.

when to use

When you need to lift the vehicle in soft ground, although it can be used on any terrain. It can often lift two wheels off the ground at the same time. Air jacks are handy for jacking in situations where you can't easily operate a conventional jack, and they can raise the vehicle a long way. They are the only jack that can be operated remotely – well, you still need to hold the hose to the exhaust, but that's not the same as getting up close and personal with a Hi-Lift. Also, the exhaust doesn't need to be that of the casualty.

when not to use

On rocky ground, or where the vehicle cannot be secured, e.g. a hill. The rocks might puncture the bag. If the bag cannot be placed properly under the chassis (not trim) or will contact sharp objects under the vehicle do not use.

how to use

Position the jack balloon, then connect the end of the nozzle to the exhaust.

- Air jacks tend to raise an entire side of the vehicle, so chock the wheels opposite to where you're lifting.
- Flatten the surface where you'll jack, ensuring it is clear of anything that may damage the air jack.
- Check the underside of the vehicle for sharp or hot objects that might damage the air jack. There should be a strong blanket or tarp supplied. Use it.
- Consider what will happen to the vehicle when a wheel is lifted. Will it move? Should it be secured with a winch? Air jacks are definitely not stable, even by jack standards.
- Dig a shallow rut, if possible, for the air jack. This stops it moving out from under the vehicle.
- Is the jack going to be tall enough? Do you need to do some building?
- Get the jack right underneath the vehicle. You may need to deflate and inflate a couple of times before you get that quite right.

- Ideally you need one person holding the exhaust cone in place, another on the throttle and another looking at the bag and how the vehicle reacts to being jacked.

- Petrol engines especially might need a few extra revs to get the jack up. Hand throttles are useful.

- The jack might leak and need a constant supply of exhaust fumes.

- Don't inhale the fumes when you deflate the exhaust jack. I don't know why people feel the need to do this, but they do. Just the once anyway.

- Not all nozzles fit all exhausts.

- Some vehicles have dual exhausts, or one exhaust with two outlets so will need one outlet blocked up with a bung. This is the sort of thing you should find out at home before you leave.

Ideally, the exhaust jack should be connected to another vehicle so nobody needs to be in or close to the vehicle being jacked. This is an important safety consideration and makes the air jack potentially the safest jack as it can be operated remotely to some extent.

Some air jacks can be inflated using an air compressor as well as, or instead of the exhaust. As mentioned, not all exhaust outlets fit the air jack nozzle so using a compressor is a good idea, and less toxic.

A Pajero about to be lifted by an air jack. The Pajero is in a rut, which is ideal for keeping the vehicle and jack laterally stable. The vehicle is secured to another vehicle by means of a winch (out of shot).

Using an air jack to raise the rear end of the Pajero so stones can be placed under the rear wheels to provide clearance. The car is well and truly against the side of the rut so there is no danger it will tip over. After we finished it was able to drive out of the problem.

hi-lift jack

what it is

A jack that can lift roughly 3,000kg about a metre, amongst other talents. "Hi-Lift" is actually a product name registered to Bloomfield Manufacturing, who make Hi-Lift jacks. There are copies, but like "hoovers" and "biros" the name has become generic in much the same way "Tirfor" has become a term for a style of hand winch.

when to use

Whenever you need to lift the car a long way, for example to stack rocks under a wheel, or cannot get under the body to lift. But there is one big problem with a Hi-Lift jack, and that is finding somewhere on a modern vehicle to use it. As in the photos, the jack works on the body of the vehicle, not under the chassis like a normal car jack. It doesn't spread the load like an air jack, either. The fact is that modern vehicles have plastic fairings all over the place, and have nowhere a Hi-Lift can be used. In some instances a bull bar can be used, but not always, and that only helps the front of the vehicle. Solutions for the rest of the vehicle include strong, rock-slider sidesteps and strong, metal, rear bumpers. There are attachments for Hi-Lift jacks that fit around some bumpers or wheels and allow them to be lifted.

Assuming you have a suitable vehicle, the Hi-Lift is probably the quickest and easiest way to jack a vehicle up, can lift the highest, and is the most dangerous. There are other uses for a Hi-Lift which include:

- **Winching:** Hi-Lifts can be used for winching too. Chapter 37 covers winching.
- **Bead Breaking:** If you need to break the bead on a tyre a Hi-Lift is one of the easiest ways to do the job. Simply place the tyre on the ground, put the jack's foot on the sidewall and begin jacking. The bead will have popped off well before the vehicle is lifted. Much better than any of the purpose-built bead breakers out there.

when not to use

If you don't have a safe place to use a Hi-Lift, don't, and in soft ground an air jack is preferable. Never use a Hi-Lift unless the vehicle is very well secured. There are many offroaders who would never use a Hi-Lift if their life depended on it and have stories to back up their conviction.

how to use

- First, secure the vehicle. Then secure it some more. Then check it's secured and will remain secured. Then make absolutely certain the jack base is on solid ground. Place the jack on a lift point that will take the weight, move the lever into position and cautiously check the balance of the vehicle. Make sure the base plate of the jack is on a flat, hard surface where it can't move.
- At all times assume the vehicle will fall off the jack, tipping it sideways.
- With Hi-Lifts there is an additional hazard; assume the handle will fly upwards without warning.
- Make sure your footing is firm. Warn everyone else too.

- Place the reversing latch into the lift (up) position. Never operate the reversing latch unless the handle has been placed against the winch spine and into its handle spring clip.
- Once the latch is in position, move the handle up and down to lift. The load is lifted on each downstroke of the handle. It will require the handle to be moved quite a way and you will hear the mechanism operate and see the mechanism rise up the jack spine.
- When you have finished lifting, be sure to place the handle back into its spring clip.
- To lower, switch the reversing latch the other way (it may take some force) and lower the vehicle back down using the handle as per lifting. The load is lowered on each up stroke of the handle.

Hi-Lifts have a shear bolt. If that breaks you must replace it, after you have taken the load off the jack.

Hi-Lifts require some force to be on the mechanism before it will lower by levering downwards, and once there is no load the lift mechanism unlocks and will freely move along the jack spine, sometimes dropping down unexpectedly.

Practice with small loads is highly recommended.

The Hi-Lift's reversing latch in up and down positions. It may not be easy to operate and people are known to use their feet. The handle will need to be moved up and down a fair way for the jack to operate; keep pulling it until you hear and see the jack operate. In one direction the jack raises, in the other it lowers on each up-stroke of the lever provided there is a load on the jack, otherwise it just drops down. When the load is raised the handle should always be stored in the clip provided.

jack comparison

Which one when? At the very least, make sure your car jack works. If your vehicle doesn't have anywhere for a Hi-Lift to jack or one of it's adaptors then it's out of the equation. An air jack makes a useful complement to a standard jack.

	Car jack	Air jack	Hi-Lift jack
Approx Cost	With car	$250	$100
Soft ground	With a flat plate	Excellent	With a flat plate
Rocky ground	Yes	With care	Yes
Suitable for modern vehicles	Yes	Yes	Rarely, few jacking points
Height	About 30cm	Up to about 50cm	One metre
Other uses	None	None	Winch, bead-breaking, panel bending and more

Unusual for a modern vehicle, the Discovery 3, when fitted with ARB's bull bar, can take a Hi-Lift jack.

Many people carry their Hi-Lifts on the roof rack. This is convenient, but not ideal as it's a fair bit of weight and the unit is exposed to the elements. On the other hand, it is always easy to get to.

1 This vehicle is hung up on a rock. It cannot go backwards or forwards. Winching forwards makes no sense. There is nobody behind to winch backwards.

2 The solution; a Hi-Lift jack. The front wheel has been raised. While the vehicle was certainly immobilised when it was on the rock, now it's free it is less stable. However, that was anticipated and we chocked the other wheels securely. The front wheel is also turned into the rock and the engine is off, which applies the steering lock, preventing the front wheel from turning.

3 Some rocks were built up under the wheel and now the vehicle is free of the rock and able to drive forwards. No damage to the vehicle and the operation took about 15 minutes.

Never work on a vehicle supported only by a jack, underneath or otherwise. Support the vehicle with a spare tyre, rocks, logs or preferably axle stands.

changing wheels

Once the vehicle has been secured (see above):

1. Remove the spare wheel and get everything needed out of the vehicle so you don't need to slam doors or climb inside when it's on the jack.

2. Loosen the wheel nuts (on the wheel to be removed). Not all the way off, just half a turn or so. Now is a good time for someone else to be adjusting the pressure of the spare.

3. Jack the vehicle. If the ground is uneven, use your spade to even it for the jack. If the ground is soft, you'll want the flat plate you carry to spread the load on the ground, otherwise the vehicle will stay where it is and the jack goes into the ground. Remember you'll need to jack the vehicle higher or dig out underneath to get the wheel back on as it'll be inflated, not deflated. Try to jack under the axle, otherwise you'll need to jack all the way through the axle's articulation. Be careful not to jack on anything that can't take the weight.

4. Use a safety wheel. Put the spare under the vehicle so if the car falls off the jack it won't go all the way to the ground.

5. Carefully remove the wheel. Try not to get mud on the wheel nuts or axle studs and remember the wheel is likely to weigh 30-50kg.

6. Refitting. If there's not enough space for the new wheel then maybe scrape out a shallow trench, or reduce its tyre pressures (if you have an air compressor) if further jacking is dangerous or impossible.

7. Tighten nuts a little way each time, working diagonally from opposite nut to opposite nut till they're tight (see diagram).

8. Lower vehicle and remove jack. Finish tightening nuts.

9. Don't forget to collect all your gear and to check the nuts after a few kilometres.

It is a very good idea to practice removing and replacing a wheel on unfamiliar vehicles while still at home. It's quite amazing what little tools are forgotten that are essential, such as the locknuts for the wheels.

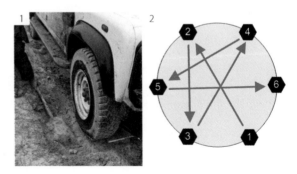

1   *As the ground is soft, rather than raise the vehicle higher we're just shovelling some sand out of the way so the wheel can come off. This is something you often need to do in ruts as otherwise you'd need to jack the wheel right out of the rut.*

2   *This is the pattern to use when doing up wheel nuts for a six-stud wheel. A five-stud is similar, just work on opposites. Don't forget to tighten again when the wheel is off the jack and again after a few kilometres.*

This Range Rover has run a tyre off a rim. It is secured by its winch to a tree stump (top right). The winch line was drawn in until tight, then the vehicle was chocked and jacked.

This Defender didn't look stuck, but it was. The vehicle was balancing on its rear differential with very little weight on either rear wheel, and heading uphill. But the diff had slid into a rocky depression, so no way was it going to be pulled back out. The solution was a quick jacking of one wheel and building rocks underneath, which provided the clearance necessary. The driver should have spotted the problem in the first place, as a slight angle off would have avoided the hangup.

difficult nuts

It's everyone's nightmare – wheel nuts you can't remove. One answer is to take a breaker bar, a long, strong lever to which you fit various socket heads to fit your wheel nuts. These are available at tools shops and a useful tool to have in any case. To prevent the problem happening in the first place ensure that the nuts are not over-torqued, and the biggest culprit there is lazy tyre shops who use high-powered rattle guns. Check you can turn each nut after any such work. If one nut won't come off, then put all the others back on tight and then try it again, with the wheel off the ground to release as much pressure as possible from the difficult nut.

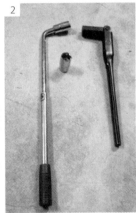

1   *A hi-lift jack being used to separate a tyre from a rim.*

2   *Factory wheel brace and aftermarket breaker bar. The latter is much stronger, longer and is more versatile as different sized sockets can be used.*

CHAPTER 36

WINCHES

Winches are great for moving vehicles that can't be moved under their own power. They aren't a must-have, but in many cases a quick winching session can save hours of digging and road building.

what it is

There are two basic types of winch:

- Hand winch.
- Power winch.

Hand winches are powered by you, or better still, your passengers. Power winches are powered by the vehicle, and there are a few variants of each style.

hand winches

The two basic categories of hand winch are ratchet and Tirfor style, or 'creeper'. The ratchets look like this:

A basic ratchet-style winch. This version doesn't have a drum but pulls through a chain so is slightly better, but nowhere near the capability of a Tirfor style. So many people have bought a cheap "comealong" because they don't want to invest in a more expensive bit of equipment. It's just not worth it.

and Tirfor-style looks like this:

A 1,600kg Tirfor-clone hand winch. The winch is pulling in – to reverse direction the long handle would be placed on the other lever. The yellow handles are for opening and closing the winch to insert and remove the cable.

ratchet winches

Ratchet winches wind on a short amount (four to five metres) of cable via a drum, are about ½ the price or less of a Tirfor clone and are somewhat limited in their pulling power and cable length. Because of this they are of limited use. You'd use one if it's all you had, but in reality they aren't for serious applications. They would be of use securing a vehicle, for example while you change a tyre, but don't expect to winch anything much up hill.

tirfors

The best hand winch is a Tirfor-style. The design was invented by Tractel, a French company, but the design patent has now expired and so there are many quality copies on the market.

The Tirfor winch is actually a hoist, which means it's rated for lifting. It usually comes in three sizes

– 800kg, 1,600kg and 3,200kg – and should be manufactured to comply with AS2741.

As the 800kg and 1,600kg winches are most commonly used, a table of their vital stats is supplied below. These figures are for the real Tirfors but clones should be the same.

Model	T508	T516
Safe lifting capacity	800kg	1,600kg
Effort on handle	35kg	48kg
Rated pulling capacity	1,250kg	2,500kg
Effort on handle	54kg	75kg
Stroke (winching in)	46mm	42mm
Stroke (paying out)	62mm	57mm
Shear pin breaks at	96kg	120kg
Maximum pulling capacity (based on shear pin strength)	2,194kg	4,000kg
Cable length	20m	20m
Unit weight (including 20m cable)	12.2kg	23.7kg
Cable breaking strength	4,800kg	9,600kg

The T516 is the favoured winch for most 4WDs, except for lightweight vehicles like most Suzuki 4WDs which can use the T508.

Tirfors work by gripping the cable and moving it along the winch, not by winding it onto a drum, which means their rated pull is constant no matter how much cable has passed through the winch, unlike a drum winch (described below). They can either bring the cable in, or pay it out, which is handy for gently lowering a vehicle down a hill.

Spare shear pins should be provided in the handle or winch unit. If a shear pin breaks the winch will still lower (pay out) but cannot winch in.

power winches

Pretty much all power winches are fitted to the front of the vehicle and are drum winches, which means the cable is wound around a drum. They differ in how they are powered:

- Electric
- Hydraulic
- Power takeoff (PTO).

electric

Electric winches are powered from the battery and are the most common, and the cheapest. You need to keep the engine running and cannot drive the winch for too long without flattening the battery, or indeed overheating the winch.

A Warn 8274 high-performance winch used for competitions. This has its motor outside of the drum unit, whereas recreational winches tend to have the motor and drum combined.

A typical recreational winch, a 9,500lb 12v electric with steel cable. The motor is on the left and the gears are on the right of the drum.

A portable electric winch used to drag my Defender sideways after it got cross-rutted (for the purposes of demonstration, of course). The "portability" is relative; electric winches are still heavy and bulky, but at least this one has more choice of directional pull than a fixed-mount.

hydraulic winches

Hydraulic winches work off the power steering and can be run for as long as required; but they do need the engine to be running. You also can't steer whilst winching. They look very similar to electric winches except that there are hydraulic hoses instead of electrical cables.

PTO winches

PTO or power take-off winches are driven directly by the vehicle's engine. They can't be retrofitted to a vehicle, so unless yours has one fitted, or the transfer case has the option and a kit is available, you're out of luck unless you're into major modifications.

portable power winches

Some vehicles fit a power winch at the back and companies like Warn have kits which allow you to mount the winch in different locations on the vehicle.

This Troopy is worth more than any other in the same condition because it has that most rare of accessories, an engine-driven winch. The state of the cable is less than impressive and should be replaced immediately.

A Hi-Lift jack can be used as a winch. You will need to remove the base and probably also take a rat-tail file to the end so a shackle fits through. It works, but because the two input and output cables aren't lined up it isn't very efficient, and you only get a metre's worth of pull before you need to stop everything and reorganise. That's why we're using a drag chain which can easily change its length.

hand winch vs power winch

If you need to winch more or less directly forwards then you can't beat a power winch. No effort, quick and easy.

If you need to do anything else, the power winch is pretty much an expensive weight on the front of the vehicle, whereas a hand winch can pull in any direction. Another major advantage is that you don't need to get the winching vehicle in position; you take the winch, and not the vehicle, to the problem. This limitation can be worked around to some degree by use of snatch blocks, but it's still a limitation.

	Tirfor (T516)	Power
Speed	Slow	Fast
Effort	Got lots of helpers?	Nothing
Flexibility	Any direction	Only pulls forwards
Cost	~ $500	~$1,500+
Safety	Slow, with very strong cable – as safe as winches get.	Cable/rope known to break – the winding mechanism is a dangerous moving part; fingers have been lost
Reliability	Simple, reliable, carried inside vehicle	Open to the elements, in the worst possible place
Pulling power	2,500kg	Varies, but maximum only with minimum rope on drum
Angles	Any angle	Limited by fleet angle (see later in this chapter)

Which one to buy? If you have only one, use a hand winch. It is cheaper and way more flexible and reliable. However, remember that plenty of people have come back from a trip using a hand winch and placed an immediate order for a power winch. Probably just as many people that have come back from a trip being unable to use their power winch because it failed or because it was inflexible, and promptly bought a hand winch.

1   Many recoveries just need the vehicle to move forwards a metre or so. A hand winch is really good for that sort of recovery.

2   Winching up a slope too slippery for this car to drive. Otherwise he could be lowering himself backwards if it's too dangerous to try to drive it. This is a long pull, not ideal for a hand winch. It is important not to winch and drive in this case as the tyres need all the lateral grip they can get and there isn't much in the way of ruts to keep the vehicle straight. The pull is also not too difficult, with no ledges and not a particularly steep slope.

3   Many winches can now be remotely controlled. I used to think this was a gimmick till I tried it. When winching the person in control is the one outside of the vehicle, so it makes sense to give them control. However, the winchmaster and driver still need to communicate. Winches can be wired so they are controlled by both a remote and switches.

4   A Hilux demonstrating a double-line pull.

5   The Defender 130 is hung up. A very quick winch backwards fixed the problem. Snatching would have been problematic as it would be dangerous to put the D3 in the bottom of the hole, and the changing elevations would also have caused problems. That was also a problem with winching as the Defender moved back it also moved down, so we had to be careful not to overstrech the winch rope. Notice the D3 is also parked before the crest of the hill so as to use the hill for additional retardation.

winch accessories

If you buy a winch, you need more than just the winch! The essentials are:

Accessory	Purpose
Gloves	Protect hands. Winch cables can cause nasty gashes.
Tree trunk protector	Goes around the tree to prevent the winch cable cutting into the bark, which would mean a slow death for the tree. It's not a good idea for the winch cable, either.

Accessory	Purpose
Shackles	You'll probably need one to connect the winch hook to the tree trunk protector, possibly another for the vehicle and one for the Tirfor. Work out how many you need and add one for luck. Use only rated shackles rated to AS2741.
Winch extension strap	Winch cables are often not long enough. Add extra length with an extension strap of 20m or more. Can also be used for towing, or extending snatch straps.
Snatch block	A pulley is a wheel around which a belt or rope can run. A block is a pulley with plates around the outside so it can be attached to something. You then feed the rope or cable through the gap between the pulley and the block plates. A snatch block can have its plates opened (see photo) to allow the rope to be inserted, which is why they are used in offroading as 4WD ropes have hooks attached and are thus too large to thread through a pulley gap. Snatch blocks are used to change the direction of pull and to increase pulling power at the expense of speed (explained later in this chapter).
Drag chains	The advantage of using a chain for winching is that its length can easily be varied. Use only chains rated to AS4344 made out of Grade 70 chain.
Winch dampener	For wire rope use a winch dampener to help stop the rope flying dangerously in the event of a break (see page 425).

1-2 *A snatch block opens up to allow a rope or cable to be placed onto the pulley.*

3 *Gloves, shackles of various sizes, a winch extension strap, a tree trunk protector and a snatch block are winch essentials. Also shown here in white is a snatch strap.*

4 *Four shackles. The largest one is rated to 8.5t and the smallest to 1.5t. The D shackle (bottom right) is not rated at all and is only kept for demonstration.*

All the winching gear kept in one strong plastic box which can be taken to any recovery site.

Drag chains can have two eyes or two hooks or one of each, which is best for flexibility. It is easy to change them over anyway. Make sure the chains are rated to AS4344.

shackles

A shackle is a metal loop with a threaded pin.

There are rated shackles, and there are unrated shackles. Rated shackles are designed for lifting and have their rating embossed on the side in raised letters. This is a lifting rating, e.g. 4.7 or 3.5 tonnes, so the shackle is designed to take a load of 4x or 6x the rating before breaking, depending on whether it is an M- or S-rated shackle, but any shackle should be compliant with AS 2741. You can use either rated bow or D shackles; the shape is personal preference.

- Never, never, never use an unrated shackle.
- The strength of the shackle is at right angles to the pin. Also ensure that the rope or hook goes around the pin, not around the D or bow. That has two benefits; a flatter surface for the hook or strap means the shackle can rotate around whatever it is hooked on easily so it always "points" the correct way.
- A rated shackle will always have a pin diameter larger than the body diameter and have its rating embossed on the side. The pin will always be unmarked.

the back-off question

Some say shackles should be done up as tightly as you can. Some say to go as far as finger-tight and then back them off. Both opinions are strongly held. Proponents of the first approach say there is no need to back it off half a turn in case it jams – it won't, and the looser pin may come out or get dirt in the thread, plus the pin needs to be fully seated for maximum strength.

Proponents of the second approach say if the shackle were in an environment where it was subject to vibration for long periods of time it should be done up tightly and then moused (prevented from coming undone). However, in recovery situations the shackles are only used temporarily and there is more risk of them binding and being difficult to undo than coming entirely loose. Backing off half a turn does not materially affect the shackle's strength which is well beyond that of the other recovery gear.

Which is correct? My view is to do them up finger-tight only and if they are difficult to undo that's nothing a screwdriver, pliers or shifting spanner can't fix and we always have those handy.

A shackle used to connect a winch rope to a tree trunk protector. The winch eyelet is not quite centred, and for best effect spacers should be used to centralise it. Never replace a pin with a normal bolt, even if it fits.

winch rope: wire or synthetic

It used to be simple. If you decided on a power winch you got yourself some wire rope. Then along came synthetic rope, and you have a choice. Look around the competition offroaders and wire ropes will be few and far between if indeed they are permitted by the organisers.

Synthetic winch rope is manufactured by a number of specialised companies, all of whom claim the same properties and advantages over wire. The rope is designed for industrial winching and some lifting applications, or anywhere where a very strong rope is required. One example is towing quarry trucks weighing 100 tonnes (that's 30+ fully

loaded Patrols!), but for 4WD winch applications synthetic rope is around eight millimetres to 12mm diameter.

synthetic advantages

Synthetic rope is stronger than wire and considerably lighter. That's a bonus, as by the time you've put a bull bar, lights and winch right at the front of your truck the suspension will be begging for an upgrade, and all that extra weight does nothing for the handling. Thirty metres of wire rope may weigh 9.5kg, but 30m of eight-millimetre synthetic rope may weigh only 1.5kg. Synthetic rope doesn't kink, although it can knot. That means if your winch packs up with the rope out, you can easily coil it, or wrap it around the bull bar, and it won't even scratch the paintwork. Try doing that with wire rope. Synthetic is also much easier to remove from the winch, inspect and replace.

So synthetic's lighter, stronger and generally good. But the biggest advantage over wire is safety.

If synthetic rope breaks it's a hell of a lot safer than wire rope, for three reasons. Firstly it's about one-seventh the weight of wire, so there's far less energy. Secondly it has a low elongation (doesn't stretch) and thirdly it's much softer than wire rope. But contrary to popular opinion, it doesn't "just drop" to the ground. I can personally attest to that, having seen a broken synthetic rope fling a rope dampener some 20m into the bush. We've also found one bloke who was in the way of a breaking synthetic rope and caught it full-force across the chest. He scored some red welts, but no skin was broken, he's fine – and very happy it wasn't wire rope. People pay good money for harder whippings, apparently. And while your hands won't be splintered, wear gloves anyway.

wire advantages

All positive for the synthetic, but the wire rope is not without its advantages. Firstly, cost. It's a lot cheaper. Secondly, abrasion resistance and general robustness. While placing wire rope over a rock isn't a good idea, it'll handle abrasion and general abuse much better than synthetic, provided you don't kink it. Synthetic rope can't be kinked.

Wire handles heat better (which is why the likes of the fire services often use it), but most synthetics have critical temperatures (when they begin to lose strength) of around 200 or even 350 degrees Celsius. If the winch gets that hot, it will be damaging itself, for example by melting its grease. If you're still concerned, or using a rope with a low critical temperature, there are sheaths to go over the first few metres of rope onto the drum.

The major cause of heat on some low-mount winches is actually paying out the rope, as the winch motor is then overriding the brake, and even this only applies to some winches.

If you already have wire rope, you'll be able to use synthetic. Either type will do the job, but put it this way – wallets tend to be quickly opened after their owners have seen a wire rope break under load.

wire and synthetic compared

	Wire	Synthetic
Cost	Cheaper	More expensive
Weight	10mm = 317g/ metre	10mm = 60g/metre
Strength	10mm about 6,000kg	10mm about 8,000kg
Length on drum	Less than synthetic	More than wire!
Kinks	Prone	Can't kink, but can knot
Heat resistance	Excellent	Weakens under extreme heat
Abrasion resistance	Good, but try to avoid it	Poor, avoid contact with any surfaces like trees or rocks
Effect of water and sunlight	The galvanising can wear away with abrasion, exposing the rope to rust – not affected by UV	Synthetics are treated to chemicals and UV – water does not affect them
Birds-nesting on drum	Kinks, severely weakens	Generally no damage, just needs untangling
Repairable?	Once kinked (strands dislocated, broken, chafed, rope badly bent), must be replaced	Can be spliced and rejoined

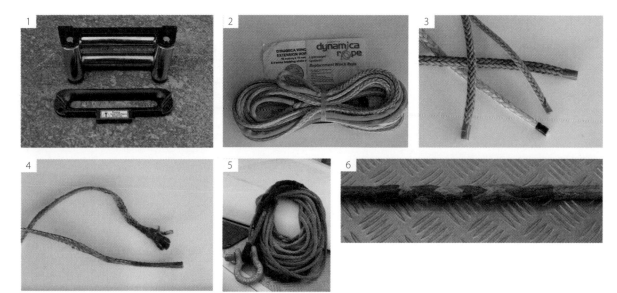

1   Synthetic rope can be used with a lighter hawse rather than roller fairleads. However, the rollers are kinder to the rope and generate less friction – try pulling a shoelace hard over your arm to see the heat that can be generated. There is little chance of the rope becoming jammed in the side of the rollers if the rollers are designed for synthetic rope.

2   Synthetic rope can also be used as a winch extension. It has the advantage of being light and able to go around snatch blocks.

3   Synthetic rope comes in a variety of diameters, colours and types. It's not a case of seen one, seen them all.

4   Cheap synthetic rope damaged by excess heat on the drum.

5   Synthetic rope can be easily coiled and stored, unlike wire rope.

6   A professional-grade splice. Damaged parts of synthetic rope can be cut out and spliced, and different types of rope joined together with minimal loss of strength, unlike a knot which loses 50% or more of the rope strength and won't go around a snatch block.

when to use

Whenever you're stuck, a winch is an option. In particular, use a winch when a snatch is not possible or is dangerous, for example if you need to move the vehicle slowly over rocks.

You don't even need to be stuck to use a winch. If there's a particularly steep, slippery descent you absolutely have to negotiate, then winch yourself downwards. Same applies for ascending the same hill, if you really need to. Winching is preferable to lots of wheelspinning or fitting chains.

Winches are also handy for moving fallen trees off tracks and even fixing vehicles, for example bending tie-rods (part of the steering) back into shape. You can also secure a vehicle on a hill using a winch.

The ute has backed into a slippery hole and can't move. The easiest way out is backwards, so a little winching was all that was needed. Pulling it out forwards would have meant the tow car sliding around and trying to drive up a slope. There isn't enough room for a backwards snatch, so the winch is the gentler approach. Before winching we checked the vehicle was not hung up on its chassis and could move when winched.

Using a winch to pull a tree out of the way. We could have used a snatch block to pull it away from the track but a straight line pull worked in this case as there was enough room to move it off the path.

This Prado couldn't make it up the hill. Snatching the vehicle up would have involved a lot of dangerous speed, the possibility the tow car wouldn't make the hill and then having to reverse back down together, plus the distance required between the cars may not have made the approach safe. Contrast that approach to the winch – the recovery car stays still, it doesn't need a lot of room to operate, speeds are slow and the whole operation is much safer.

when not to use

There isn't really a time not to winch if a recovery is in order. However, you do need something like a tree or large rock to act as a winch anchor, so if you're stranded on a flat beach winching won't work unless you use a deadman anchor or similar. Power winches are only any good for pulling yourself forwards.

how to use

winching physics and geometry

All winches with drums – which are most power winches – can only produce the maximum pulling power with a small amount of rope on the drum. As more rope is wound on, it increases the diameter of the drum, which reduces the effective pulling power.

Layers on the drum (8mm diameter wire rope)	Pulling strength (kg / lb)	% loss relative to maximum
1	4,323 / 9,500	0
2	3,923 / 8,621	9
3	3,595 / 7,900	17
4	3,359 / 7,382	22
5	3,150 / 6,922	27

Pulling strength vs turns on the drum: Warn 9500XP 12v electric winch. The table above assumes a suitable supply of electricity and the winch operating at optimum efficiency, so should be seen as a maximum.

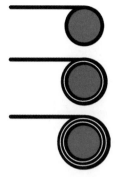

The three diagrams show how the drum diameter effectively increases as more cable is wound on. The speed of the pull also increases, but in practice the extra power required to rotate the greater diameter drum means the line speed doesn't change very much unless there is little load on the winch.

Load (kg)	Amps	Metres/min pull
0	70	11.6
910	175	5.1
1,818	262	3.9
2,720	335	3.1
3,630	425	2.7
4,310	480	2.3

The table basically says that any form of winch load is asking a lot from your vehicle's battery. That means you need to run the winch intermittently to ease the load on the battery, and anyway electric winches will need time to cool as they run very hot very quickly. It also means it's a great idea to minimise recovery loads.

If your winch isn't powerful enough to pull what you want it to, and even if it is, but you wish to make its job easier, then there are two options:

- Make the pull easier. Lighten the vehicle, dig it out, build the road, drop tyre pressures.

• Increase the winch's effective pulling power; spool more rope out to create a smaller diameter drum or use snatch blocks.

using snatch blocks

This is a simple winch pull. A vehicle is stuck (the "casualty") and it is self-recovering with a winch (the winch shown here is electric, although it could be any other type).

Example 1: Straight-line pull. 1 x weight. Load on winch anchor is the load of the weight.

The force required to move the vehicle is 300kg, and the winch generates 300kg of force. Actually, just a fraction more than 300kg, otherwise the forces would be perfectly balanced and the casualty wouldn't move, but we'll call it 300 for the sake of simplicity.

Example 2a: Double-line pull, half the effort required for the same pull.

Now if we add a snatch block and attach the winch rope back to the casualty we halved our effort, so to generate 300kg of pulling force the winch needs only generate 150kg. This is known as a double-line pull, but there is a disadvantage. The winch now needs to pull in twice as much rope to move the car a given distance, so in theory we've halved the speed of recovery. Except of course in most cases we haven't, as the table above shows that the more load on an electric winch, the slower it runs, so

although it has twice as much rope to pull it is now pulling it in quicker than it would on a single line pull. The same would be true if it were a human-powered winch. There's another factor too, and that's the inefficiency of the snatch block, which uses between five and eight percent of the pulling power, so the actual effort required from the winch is not half, but more like 160kg. Still, the basic principle is that the winch load is about halved, but speed of recovery is not halved. In an extreme case, if the single-line load were 3,990kg on a 4,000kg winch then the winch would be groaning along, barely moving. However, if the snatch block were used that would become around 2,000kg, which the winch could deal with much more easily. So in that case the double-line pull speed would be quicker than the single line.

A side bonus is that because we now have a lot more rope off the drum the winch is even more efficient anyway – remember that this wouldn't apply to a Tirfor winch with no drum. The examples below, for clarity, ignore the five to eight percent loss per snatch block.

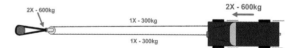

Example 2b: Double-line pull, doubled pulling effort.

Another way of looking at it is to assume the winch still generates 300kg of pull, in which case the recovery force is now 600kg. However, winches don't work like that; the pulling power they generate is proportional to what's required, it's not a fixed amount. For example, if you need to generate X force on a hand winch to move a vehicle, you'll generate X force, not two or three times X, otherwise the vehicle would accelerate rapidly. This means snatch blocks should be thought of as reducing the winch effort to move a given load, not really increasing the power of the winch. They would only increase the winch's pulling power when the load gets beyond the single-line pull rating of the winch.

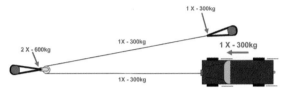

Example 3: Double-line pull but no benefit for the winch.

This is an interesting setup. There is no benefit to the recovering vehicle beyond example 1 – the winch has to generate the full 300kg of force. However, the tree we're using has to withstand 600kg of force. If this seems strange then turn this book 90 degrees clockwise so the vehicles are pointing upwards, and imagine the vehicles hanging loosely, vertically suspended. In example 2a there are two ropes supporting the vehicle, whereas in examples 1 and 3 there is only one. The vehicle "weighs" 300kg, which is the force we say is needed to move it, and in examples 1 and 3 that 300kg is on one rope. In example 2a that 300kg is split over two ropes, hence half the load.

There is little practical benefit to this arrangement in example 3 except that you can get more rope cable off the drum, but you then are better off simply using the setup shown in example 2a. The example 3 setup is sometimes rigged in the belief it will give the advantages shown in example 2a/2b and 4, as all of these offer mechanical advantage. It is sometimes stated that unless the winch rope

is attached back to the winch vehicle there is no advantage. That is only correct when the winch car is recovering itself. When the winch car is stationary and recovering another vehicle you get the advantage whether or not the rope is secured to the car, as the next example shows.

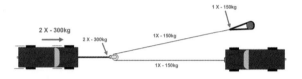

Example 4: Straight-line pull. 1 x weight. Load on winch anchor is the load of the weight.

This time we are using a car with a winch (on the right) to recover a car without a winch. The winch is attached to a tree, just like in example 3, but in this case there is a mechanical advantage. Again, turn the book so the car being recovered is vertically suspended and you can see that the casualty is "dangling" by two ropes, so the load is halved. If the casualty were to stop being a casualty and become an anchor point so the winch car was self-recovering then we'd be back to example 3. We could modify example 3 and terminate the winch rope back at the vehicle instead of the tree. We'd still get the advantage, but then we'd have 300kg trying to pull the recovery vehicle forwards and it may not have enough traction to resist.

So far all the examples have used just the one snatch block, but more can be used. The practical limit for offroading is two – while more can be used you tend to run out of rope and anchor points. Though the extra block loses another eight percent of effort to make a total 16% wasted, we'll again ignore that for simplicity in the following diagrams. Also, each snatch block would need to turn the rope 180 degrees to get full advantage of the pulley, and the diagrams aren't quite 180 degrees; again that will be ignored but in practice factor in these losses of efficiency.

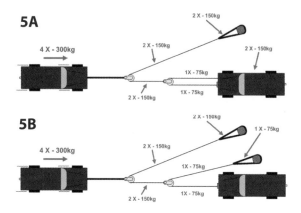

Example 5: Two blocks, reducing effort by a quarter in both examples 5A and 5B.

Again, to make sense of the diagram turn the book so the casualty is being moved vertically upwards. The only difference between 5A and 5B is that in 5B another anchor point is being used, which reduces the load on the recovering car as it has now only to resist a load of 75kg, not 150kg.

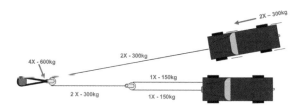

Example 6: Two blocks, but only halving the effort. The block against the tree is only redirecting the load in exactly the same way as example 3. The block closest to the winch

car is the one giving the advantage, and again it makes no difference to the mechanical advantage (in this case) whether the second point is anchored to the winch car or not. However, if the second anchor point is not on the vehicle then the load on the vehicle is halved, which is a useful point if the winch car has little traction.

This final example shows two snatch blocks rigged but in such a way that the load is only halved, not quartered. If the book is turned so the casualty is being winched vertically it can be seen that it pulls down with 300kg of force, and as the winch car is not moving, the winch car has 300kg of force exerted on it, too. The two 300kg forces combine to place a load of 600kg on the anchor point. However the winch car has split its 300kg load into two, or 150kg each.

The point of all this is that snatch blocks can certainly reduce the effort required by the winch, and by significant amounts, but they do take some setting up, especially double block pulls. Very rarely will a recovery need more than a double-line pull, so the examples with a single snatch block are the ones most likely to be used in the bush. With three blocks the efficiency losses become significant, and you need a lot of rope to make it work.

However, you may need to change the direction of pull, and a classic example is when you need to winch a casualty up a hill. You could have the winching car face down the hill and pull upwards, but often you'll simply pull the winch car downhill. The problem can be solved by backing the winch car down the hill and using a snatch block on a tree so both casualty and winch car are facing uphill, similar to example 6 and photo on page 424.

1 A broken vehicle in 2WD could not reverse up this slippery incline which also featured some awkward turns. Here we are not gaining any mechanical advantage as we don't need to, but we are reversing the direction of pull.

2 Once past the tricky bit we could reposition the Defender but again used a redirection. The load on the tree is about 1.4 times the actual pull as it's about a 90 degree angle. A winch recovery is far safer and less stressful than trying to tow the vehicle out mainly because you can angle the winch exactly where you want it and everything moves slowly and easily.

3 A triple-line pull. This needs a pulley block capable of taking a load at either end (see here at the casualty end), which most 4WD ones cannot do. This unit was sourced from a hoisting shop.

snatch block size

The size of the snatch block is important. Rigging guidelines say that the snatch block should be at least 20 times the rope diameter with a groove depth of 1.5 times rope diameter otherwise strength will be reduced. Tirfor-style hand winches cannot be used with standard-issue 4WD snatch blocks as they have a much greater wire rope diameter, and have a special core that should not be bent. Snatch blocks for Tirfor-styles do exist but are much larger in diameter.

anchor point loads

The load on an anchor point may be more than the recovery load, even if it's a 90 degree pull.

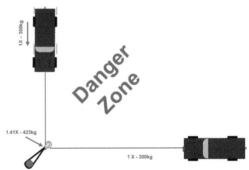

A simple redirection of pull, often used offroad. There is no mechanical advantage but that's not the point as in this way the winch vehicle can be positioned somewhere other than directly in front of the casualty. However, although the casualty load is 300kg, the load on the anchor point is 1.41 times the load or 423kg, considerably more than the actual load. This is often not realised and insufficiently strong anchor points are used. The table shows the load factors. The anchor point force will be halfway between the strap's angle, as when two equal forces act in different directions the resultant force is halfway between the applied forces. This is something to bear in mind when setting up the recovery. The particular danger zone for a redirect pull is shown in red.

The table below shows the angle of the cable passing through the block, and the load factor. It shows that only when the angle is 120 degrees is the load on the snatch block equal to the weight. Even at that angle there is still a loss due to friction.

Included angle – the angle between the rope coming in and going out of the snatch block (degrees)	Load factor
0 (exactly doubled back on itself)	2.00
10	1.99
20	1.97
30	1.93
40	1.87
50	1.81
60	1.73
70	1.64
80	1.53
90 (shown on page 424)	1.41
100	1.29
110	1.15
120	1.00
130	0.84
140	0.76
150	0.68
160	0.52
170	0.35
180 (a straight line pull)	0.00

This table is not reversible, i.e. the figures for 10 degrees cannot be reversed to work out the figures for 170 degrees.

The important point is that changing the direction of pull:

- Places a great load on the snatch block and its anchor
- Loses you some efficiency due to friction
- Safety note; the danger zone changes compared to a straight pull – see diagram for an example.

fleet angle

Another problem with drums is the fleet angle. The rope must be wound on evenly, otherwise it bunches up and quickly increases the diameter, possibly to the point at which the winch cannot wind any more rope on. The way to avoid this is to ensure the cable goes almost straight onto the winch, at a shallow angle. This is called the "fleet angle" and it should be five degrees or less.

If the cable starts to bunch up it may slip off the bunch and that shock load can damage the winch or break the cable.

Often you can't pull directly ahead. Not ideal, but it can work for short pulls. This is where not having a lot of rope on the drum is an advantage. Notice the dampeners (explained later) on the rope.

setting up

first steps

Make sure the winch actually works and, if powered, that you have the control cable, or the handle if a hand winch. Collect all the kit you need; tree-trunk protectors, shackles, gloves. It is best to keep it in one spot on the ground. Check the rope and cable for damage as it comes out. Keep the winch car's engine running to maintain the battery's charge.

anchoring the winch

Trees

No winching is going to happen unless you have something immovable to use as a winch anchor. Usually this is a sturdy tree, or if the winch vehicle is recovering another vehicle, it may be able to hold itself still if a slope can be used. Any tree with a trunk diameter of more than about 30cm will do, but find a larger one if you can. Sometimes two or more smaller trees can be used together by using a winch extension strap around them all.

Use a tree-trunk protector (or two) and place it as low as you can to reduce leverage on the tree. If you don't have one, a snatch strap wound several times around the tree will suffice but is not ideal, a winch extension strap can also be used, especially if it's a very large tree.

If the strap is likely to rise up the tree under load, as it may do if the bark is wet and slippery, or the trunk is angled, then wrap the strap around the tree once. Make sure you leave enough length for this to avoid too great a load on the strap by increasing the included angle (see "Anchor point loads" above). In general however, avoid this in favour of a shallower included angle.

Other anchors

If you cannot find a tree, then there are alternatives. These include:

- A portable anchor
- Vehicles
- Rocks
- The spare tyre or a log.

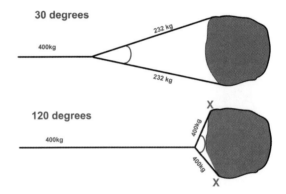

The top diagram shows an anchor with an included angle of 30 degrees. As the anchor point straps are not parallel, the 400kg recovery force translates to more than half of the load, or 232kg in this case, and a force of 60kg pulling each strap inwards. No bridle ever halves the total recovery force on the recovery points – it's always more than half. As the included angle increases the relative forces build up to the stage where they are equal to the recovery load, and this happens at 120 degrees where the single recovery force of 400kg translates to 400kg of tension in each arm of the strap, with 174kg force pulling each strap arm inwards. Another point to note is that the relatively sharp points marked with a red X are weak points. The perfect anchor is a perfect circle, but trees are never quite that perfect.

1   Portable anchors create a winch point on soft ground. They work effectively only in specific conditions where the ground is soft enough to allow the anchor to dig in, but hard enough for it to grip. Usually, sand is too soft, dirt is too hard. You do see anchors on competition trucks but that's often because there are specific tasks requiring them to carry anchors, not because they're generally used for recovery.

2   Sometimes the winch car itself needs securing. This vehicle is engaged in removal of abandoned cars from a state forest as a free club service to the community.

3   Chains are useful for dragging things that would damage a strap, such as this abandoned vehicle a club removed from a state forest.

4   A ground anchor secured by pickets. Effective, but not easy to carry around.

5   A drag chain laid out on the ground and secured with 10 tent pegs. The method is to use a slight "V" shape, drive the pegs in about ¾ of the way and put a little tension on the system, then drive the pegs home. It's not super-strong but it can be more

than enough for a winch pull, especially if you can put it on a slight incline relative to the winch car as opposed to dead level. You can use more than one drag chain too.

6   If you need to join two tree-trunk protectors you can use the method for snatch straps described in Chapter 34. This saves using a shackle.

7   Winches can be used to right rolled vehicles. This one ended up on its side during a navigation exercise. It was easy to right using a Tirfor-clone hand winch. The track was too narrow to bring an electric winch on a car to bear, whereas the hand winch is easy to position for best effect. Very little physical effort was required and the vehicle was able to drive on. Nobody was hurt. When righting a vehicle generally hook onto the chassis rails and pull, don't try to use the bodywork or a B-pillar.

You can coil straps around trees to stop the strap sliding, although this is a rare problem. More common is the need to shorten the strap, especially if it's a winch extension strap. The photo shows an incorrect setup as there's no need to coil the strap, and it has created too great an included angle.

1   You can thread a tree-trunk protector through itself as shown, but if you do be aware that you reduce the strength by at least 50%. It is better to use two protectors, joined together (see Chapter 34) or even a winch extension strap.

2   Several small trees can be used instead of one big one, but that usually requires a strap longer than standard tree trunk protector. Here we have joined two to make it double the length. If we used just the one the included angle (see earlier in this chapter) would have been too great, and placed unnecessary stress on the trees and the strap.

Rocks

Rocks can be used provided they are large enough not to move and small enough to get a strap or drag chain around. That's rare, but not unheard of.

Ground anchor

A portable anchor is a device that looks like a plough. You basically jam it into the dirt and start pulling; the winch then pulls the anchor into the ground.

You can also bury the spare wheel to make a deadman anchor, which should be so named because you're nearly dead by the time the hole is dug. I have used a deadman anchor just once and would suggest that the effort required to dig the hole is often better put to digging the vehicle out. Australian soil is not usually easy to dig and if you're in sand refer to chapter 20, for an easier way to recover vehicles than winching with a deadman.

Vehicle

Another anchor option is another vehicle which has the advantage of being portable. The driver should be in the anchor vehicle with the engine running and foot pressed on the brake as a park brake and engine braking cannot be trusted. Vehicles do not make good anchors if they are being pulled downhill or even on the flat. It is important to chock the wheels, dig them in and attach the vehicle to a tree or other object.

1   *A big, heavy tree. So big we needed two tree-trunk protectors to go around it, joined by a shackle. This was a major winching operation to retrieve a Jeep that was some distance down the track and needed winching upwards. If the recovery car (Defender) was driven down the track, facing the Jeep, it would have been difficult to sufficiently secure the Defender to recover the Jeep; and after the recovery the Defender would then have to be reversed up the hill. Instead the Defender was reversed down the hill and we used a snatch block to angle the pull towards the Jeep. This gained no mechanical advantage but it didn't matter, the Jeep didn't need much pulling. Once the Jeep was recovered both vehicles were able to drive forwards up and out of the track.*

2-3 *One Patrol recovering another. The recovery vehicle is facing slightly downhill on muddy grass, so there was little traction. The solution was to dig little ruts for the front wheels and roll them in, adding a flat stone to help keep the wheels in the ruts. This operation greatly improved the recovery vehicle's ability to hold the other vehicle. There is little point doing the back wheels, you're better off spending the effort on the front wheels, and don't forget to fill the hole in once you've finished.*

If both the anchor vehicle and casualty have a winch then in theory it doesn't matter which one does the winching. In practice it is better to have the casualty winch as that way if the rope touches the ground or anything else it just touches and does not rub – when the casualty winches the rope doesn't move, the casualty moves along it.

operation

paying out the cable

If you are using a power winch put it into freespool by turning the clutch handle 180 degrees. This should not require much effort but if it does operate the winch drum in either direction for a fraction of a turn. You can simply reverse the

operation of the winch but it is quicker to freespool it out, and it also means less battery drain for electrics. Electric winches typically work against their brake when paying out which only generates heat.

Electric winches have three modes of operation; in, out and stopped. While the line speed is pretty slow sometimes you want it even slower and the trick there is to flick the switch up for a fraction of a second a few times, or "pulse" the winch.

If you are using a Tirfor-style hand winch then pull as much cable through the winch as you can before you lock it for pulling. If you need to pay out (reverse direction) a Tirfor-style under load then put the handle on the other lever and then move

1-2 Under-vehicle view of a winch clutch lever. The winch will have marked on it which way is engaged and disengaged. The clutch cannot be operated while there is tension on the winch rope.

3 You can simply wire in controls for the winch so the driver can operate them. Here are an isolator switch and an in/out switch. There is also an in/out switch on the bull bar. Much easier than messing around with a long lead which is often lost.

4 Always leave at least five turns of rope on the drum, be it wire or synthetic. This is the first layer of rope and the winch is operating at its most efficient.

it back and forth – the winch will reverse direction and let the cable out as opposed to bringing it in.

Winches can also be used to lower vehicles down hills. Be careful with this process when using an electric winch as most electric winches reverse against their brake, which means they quickly become very hot even though there is little apparent load on the winch. It can be done, but frequent rest periods are required. It is not a good idea to use a double-line pull as all that does is increase the number of revolutions the winch needs to make to move the vehicle a given distance, and you're trying to avoid that because of the brake problem.

An LC100 being lowered down a difficult pinch. The 80 Series at the top is well secured, and the LC100 driver is in first low, braking so that the rate of descent is controlled by the winch cable payout. This keeps the cable taut and not shock-loaded. It also means more of the LC100's tyre traction can be used for lateral grip so it doesn't slide sideways.

winching in

Once everything is connected and ready to winch, take up the slack, then pause. Perform a final check that shackles are correctly oriented, recovery points used, anchor points are correct, no straps are twisted, no rope has jumped out of snatch blocks and everything else is in order. Then give the command, "Clear winching!" so everyone knows the winch operation is in progress. The winch vehicle should have its engine running at all times to run its alternator which keeps the battery's charge up. The alternator will charge the battery at idle but increasing the revs to 1,500rpm or so will help it. For the same reason leave the engine running after winching is complete so the battery can be charged.

Never be afraid to stop the winching and re-rig if it doesn't seem right for any reason.

On drum winches make sure there are at least five turns of rope on the drum. The little grub screw used to attach the rope to the drum is there only to locate the rope, not take any weight.

The second layer goes on, nice and tight and correctly lined up.

location of drivers

Drivers should be in both vehicles, recovery and casualty, whether hand or power winches are being used. The casualty will need steering, possibly assisted by driving and brakes from time to time. The recovery vehicle may need its brakes applied and the winch operator is much safer inside the vehicle than outside, not just in the event of a cable break but also if the winch vehicle starts to move.

driving and winching

Winching is different to snatching because any load should be gently and evenly applied. That means the vehicle should not assist, as a general rule, because it might overrun the cable and as it slips back that will shock load the rope, potentially causing a break. Even if it doesn't, for a turn or two the rope is going on under no load and that may cause the rope to tangle or bird's-nest. That said, if the driver is careful the casualty vehicle can drive. In automatics this may mean just leaving it in drive, and very little or no throttle. Manuals would be at

idle, with the driver just gently lifting the clutch up. The wheels don't need to spin, nor does the vehicle need to be able to move of its own accord in order to assist with the recovery.

The trick to driving and winching is to listen to the winch motor. When it starts to strain you can drive. As soon as it sounds like the load is easing, and you'll hear this, then stop driving. You may even need to apply a little brake pressure to keep the rope tension, particularly when in rocks. It's not unlike being towed and keeping tension in the towrope.

Another point about driving and winching is traction. The circle of traction was explained in Chapter 12 in connection with skids, but it's just as relevant for winching. If you are on a slippery sideslope and decide to drive the wheels then you are using some of the tyre's grip for going forwards, when you probably really want to reserve it all for lateral grip. Therefore, don't drive and winch when you need maximum lateral grip.

1   The rule of never driving when winching can be broken, but if it's done incorrectly more than the rule gets broken. Mud recoveries are a good case of being able to drive and winch. Here the D3 is in thick, treacly mud and it is well bogged. So I'm winching in, but also in first low and driving. There's no chance of overrunning the winch cable in this situation, but the driving wheels are helping reduce the winch load.

2   *Two people on a hand winch. It is best to let one person pull the lever towards them, then the other pull it back – alternating effort, rather than both people try and push and pull the lever at the same time.*

3   *This is a competition vehicle at Vic Winch demonstrating just how powerful winches are. Even a recreational winch could do this, albeit a lot slower.*

4   *Always use a tree-trunk protector (or two) to protect the tree and your own gear. Place the strap as low as possible. This winch setup uses a tree a long way from the recovery vehicle so plenty of rope is taken off the drum, making for an easier winch. As usual, the fleet angle is off so the pull can't be that long. Often the anchor point needs to be changed during a winching operation.*

continuous winching

Competition winching shouldn't be taken as an example of how to winch for recreational users. Comp winches may cost $10,000 or more, be driven by two or more batteries and be designed for high-speed continuous operation. No recreational electric winch is designed for that sort of continuous duty because they overheat quickly. A good rule is to operate the winch for no more than 20 seconds, and then give it just as long a rest to cool down. This also allows the alternator to keep the battery charge up. You'll need to be carefully monitoring how the operation is going anyway so frequent breaks are a good idea.

safety

general

- **Never cross or touch a rope that is "live" or connected at both ends for recovery purposes.**
- Move all spectators well out of the way. The safest locations are out to one side of the winching operation – think where things will go if they break.

- Handle the cable as little as possible. If you need to manually feed it on to the drum do so from at least 1.5m away from the winch itself. Wear gloves to protect your hands and even then do not permit the rope to run through your hands as a burr could catch on a glove and take your hand with the rope – which is why you're 1.5m away from the hawse in the first place. Use a hand-over-hand approach.

- Do not approach a taut rope unless it is slacked off.

- Never shock-load a winch.

- Check your anchor points are strong enough.

- Never be afraid to stop and re-rig.

- Always spool rope onto a drum under tension.

- Regularly check the winch rope spool onto the drum.

- Keep at least five turns of rope on a drum.

winch dampeners

A winch dampener is a thick, flexible piece of material designed to prevent a winch rope whipping around in the event of breakage (see image on page 425). Opinions on their utility vary. In the case of synthetic winch rope; the weight of the rope, its limited elasticity and its soft nature mean that damage or injury in the event of a breakage is unlikely, even though it doesn't just drop to the ground when broken. Personally, I think the dangers of constantly approaching the rope to reposition a dampener on synthetic rope outweigh the advantages.

Wire rope is another matter and is considerably heavier, more elastic and can do some significant damage so the case for a dampener is more clear cut. Before approaching to reposition a dampener ensure the cable has stopped and the vehicles are stabilised.

shock load

A shock load is a sudden force placed on a component. In the context of winching this usually means the casualty rolling backwards with the winch rope slack, then having its progress abruptly stopped by the rope becoming tight. Shock loading must be avoided where possible as it places great strains on all components. One example; if a 2,600kg vehicle is on a 30 degree slope it will take about 760kg of force just to hold it steady on that slope and a little more to start it off and move it upwards. If it then rolls backwards with no braking effect – as may happen if you drive forwards and then slip back – after 300mm of roll it will be travelling at 1.5km/h. This isn't very fast, and if the vehicle was gradually brought to a halt there would be no issue. However, there is not much elastic in winching gear so the stop is sudden – think about letting the brakes off and rolling back a foot on a really steep hill into a brick wall. The force is proportional to the speed the vehicle reaches as it rolls back, weight of the vehicle and especially how quickly it is brought to a halt. Using our example of the 2,600kg vehicle on a 30 degree slope then if it rolls back 300mm and stops over another 50mm which it will do in 0.25 seconds then the shock load is in excess of 4,500kg – which is uncomfortably high and why shock loads must be avoided at all costs. Doubling the stopping distance to 100mm halves the force to around 2,250kg, which is still significant.

maintenance

power winches

All power winches need to be used regularly – every month or so. They should also be serviced every year by a winch specialist. It is very common to see someone fit a winch, drive round with it for several years and then when it's finally needed – it doesn't work.

Whenever a new cable is fitted to a power winch it must be spooled on under tension, as the layers will be too loose which could lead to birds-nesting. Even if the spools look nice and tight packed this tensioning must be done as all rope, wire or synthetic, stretches a little under its first tension. The solution is easy; freespool the rope out till five turns are left on the drum, then winch it in under tension. A slight incline is fine, or even on the flat if you hold your foot on the brake lightly. There should be enough tension to cause the winch motor engine to change note, but nowhere near so much that it strains.

hand winches

Tirfor-style winches need little maintenance but should, like all recovery equipment, be stored where they won't be damaged or rusted, lightly oiled and used every now and again.

Equipment

For ropes check the following before use:

- Knots
- Frays
- Cut strands
- Rot

- Mildew
- Sun
- Chafing
- Rust (if metal)
- Crush
- Effects of excess heat.

Webbing, such as tree-trunk protectors, snatch straps and winch extension straps should be checked for:

- Abrasions
- Grit, dirt

- Label, tag, stitching, eyes
- Cuts, tears.

All recovery gear should be stored in areas that are:

- Clean, dry and dust free
- Well-ventilated
- Away from sunlight
- Away from chemicals, oils, acids
- Free from vermin.

Any wear and tear around or near the eye of a rope is dangerous and the rope should be discarded.

1 Wire rope irreparably damaged by being flattened after being wound on the drum. This is now a dangerous weak point and kink.

2 Keeping spare wire rope inside a motorcycle tyre is not a bad idea

3 If you are going to use a hook, use one with a proper safety hook like the larger one in this photo. The smaller hook uses a flimsy bit of tin. Otherwise forget hooks and just use a shackle.

4 If you must run moving rope over things, then ensure the surface is at least smooth and use something soft like bark to protect. This will, however you play it, rapidly wear your rope.

CHAPTER 37

TYRE CHAINS

Chains mean traction – in the right places.

what it is

Tyre chains are links of metal that fit around a tyre. The purpose is to create a super-aggressive tread pattern that bites into soft surfaces and all types of ice, providing traction where there would otherwise be none. Chains can be effective in mud, snow and ice, but must be removed for rocks and cannot be used on hard surfaces, or at anything other than a slow speed. So while road tyres with chains can outperform extreme offroad tyres, running road tyres and relying on chains for traction is not a practical solution. Chains are for specific low-traction situations, not general all-terrain use.

diamonds and ladders

The two main types of chain are diamond or ladder pattern. Ladder patterns give better fore and aft traction, but little resistance to sideways forces. While diamonds make a massive difference to forward traction, ladders can "paddle" you out through mud that diamonds can't manage. On the other hand, diamonds are a better all-rounder as they have lateral as well as longitudinal grip and make a huge difference to traction over a standard tyre.

There is also a V-bar pattern which looks the same as the ladder, but the chain links have small metal V-shaped bars. This gives incredible traction and grip in all directions, but is expensive. Most users will go for the all-purpose diamonds, which come in two types; square section and round section.

The squares have hard edges on the links, and the rounds have additional, loose links. The purpose of both designs is to break into and bite the ice.

choosing a chain

Whichever type of chains you choose make sure they fit your tyres before you leave the shop; good retailers combine that check with a fitting demonstration. Chains should be available for all standard 4WD wheel sizes, but anything above a 33" diameter will be difficult to find. The correct chain is related to the diameter of the tyre, not the rim, so if you run a 17" rim then a 16" rim chain could still work. You'll need to calculate the overall tyre diameter (Chapter 7). That gives only a theoretical diameter, and there will be overall-diameter variation between tyre types and manufacturers. The shape of the tyre makes a difference, too; those with squarish tread block will need more length of chain to fit than those with sloping tread blocks. Ultimately, the only real check is by fitting the chains. Look also for the construction; you want hardened steel.

when to use

Ideally, you'll fit chains to all four wheels, possibly with diamonds at the front for steering and v-pattern at the rear for traction, but if you only have one set you need to decide which set of wheels will be chained up. This question is an excellent way to start an argument and is right up there with "if you have one locker, front or rear?" The answer is really terrain-dependent. On uphills chains on the rear work as that's where the weight is, downhill you want them on the front, and that's better for braking and steering too. Overall, we'd generally fit them on the front if possible, but some vehicles cannot fit them to some axles, or even take chains at all, or only with certain tyres. If your tyres are taller or wider than stock you'll definitely want to check clearances, so do all this before you set off. If a vehicle biases drive to an axle, for example some softroaders, the chains should be fitted to the wheels of that axle. Incidentally, it's always interesting to see people fitting their only set of chains to the front wheels of Commodores, not a great idea as those vehicles are rear wheel drive.

The question of chains in mud is a mixed one. Certainly chains chew up the surface of a track, something responsible offroaders avoid, but so does wheelspinning madly up without them, when instead you could gently crawl with chains. The best way is to think about the most responsible way to traverse the terrain, which may in fact be with chains, or winching or turning back.

For ice and snow the case for chains is clearer as there should be enough of a layer to prevent track damage. Mud tyres can provide quite good traction with snow, but chains are better, and miles ahead in ice where no rubber will be any good and will instead just skate over the surface. Snow chains could be thought of as ice chains.

when not to use

Chains aren't much use in rocks and should never be used when the track will be damaged, or at any speed over about 20km/h. Chains do increase tyre diameters, so if you have oversize tyres watch for rubbing on full lock or at maximum suspension flex; chain rubbing will damage a car much more than tyre rubbing. Keep checking the chain fit, as if the chains come off and are flung around by the wheel you can expect some serious damage. Never drive on a hard surface with chains as traction will be much reduced and you'll also damage the chain.

how to use

Once you have chains on your car you'll need to change your driving style. Chains aren't made for speed, so keep to 20km/h or less and be gentle with the controls, as befits slippery conditions anyway. You won't need much momentum as you'll now have more traction from the wheels than you thought possible, allowing gentle crawls where before you'd have spun. Tyre pressures may be reduced with chains as the overall tyre diameter won't change significantly, and you may need the flotation if you're going to try driving over rather than through snow. The steering will feel heavier too. Cross-axle lockers can be used with chains on either axle and you should always lock centre diffs. If you don't, then drive is likely to go to the unchained axle. High- or low-range can work but, given the speed restrictions with chains, low-range is probably best, even if you're in third or fourth low.

fitting chains

You absolutely must practice fitting chains before you leave, unless you particularly enjoy fiddling around in cold and wet conditions inventing new oaths. It also means you can check they actually fit; tyre size variation being what it is, you may be surprised. For example, our chains just fit a slightly worn 235/85/16 Cooper STT tyre; a new tyre is very hard to get them around and the next chain size up is too loose. The same chains were perfect for a new

1   Lay the chain out flat, with the block about ⅓ of the way along from the front. Put your flat plate under the block so it doesn't sink into soft surfaces. Make sure the chain is facing outwards!

2   Drive the car onto the block and lift the chains up and over the tyre. You should find you're able to drape the chain over the front of the tyre so it will join at the front, not at the top; that's why you put the block ⅓ of the way along, not halfway. This makes the latches a little easier to get to.

3   Fasten latch at the back of the tyre.

4   Fasten latch at the front. Note the choker (inner) chain with the rubber strap at the end, that's next.

5   Pull the choker chain tight and fasten the inner hook. Tidy away the slack by hooking the loose end somewhere and pulling the black rubber tight. Then double-check your work. You don't want to get it wrong. Drive a few tens of metres, stop and take up the slack again. Do this twice. Removing is the reverse of fitting, and easier. Ensure the chain is entirely off the wheel; never "drive it off".

6   Our block of wood rests on a small plank with two ribs screwed in. Without this the tyre tends to push the block off the wood, and without the plank the vehicle will push the block down into the soft ground.

Kelly MSR in the same size. Chains can be custom-made or modified if no off-the-shelf sizes exist.

Chain fitting equipment; you'll need a tarp, a wooden block, a flat plate for the block and gloves.

Stop somewhere safe, flat and away from traffic and secure the vehicle firmly. Don't wait until you're stuck; fitting chains in a rut is not easy. Don't air right down either – while in theory that makes the chain easier to fit the sidewalls also start to bag out and the tyre won't sit on the raised block as firmly.

There are several types of chains and several ways to fit them. On the previous page is one method we find to be effective for our diamond patterns on a 4WD. Alternatively, sometimes the chain can be laid out and simply driven on without the use of a block.

right side of the law. Chains are one of these things that don't seem expensive any more when you're trying to drive an icy road on a mountain.

A lighter-duty chain with a plastic guard over the inner.

Tarp, beanie, gloves, jacket and stopped in a clear, flat area before it gets too difficult.

maintenance and care

When you have finished with your chains wash them, give them a light spray of WD-40 or similar and store them in a dry box. We keep a set of gloves in there as well. You can buy chains from a number of retailers, or hire them. The quality is crucial because the chain will have tonnes of 4WD weight on it in very cold conditions, so if the design and metal quality is not top-notch it will fail and the damage caused will be catastrophic. Don't buy or use cheap chains.

Chains aren't cheap considering you use them rarely, but a well-maintained set will last for years and hold its second-hand value. They will also see you on the

This climb would not have been possible without chains. Although there is a weight shift rearwards, the Defender still climbed with chains only on the front wheels. The front wheels were able to compact the snow for the rears. Tyre pressures were lowered to reduce sinking and therefore lessen rolling resistance.

1   Off-centre, incorrectly fitted chains. These are diamond pattern.

2   While chains are amazing in the snow, they are no substitute for the usual gear such as shovels, winches and the rest.

3   V-chains; a ladder design with extra bite.

4   On the left is a chain with squared links, which can bite into the ice. On the right is a chain with rounded links which don't, so there are loose links to do the biting.

Chains are by no means essential for many snow drives, but should always be carried just in case.

chains and the law

If the law says you have to fit or carry chains, then you must, and they must be appropriate for your vehicle. If not then you are not only risking your own safety and that of others, but also demerit points and you're probably invalidating your insurance. You must fit chains when directed by a sign or by an authorised officer.

Victoria and NSW have, as you'd expect, different regulations despite the snow being exactly the same.

Victoria has four levels of alpine road conditions with all vehicles required by law to carry chains:

1. Open to all cars.

2. 2WD require chains, 4WD don't.

3. 2WD access closed, 4WD require chains.

4. Closed to all traffic.

NSW has only three with only 2WD vehicles required to carry chains by law:

1. Open to all cars.

2. 2WD require chains, 4WD don't.

3. Closed to all traffic.

Keep the speed down when you fit chains.

However, NSW are in the process of changing their rules. While 4WDs may not be required to carry or fit chains that doesn't mean to say it isn't a good idea, as ice is ice and 4WDs can slip there too. As ever in Australia, what's legal in one state is not necessarily the case in another.

CHAPTER 38

TRACTION DEVICES

what it is

Traction devices are anything you can place under the wheels to:

- Improve grip
- Increase clearance
- Reduce axle flex to put more weight on the wheels
- Create a ramp.

These are self-recovery devices that do not require another vehicle or winch anchor point, although they may be used in conjunction with winching operations. Solutions include:

- Specially-made devices
- Rocks
- Wood (logs/sticks/branches)
- Car mats.

The specially-made devices are the focus here. Most of the systems on the market fall into the following broad categories:

flexible traction mats

These are light, linked tracks designed for soft surfaces. They do not spread the load well and cannot be used on hard surfaces, but they are better than nothing, and roll up tightly so are easy to carry.

bridging ramps

Designed to take the weight of a vehicle's wheel across a gap, these can also be jammed under the wheels to provide flotation or to create a ramp. Their strength and purpose means they are bulky and heavy. Can be used on any surface.

traction ramps

Much the same as bridging ramps except they are lighter as they aren't designed to take the weight of a vehicle, and are more oriented towards flotation and traction. Soft surfaces (e.g. sand, mud, snow) only.

inflatable traction aids

An inflatable sort of traction ramp. Light and small, but cannot bridge, only fill in gaps. They cannot provide the sort of flotation a traction ramp can manage, but are better than a flexible traction mat. Can jack up a vehicle by placing under a wheel then inflating. Can be used on any surface. The most versatile of the traction aids; a jack of all trades but master of none.

There is no reason you cannot mix devices in a recovery. The combination of inflatables and traction ramps can be especially powerful.

Yellow bridging ladder, orange traction ramp, black flexible traction mat and red/black inflation traction aid. Ideally you'd take them all, but usually you need to choose based on the requirements of the trip. These particular bridging ladders are also known as "waffle boards".

when to use

This depends on the device; but any time you need a bridge, flotation, weight on a wheel, or are stuck. Careful use of bridging ramps and inflatables can see vehicles climb amazing rock ledges, or reduce the risk of damage. Traction ramps can have you out of sand bogs in a jiffy. Sometimes using them before you're stuck is a great idea too.

when not to use

Traction aids tend to be quick to set up and safer than winching or snatching as there are no external forces on the casualty vehicle, so should be preferred over those methods. The only time not to use them would be for the wrong purpose, e.g. using a traction ramp for a bridge. Sometimes winching is better as that can hold the vehicle steady, whereas with all these aids you are putting something between the tyre and the ground which can destabilise and can be a particular problem on sideslopes. However, some bridging ladders can be used to stabilise a vehicle in some situations, for example where it would otherwise fall into a hole.

how to use

Every traction aid will have tips and tricks specific to its operation. The better ones have comprehensive instructions, videos and websites. Review these carefully. The descriptions below are necessarily generic.

soft ground

Dig away the ground in front of the wheels to form a shallow ramp. It's best in these situations to spend time on the preparation job, clearing away soil from the vehicle and making a shallow exit, than to keep trying to drive out after every spadeful of dirt or sand, as each try tends to undo a fair amount of work.

Place the device hard up against the front of the wheel. Ensure the chassis is clear of the ground. Gently idle up and out in first low. Do not attempt a fast drive out – either you've got the clearance and traction or you haven't, and if you haven't then speed won't fix the problem. Inflatables may be able to be placed under a wheel and then inflated.

The traction device is quite short, and there's no point driving off it and getting instantly stuck again. So take steps to ensure that doesn't happen, for example by lowering tyre pressures. It might also be the case that once clear the vehicle cannot safely stop, so helpers might need to enjoy a stroll to catch up with their spades and the traction devices.

If you have only two aids, then in general put them in front of the front wheels, not the rear. This way the fronts grip, and shortly after the rears get to use them too. If you place the ramps at the rear only the rear wheels get any benefit.

hard ground

The problem here is not likely to be traction but a lack of clearance. If the vehicle is running out of axle flex and thus unable to progress, either place the aid under the wheel in the air or at its diagonal opposite. Either placement will improve the situation. A slightly different line can be taken once the aids are considered. Inflatables may be able to be placed under a wheel and then inflated. Again, once in place drive slowly out of it.

1-5 *The inflatable PillowTrack in operation. The Prado was running out of suspension flex, but with the PillowTrack in place the vehicle was able to place some weight on the wheel and thus drive up and out. The device is inflated by mouth or with a compressor.*

6 *Even the humble rock can provide enough extra clearance or traction to see a vehicle through.*

This would have been a tough recovery without traction ramps. It's soft sand near the water, off camber and up a hill.

The recovery was effected by very carefully idling the vehicle up over the Maxtrax ramps, then digging into the sand to create ruts for the other vehicles. The ramps can also be laid on the ground, flat, ready for vehicles to drive over at speed instead of waiting for them to be stuck.

maintenance and care

Keep them clean and inspect for damage such as cracks or leaks which will cause the device to fail under pressure. Avoid contamination with oils or other chemicals and prolonged exposure to sunlight.

1   *Traction ramps have the advantage of not relying on any other vehicle. Unlike a winch, they are simple, reliable and don't need an anchor. If this Defender became bogged (he didn't) winching would have been very difficult. Getting another car to it would be hazardous. Traction aids are the solution.*

2   *Flexible traction ramps being used, unsuccessfully, to provide extra grip on a slippery uphill*

3,4 *The Patrol ran out of approach angle coming out of this rut. Two Pillowtracks in the ditch solved the problem. A bridging ramp would also have worked well here.*

Every recovery device is more effective if you dig the vehicle out first. The forces required to recover are far less, which translates into better safety.

Freelander 2 out of clearance, but bridging ladders are enough to make the difference.

Bridging ladders used to make a steep ascent shallower. Without the ladders the Defender ran out of approach angle.

1,2 Defender out of clearance. It can winch itself, but to reduce the load on the winch (and therefore increase safety) a set of traction ramps are used for extra clearance.

CHAPTER 39

OTHER
RECOVERY
GEAR

drag chains

what it is

A strong chain used for a variety of purposes. The relevant standard is AS4344, and the chain rating is half the designed breaking load, therefore the chains are not for lifting purposes (hoist chains are rated to Grade T). Only buy chains rated to AS4344 – these will be marked on the chain.

when to use

Drag chains are useful for, well, dragging things. Specifically, fallen trees lying across the track. The chains cut into the bark of the tree, so the tree can be dragged with people or a vehicle.

Drag chains can also be used for winching and are particularly useful because their length can be easily varied by changing where you hook the cable back on itself. They are invaluable with short-action winches like Hi-Lift jacks.

when not to use

Drag chains should never be wrapped around a live tree because they will cut into the bark and damage it. Use a tree trunk protector instead.

You can use drag chains for towing if you have to, but they have no "give", are heavy and any dragging on the ground will damage the links. For these reasons never include them in any snatching process.

how to use

Just pay out the amount required and hook the chain back on itself. You can either create a choke hold or a plain loop (see photos). Use the choke where you can as it is a more secure grip. The loop works when you may not be able to easily remove the chain after you finish moving the log – you can simply unhook it and use the vehicle to drag the chain back out from under the tree. Never tie knots in a chain, and never shock load it.

maintenance and care

Drag chains, being metal, should be kept free of dirt and moisture, and never carelessly dropped or thrown around as this fatigues the metal links. Keep them in a canister or canvas bag, not lying around loose. Check for cuts, cracks, corrosion or damage to the links such as elongation or other deformities.

You can either use a choke hold, where you thread the end of the chain through the eye (if your chain doesn't have two hooks), or hook the chain onto itself. The former has the advantage of tightening onto the log, the latter the advantage that once finished you simply drag the chain out from under the log to retrieve it.

1   A large tree, so we've turned the Defender around so it can pull driving forwards, not backwards. As the tree may swing round and hit the vehicle we've lengthened it by using a tree-trunk protector.

2   Choke hold on a log to be dragged with the chain set a couple of feet down the log.

3   Chain used with a Hi-Lift jack. The Hi-Lift can only pull a metre at a time so the chain's ability to vary its length is perfect.

4   A complex winch setup where we had to recover a vehicle behind the Defender. Getting the snatch block lined up needed some variation in length so again the chain's ability to change length makes it indispensable.

5   A simple, strong bag filled with small logs, earth, rocks and whatever else you can find can make a decent makeshift fill-in for ditches or to get greater clearance.

Drag chain and winch used to pull an old engine out from a shed as part of bushfire relief operations.

Drag chains can even be used as a makeshift anchor (Chapter 39)

axe, saw, chainsaw

Not really recovery devices, but useful for moving fallen trees out of the way. While a chainsaw is definitely best they are relatively expensive, require training, PPE (Personal Protection Equipment such as gloves, earmuffs, hard-hat and chaps) and are bulky. A good alternative is a quality bowsaw, axe, gloves, drag chain and a winch. A few people working with some of these tools can remove apparently impossible trees in short order, although the chainsaw is quicker and can demolish even larger trees. The drag chain can be used without a winch as the vehicle can simply pull the tree out of the way, but a more effective method is to use an offset pull with a winch and snatch block to move the tree away from the track.

Personal Protection Equipment – gloves, helmet, eye protection, chaps and work boots. On chainsaw training courses you get shown enough photographs to make this investment.

A sharp bowsaw can deal with smaller logs quickly and effectively.

Sharpening a chainsaw's chain is not difficult and essential if the saw is to remain efficient. I generally sharpen mine a little after every heavy use of the saw which may be once a day. A little, often, is better than a major sharpening infrequently.

spades, shovels and picks

A spade is a digging tool with a "gooseneck". A shovel is for shifting loose dirt. Ideally you want both, but in practice, go with the spade. The spade is not as efficient as the shovel for moving loose dirt, but the spade is far superior for digging which is more important. A pick is a tool designed for breaking earth. You definitely can't shift any loose material with it. Of the three, take a spade. Some tools are multifunction and have different heads for picks, shovels, spade and axes.

You will certainly need to dig if you are bogged in sand, and quite often in mud. Spades can also be used to reshape a track, even slightly, such as creating a small terrace on a side angle. However, keep any track changes to a minimum for environment considerations; if you can't drive it without a lot of digging, find another way or winch.

1 & 3 Shovels are best carried outside the vehicle either on dedicated carriers or on roof racks, as they are long and get dirty.

2 This shovel has an extension handle, very useful for sand work. The shorter handle is best for digging earth. 4WD kit should be as versatile as possible.

4 Shovels are essential in sand and very useful everywhere else.

SECTION 4

GOING TOURING

CHAPTER 40

CHOOSING A 4WD

This chapter does not tell you which vehicle to buy. Like the rest of the book, it informs you so you can make your own decision. The advice and examples are generalisations, and everyone's different, with different needs. However, we have to start somewhere, so the basic assumption is that you want a vehicle in which you can travel offroad to some extent, through the likes of sand, forest tracks, desert dunes, the Outback and beyond.

With that said, the vehicles on the market can, loosely, be categorised as follows:

Type	Description	Examples
Old Wagons	Medium-large wagon, sometimes with 7 seats, generally dating to pre-electronic days, generally pre-2005.	80 Series, most 100 Series, Pajeros before 2000, Discovery 1/2, Nissan Patrol up to Y62, Jackaroo
Modern Wagons	As above but newer with electronic aids such as traction control, safety features like side airbags, typically 2005 onwards.	Discovery 3/4, Prado 120/150, Pajero NP onwards
Old Utes	Utes with no electronic driving aids, typically prior to 2007-9	Holden Rodeo, Ford Courier
Modern Utes	Utes with electronic driving aids, specifically traction control and stability control (Chapter 9), typically from 2009 onwards	Ford Ranger PK, VW Amarok
Luxo-Wagons	Expensive, premium luxury 4WDs, all wagons.	Range Rover, VW Touraeg, any BMW or Audi , any Lexus
Softroaders	Offroader without low-range designed for light-duty work	Freelander, Santa Fe, Captiva, CR-V, Kluger, Subarus and many more! Some Luxo-Wagons fall into the softroader category too, mostly defined by whether they have low-range or not.

The Discovery 3 is a Luxo-Wagon with immense all-round capabilities, but is expensive and complex. The Subaru XV is a Softroader with rough-terrain capability, the Jeep Wrangler is a great fun offroader as is the FJ Cruiser. The Ford Ranger is a Modern Ute and the 80 Series is (was) an Old Wagon until it was modified, as you can do with those cars!

Here's a general summary of the choices:

- **Old Wagons:** Simple, cheap to buy and sufficiently capable, these are the default choice for many. They can be made very capable with investments such as cross-axle locking differentials, suspension lifts and tyres, but their age means some money may well need to be spent. Safety and driveability is not up to modern standards but that doesn't matter – they're good enough for most people and they'll get you around Australia just as well as the newer cars. Budget extra money for a thorough servicing and parts replacement.

- **Modern Wagons:** The main reason to buy newer wagons is for safety, refinement and handling. You don't need to modify these vehicles as much as the older ones to get the same level of offroad capability as the new ones have effective traction control, stronger engines and more assured handling. They are also more city-friendly.

- **Old Utes:** These vehicles can be really basic. Although they get places on and offroad they aren't in the same class as Modern Utes or any wagon as they lack clearance, power, suspension articulation and traction aids. Handling or safety is nowhere near as good as newer cars, and towing capacity is often limited. But they'll still get you around Australia, they're cheap and they can certainly take a load. For some people, that's all you need.

- **Modern Utes:** These vehicles are encroaching onto wagon territory in terms of handling, offroad capability, safety and towing ability. Anyone considering a new wagon should look at a new ute, and consider the advantage of the huge loadspace combined with a cheaper driveaway price.

- **Luxo-Wagons:** Almost by definition these vehicles are not for modifying, which limits potential. But with the right tyres and recovery points the more offroad-oriented versions will go pretty much anywhere and in considerable style and comfort. Many retired couples treat themselves to such a car and why not, you've earned it! If you are looking for your dream car, don't accept someone telling you 'you can't go bush in that', but do be aware these cars are not designed for continuous, hardcore offroading, and are difficult to accessorise.

- **Softroaders:** As with the Luxos, don't be told that you can't take these bush. But, if you do, be prepared to go slower and have to turn back more often, and to suffer increased maintenance bills. If you're serious about offroading and looking at a softie to save money you're often better off with a cheaper low-range wagon, even a secondhand one.

There is always at least one exception to the rule – for example some VW Amaroks have no low-range yet are almost as good as the low-range vehicles, the Range Rover is one of the few luxury vehicles with real offroad capability, the Suzuki Grand Vitara is one of the few sharp-handling smaller 4WDs (and it has low-range too!), and the Land Rover Defender is an exception to just about every other vehicle on the market.

For a more detailed consideration the next step is to look at the various attributes required of an offroad touring vehicle.

the essentials

tyres & recovery points

There are very few non-negotiable factors for any of the vehicle types, but two absolutely essential ones are tyres and recovery points.

- **Tyres:** If the car comes with a space-saver spare then you must take a full-sized spare on a full-sized rim, and that may not fit in the space-saver storage location. You then need to fit a rear carrier, or put the spare on the roofrack. This is not a recommendation, it's a requirement. You also need to ensure that offroad tyres are available for your vehicle (Chapter 7).

- **Recovery points:** Fit a towbar at the back and recover from that (Chapter 32). At the front, you must have solid recovery points connected directly to and in line with the chassis. Screw-in recovery eyes are not acceptable. If the car doesn't have a front recovery and cannot be modified to suit then it is not an acceptable offroad tourer and should stick to well-formed dirt roads.

Immediately rule out any vehicle that fails these two basic tests. The two classes of vehicles that are most likely to have problems on these fronts are the Softroaders and Luxo-Wagons.

what's best for you

Now the essentials are out the way it's a question of balancing cost and capability in certain areas.

accessory and modification potential

You may decide you don't need any accessories at all. This is fine, but many people change their minds later and it'd be good to keep the option open. The first thing to do is to ensure any design flaws specific to that model for offroading – for example, differentials prone to breaking, or weak doors with spares on the back – are fixed. If you want an easy time of vehicle setup, have a flick through the catalogues from the likes of Ironman, ARB, TJM and Opposite Lock and if you don't see your make and model listed then reconsider; the expertise and gear may not be readily available out in the market. Typically, the newer the vehicle the harder it is to fabricate a solution.

The Luxo-Wagons and Softroaders tend to be weakest on the accessory front. Very new wagons may also be a problem if the aftermarket waits to see demand, although for popular offroad models accessories are developed in time for the vehicle release. Note that some accessories for a given vehicle may not fit all variants of that vehicle – for example, snorkels may fit diesel vehicles but not the petrol-engined equivalent, and the same for dual battery kits. Generally, the diesel auto mid-spec models are the ones most likely to be targeted by accessory developers.

fuel

In remote areas 95 or 98 RON petrol is not always available, and neither is LPG, but diesel is never a problem. This is not to say all tourers should be diesel, far from it. However, don't buy a car that drinks only premium petrol, or relies on LPG, and expect to have the flexibility of remote servos enjoyed by the diesels. Diesel engines are also significantly more efficient under touring conditions of heavy loads in rough terrain, which translates to extra range. In terms of pure offroad capability there is very little in it; the driver will make the difference.

auto/manual

There is no longer any logical reason to buy a manual. In general, modern autos are just as fuel efficient as manuals, if not more so, and are easier to drive and more capable both on and offroad. Automatic transmissions are also now very reliable. Manuals may be slightly cheaper and technically even more reliable, but the main reason to buy a manual is because you enjoy shifting gears yourself, not because there's any advantage in capability. Increasing numbers of modern vehicles will be auto only, particularly softroaders and Luxo-Wagons, and the Australian market is known to prefer autos.

body style

Here you're mostly looking at short or long wheelbase wagons, or in the case of utes single, dual or extracab. The shortie wagons are not popular in Australia because we don't need their manoeuvrability, the price difference isn't much compared to the long wheelbase wagons and shorties are limited in carrying bulk loads. In places like the UK and New Zealand shorties make a lot more sense. But on the other hand, if there's just two of you, a shortie might be all you need.

Shorties are cute but impractical.

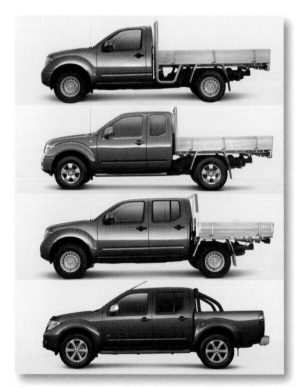

The ute variants simply play off cabin space against loadspace. The problem with the singlecabs (top) is that you can't really recline the seats and there's little space for gear like cameras, bags and coats. Most tourers tend to go for the extracab (second from top), which may have small seats behind the front row, or the dualcab (bottom two). Loadspace even in the dualcab isn't a concern unless you're looking at carrying a camper setup on the tray, in which case the extracab may be the way to go. The higher spec levels tend to be available as dualcabs only, with singles only available as low-spec models. Utes also have the advantage of being able to swap trays, as shown in the bottom two images. The top-spec models also typically have more powerful engines and may be auto-only. Generally, the utes are not as well specified as wagons.

reliability

Let's address the big question. You might be thinking of a Luxo-Wagon but are concerned about reliability relative to an Old Wagon or simpler vehicle. There is no simple answer, but here are some facts to help:

1. The more complex the vehicle the greater the chance of failure of some description.
2. You can't quantify something as abstract as 'reliability'.
3. The question isn't 'Which is most reliable?', but 'Is it reliable enough?'.

It's not easy to make a decision based on reliability. Taking point 1, a new 79 Series Cruiser will have a lower chance of failure than a Discovery 4, for example, because the latter has more things to go wrong, such as air suspension, and relies on electronics to operate. But how much more reliable will it be? Nobody can say, exactly. So point 3 comes into play and the question is then 'Is the D4

reliable enough?'. Or, let's say instead of reliability you're talking about range from a single tank: you need 550 km and you're comparing two 4WDs which run 600 and 700 km. One's better that the other, but both meet the need, and much depends on how you drive – it is hard to measure the advantages (point 2).

So here's some general advice. If you want to absolutely maximise reliability and ability to recover then buy a new, simple, manual vehicle at the lowest possible trim spec (a ute, 79 or similar while they're still on the market) take spare parts and learn how to fix it. The vehicles least likely to cause issues are the simplest and newest ones. The most problematic are the Luxo-Wagons and Softroaders because of their complexity and because their design focus is not on heavy-duty offroad work. Utes do well on reliability because they are often designed with commercial operations in mind, whereas wagons are not, so perhaps a Modern Ute is the best blend of reliability and modern capability.

However, most people will be willing to trade off some reliability for other features, in the same way that we take only two spare tyres bush, not three or four or five. In general terms, if you take a Luxo-Wagon bush that is well prepared, drive it carefully and have a backup plan, then you can comfortably travel Australia. You may encounter issues that simpler vehicles don't, but that's the price you pay for the choice you make. Lots of people travel the outback in top-end vehicles with no problems at all.

The final point to consider is that, regardless of your vehicle's reliability, you should always plan for it to malfunction at the worst possible time.

costs

Fuel economy is just a small part of the cost equation. Here are all the costs you need to consider:

- **Purchase cost:** This ties up more money in the car.

- **Accessory cost:** Consider not only how much accessories cost, but how many you need to buy. For example, Prados have both standard long-range tanks and spares on the back wheel, and the Discovery 3 has neither. Factor in 'design flaw' modifications (see 'Accessory and modification potential' above). The typical offroad driver spends around $10,000 on modifying their vehicle, but that figure may vary from $5,000 to $50,000. Refer to Chapter 40, and leave room in the budget for the kit-out.

- **Servicing cost and spare parts:** Remember to use the arduous-use servicing schedule which means servicing will be about twice as often as normal. Offroad tyres wear out more quickly than standard rubber – in fact, as touring 4WDs are typically heavier than standard, everything else wears out more quickly, even just driving around town, from brake pads to suspension. And if you have height-adjustable suspension it'll cost more to run over a car's lifetime than simple metal springs.

- **Depreciation:** If you sell the car having done some offroad work, and potentially at high mileage, this may be a problem. Selling a Defender which has done a lot of offroad work isn't a problem, but selling a Kluger in the same condition would be.

- **Fuel:** If fuel costs $1.50/L and you drive 20,000km a year over 5 years then a 2L/100km saving will translate to $900 per year, or $4,500. That saving could be wiped out by the cost of extra accessories on the more fuel-efficient vehicle, or a big maintenance bill, or depreciation. Consider the bigger costs, not the headline fuel figure, and estimate the ADR81/01 figure plus around 50% because all those modifications you make do nothing for efficiency.

In short, it is best to spend less of your budget on the car itself when it comes to offroading than you'd spend on a roadcar – let's say you have $60k to spend, maybe go for a $45k car, $10k accessories, and save $5k for extra servicing, maintenance etc., instead of $59k on the car and then no money to run it offroad.

offroad capability

The first and most important point is that all the low-range vehicles are capable of reaching most offroad touring destinations in Australia, but Softroaders need to be singled out as having significantly lower offroad capability than the other types. Chapter 28 has more details, but in short you'll get a softroader to many places, but not all, and it will be slower, with more wear and tear on the vehicle, particularly when loaded.

In general, the newer vehicles are more capable than the older ones, and wagons are better both on and offroad than the utes, though the gap is narrowing with Modern Utes. The Luxo-Wagons are a bit of a mixed bag, from the likes of the BMWs with little capability to the Range Rovers and LX570s which can hold their own against the hardcore Jeep Wrangler.

onroad ride and handling

'Ride' refers to the comfort of your travels, the 'waftability' of the car, expanded here to include the ability to cruise over long distances. 'Handling' is the car's ability to be hustled quickly – the zest the enthusiast driver craves.

The Luxo-Wagons are clear winners in both categories, followed by Modern Wagons. Softroaders tend to have a nice enough ride (when lightly loaded over smooth terrain) but are by no means sharp handlers. Bottom of the pile are the Old Utes which neither handle nor ride comfortably. The Modern Utes approach, but don't quite match the Modern Wagons.

It is important to note that the standards for ride and handling increase year on year. A ute of today might not score highly for ride and handling, but that's compared against today's wagons, for example. Compare the same ute to the wagons of a decade ago and it'd be right up there – and a decade ago people managed to drive long distances just fine. In other words, even the 'worst' car in a review may be better than what you need.

family and around town

The Softroaders win this one, being nimble, safe, efficient, easy to drive and park. Next would be Modern Wagons and Luxo-Wagons. Any ute is less than ideal as rear visibility is poor, turning circles are wide and the vehicles are relatively long. Luxo-Cars may have height-adjustable suspension which is a bonus in cities.

safety

If you want a safe 4WD look for a high rating from ANCAP via www.howsafeisyourcar.com.au. In particular, check for the availability of electronic stability control (Chapter 9) and side airbags. What you're also looking for, in general, is a new design, not just a new car. For example, a 2005 Discovery 3 is likely to be safer than a 2007 Pajero as the Disco was completely redesigned from '05, whereas the '07 Pajero is on much the same base as the '00 model. That said, cars are continually updated and often this includes extra safety equipment, so the newer the vehicle the safer it is, both in terms of preventative safety and post-crash safety. The safest vehicles will be the Luxo-Wagons, followed by Modern wagons, Softroaders and Modern utes. The least safe are Old Utes, then Old Wagons. But for most people, any vehicle with stability control and side airbags will be safe enough. The final factor is size –it's hidden in the safety ratings, but all else being equal the bigger the vehicle the safer it is in a crash.

space and carrying capacity

The utes have a clear win here, with acres more room once a canopy is installed, and significantly higher payloads (Chapter 6) than the wagons. Everything else will be space limited by comparison, particularly the Luxo-Wagons and Softroaders. As with most things 4WD, buy something with more capacity than you need. It is not a good idea to pack so that you use every last cubic centimetre of space – you're likely to be close to overloading the vehicle, things never pack away neatly in the bush, and you won't have any emergency carrying room. Rather than jamming things in, look at a bigger vehicle or tow.

This photo shows how much longer a ute is relative to a wagon, with its significantly longer cargo area. But you need to budget for a canopy too!

towing

You don't want to be using the vehicle at its maximum towing capacity, so if you have a 2500kg trailer that's best towed with a 3500kg rated vehicle you have some capability in reserve for hot or difficult conditions. The leaders here are the Modern Wagons and the Luxo-Wagons. Modern Utes do quite well, but some of them cannot tow their full rating while at their GVM. Softroaders are not a good choice for heavy towing, lacking offroad capability and the basic towing capacity, and the older vehicles start to lack grunt, if not outright towing capacity. The newest vehicles incorporate electronic trailer stability control to correct sway (Chapter 30) and cameras to help guide the vehicle for hookup.

The Discovery 4's rear camera projects a line showing where the towball will go, just one of several useful trailer hookup tricks. This sort of device cannot easily be fitted aftermarket. Anything that makes trailer hookup easier is a known and proven marriage saver, next to easier navigation systems.

other considerations

Here are some more things to think about:

what about a trailer?

A trailer can change the whole equation, and whether you intend to tow should have a direct effect on your choice of vehicle and how you modify it. Trailers can be pulled over some very rough terrain (Chapter 30) with the right vehicle – for example my Defender has pulled trailers over terrain I could not drive a Freelander over (and I tried, hard!). All of a sudden you don't need as much carrying capacity, so a short wheel-base softroader can beat a ute for load. The advantages of trailers are space for gear, a stable and comfy base to set up camp and the ability to have the trailer permanently set up ready to go – no packing required, just back the car up and off you go. The disadvantages are the cost of the trailer, restrictions on some routes, reduction in offroad capability and the extra fuel (10-20%) required to pull it. In practice, the advantages often outweigh the disadvantages and trailers are very much an option for touring offroaders.

new or secondhand

A secondhand vehicle offers significant savings and may come with lots of offroad gear already fitted. It may well have been used offroad but if it's been well looked after, and you check it out thoroughly (Appendix A), then that need not be an issue. It could in fact be a real bargain, as you will make a great saving on accessories and won't have to pay for them to be fitted. High country miles may not be a problem either and could mean less wear on the car than lots of short city trips or school runs.

A new vehicle will offer factory warranty, but that will be invalidated to some degree through modifications. There is no hard and fast rule, and good luck getting anything in writing, but in general most manufacturers of mainstream low-range vehicles do honour warranty if you use the car offroad. The exception is modifications where the modified part isn't warranted, and neither is any effect it may have caused. For example, put a suspension lift in, break a CV joint and you may find the manufacturer disclaims responsibility on the basis of additional stress on the joints. Softroader owners can expect more trouble with offroad claims than purpose-built vehicles such as utilitarian low-rangers.

trim level

It is a personal decision as to whether to go for the base 'poverty pack' model, GX, or the top-end luxury version of the same vehicle, so here are some pointers to help.

- **Don't write off the basic models:** Base models these days may include cruise control, aircon, electric windows and mirrors, reversing cameras, central locking, satnav, Bluetooth for phones, adjustable seats and more. Not so long ago that used to be the province of luxury trim levels. And these days all vehicles have lots of safety features, whereas before there was a strong bias towards safety features in top-end trim specs.

- **Look at whether it'd be cheaper to add certain features you want aftermarket:** Satnav is an excellent case in point; a cheap Android or Apple tablet can navigate you very well and there are specialists who can make it look like it's part of the original car.

- **Be aware of the disadvantages of luxury models:** Remember that luxury models are more complicated. They may have slightly different parts to standard cars and these are typically more expensive. The Luxo model may in fact take you backwards with 19" rims when you really wanted 17" (Chapter 7), and accessory manufacturers typically produce their products for the mid to lower spec vehicles, so higher spec models may miss out or have features lost such as front parking sensors. The Luxo spec will also be heavier (Chapter 6), 2635kg for the 200 Series GX vs 2720kg (85kg), for example, and that typically means a reduction in payload. Luxury specs also tend to depreciate faster than more mid-level models.

- **On the other hand, consider their advantages:** The Luxo models can provide useful capabilities such as towing hookup aids, and HID (bi-xenon) headlights (Chapter 40). The more highly adjustable seats can be useful too – if the seat's not right then don't buy the car – and these days the seats are very much part of the overall safety design so are not always easily swapped out. Leather seats are also easier to clean than cloth. Luxo models may also have better soundproofing, audio systems and other little conveniences such as keyless entry and central compartments with coolers that don't always show up on the spec sheets, and these can combine to make what is apparently the same vehicle quite different in real life. Aftermarket equivalent accessories won't be warranted, and may not be as well integrated. Top-spec models have even more safety features – extra airbags, active safety systems such as autonomous emergency braking (AEB) so the car stops for you in an emergency, active cruise control and more.

- **Check that the features you need are available in each model:** There may be transmission and engine options only available in one trim level. For example, if you must have a manual you are unlikely to find that option in a luxury spec, and if you prefer a simpler, less powerful engine, you may not need the powerful engine offered by a Luxo.

But in the end, you're buying a car to enjoy and be proud of. If there is a feature on the Luxo list you want then by all means buy the car, and don't let anyone talk you out it. Your touring 4WD is more than just a car, it's a way of life and it has to be right for you.

new car factory options

Mostly the factory accessories are just bling, and the ones that aren't bling are typically not as good as the aftermarket, and more expensive. But there are a couple of caveats – firstly, factory accessories won't affect warranty, and secondly there may be options that you really need to specify before the car is built. An example is the e-locker (cross-axle differential lock) in modern Land Rovers. Carefully peruse the options list!

A factory-fit spare carrier was an option for Touaregs and one well worth taking.

what you'll actually do

All the advice in this chapter is logical. But cars are mostly a purchase of the heart. It is my belief that since cars can give us so much pleasure of ownership you should buy the car that makes you happy, which is not always the car of logical choice. So buy what you want, enjoy the vehicle while being well aware of any disadvantages.

There's a variant of Modern Wagon – ute-based budget wagons such as the Challenger and Colorado 7. These wagons are more basic and less refined that the likes of Pajero and Prado, but offer good levels of safety, offroad capability, and (usually) seven seats, making them a viable choice for tourers.

A Hyundai Santa Fe leading a group of Nissan Patrols. That weekend I looked for the hardest possible tracks in the area of Robe, but the Santy conquered all, and even recovered a Patrol. Who needs a Patrol? Well, we all do. I had to use every last skerrick of my experience and knowledge to get the loaded Santy over through the harder sections whereas the Patrols cruised for the most part. As usual, softies can often get there but there's no question they do it harder.

The Ford Ranger PX (foreground) and precedessor PK, Old Ute and Modern Ute. Both are part-time 4WDs with ostensibly similar suspension, but there's a world of difference in handling, safety, towing, on and offroad capability, as well as general refinement.

CHAPTER 41

VEHICLE ACCESSORIES & MODIFICATIONS

You can spend a fortune, but you don't need to. There are just a few must-haves, and the rest is up to you.

A "modification" is typically the replacement of an existing part, like new suspension or tyres, or something extra directly related to vehicle capability. An "accessory" is typically something not permanently attached to the vehicle, like a fridge, or not directly related to vehicle capability, such as a winch. However, these definitions are by no means fixed and nor are opinions about what's best. Ask 15 people for opinions on accessories and modifications and you'll get 30 answers. However, I have split this chapter into three sections:

- **The essentials:** The first items a touring offroader should buy (in my opinion) and why.

- **Beyond the basics:** Useful stuff for touring, not as critical as the essentials, but still kit you'll mostly need (or want).

- **The specials:** Major changes to the vehicle.

Within each section the kit is listed in approximate order of importance.

It's very tempting to go for the sexy kit first, like locking diffs, big lift-suspension upgrades and so on, ignoring things like cargo barriers, fire extinguishers, radios and first-aid kits. Don't fall into this trap; get the safety equipment first. You'll be glad you did. I've seen a vehicle go up in flames, all of a sudden. I've used my first-aid kit many a time. After those sorts of experiences you become very, very glad you had the right safety gear with you.

The second area to concentrate on is basic recovery gear and essential mods. The argument

"if I get the lockers I'm less likely to need recovery" doesn't hold – you'll ultimately still need recovering. The more recovery gear you take, the more options you have. The more options you have, the safer you are.

Finally, and only once your touring gear is complete, you can start to look at improving your vehicle's offroad performance with lockers and so forth, and extra recovery gear and touring accessories. However, it must be said that pretty much any low-range 4WD with decent tyres and a small suspension lift can be driven into almost any offroad touring destination in Australia. There is, in my opinion, no need to highly modify a touring vehicle with giant tyres and the like.

You may also need to fix design flaws with your vehicle, for example adding a long-range tank if it's a thirsty petrol engine with little fuel capacity, or a spare wheel carrier. The type of trips you do will have an influence; anyone planning on spending a lot of time in Cape York should prioritise a snorkel, whereas someone planning a lot of easy beach driving need not worry about mud tyres and someone who is going to tow will need a visit to a suspension shop pretty quickly.

is it legal?

Make sure your vehicle complies with the relevant authority's road rules. Some modifications, for example extra lights, larger tyres and suspension mods, may breach road safety regulations. While there are some very good experts in the industry, there are many who subscribe to the "fit and forget" principle and either don't know or don't care about any regulations. The onus is on you as an owner and you should inform your insurer in writing, as it does affect their risk and in any case you'd want the modification covered. Don't assume that all Australian states and territories operate the same road rules and laws. They do not, for reasons which are well beyond my ability to understand – the roads and conditions look pretty similar all round – so what's legal in one state may well not be in another.

planning

Many accessories and modifications are dependent on each other, and you don't want to have to re-buy kit or undo work. For example, think about buying a bullbar with a winch option, just in case, and buying suspension that can take more of a load than you first consider. This also applies to electrical work – nobody ever removes wiring, so plan out the extra electrics with a good-sized fusebox and heavy-duty wiring.

buying tips

You get what you pay for, and with some of the mods above you're talking about safety. Compromising on tyres, suspension, cargo barriers and recovery gear is a very bad idea. And beware of cheap goods, often from larger outlets. Cheap driving lights will fall apart. Cheap air compressors will take forever to inflate a tyre, and then overheat.

How do you choose? Use this guide, talk to experienced people, ask on discussion forums, read the magazines and best of all join a club (Chapter 42) and see what others use.

OK, you might not want quite the amount of navigation devices, radios and assorted electronics crammed inside this cockpit but it does illustrate the value of planning a fit-out and whenever you work, assuming you'll want to add more kit later.

the essentials

recovery gear

Essential, and covered in Section 3. The driving techniques (Section 2) cover specific gear for specific terrain. Chapter 36 covers winching.

A good starting point is an all-in-one kit sold at any offroad retail shop or show.

fire extinguishers and first-aid kits

What it is	Something that puts out fires and therefore saves lives, vehicles, forests etc. A first-aid kit is exactly what it sounds like.	
Why you'd want one	I've seen a vehicle catch fire. It was sitting idle, engine off, key out. Had been for about 20 minutes. I've also had one of my own vehicles catch fire after a battery came loose and shorted. Lesson learned. Now I carry a big fire extinguisher, easily accessible. In some cases carrying one might be a requirement for access to some areas.	
Tips	Get a fire extinguisher designed for typical vehicle fires. These tend to be electrical, although occasionally dry grass can collect and ignite. This means a powder extinguisher, but remember that these are not good for cooking oil fires, which is where you'll need a fire blanket, a good item to carry in any case. The first-aid kit should be designed for remote areas. Items in the first-aid kit should include infection control items, saline to clean eyes or wounds, bandages, gauze, dressings, burns sheet, sharp scissors and more. Do a first-aid course and follow advice. The first-aid kit should be complementary to your survival kit as many items, for example a thermal accident blanket and sharp knife, are common to both. Both items should be very easily accessible and the location known to everyone in the convoy.	

survival kit

What it is	The bag you'd grab if the vehicle goes up in flames.	
Why you'd want one	If it all goes wrong and you need to spend some time out in the bush.	
Tips	The best advice is from specialist survival courses, but ours includes a small first-aid kit, Swiss army knife, notepad and pencil, hand-powered torch, flint, newspaper, compass, four thermal blankets, fishing wire, water purification tablets, whistle and gloves. The priorities are shelter, warmth and water – humans can go a long time without food.	

cargo barrier

What it is	A metal mesh between the rear of the vehicle and its occupants. See below for photos.
Why you'd want one	To stop the contents of the rear flying forwards and injuring the occupants in the event of a crash, and to make the rear storage compartment an easier place to store items. A cargo barrier also acts, to some degree, as a rollover cage, helping prevent deformation of the cabin. Cargo barriers are great. Get one.
Tips	Make sure your cargo barrier is compatible with side airbags if they are fitted to your vehicle. If necessary, holes can be cut in the barrier for child restraint points. Some barriers are half-height and thus lighter. Some can be positioned in two locations, behind the second row and behind the first row.

Our Discovery has to transform from seven-seater to offroad tourer. Fitting the cargo barrier, rubber mat, storage system and fridge (no slider) takes only 10 minutes.

Cargo barriers are typically held in place by four mounts secured with removeable thumbbolts. Thin things like tarps can live between the second row and the barrier – use every little bit of space!

The shelf system, secured by turnbuckles.

interior storage systems

What it is	A set of shelves, trays or drawers that convert the back of the vehicle into a storage system. See start of this Chapter for more photos.
Why you'd want one	Even with a cargo barrier, you definitely need to subdivide the space in the back because: • It gives easier access to get things in and out without removing lots of gear • Some things will need bolting down, like the fridge • You'll need to segregate dirty/oily things from clean things • This efficiently uses space up to the top of the vehicle
Tips	There are as many storage systems as there are 4WDs. There are several manufacturers that provide off-the-shelf (no pun intended) systems, with different options, but many people just head down to the local hardware shop and put something together themselves. Many systems have pull-out drawers. Others are just shelves which you put removable storage containers under and over. I'm a fan of the latter as it means that I can take all my winch gear in a ready-packed box to a recovery, or just pull out a toolbox and take that somewhere too. With a drawer you can't do that. Our gear lives in boxes and the boxes get loaded into the vehicle's shelves depending on where we're going – see previous page for the photos.

In a touring 4WD every little bit of room is precious, and you do want to keep things from sliding around offroad.

A popular modification to rear doors is a simple fold-out table.

tyres

What it is	Replacement tyres (Chapter 7).
Why you'd want one	There aren't many must-have accessories but this is one of them. The standard tyres on a 4WD are passenger tyres and are not designed for offroad use. They will puncture too easily and provide insufficient grip. A change to a Light Truck (LT) construction tyre should be seriously considered, as should a change to a tread pattern of at least all-terrain. If your vehicle is the likes of a ute or has fairly strong tyres designed for a load there is less need to swap tyres, but if you have a high-performance 4WD with high-speed, low profile tyres then it is extremely important that you change these before you go bush. Check also whether the vehicle has a TUST (temporary use space tyre) and if so, get a real spare.
Tips	It's a sad fact, but many tyre shops are not particularly familiar with the regulations. Make sure you do your own research and remember the regulations vary state-by-state. If you are considering changing rim sizes do that at the same time and sell the old kit as a set. Often changing down a rim size means a cheaper tyre which offsets the cost of the changeover.

Road and all-terrain tyres.

suspension

What it is	Replacement springs and shocks (Chapter 5).
Why you'd want one	The standard 4WD suspension is not designed to have the vehicle be loaded up and driven offroad. Sounds surprising? Consider how many people actually use their 4WDs offroad or even to carry a great weight. So the manufacturers don't bother spending the money on heavy-duty quality suspension. They only need to make a favourable impression on the test drive, which is done lightly loaded on bitumen.
	Ever seen a standard 4WD, fully loaded, driving along with the nose pointing skywards? That's standard suspension. Don't trust it to take a fully loaded 4WD into the outback.
	Of course, if you do light-duty offroading, don't venture into the outback and don't load the vehicle up too much then standard suspension may be perfectly adequate, especially if the vehicle is relatively new.
	However, if you do go for aftermarket kit, consider a small suspension lift, at the very least to have the vehicle riding at normal height when it's loaded.

Tips	Only buy suspension from people who ask careful questions about what you'll be doing with the vehicle and what else you'll fit to it. For touring purposes both mono or twintube designs both work perfectly well (see Chapter 5). A bigger diameter tube is not necessarily better as there are other means of dissipating heat, such as the type of oil used, and for most tourers every quality shock should resist fade so the differentiators are based on suitability for the purpose and quality. Suspension tune is also quite subjective, as some prefer a stiffly responsive ride, whereas others prefer a waterbed approach to their vehicles.
	A two inch lift is a good idea as by the time the vehicle is loaded it will be close to normal. Buy suspension based on the vehicle's end-state, not what it looks like before you finish kitting it out. Tourers do not generally need remote-shocks or expensive comp suspension. Remember stone guards, get an alignment done, inform your insurance company and get springs as well as shocks. A good suspension setup is worth its weight in gold. If there is a choice, err on the side of the stiffer setup as it is better to suffer a slightly harsher ride unloaded than to be scared by a too-soft setup when towing or laden. Consider helper airbags when towing or laden.

A typical aftermarket kit - four springs and shocks. This works up till around 2" of lift, after which extra parts are typically needed and the job becomes more complex, usually requiring engineering approval to be legal.

Replacement suspension on a Terracan, with a small lift and thus no additional work needed beyond the springs and shocks. Aftermarket suspension is usually coloured differently to the grey or black of the original gear. Beyond lifts of about 2" the modifications for a legal and proper job start to add up and become both complex and expensive.

Remember also that the average touring 4WD has accessories fitted so is heavier that the stock vehicle (Chapter 6), and this by definition means it needs different suspension.

Your 4WD's suspension is simply not designed for carrying heavy loads over uneven terrain for hours on end, and even aftermarket gear wears out. A suspension upgrade is very important for safety and transforms a loaded vehicle when offroad or on dirt roads, and particularly when towing.

Even aftermarket suspension wears out over time so should be replaced after approximately 100-200,000km depending on use. New suspension can transform a vehicle and make owners reconsider sale.

tools and parts

What it is	For fixing and modifying
Why you'd want one	All sorts of reasons. You can tow a trailer with the contents of your local tool shop, or just take the basics which is closer to what you'll really need on a trip. Essentials are:

- Shifting spanners (two sizes)
- Flat and Phillips head screwdrivers
- Knife (best as part of a Leatherman or Swiss Army knife multi-tool (not a cheap version!))
- Socket set
- Pliers
- Hacksaw
- Hammer
- File
- Multimeter
- Mole wrench
- Wheel brace and breaker bar

Not tools, but useful repair items:

- Workshop manual
- Cable ties
- Fuses
- Electrical wire
- Hose clamps
- Thread lock
- WD-40
- Jump leads
- Nuts, bolts, screws
- Emergency windscreen
- Tyre repair – or at least plugs
- Allen keys

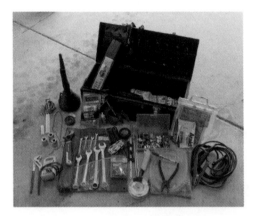

Some tools and their box. I have a separate set of tools just for the car which always live in their box, so I don't find I've "borrowed" a tool from the kit and forgotten to replace it.

Spare parts you may wish to take are dependent on the particular vehicle and trip but there are a few points true to all trips:

- Prevention is better than cure. Replacing items like hoses and belts before you go (and maybe carrying the old ones as spares), plus a good pre-trip service is better than carrying a lot of parts.
- There is no point weighing your car down with everything as all that weight will just increase the chance of a problem. Don't take esoteric parts that would require a complex vehicle to be taken to a dealer anyway.
- By far and away the most common reason vehicles are immobilised is a tyre problem. Take an extra spare and learn how to carry out repairs.

	That said, there are some spares which should be considered for all longer trips:
	<ul><li>Air filter, fuel filter</li><li>Extra spare tyres</li><li>Difficult-to-get fluids (vehicle dependent)</li><li>Hoses, belts</li><li>Workshop manual</li></ul>
Tips	Even if you can't use all this kit, someone else may be able to.

air compressor

What it is	A portable pump for your tyres.
Why you'd want one	To reinflate tyres after dropping pressures, or to re-seat a tyre on rim after it comes off. There are plenty of other uses for compressed air around the household.
Tips	Compressors can be permanently mounted to the vehicle or portable, in a case. Permanent mounting positions include under the bonnet or inside under the seats. The advantage of permanent mounting is that it may not take up cargo storage room, but this obviously limits flexibility. Some aftermarket accessories, notably ARB's AirLockers, require a compressor which can then be used for other purposes such as inflating tyres. Most compressors are 12V electric but there are quicker ones driven by the engine. Make sure you mount the compressor in an area where it can dissipate heat and get a clean supply of air. Do not buy cheap compressors which simply fail and cut out after the first tyre, it really is one of the classic offroading false economies. Buy only from reputable brands. This lesson is learned again and again. Quality modern compressors should all be able to re-seat tyre beads. Consider also extension hoses if you tow trailers.

If you use a trailer then the standard hoses may not reach all the way; this is one solution or just use a longer hose. I made my own hoses up, preferring the long coiled hose to the wriggly yellow one supplied.

1   Portable compressor. When using a compressor always run your engine as compressors can quickly flatten batteries. The extra couple of volts also means the compressor runs more quickly, reducing air-up time.

2   Under-bonnet compressor. Bonnet open so it can get lots of cool, fresh air which makes it more efficient.

3   Attachments for different purposes.

4   Under the seat is another popular location for a compressor.

5   One way to inflate tyres is to use a compressed air tank, either a scuba one you get refilled, or a temporary one kept up to pressure by a conventional compressor. This vehicle has large tyres so needs a lot of air quickly.

mud mats

What it is	Heavy-duty rubber mats with raised edges, which prevent any mud, water, sand or other material from leaving the mat.	
Why you'd want one	Mud, sand and all sorts of terrain are fun. They're more fun outside the car than in, but you can't always clean your feet before you get in. That's where mud mats come in, collecting all the great outdoors before it gets stomped into your vehicle's interior.	
Tips	Another advantage is that they make handy recovery mats if placed under the wheels, or just as work mats that you can drop small nuts and bolts in while out in the field and expect to see them again. Recommended.	

uhf radio
(in car, handheld)

What it is	A CB radio. Allows communication between people, either fitted in the car or just carried as a handheld.
Why you'd want one	Communication; safety, fun, planning, decisions.
Tips	A handheld and an in-car unit are ideal. Make sure you get one of the new 80-channel units.

tyre gauge

What it is	A means of telling you what pressure is in your tyres!
Why you'd want one	Difficult to think of why you wouldn't, given the importance of tyre pressures. You CANNOT accurately gauge pressures to the precision you need by eye, or feel, or a kick.
Tips	It's best to get a gauge that has decent measurement intervals of under 40psi. Some gauges go up to 80-100psi, so as the maximum pressure you're likely to have in your tyres is 50psi, their range isn't useful. Buy at least two – they're so cheap and invaluable you should have a spare, and then two people can work on airing down at the same time.

That completes a very basic kit list for a touring 4WD.

A Volkswagen Touareg V10 diesel with a nice array of aftermarket and custom-built accessories. While not a mainstream offroader the Treg is pretty capable and with some research can certainly be nicely decked out.

Similar but not identical. These two JK Rubicons have different tyres, suspension, accessories, interior mods and much more, all tailored to the owner's exact needs and tastes. Popular vehicles like the JK have a huge range of mods.

beyond the basics

It won't be long before you consider most of these essential, but prioritise depending on the trips you plan.

snorkels

What it is	A relocated air intake, waterproofed such that air can only enter through the intake.	
Why you'd want one	The primary purpose of a snorkel is to prevent the engine drinking water. Engines work by compressing gas as the engine's piston moves upwards. The mixture is then ignited and the resulting explosion forces a piston down, producing power.	
	If water is drawn in with the air the piston attempts to compress a mixture of gas and water. The problem is that water is incompressible, the engine goes bang and there are sad faces all round. This is known as hydraulic lock, or just "hydraulicing" your engine.	
	Fitting a snorkel means the air intake is very much higher than it was before, so water cannot get in the engine, or if it can then you're not going anywhere anyway. There is no guarantee the engine will run if completely submerged, especially if it is a petrol engine, but at least it is less likely to turn itself into scrap metal. However, as the price of a new engine may start at a few thousand dollars and rise steeply from there, spending $500 on a snorkel is cheap insurance.	*Snorkels are popular and with good reason…it's cheap insurance.*
	The snorkel manufacturers do claim other advantages such as cleaner air from higher up, and some people notice improved performance due to the ram-air effect, especially those that own older diesels.	
	Snorkels may increase noise slightly, either through induction noise caused by the air being sucked in, or through drag. A well-designed snorkel should not cause visibility problems.	

Tips

Although the dictionary definition of the word "snorkel" makes reference to water and submersion, not all "snorkels" are actually watertight. Before you buy any snorkel, particularly vehicle manufacturer options, make absolutely sure it is designed – and fitted – to have a watertight seal so the only air coming in is through the top of the snorkel. Anything named "Raised Air Intake" (RAI) is definitely one to be cautious about. But while a proper snorkel may solve the hydraulic lock problem, no snorkel turns your car into a submarine. Consider a snorkel as insurance, as opposed to a deep-sea fishing permit. You never know when that water will be a little deeper than planned, or when the vehicle may tip sideways a little.

Another point to remember about choosing a snorkel is availability. Brand new models often need new designs as engines change, as do body panels, and sometimes snorkels are available only for one engine or transmission type. By and large snorkels are not available for softroaders, which being relatively low are the cars that need them the most. As ever, double-checking saves disappointment. Once fitted a snorkel should not be removed, as there will probably be an unsightly hole in the front three-quarter panel and along the A-pillar.

A raised air intake, not a snorkel. It can be waterproofed aftermarket which increases induction noise but that's only noticeable with the window down. Note the waterproofing doesn't turn the D3 into a submarine.

Some snorkels have adjustable heads that can be turned - handy in tight overgrown conditions, or to change to a precleaner (see previous images).

A snorkel with a pre-cleaner which collects dust before it gets to the engine. These are effective.

breathers

What it is	A set of pipes which allow air inside the diffs and other components to breathe.
Why you'd want one	Diffs are metal, and they get hot. Therefore, they expand and leave tiny gaps where fluid can get in. The good example is a water crossing; hot diff into cold water means cold water into diff. And water is not known for its lubrication qualities, so eventually the diff may be damaged. Part of the answer is a breather which permits the diff to "breathe" through a long pipe, usually routed to the top of the engine compartment. It's a cheap and simple mod; make sure you do it.
Tips	Some vehicles already have good breathers, some don't. Your 4WD mechanic will know, in fact a good test is if they can answer the question immediately and know what you mean.

water storage

What it is	Storage for water. Can be tanks or bladders, and these come in all sorts of shapes and sizes, including some that can be custom-made for inside or outside the vehicle.	
Why you'd want one	You need water to live, so best take some with you.	
Tips	Use only food-grade hoses, available at any hardware shop for water storage filling. It is best to have at least two separate water sources rather than one large one, in case one is lost or contaminated. Grey water can be kept and reused, leaving pure water for drinking and cooking only. Water is heavy and prone to moving, so ideally store it low and central. One good thing about water is that the shape of the container doesn't matter, and as long as a hose can be run to it then it can be located in difficult-to-reach places.	*A water tank that fits behind the rear seats of a Patrol. The good thing about water is that it can fit into odd spaces.*

1   *This LC100 has an under-body tank split for fuel and water, with a pump and a hose.*

2   *A flexible water bladder, secured into the second-row footwell.*

3   *Another second-row solution, but this time made of solid plastic.*

4   *A 50L sill water tank on my Defender. The pump is a hand pump, but very effective and easy to use so no need to bother with yet more wiring and another electric motor. If need be we can drain the tank directly.*

long-range fuel tanks

What it is	Replacement, and/or additional fuel tanks. There are two basic types of long-range tank; replacement and auxiliary. Replacement tanks see your existing tank thrown away and a new one fitted, gaining extra volume by utilising unused areas under the chassis and perhaps relocating some components. Auxiliary tanks are an additional, entirely separate tank, and the fuel is generally used in one of two ways; either there is a transfer pump into the vehicle's original fitted tank and a separate gauge for the aux, or the engine is set up to feed from either tank by means of a switch, which also switches the fuel gauge. Our preference is for the former, because that way the aux tank can be entirely run dry by the transfer pump.  *Aux tank fuel gauge and pump transfer switch on a D3.*

The alternative is jerry cans, which are bulky and heavy, and so difficult to store. Fuel is also an unpleasant fluid and, in the case of petrol, particularly dangerous. Jerry cans are a viable option and cheaper, but long-range tanks are better. Long-range tanks also keep the considerable weight of the extra fuel down low, where it needs to be.

Why you'd want one	To go further, or longer without refuelling.

Australia is a very big place. Let's take the Simpson Desert as an example. That's about 600km worth of sandy driving, and chances are your stock tanks wouldn't even let you make it if it were bitumen. Even in somewhere like the Flinders Ranges where fuel is never more than about 100km away, it is handy to have the extra range in case the next place is closed or out of fuel.

Long-range tanks pay off even without a big trek. For example, on a recent trip to the Otways, hardly the middle of the outback, we left home in a test ute with a full tank and arrived at camp with about half, so we could, if we went back the same way, just make it back. The nearest town was more than half an hour away, we weren't sure if they had fuel or what time it was open and it's just a hassle you don't need when you should be relaxing by your tent.

Had we had a long-range tank we could have just driven anywhere and everywhere that weekend without worrying at all about fuel. The extra range means we can refuel when we want to, not when the car demands it, something also useful on higher-speed trips when towing. When you pull in for a break, who wants to queue with everyone else at a servo on a public holiday? With a long-range tank you avoid all that waiting and go straight to your relaxing. Nobody enjoys a trip having to keep one eye on the gauge, and our long-range gives us complete peace of mind should we need to extend the trip, turn back or change plans. That, for us, is the main reason we prefer cars with long-range built in.

A 65L sill tank on a Defender. The filler point is to the right of the rear wheel.

A common location for an aux tank is under the cargo bay. Sometimes spare wheels need to be relocated onto carriers, but not in the case of this Patrol.

Tips	The long-range tank is more expensive than jerry cans, but doesn't intrude into storage space, is easy to fill, doesn't require a stop to empty, is a lot less dangerous and the fuel is harder to steal. Most of them are between 60 litres and 120 litres, equivalent to three and six cans, respectively. Some tanks can be split between water and fuel. Ensure the tank does not reduce departure angles.
	If you do use jerries then observe the safety precautions, particularly with petrol which is an effective way to create a nasty explosion. Because it is the vapour that explodes, always fill cans – don't half fill them leaving plenty of vapour room. However, allow a little room for expansion, especially if you store them in the heat on top of a rack and secure them properly.

Y-filler on a D3. Insert the nozzle in the front part to fill the primary tank, angle it back into the other part of the Y to fill the aux. There is a pump to move fuel from aux to main.

bash plates, diff guards and other protectors

What it is	Metal plates under the body that protect components such as the transfer case, fuel tank and differential from damage. The impact is absorbed (well, taken) by the plate, not by the expensive transmission.
Why you'd want one	If you're going offroad, you will run out of clearance at some point, no matter how much you have to begin with, and when you do, you want it to be nothing more eventful than a scraping noise, rather than damage to anything important. So protection is very, very important. You might think that it's all a moot point, and 4WDs have this already. Not so. Every vehicle is different, but most 4WDs do need either new, or replacement bash plates. Your local 4WD shop or club can provide model-specific advice. *Aftermarket bashplates are usually stronger than the originals and protect more parts. Some original bashplates are just plastic.* The good news is that as long as your vehicle is reasonably popular, there is bound to be the protection you need readily available. For example, the NM Pajero's front bash plate isn't all that strong and so there are stronger aftermarket equivalents for it. In fact, many new 4WDs have very poor "bash plates", sometimes just plastic guards which are just cosmetic or there to marginally improve the drag coefficient. Diff guards are guards for the differential (Chapter 3), and there are also sill protectors.
Tips	If there are none available for your vehicle ask your 4WD shop to custom-fabricate what you need. Some vehicles need plates more than others; it all depends on the original clearance, quality of the plates and use of the vehicle.

tinted windows

What it is	Nothing to do with 4WD per se, it's just tinting of the windows.
Why you'd want one	Tinting your vehicle's windows means it won't heat up as much inside, which means less air conditioning and less fuel used. You might consider tinting the rear windows even more, as when it's full of gear you can't see out of them anyway.
Tips	There are legal limits on how far you can go with tinting. Stay within them, and as ever, don't assume the people doing the tinting know the regulations. Tinting does slightly reduce visibility. If you stack gear against a tinted window you will damage the tint, so it is best to cut some cardboard or similar in the shape of the glass to protect it. This also helps with prying eyes.

bull bars and nudge bars

What it is	A replacement, or supplementary bumper bar.
Why you'd want one	The original intent of these bars was to protect the vehicle in the event of a collision with animals, particularly kangaroos. They are also a useful place to mount winches, lights, antennae and especially sand flags.

A good bull bar means the difference between limping home and having a vehicle entirely disabled. However, many people fit bars for cosmetic reasons. There are three types of bars:

- A nudge bar fits over the existing front bumper, and covers part of the bumper.

- An over-bumper bar is the same thing but covers the entire bumper.

- A bull bar replaces the front bumper entirely.

Nudge and over-bumper bars are largely cosmetic, excepting the fact they can be used to mount some lighter accessories. They provide little to no protection against impact with roos, and often decrease approach angle. Bull bars usually improve the approach angle.

You don't need a bull bar to drive offroad; the justification is that you may need one if you travel in areas where animal impacts are probable. If you need a bull bar, get a real one.

There are three types of bull bar construction:

- **Steel:** Steel bars are stronger, cheaper and heavier. They are more readily repaired and most can take a winch mount.

- **Alloy:** Alloy bars are lighter, more expensive and probably look better. They too can take winches but need a special mounting kit to do so, and are not as strong as steel.

- **Plastic:** Plastic bull bars are made of reinforced plastic, and like alloy bars, need special mountings for winches. They are the lightest, but not the toughest and there are some concerns that they bend so much they are ineffective.

A black steel winch bull bar, which adds 41kg to the D3 (excluding winch).

Bars can often be colour-coded.

A cheap over-bumper bar which is easily bent, possibly causing more damage than otherwise would have been the case. Avoid. They aren't even strong enough to properly mount accessories.

Tips	If your vehicle has airbags, ensure that the bar is airbag-compatible. Consider new bars only, as that way you are sure of their history. It also means they are compliant with the latest Australian Design Rules (ADRs).

Bull bars may be offered by the manufacturer, or by aftermarket companies. In general, the manufacturer options are more expensive and less functional than aftermarkets, but do tend to be crash-tested and certified to the same safety (ANCAP star) ratings as the original vehicle, whereas aftermarket bars typically are not. This doesn't mean to say aftermarket bars are unsafe, far from it, but if you're after proven compliance factory bars may be the only option.

Steel bull bars don't weigh as much as you may think. The bar on my Discovery 3 weighs 55kg, but as 14kg of trim and bracing needs to be removed to fit it the net weight gain is 41kg.

Even if you don't plan on fitting a winch, buy a winch bar as you may change your mind and it will be a little extra resale value.

Cheap nudge bars are simply not strong enough to mount accessories like sand flags and often vibrate too much for driving lights.

There are "trade" or "commercial" bars which do the same job as standard bars, but don't look as pretty. The "deluxe" bars again do the same job, but are more carefully styled. Spend the money if looks are important.

Not all bull bars cater for things like front cameras or reversing sensors. Ask carefully what (if any) function you will lose as a result of the bar, especially if you have a luxury model vehicle. Not all bull bars for modern vehicles can be fitted to each model, for example different trim or engine specifications.

Colour-coded steel winch bull bar with integrated side protection and side rails.

A decent quality nudge bar, weighing only eight kilograms. Not a lot of protection but better than nothing and strong enough for accessories.

Cosmetic-value only nudge bar decreasing approach angle.

If your vehicle has airbags, make sure any bar is airbag-compatible.

rear bars and wheel carriers

What it is	A replacement rear bumper bar, optionally with a wheel carrier, or a carrier that mounts onto the chassis and preserves the existing rear bar. See also Chapter 7.
Why you'd want one	There are problems with mounting the spare under the vehicle: • How do you get to it if you're bogged, or at an angle that makes it difficult? • The spare is vulnerable to damage from being dragged over rocks. • Potentially reduces departure angle. • In some cases, the vehicle must be unloaded before the spare can be accessed. Some vehicles, such as Defenders, have weak rear doors and need spare carriers even though they have door-mounted spares. Relocating the spare also means you can add a shovel holder or rubbish bag on the back, and frees up space for an extra fuel tank. However, spare carriers are more trouble to open as they need to be opened before you get to the door, it raises weight higher and reduces visibility.
Tips	Make sure your carrier does not make your vehicle unroadworthy by reducing the angle at which the light can be seen from it. Get a written statement from the supplier and if they are unwilling, don't buy. Some carrier arms can be removed and replaced easily. A gas strut or similar to hold it open is essential. Dual carriers are great, but very heavy even without two tyres fitted. Some rear bars replace the entire rear bumpers, and have towbars incorporated.

Spare wheel carrier (weight 30kg) on a Discovery 3.

Dual carrier and replacement rear bar on a Patrol GU, with work light.

Rear carrier on a Defender, which opens with the door.

dual battery

What it is	A second battery, in addition to the vehicle's starting battery.
Why you'd want one	The battery in a vehicle is there to start the engine, which takes a lot of its power. It also supplies the vehicle's electrical needs when the engine isn't running, thus providing power via the alternator. Many 4WD owners fit a second battery because they find that they are running down the starter battery with all their accessories when the engine is off.

The controller (isolator) for a dual battery, which decides which battery gets charged first and protects one battery from flattening another. Next to it is an aftermarket fuse box.

Examples of additional electrical load:

- Electric winches (these can drain batteries quicker than the engine can recharge them)
- Fridge
- Radio equipment (UHF, AM, HF etc.)
- GPS equipment
- Laptop computers, tablets, phones, gadgets
- Lights (interior and exterior spotlights)

The list goes on.

There are two basic types of battery; deep cycle and high-current discharge (starter). A deep-cycle battery is designed to give a fair bit of power over a long period of time, and can be discharged and recharged without damage. A starter battery should never be fully discharged, but can give a large amount of power over a short period of time. Which is what you need for starting an engine. The deep-cycle is better for running accessories.

Dual batteries on a Discovery 3 with covers removed for clarity. Top right is the starter battery and top left in yellow is the secondary. Also visible in front of the starter is an air compressor. The D3 doesn't require a second battery mount, unlike most other vehicles. The location of the battery is a consideration as it must be reasonably well ventilated and not get too hot – difficult in an engine bay.

So what do you get, and do you need one?

If you don't camp, or have an electric winch, then a dual battery is not going to be that useful to you as the vehicle's existing battery should supply all your needs for the short periods of time you'll be using the vehicle without the engine running. You could always upgrade the single battery, which is a much cheaper alternative than a full dual battery system.

If you are a keen camper, a deep-cycle is probably the way to go, as the vehicle will be a stationary powerhouse for at least a day between camps and probably longer. Another camping option is a battery pack, which is a portable battery source.

The situation is complicated by an electric winch. The winch really needs a starter battery, but your other needs might require a deep-cycle. There are options, such as a triple battery system, upgrading the starter motor and using that for the winch too, or using another starter as the second battery. The last one sounds contradictory, but while a starter battery isn't as good as a deep-cycle for days of non-engine operation, it will probably do for most uses for a day or two quite comfortably.

How the batteries should be connected is another issue. They should not be connected in a way that means that you can accidentally flatten both batteries. Each battery should be independent from the other, and for that you need an isolator. The alternator usually charges the starter first, then the secondary. Many people have monitors which permit them to see the state of the battery's charge.

Modern vehicles are extremely sensitive to changes to their electrical systems, and may have alternators that charge only under certain conditions. These vehicles require special care with any modifications, and the best advice is to leave the factory wiring as standard as possible.

The quality of internal wiring may also be a cause for concern, for example the rear socket is often not designed for the continuous load of running a fridge. When fitting a dual battery it may be a good idea to have some extra, heavy-duty sockets installed and maybe make them independent from the ignition too.

The best idea is to talk it over with a competent dual battery expert. Make sure you've listed all your electrical requirements before you start the conversation.

Even when bush camping you need electrical power; cameras and MP3 players to recharge, laptops to work on, lights, fridges and more. And, it's nice to be able to start the car in the morning.

Solar technology is rapidly improving and can make a significant difference to bush electrical supplies. As solar power is somewhat variable it is best used to charge batteries when the conditions are right, then have appliances draw down from the battery storage. This solar panel is about A4-sized and can recharge smartphones, but there are much larger versions which can power campsites.

Larger solar panel useful for powering a campsite.

roof racks and roof pods

What it is	A roof rack is a flat metal area mounted on the roof for carrying kit. Roof pods are enclosed storage pods mounted on the roof.	
Why you'd want one	You can never have too much space in a vehicle, and after you fill the interior the only way to go is to use the roof, tow a trailer or leave something or someone behind.	*Terracan with a roof pod. These are easy to load, somewhat secure, but limited on space and don't provide much in the way of drag advantage over a normal rack.*
Tips	Roof storage raises the centre of gravity of a vehicle, which worsens on-road handling, reduces side-angle tolerance and increases fuel consumption. Something else to consider is the roof loading rating. That may be as low as 50kg, or as high as 200kg. You need to subtract the weight of the storage system from that, so a 45kg roof rack on a 75kg rated roof gives you only 30kg load capacity. The rating is also usually for bitumen driving; so any form of offroading is going to increase the load dramatically as the vehicle rides corrugations, dips and potholes. The other side of the coin is that the roof is likely to support more than that load when the vehicle is not moving. The total load on the roof, and that of the storage system, will come out of the vehicle's overall payload (see Chapter 6). However, the roof is a very useful place to store light, bulky items such as tents, camping chairs and prams. It is definitely not the place for heavy items like fuel, tools or water, but if there is no choice then be aware of the effect on the vehicle's handling and the stress on the roof mounts. Alloy racks are as strong as steel and far lighter, so are recommended, as are those with mesh floors.	 *Many vehicles have cross-rails and baskets can be bolted on top. This Forester owner has taken the precaution of moving his spare wheel onto the roof so it is easily accessible. If it were just the spare then it could have been secured direct to the cross-rails.*

Additional mesh added to a rack with widely-spaced cross-rails. A tough canvas bag makes loading smaller items on a rack very easy.

1-2 Dual-cab utes with canopies must not use full-length roof racks as the rear cargo area will move relative to the body. This ute has a short rack and cross-rails at the rear. Tradie racks fit on the canopy and extend over the cabin but are not fixed to it.

3 The lesser-spotted Long-Tailed Defender. Even if you don't need the space, racks are ideal for carrying firewood, chainsaws and other items you don't really want inside, or as emergency carrying capacity.

4 This step uses the spare wheel. Others fit on the rear of the vehicle.

5-6 This table slots neatly underneath a roof rack. Racks can be mount points for many other accessories.

7 This is a spare wheel holder. There are other holders for common items such as jerry cans, gas bottles, shovels and Hi-Lift jacks. Also visible in the shot is a wind deflector which dramatically quietened the noise from the rack. It is worth experimenting with even quite small pieces of flat metal to see what difference is made.

Why not just make the roof rack into a bed? Easy to set up and sturdy, but you need to pack the car up to move it so not great for base camping, and it's windier that high up.

driving lights

What it is	Additional illumination for your vehicle. There are two basic styles: • Spotlights, or pencil lights which illuminate a long distance ahead, for cruising • Wide angle or spread-beam light for low-speed 4WD work. There are two basic types: • Halogens • HID – High Intensity Discharge HIDs are far superior to halogens; they create more light for a lot less power, run cooler and their light is whiter. Halogens are cheaper. Refer to Chapter 26 for night driving techniques.	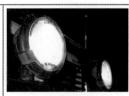  *HID driving lights.*
Why you'd want one	For urban driving your headlights are more there so others can see you. For 4WD trips you need them to light the way. The Australian Government hasn't yet put streetlights or cat's eyes everywhere, so extra illumination is very useful. It's especially useful in forests and in places where the road is not very distinct. Normal headlights aren't built for that sort of environment and they're not designed to throw light to the sides of the vehicle, which is what you want when you're offroad in low-range.	
Tips	Like every modification, the biggest and most expensive isn't necessarily the best. The quality of the globes and the reflectors (parts that reflect light from the back of the casing and so make the light directional) make a big difference. Another option is to improve your headlights by replacing the bulbs. Sealed beams are an idea if you do a lot of water crossings at night, as most of the energy supplied to any light goes into heat, not light. Immersing a hot bulb in cold water leads to a broken bulb. You cannot legally upgrade your normal headlights to HIDs without fitting a self-leveller as HIDs are so bright the law says they must be auto-levelled. You can upgrade some halogen auxiliary driving lights to LED, but beware cheap kits as there are significant currents involved. Fit transparent plastic covers to your lights to protect them from stone chips, not solid covers which you need to remove and store inside, or lose. While roof-mounted lights may seem attractive, they are not road-legal. Ignore any lights with a blue tint. These are just bling as the tint decreases the available light, but HID lights will always have a natural white/blue output.	 *A kit to upgrade halogen driving lights to HID.*  *LED lightbars offer low current draw and a wide, bright light.*

cross-axle locking differentials

What it is	Locking differentials (Chapter 3).
Why you'd want one	Massively improved offroad capability for vehicles without modern traction control.
Tips	There is a misconception that lockers are just for the hardcore. Not true. They can turn a hard track into medium and a medium into an easy, so they certainly have a place on a touring vehicle. Avoid the auto-lockers (see Chapter 3) and select from the range of manual lockers. However, if you have a new vehicle with good traction control a set of lockers will make little difference to the overall capability. De-prioritise if you're mainly driving on the flat or in sand.
	Now the big question; front or rear if only one set? There's no fixed answer and this is another Holy War, but if pushed my recommendation is rear. The rear axle is stronger, there's no CV joints to stress and you're more able to steer with a rear locker than a front. One exception is when you have a strong LSD in the rear, e.g. Patrols, and want to complement it with a front locker. The real answer is therefore dependent on your vehicle and intended use.
	Some vehicles have optional factory-fit lockers (Pajero, Triton, Amarok, LC76, Discovery 3 and 4 and more) and these are always worth ticking the box for as they are then under factory warranty.

A modern LC200 and a new, but not so modern, LC76. The 200 has excellent traction control as standard, and therefore has little need of lockers. The 76 has no traction control, but can be fitted with factory (or aftermarket) lockers, devices it benefits from far more than the 200. You can always fit lockers to the 200, and then have the best of both worlds, able to switch between traction control and lockers depending on the terrain.

rock sliders

What it is	Protection for your sills as you slide over rocks. Also known as siderails.
Why you'd want one	Resale value, so you can open the doors afterwards.
Tips	Rock sliders help you get in, and out of the vehicle, and can protect door sills. The only ones you should buy are heavy-duty versions that can take the weight of the vehicle as it slides over a rock. Anything less will simply be bent.
	Some people store compressed air inside the slider, which is a neat idea. Make sure the slider is properly connected to the chassis, and Hi-Lift jack points are a good idea, as is non-slip coating on the top.
	Vehicles with side airbags cannot fit rock sliders as, at the time of writing, no sliders had been certified for airbag compliance, unlike bull bars. Many people do not run them and just take care over rocks.

A strong siderail. This is also connected to a side protection bar and the bull bar.

winches

What it is	A device for moving the vehicle without driving its wheels. Refer to Chapter 37.
Why you'd want one	Easy recovery! Remember it is not a license to drive anywhere you want and then expect to be easily got out.
Tips	Chapter 37 describes winching operation in detail, and covered here is sizing. As Chapter 33 describes, the maximum recovery load is likely to be around 1.5x the fully loaded vehicle weight, and that is an exceptionally difficult recovery with no driving assistance from the casualty. Most recoveries are likely to generate forces no more than approximately order of half the vehicle weight, although you should always allow a significant safety margin.

As an example, if a 4WD with a GVM of 3,500kg tows a trailer of 1,500kg then we have a total of 5,000kg to move. That is at the maximum end of the weight scales, and typical recovery loads will be 2,500kg.

There are two basic types of winch; power (usually electric) and hand winches.

Electric winches
Warn's website lists various specifications for their electric winches, some of which are reproduced below:

Winch	Weight (kg)	Pull force (kg)	Current (amps)	Line Speed (metres per minute)	Pull force (kg)	(kg)
		Layer 1 on drum/performance			Layer 4 on drum	Mech adv + 1
M12000	62	5,440	440	1.18	4,432	10,336
9500XP	39.5	4,313	480	2.30	3,359	8,195
XD9000i	38.5	4,080	460	1.94	3,180	7,752
Tabor 9000	36.6	4,080	464	1.55	3,180	7,752
M8000	34	3,630	435	2.44	2,826	6,897
M6000	34	2,720	465	3.05	2,118	5,168

Weight is inclusive of wire rope.

Mechanical advantage is double the Layer 1 force with an allowance for snatch block loss.

If we have our load of 5,000kg, and assume we'll need 1.5x the effort to move it, then even a 9,000lb (4,080kg) winch is sufficient with a snatch block, and 10% has been taken off for efficiency loss. That would generate enough force to pull a large 4WD plus trailer out of a boggy uphill, with no casualty assistance. Clearly not something you'll often need to do, so even the smaller winches would be fine for most recoveries. Rig a second block and you've got even more pulling power. The table above indicates some of the differences between budget and premium winches with the Tabor 9000 and the XD9000i which are rated the same, but the XD uses less current and has a quicker line speed. It's also two kilograms heavier and you can bet that's gone on quality.

Summary; a 8,000lb to 9,500lb winch with a snatch block or two is all you need for recreational offroading, even a 6,000lb winch will work, and not all winches rated the same are the same.

Hand winches
The 1,600kg Tirfor-clone models to AS1418.2 are recommended. The lower-rated models are sufficiently rated for most purposes but the Tirfor 516 is easier to operate as it has a longer handle. The smaller ones work well with small, light vehicles such as shortie Suzukis.

How much rope
Winches can often take up to 40m of rope. However, to get this amount of rope on takes careful spooling, and while that's no bad idea it also means you need to take a fair bit of rope off the drum to maximize efficiency, and if you need to winch at a large fleet angle you can't do that. On my winches I run only 20m of rope which is easy to spool, means the winch runs with minimal layers on the drum and the fleet angle can be large for very short pulls. The disadvantage is that the rope is short – but that's easily fixed with a synthetic rope winch extension which, unlike a strap extension, can go around snatch blocks. Very often 20m is more than enough for a pull anyway, and 20m of rope is a lot cheaper than 40m.

other accessories

There really is no limit to what can be done to a 4WD touring vehicle. Here are some more ideas.

Even if you don't tow, a towbar makes a great recovery point (but never loop a strap over a ball, insert it into the tongue). They also make handy steps.

Awning mounted on the roof rack. Some extend out the back instead or as well as.

1   Canopies are ideal for touring dual-cab utes, if you don't want the expense of a custom-made rear. Utes are great for carrying, have huge cargo capacity and a better payload compared to the typical wagon. The small cabin is also easier to heat and cool. Modern utes now handle almost as well as wagons and are just as safe onroad, albeit not as refined or manoeuvrable.

2   Canopies have two types of window, pop up or slide back.

3   Heavy-duty clutches. If a part wears out, consider a stronger aftermarket version rather than just another original

4   Seat covers. Check they are compatible with in-seat airbags if fitted.

5   CTI, or Central Tyre Inflation. The ability to adjust tyre pressures on the fly.

6   Swaybar disconnect (see Chapter 5). Check roadworthy rules.

7-8 In-car smart devices are very useful for navigation, area research, radio, music streaming and much more. A good mount is essential for usability and safety. There are many specialist aftermarket mount companies – don't buy cheap!

9   Some people pull the second row out entirely and use it for storage. You will probably need to advise your state roads authority and your insurance company if you do. In fact, advise your insurance company about every modification and accessory.

10 It is not usually possible to see out the back of a touring 4WD, so cameras are invaluable.

11 Engines can be modified; bigger exhausts, changing turbo boost, extractors…the options are unlimited. Consult a specialist to discuss options specific to your vehicle. Be cautious of major power increases as these mean changes elsewhere, and engine longevity may be compromised.

12 An aftermarket tyre pressure monitor. The gauge stays inside the cab and the monitors replace the valve caps, transmitting pressure and temperature information by radio. Very useful and interesting, but doesn't negate the need to manually check tyres for damage and wear patterns.

13 Aftermarket steering damper to reduce the effects of wheel kickback. Often used in conjunction with larger tyres.

14 Let the world know your allegiance. This one has a message.

15 Bead locks are used to secure a tyre to rim. They are not really required at pressures of more than 15psi provided you are not driving like a bat out of hell, and you can go as low as eight psi if you're nice and gentle. Very large tyres such as those fitted on comp cars must be deflated a long way to air down, often below 15psi. Funnily enough, these cars tend to be driven with a bit of brisk pace. Hence the popularity of bead locks such as this external set shown here in orange around the rim. These are not road-legal. The internal bead locks which are similar to a small-diameter inner tube are legal, but the rim needs modifying for a second valve and that rim mod may not be legal. For recreational users there are other priorities and even if you do pop a tyre off a rim it's not a big problem to pop it back on again.

the specials

You can go further than just bolting on accessories and start to modify the entire vehicle, swapping out engines, suspension, changing the chassis and more. However, most offroad tourers just need to change components. The only limit is your imagination and wallet, although modern vehicles with monocoque chassis and electronics such as stability control are increasingly difficult to modify.

things to remove

These are components that are often on 4WDs and shouldn't be for offroad usage.

Sidesteps	If they are lightweight, made of alloy, and are the lowest point on the vehicle, remove them as they'll only be broken and retard progress offroad.
Cosmetic nudge bars	Often these are very weak, just for looks and simply reduce the angle of approach.
Rear towbar and/or tongue.	Remove if it gets in the way of a recovery point or if it decreases the departure angle.
Low-profile, high-speed tyres	Too weak for the bush (see Chapter 7).
Mudguards & trim	Most factory mudguards will fall off shortly into the bush, as will various other minor bits of cosmetic trim.

Either you take them off or the bush does it for you. If you want sidesteps get strong steel ones attached to the chassis (see Chapter 40).

choosing your kit

If nothing else this book should make apparent the huge variety of gear available on the market. The book cannot give specific advice for your situation and vehicle, only explain the principles which allow you to make a call. The best places for advice are a good 4WD shop and a 4WD club – not a factory dealer, with few exceptions. However, even in those places you will find conflicting advice, so either one party is wrong or there's a misunderstanding. For example, I regularly see owners who have been advised that a certain tyre specification is "ok" when in fact it is not road-legal and a simple review of the regulations would have easily shown that fact.

So what can owners do? The only answer is do your own research and whenever anyone tells you something, ask why that is so. If they are unable to explain why then they're just following a rule without understanding – they may be wrong or right in a given situation but have no way to know.

When discussing almost any 4WD accessory the true professional never recommends until they have a good understanding of your vehicle, intended use, budget and general situation. Beware anyone that launches into fixed recommendations about the likes of tyres, winches, pressures and more. The good advisers instil a sense of confidence in the buyer, are not dogmatic, can admit when they are wrong and take the time to explain the whys and wherefores as they are confident in their skills and knowledge. They will explain the downsides as well as the upsides, not pretend the product is perfect. Look for those people at 4WD shops. They will be busy.

1   Land Cruiser lengthened and crossed with a camper trailer.

2   Discovery 2 converted to a ute.

3   Patrol GU wagon converted to a dual-cab ute for competition use, no change in wheelbase. The vehicle is lighter as a result.

4   No change in wheelbase, but the modifications required to get 37" tyres on the Jeep are extensive.

5   Wrangler TJ converted to a ute using a kit.

6   A solid axle swap (SAS) for much-improved articulation at the front.

It is a good idea to plan your accessories so you don't need to re-buy. For example, don't buy a non-winch bull bar then a winch; or a towbar then a rear bar with a built-in towbar. Create a bit of a roadmap, then work through it. Getting multiple accessories fitted at the same time also saves on cost.

CHAPTER 42

HOW DO I START?

So you're interested in exploring Australia by 4WD. Where to start?

If you've read this book you've got the theory out of the way. Practical training is the next step, where you can put the theory into practice.

4WD training courses

Nobody is born knowing how to drive offroad; therefore, you need training. The alternative is just learning by osmosis, which tends to be hard on your vehicle and passengers. In some cases, even existing knowledge and skill will work against you. For example, race drivers may be taught fixed-input steering, but that doesn't work well when you're in low-range territory. On the other hand there will be new techniques – such as stalling the vehicle intentionally, or pulling away in any gear other than first – which go against your understanding of what is the correct technique for a road car on roads.

The first step is to select a training course. Most 4WD training courses focus on slow-speed obstacles and terrain such as sand, rocks and hills and are designed around the national competency standards like SISODRV302A (previously SRODRV001B) – ask if your course gives you this nationally recognised qualification. 4WD training courses will assume that you can drive the 4WD reasonably competently on the road, but have no offroad experience. If you want on-road, or dirt road training any advanced driving school should be able to offer that as the skills are essentially the same as a normal car, although a 4WD-specific slant is preferable.

The 4WD course itself typically starts with a theory session, where various driving techniques and 4WD systems are explained, followed by a practical where trainees drive set-piece obstacles under supervision. There's a lot to learn, so we recommend courses of at least one full day, and the training should be viewed as a base for further learning and definitely practice. Most training organisations offer specialised courses, for example camper trailers, snow, sand driving, advanced offroad, recovery and winching. Select from these only when you've completed the basics.

preparation

To get the best out of any training you need to prepare. In particular; thoroughly read the owner's manual for your vehicle – the instructor may or may not be familiar with your vehicle and there are many variations within models. Then read up on 4WD techniques and theory – especially 4WD systems, as this is difficult to understand and explain. If you can understand the concept of a locking centre diff, traction control and windup you'll find the theory much easier to follow and your owner's manual will make sense.

Finally, prepare for the day. You'll be outside, so come with clothes suitable for all weathers. Make sure your vehicle is properly serviced, has a full tank of fuel, anything inside is tied down and the tow tongue removed. Bring a tyre pressure gauge and your recovery gear, plus lunch (if not supplied), plenty of water and a small notebook and pen. During the course ask questions, pay attention and, importantly, try things even if they look difficult. Instructors have a well-developed sense of self-preservation, and even if you think that hill looks impossible they wouldn't suggest you attempt it unless they were sure you, they and the car would emerge unscathed from the other end. So as you're in a controlled environment with a professional, that's the time to push your personal level of comfort. Once the course is over, it is important to consolidate your learning by re-reading your books and magazines, then going on an actual offroad trip.

types of course

There are many operations offering 4WD training, and they can be loosely divided into 4WD clubs, specialised offroad operations and driving schools. Most clubs offer training at substantially reduced costs compared to commercial operations as the instructors are volunteers, but this doesn't necessarily compromise quality. Clubs tend to have experienced offroaders, familiar with the local tracks and, if it's a single-marque club, the vehicles, too. On the commercial front, many advanced driving operations have a 4WD course, but in some cases the trainers don't have much of an offroading background, so ask the trainers when they last led a trip or had to lead a recovery and what happened. The specialised offroad outfits are sure to have offroad-experienced operators and may also offer other services such as tag-along tours. In any case, have a chat to the trainers, see how willing they are to talk things over and how much knowledge they have about your vehicle (it helps if you've read up on it first). There are two specific examples where lack of instructor knowledge may be an issue; softroaders and technologically advanced vehicles like newer European vehicles. Ask if they have references you can follow up, or testimonials. You want to be trained by someone

who does this all the time for real, not just in artificial environments. If you have any special needs, for example limited mobility, bring those up as well. Choose your training provider based

on how comfortable you feel with them and their knowledge of your vehicle and needs, not so much on price and location – quality training will pay for itself many times over.

your first trips

Don't rush out and attempt the Canning Stock Route as your first trip. Instead, try working through this plan:

- **Daytrips:** No camping, just out in the state forest, sightseeing. Take lunch.

- **Overnight camping:** Somewhere not too far from civilisation or home so you can cut and run or fetch something you forgot. Start building up lists. This is the point at which your cheap kit will fail and you'll buy quality gear next time. You may also end up leaving things at home you thought you'd need.

- **Longer weekends, further out:** By this time you should be confident that you can go away, nothing will break, nothing will be forgotten and you'll have developed routines which mean time saved and less stress, so you can better enjoy the experience.

- **The big treks:** Now you're ready for the longer journeys, but again these need a different mindset and preparation as you could be living out of the car for three weeks or so. If you build up slowly there won't be a problem.

Try to do one trip a month to build up your routines and skills. It really does get easier with practice.

My view is that the longer the trip, the easier it should be. That means do your hardest 4WDing on the day trips. That's the time to extend yourself and your vehicle, so anything you find on the long trips is no longer daunting – you've done harder. If you get it wrong or have a problem on a daytrip it won't destroy a holiday.

The longer the trip, the greater the preparation needed. For trips of a week or more consider a pre-trip inspection by a 4WD workshop. The workshop will give your vehicle a proper inspection to minimise (not eliminate) the chances of anything going wrong. However, I don't like to collect my car and then head straight off into the unknown. Mechanics are human, so they make mistakes. A little driving before you set off increases the chances of any basic mistakes being found. You don't want that grief when you turn the key of a fully loaded 4WD complete with family, bound for adventure.

One of the many lessons you learn when starting out is that the guy ropes and pegs supplied with most tents are junk. Here is a photo of a decent rope, a peg not made out of spaghetti and, importantly, a spring tensioner. When you learn this sort of thing it's fine if you are on a weekend trip when it's just the one night, but not so good if it's the first night on a three-week holiday.

Don't assume fuel will always be available where you need it, or when you want it.

This book is not about camping, but there are two points worth making; firstly, quality really does count with camping gear and, secondly, the best place to buy it tends to be at smaller, more specialised shops. A good tip is not to buy "4WD camping gear" from the big stores but to purchase hiking gear, which tends to be better quality, lighter and stronger. In general, buy the smallest and lightest of everything. For example, many people buy one giant gas-powered cooker when they could take three smaller hiking cookers for half the weight and space, then have three stoves instead of one (or two backups). And do you really need that director's chair with two fold-out tables, when a smaller, less ornate chair would do? Another example; we find a few simple battery-powered LED lights are more effective, cheaper, smaller and lighter than single, bulky lantern.

One piece of advice you'll often see is not to go offroading alone, and that means don't go with only one vehicle. But where do you find others if you have no offroading friends, or none with any experience? There are two main choices:

- 4WD clubs
- Tour operators

clubs

What is a 4WD club? Like any club, it's a collection of people with a common interest. The "common interest" isn't just as vague as "4WD", either. There are more than enough people with 4WDs who use them to form a club for almost everyone. Here are some examples:

- **Family clubs:** Mainly into touring, often with the entire family.
- **Midweek clubs:** Popular with retired people, they focus on trips during the week off-peak periods.
- **Hardcore:** Concerned with the deepest, steepest, hardest terrain!
- **Marque-specific:** They specialise in a given type of vehicle or model, e.g. the Pajero Club, Nissan Club or Land Rover Club. Some marque clubs are very focused on their marque while others started that way and ended up broadening to accept any other 4WD vehicle.
- **Vehicle type:** Some clubs focus just on softroaders, as many 4WD clubs don't permit vehicles without low-range.
- **Association based:** For example CFA, schools, RAAF, Scouts and clubs that are part of some other larger organisation.
- **Regional:** Clubs in less-populated areas cannot afford to specialise so tend to welcome anybody and anything.

Most clubs are a blend of two or more of the above and each club has its own demographic and culture. No two are alike.

Some marque-specific clubs forge relationships with the manufacturer.

At the centre of Australia on a club trip.

Beach driving is one situation where you'll be glad others are along too.

Sometimes it's fun to meet and chat with owners of the same vehicle.

why join a club?

Lots of reasons:

- **People:** It's a lot more fun and a lot safer to explore in company. Workload and worries are shared. You have a ready-made group of friends ready to explore with you.

- **Training:** You'll get training which is usually as good as anything you pay commercial rates for. It's cheaper because the instructors are volunteers, but those volunteers have passed theoretical and practical examinations. Many clubs also offer training in bush cooking, navigation, photography, towing and other skills.

- **Experience:** Once you've done a training course, you could go off on your first trip. Inevitably, however, there's a difference between training and practice. Best to continue to learn with experienced friends. The first recovery you do can be daunting! Many clubs have special first-time-after-training trips.

- **Modifications and accessories:** What really works? The club members can provide the real story, especially if you join a marque club, and everyone is always happy to show off their vehicle!

- **Access:** Some areas are available only to organised club trips.

- **Discounts**: Most clubs have a discount scheme with local 4WD service providers.

- **Public liability insurance on club trips:** If you lead a trip of friends outside a club organisation, you may have a duty of care and therefore be potentially at legal risk.

- **Equipment:** Many clubs have equipment for loan, for example: satphones, winches and other items which are either free or available for a nominal fee.

- **Non-4WD events!** Bowling, karting, dinners, film nights...it's social, not just low-range all the time.

- **Knowledge:** Thinking about the Simpson? The High Country? Stockton? Cape York? As a club member you'll have access to people that have been there, done that; either in your own club or others. Worried about travelling

Clubs often run competitions; precision driving, navigation, sometimes not even related to a vehicle. Photography is a common offroader interest, as is bush cooking.

There's far more to 4WD clubs than just driving. Many operate rural response groups which come in after disasters such as floods and fires to help rebuild. Offroaders tend to have many useful skills, can get anywhere and are entirely self-sufficient so their help is appreciated and it is immensely rewarding, giving participants a rich sense of achievement.

with children? Talk to those who do it every weekend.

- **Competitions:** If you're keen to compete there's a wide range of competitions varying from easy to very, very difficult.
- **The environment:** 4WD clubs and the umbrella organisations fight to keep tracks and forests open. They do this with a part of the membership fee you pay. The more club members, the bigger the voice. So just by joining you are helping keep Australia available for 4WD touring.

To select a club visit several at their monthly meetings, and more than once. You may well be able to go on a trip as a guest. If they have New Members' trips, sign up for those.

why would you not join a club?

The cost is only about $150 per annum and the discounts and contacts usually pretty much pay for that each year, for us. Are you worried about politics and bitching? Let's be honest, you'll get that if there are more than two human beings in a room. 4WD clubs are no different to any other club, company or collection of humans. So don't let it worry you; the vast majority of people have a lot of fun with their club. However, clubs aren't for everyone and many appreciate the solitude of the bush. Many others join a club, establish a network of friends and then travel with those and withdraw from the club.

club associations

state bodies

Most clubs are affiliated with the state's 4WD club peak body. These exist to represent the interests of the clubs, for example fighting track closures where appropriate, standardising driver training and working with the environmental authorities and other bush users.

Club members removing abandoned vehicles from a forest. No charge to the rangers.

Jeeps at a Jeep muster

Remote travel is definitely when you want company.

Disparate vehicles, all members of the same club.

Several clubs supported an event to get terminally ill young people out into the bush.

4WD clubs are nothing if not social.

international bodies

There is also an international body, although it's not well known in Australia as it's mostly USA-focused. However, it could be useful to find contacts overseas. The organisation describes itself thus:

The United Four Wheel Drive Associations Inc. (UFWDA), is a group of State, Regional, Provincial and International 4WD Associations in the United States and around the world that also encompasses various 4WD clubs and businesses.

UFWDA acts as your voice to keep 4WD roads and trails open so that you can continue enjoying four wheeling in the great outdoors. Through its united efforts, the opinions and beliefs of four wheel enthusiasts are heard by land management agencies and our elected officials. By sharing information through international and local memberships of UFWDA, answers to 4WD related matters can be sought and disseminated.
www.ufwda.org

tour operators

commercial tours

Not everyone wants to join a club, not everyone has a group of offroading friends and solo tours aren't as much fun or as safe. The answer is a commercial tour, often known as a tag-along tour. These are professionally organised trips for 4WD owners. You bring your own vehicle, there is a fixed itinerary, a few staff and off you go. Tours may be catered or self-catered and accommodation can vary from camping to motels.

Operating these events isn't cheap compared to a club trip, but on the other hand you get a guide who is often a master bush mechanic, everything is arranged, safety precautions and equipment are available, there's backup at home base and in short the guide is a professional who wants you to come back so ensures you have a good time. Convoys range in size but are typically from six to 10 vehicles. Tour operators do the same trip many a time so really know the area well and often have access into places the public wouldn't normally see. Each trip is a little different and some people go on the same trip again and again because each time there's variation that keeps the interest alive. Repeat customers are a big part of a tour operator's business.

These trips are also handy if you want to go somewhere and nobody in your club is planning a trip there. However, people in other clubs may be, and reciprocal membership isn't usually a problem. There will be a set number of tours per year, but most operators will run specials on request if numbers permit.

Self-drive 4WD tours operate all around the world. This one is a Trailmasters expedition in Morocco.

charity tours

Some 4WD tours are run for the benefit of charities. These are typically organised by highly experienced offroaders in a similar manner to the commercial tours, but using volunteer staff, sponsors and the participants' money is typically entirely donated to charity. These tours provide another way to see Australia by 4WD with other people, but there aren't as many tours as the commercial operators provide and nowhere near as many as the clubs. Nevertheless, it's another option and having been peripherally involved with the Drive4Life series I can definitely recommend that set of adventures.

gatherings

There are many other offroading events which are open to all comers. Examples are marque-specific gatherings where anyone with a certain type of vehicle is welcome to socialise, go on trips, inspect other vehicles and participate. Often these are organised by clubs but there is usually no need to be a club member to attend. Sometimes they are field days with stalls, expert demonstrations, talks and fun competitions. These events are publicised through magazines, the club network and especially online forums.

Land Rover owners converge in the Flinders Ranges every Easter.

The Drive 4Life 2009 event in the Victorian High Country, for the benefit of Northcott Disabilty Services. Held over a week, five groups of about 10 vehicles were led around the best of Victoria's mountain regions for a payment of $1,000 each, all of which went to Northcott with sponsors meeting the remainder of the costs. At the time of writing Drive4Life had raised over $250,000 for the charity. I covered the event for a magazine and looked at my article again to see how to summarise it for this book. I pulled the following quote: "As one veteran put it 'it's amazing how in just a week you can make new friends'. Most people, when asked, had a tough time deciding which was the best part for them and it generally came down to a tie between the scenery, the driving and always the people which really sums up what offroad touring is all about."

Touareg owners meeting for real, after meeting on a web forum www.clubtouraeg.com

Possibly the largest gathering of Mitsubishi 4WD owners in Australia, ever?

REFERENCES

APPENDIX A:
second-hand vehicle inspection list

Buying a new car is easy; it's the dealership or nothing. You can also find pre-loved models there as well, or at auctions or from private buyers. The best value for money can (and the emphasis is on "can") be found at auctions. The downside is risk, having to wait for a suitable model to turn up then being quick off the mark. Buying from a dealer, especially a larger new-car operation does give you some peace of mind and it's an easy, quick way to buy a vehicle. Private buying (and selling) is more work and riskier, as there's no warranty nor any returns, but without business overheads you can save money. But how to reduce the risk of buying a dud?

The simple answer is to do some homework and get a mechanical check. Any state motoring organisation will do one for you but it is best to have 4WD specialists who know that particular vehicle give it the once-over. However, there's no point just bringing a vehicle straight to the mechanic and paying them to find obvious faults you could have picked up yourself. Think of it this way; you can't tell if the car is good, but even the least mechanically minded may be able to tell if it's bad. Here's a list of items to check over before you get the final say from your mechanic.

arranging the inspection

- Check your insurance covers you for test drives.
- Make sure the car will be in a well-lit area, not a garage, there is time for a test drive, somewhere where you can go to 100km/h and the engine is cold.
- Do a REVS – Register of Encumbered Vehicles (REVS) – check. In Victoria, that's www.vehiclestatuscheck.vicroads.vic.gov.au. This will check the VIN against finance owing and tell you whether the car is stolen or written off.
- Drive other, similar cars. If you don't have even a little experience with the model you won't be able to tell normal idiosyncrasies from problems.
- Research particular problems, e.g. location of known rust spots.
- Check service intervals; if you buy a car at 97,000 you may be up for a big service bill at 100,000.

before you leave

- Wear old clothes as you'll be down and dirty, but still look smart to make a good impression even though you're the buyer.
- Take a torch, camera, rag and a notebook. Use all four liberally.
- Write out a checklist of everything you want to test.

questions

- When did you buy it?
- Why are you selling it?
- What work has been done to it?
- What is the accident history of the vehicle?
- What are the known problems?

when you arrive

- Check VIN and engine numbers correspond to the documentation.
- Sight the registration papers.
- Review the service history and check it matches the owner's description.
- View receipts for other work and accessories you see on the vehicle.
- If there is a roadworthy certificate then ensure the vehicle was assessed in the condition it is presented for sale. You may need to call whoever did the assessment.
- Check the age of the car on the build plate is consistent with that advertised. It is not unknown for '05s to become '06s.
- Take lots of photos, inside and out, so you can compare the car against others later on and so that when you come to collect it you have evidence of any changes, e.g. accessories removed.

exterior

- Check tyres for even and consistent wear and damage, including the spare. Check the rims for cracks and damage. Check the nuts are the correct type for the rim. All the tyres should be the same model and size.
- Inspect under-body for signs of damage, fluid leaks, loose components and rust and the CV boots. Beware excess cleaning or detailed products applied to mask rust.
- Check all under-bonnet fluids as per owner's manual – e.g. brake fluid, oil, coolant, power steering. Oil should be within limits. Hoses should not show signs of fatigue like cracks. The engine bay should be clean, but beware spotless engines which may have been steam-cleaned, leading to problems later. Inspect the radiator for damage.
- Inspect battery for signs of wear, corrosion and that it is firmly in place.
- Check body panels for fit and signs of respray; does the colour match exactly? Are there any ripples, flecks of paint on trim from overspray? Are the gaps between panels consistent from top to bottom? Open the doors and check the sills too.
- Check for body panel damage, scratches, rust, loose trim, missing fasteners.
- Operate and check the fuel filler cap.
- Check windows and windscreen for cracks and stars.
- Check central locking works and, if an alarm is fitted, set it off by rocking the car.

interior

- Check all electrics and accessories work; radio, mirrors, seats, lights, horn, winch, driving lights, dashboard lights, power windows including one-touch operation etc.
- Check condition of seats, removing seat covers if necessary, including the third row; and operating controls.
- Inspect seatbelts for damage; fraying or wear, and that they can be locked and retracted.
- Make sure the jack, wheel brace and towball are included.
- Check all the doors shut, open and lock including child locks.
- Lift up carpets and check underneath for signs of wear.
- Are the driving seat and controls consistent with wear for the mileage?
- Check the mileage against that advertised.

driving

- Check the engine is cold by placing a hand on the bonnet, then have someone start it while you inspect the exhaust for excess smoke. In general, keep nostrils open for odd smells.
- After checking the radio and CD player works on all speakers, switch the radio off as it will mask other noises that are important.
- Check the air conditioning and heater works.
- Open the bonnet and listen to the engine – there may be unusual noises, maybe noisy tappets that need replacing or slipping belts.

- Get in and drive. Turn at full lock with windows down, radio off; any clicking noises from the CVs? Is it difficult to turn? The turning circle should be the same clockwise and anti-clockwise.
- Reverse in a circle.
- Engage low-range (drive in a straight line if on hard surface).
- Brake hard on a flat and non-cambered surface, make sure the car doesn't pull to one side.
- Labour the engine in a high gear at low speed, without being excessive, to check for clutch slip.
- On automatics, check all gears can be engaged, second gear start works and the overdrive can be shifted on and off.
- Drive at 100km/h, checking for excess wind noise. Operate wipers at speed.
- Check the cruise control works.
- Drive at 60, 70, 80, 90 and 100km/h for a few moments, checking for vibration at each speed to see if there are any balance problems.
- Check accessories like rear lockers (make a small turn a few degrees and check for tyre squeal).
- Drive for at least 20 minutes to warm the vehicle up.
- Do at least one warm start.
- Drive over speed bumps at normal speeds and see how the suspension responds.
- When warm, accelerate to redline and note any abnormality.
- Check the park brake will hold the vehicle on an incline or, on the flat, that it is difficult to pull away (this is a test to do on your own car first).
- The vehicle should track straight with the steering wheel straight.

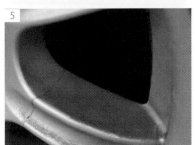

1-2 A factory dealer is the easiest, quicker and least risky approach to buying a vehicle. However, selling and buying privately you can get a better bargain.

3 Check all VIN records correspond and the dates match to those advertise.

4 Modern cars have lots of features. Check each one carefully, it could be a bargaining point if it doesn't work.

5 A wipe of a rag reveals a cracked alloy rim.

6 Bull and nudge bars should be airbag compatible where required.

You don't need to be a mechanic to spot brand new parts, fluid leaks, worn belts, loose batteries, bent mounts, saggy soundproofing, rust or shoddy wiring. If there are other choices, move on. If you need that car, ask your professional how bad it really is.

index of topics

DISCOVER AUSTRALIA WITH BOILING BILLY

4WD GLOVEBOX GUIDE

ISBN: 9781922131423 (spiral edition) $24.99

An ideal companion to the *4WD Handbook*, the *4WD Glovebox Guide* summarises key content from the *4WD Handbook* for use in the field, and adds information on communications, navigation and journey management.

4WD TOURING GUIDES

This fully updated series of 4WD touring guides explores the very best of Brisbane, Melbourne and Sydney's off-road destinations. Each A4 guide includes detailed track descriptions, things to do, and details on picnic and camping areas.

4WD Treks Close to Brisbane
ISBN: 9781921874840 $39.99

4WD Treks Close to Melbourne
ISBN: 9781922131126 $39.99

4WD Treks Close to Sydney
ISBN: 9781922131454 $39.99

about the author

Robert Pepper is a freelance motoring journalist, author, photographer and driver trainer based in Melbourne, specialising in offroad vehicles and navigation. His first book, *GPS Vehicle Navigation in Australia*, was first published in 2002 and is now into its second edition. He has had over 500 articles published in 16 magazines and newspapers in Australia and around the world and has twice judged Overlander 4WD magazine's 4WDOTY annual awards. Robert is closely involved in the 4WD club movement at several levels from leading trips ranging from day journeys to outback treks, organsing events such as abandoned vehicle recovery days and helping form responses to industry and government changes affecting offroaders. Robert is also a senior instructor with 4WD Victoria, has rewritten the basic training course, created a towing course and an advanced vehicles course from scratch. He also trains commercially, having been on both sides of manufacturer demonstration days. Robert has also conducted training on navigation, photography and vehicle dynamics, teaches instructors how to teach, has competed in the Outback Challenge and other winch competitions, won the CruiserKhana offroad precision driving competition, has run part of the Pajero Challenge 24-hour navigation exercise and has been a guest speaker at many club meetings and events on various topics. Prior to his involvement in offroading Robert was a private pilot with an interest in aerobatics and a gliding instructor qualified in the UK and New Zealand, but he has an interest in most things with wings, wheels or sails.

The author, during field research.

acknowledgements

Books of this nature may have just the one name on the cover, but in reality many others contribute. I would like to thank everyone who has helped me put this together, and that starts with every instructor who's ever taught me, every student I've ever taught and the members of every trip I've been on or led. Every time I go out there's something else to pick up or consolidate.

Many people in the industry have assisted me with technical articles for magazines over the years and much of that is reflected here. It's a long list of business owners, technical staff at car manufacturers, engineers and mechanical shops, but whenever I am in need of advice a few names spring to mind; Alan Johnson of PiranhaOffroad, John Pfeffer of Exclusive Tyres, John & Julie Eggenhuizen of Getabout 4WD, everyone at Ironman 4X4 and ARB Corporation.

Many people have helped me test vehicles and products and set up photographs, and have generally contributed to this book. The list is long and distinguished but I must acknowledge Jason Buettner, Sean Daley, Ian Salmon and of course my wife Muriel who is behind the wheel in many of the shots after I'd hopped out and said "this would be good place for a photo, now go drive!"

I would also like to thank my proofreaders, foremost amongst which is my father who combines the rare attributes of attention to detail, incredible technical knowledge and a sharp eye for vague explanations. Elena Ashley ploughed through many chapters for me, even though I probably find reading her books more pleasurable than she does mine. Having Bec

Daley read most sections through carefully was most appreciated. Paul Tanner took time out from S6 to assist, and I should even "credit" him with one of the asides.

No manufacturer or organisation has paid to be a part of this book's editorial content and no specific products are recommended. I have tried to avoid brand names but there are one or two unique products that don't really have generic names.

While everyone's assistance is much appreciated, any errors are mine alone.

On the support website you can find the Glossary, updates and clarifications, along with various other information to complement this book-plus news, views, comments and information on all matters 4WD!

**Support website: www.4wdhandbook.com
facebook.com/4WDHandbook**

 **Find us on
Facebook**

Ultimately, this book is about getting you out to places like this and safely back again.